ADORATION AND ANNIHILATION

ADORATION
AND
ANNIHILATION

The Convent Philosophy
of Port-Royal

JOHN J. CONLEY, S.J.

University of Notre Dame Press

Notre Dame, Indiana

Library of Congress Cataloging-in-Publication Data

Conley, John J.
Adoration and annihilation : the convent philosophy of Port-Royal /
John J. Conley.
    p.   cm.
Includes bibliographical references and index.
ISBN-13: 978-0-268-02296-9 (cloth : alk. paper)
ISBN-10: 0-268-02296-8 (cloth : alk. paper)
1. Jansenists. 2. Port-Royal des Champs (Abbey) 3. Philosophy,
French—17th century. 4. Arnauld, Jacqueline Marie Angélique,
1591–1661. 5. Arnauld, Agnés, 1593–1671. 6. Arnauld d'Andilly,
Angélique de Saint Jean, 1624–1684.   I. Title.
BX4730.C66   2009
273'.7—dc22
                                                    2009006984

Dedicated to the memory of my beloved mother,

Mary Broderick Conley

(1924–2002)

CONTENTS

Preface   *ix*

Abbreviations   *xiii*

CHAPTER 1
Introduction: A Convent Philosophy   *1*

CHAPTER 2
Mère Angélique Arnauld: Virtue and Grace   *43*

CHAPTER 3
Mère Agnès Arnauld: Adoration and Right   *113*

CHAPTER 4
Mère Angélique de Saint-Jean Arnauld d'Andilly: *175*
Persecution and Resistance

CHAPTER 5
Conclusion: A Nocturnal Philosophy   *237*

Appendix A. Lettres de la Mère Angélique Arnauld à Antoine   *250*
Arnauld

Appendix B. Mère Agnès Arnauld, *Pensées sur le chapelet secret*   *261*
du Saint-Sacrement

Appendix C. Mère Angélique de Saint Jean Arnauld d'Andilly,   *266*
Sur le danger qu'il y a d'hésiter et de douter, quand une fois
l'on connaît son devoir

Notes   *273*

Works Cited   *297*

Index   *304*

PREFACE

Number 169 Rue Saint-Jacques is a plain brown door on a narrow lane of restaurants, shops, and apartment houses in the shadow of the Sorbonne. When you punch in the proper code, the oak door opens and you walk into a small cobblestone courtyard. When you push in the second code, a glass door opens and you enter a dark tiled entryway. You begin to walk three flights up a sloping wooden staircase as you hold on to the rusted iron railing. At the third floor you press the buzzer next to an unmarked black iron door. After a long pause, either Valérie or Fabien opens the door, greets you, and guides you to a seat at the cramped red table where scholars (a maximum of eight) study Jansenist manuscripts under the gaze of the plaster death mask of Blaise Pascal.

The secluded library is the Bibliothèque de la Société de Port-Royal, the world's finest collection of Jansenist manuscripts and print material. The space is tiny: five rooms stuffed to the ceiling with gray cartons of handwritten letters by Port-Royal nuns and gilded eighteenth-century editions of Jansenist texts. The valiant staff is also tiny: two professional librarians, Valérie Guittienne-Mürger and Fabien Vandermarcq, in total. Around the small readers' table over the years I have met the virtuosi of scholarship on Jansenism: the historians Dale Van Kley, Monique Cottret, and Ellen Weaver; the literary critics Jean Lesaulnier, Philippe Sellier, and Nicholas Hammond. Oddly, I have yet to meet another philosopher there. At 4:00 tea in the library, where we stand as Valérie pours the tea and readers offer various cookies, we excitedly exchange news about the latest treasure discovered in the archives. As our friendships deepen, we discuss the mysterious pull of the Port-Royal convent that has brought us again and again to the attic library.

The hidden library is more than an intellectual cenacle of conservation and research; it is the soul of the Jansenist movement. Its collection goes back to the Boîte à Pierrette, an eighteenth-century fund established by Pierre Nicole to succor persecuted Jansenist refugees and to shelter their proscribed books and papers. By the early nineteenth century the collection had landed in the Rue Saint-Jacques apartment it still occupies. Generations of librarians turned the archive into an institution with a mission: the defense of the Jansenist movement against the libels of its persecutors. The scholarly tomes of Augustin Gazier (1844–1922) and his niece Cécile Gazier (1878–1936) represent the summit of the library's polemical campaign to rehabilitate the vanquished witnesses to the truth concerning God's grace.

In more irenic times, the old theological quarrels have evaporated; Valérie and Fabien insist that they are delighted to have a Jesuit around the table. But the scholars at the Rue Saint-Jacques are aware that more than intellectual curiosity has drawn us to the written memory of Port-Royal. When I began to read the letters of Mère Angélique de Saint-Jean, transcribed in a beautiful copperplate hand by the librarian Rachel Gillet, I noted her various arguments on virtue. But it was her own courage under persecution that attracted me to her. Mère Agnès's relational account of the virtues possessed a theoretical complexity, but it was her concept of the mystical annihilation of self that challenged my own methods of prayer. Mère Angélique's writings on the grace of suffering for the truth had a clear Augustinian framework, but it was her sympathy for all those persecuted for the sake of conscience that elicited my admiration. My criticisms of the nuns' philosophy in the following pages are unmistakably Jesuit: the nuns' theory of divine causation and grace crushes any substantial human freedom. But like many pilgrims to the library on the Rue Saint-Jacques, my research bears witness to the enduring power of a scholarly community of women who risked all on God's grace.

Many persons and institutions have assisted me in the gestation of this monograph. I thank Loyola College in Maryland for awarding me the Henry J. Knott Chair of Philosophy and Theology, which has facilitated my scholarly research. I thank Fordham University and the National Endowment for the Humanities for grants and sabbaticals that have permitted me to pursue archival research in France. I thank the staffs of the following libraries for their professional courtesy: Bibliothèque Nationale de France, Bibliothèque Mazarine, New York Public Research Library, Fordham University Library, and Yale University Library. I thank the Rev. Joseph Koterski, S.J., the Rev. Christopher Cullen, S.J., and Dr. Catharine Randall for their kindness in reading early drafts of the manuscript. I thank the members of the Society for the Study of Women Philosophers. Their conferences permitted me to present early versions of my research on early modern French women philosophers, and their members have encouraged my research in this area. I especially thank the librarians and readers of the Bibliothèque de Port-Royal. Their high standards of scholarship challenge all of us, and their passion for things Jansenist turns our scholarly chores into a mission of love.

ABBREVIATIONS

ACR	*Avis donnés par la Mère Catherine Agnès de Saint-Paul, Sur la conduite que les religieuses devoient garder, au cas qu'il arrivât du changement dans le gouvernement de sa maison*
BNF	Bibliothèque Nationale de France
CCPR	*Conférences de la Mère Angélique de Saint Jean sur les Constitutions du monastère de Port-Royal du Saint Sacrement*
CPR	*Les constitutions du monastère de Port-Royal du Saint-Sacrement*
CS	*Le chapelet secret du Saint-Sacrement*
DHD	*Sur le danger qu'il y a d'hésiter et de douter, quand une fois l'on connaît son devoir*
DRSB	*Discours de la Révérende Mère Marie Angélique de S. Jean, Abbesse de P.R. des Champs, sur la Règle de S. Benoît*
EC	*Entretiens ou conférences de la Révérende Mère Marie-Angélique Arnauld, abbesse et réformatrice de Port-Royal*
EPR	*L'esprit du monastère de Port-Royal*
IRP	*L'image d'une religieuse parfaite et d'une imparfaite, avec les occupations intérieures pour toute la journée*
LMAA	*Lettres de la Mère Agnès Arnauld, abbesse de Port-Royal*
LMASJ	*Lettres de la Mère Angélique de Saint-Jean*
LMMA	*Lettres de la Révérende Mère Marie-Angélique Arnauld, abbesse et réformatrice de Port-Royal*

Ms. Maz   Manuscript of the Bibliothèque Mazarine

P.R.   Bibliothèque de la Société de Port-Royal

RPR   Réflexions de la R. Mère Angélique de S. Jean Arnauld, Abbesse de P.R. des Champs, Pour préparer ses soeurs à la persecution, conformément aux Avis que la R. Mère Agnès avait laissés sur cette matière aux religieuses de ce monastère

SC   Sur la conformité de l'état où est réduit P.R. à l'état de Jésus-Christ dans l'Eucharistie

CHAPTER 1

INTRODUCTION

A Convent Philosophy

The thesis of this book is simple. In the seventeenth-century convent of Port-Royal, three nuns, Mère Angélique Arnauld, Mère Agnès Arnauld, and Mère Angélique de Saint-Jean Arnauld d'Andilly, produced a literary corpus of serious philosophical significance. Openly declaring themselves "disciples of Saint Augustine," the nuns developed their own neo-Augustinian philosophy, notable for its original treatment of the divine attributes, moral virtue, and personal freedom. The philosophy of the Arnauld nuns is not simply authored by women; its portrait of God as incomprehensible mystery, its ascetical concept of the virtues, and its defense of conscience reflect the distinctive culture of vowed women devoted to contemplation in a cloistered convent.

If these Port-Royal nuns did indeed construct such a major variant of baroque Augustinian philosophy, why have we never heard of them before? The reasons are multiple. The literary genres in which they present their arguments reflect a conventual culture few contemporary readers can easily penetrate. Arguments on the incomprehensibility of God or the illusions of prudence are embedded in letters of spiritual direction, abbatial conferences, devotional manuals, biblical glosses, commentaries of monastic rules, and

funeral orations. These are not standard philosophical treatises. We experience some trouble recognizing the philosophical argument in Montaigne's essays or Pascal's maxims, but identifying the philosophical concerns in the arcane monastic genres of Port-Royal requires a greater asceticism.

Related to the problem of monastic genre is the heavily theological content of the nuns' writings. Certain recent efforts to expand the canon of modern philosophy to include the works of heretofore neglected women philosophers have omitted women perceived as too religious in their preoccupations. In her influential anthology of modern women philosophers, Mary Warnock excludes authors "who rely more on dogma, revelation or mystical experience than on argument."[1] Unsurprisingly, not a single nun survives this secularist cut. If predominantly theological works are dismissed a priori as unphilosophical, the writings of the Arnauld abbesses, focused on controversies concerning the dogma of grace and the dogmatic authority of the church, will remain invisible in the history of philosophy.

The philosophical contribution of the nuns has also been eclipsed by the extraordinary philosophical stature of the male clerics and laity who closely collaborated with the Port-Royal nuns. Blaise Pascal and Antoine Arnauld are only the most prominent of a constellation of philosophers, theologians, historians, and artists who allied themselves with the convent. If the nuns are cited in the history of philosophy, they inevitably appear as the auxiliaries or disciples of an Arnauld or a Pascal. Their own philosophy and the gendered originality of that philosophy have disappeared.

Influential literary portraits of the convent have also marginalized the nuns as philosophers. Sainte-Beuve's *Port-Royal* and Montherlant's drama of the same name depict the nuns as victims of political forces determined to crush them.[2] The nuns' arguments on God's incomprehensibility and the ethical limits of state power are reduced to emotional pleas in the midst of persecution. The reasons given for God's inaccessibility or the arguments developed for constraints on civil authority fade away.

The invisibility of the Port-Royal nun in the philosophical canon also stems from our longstanding blindness to the philosophical arguments developed in social sites dominated by women. Only recently has the moral philosophy elaborated in the Parisian salons of

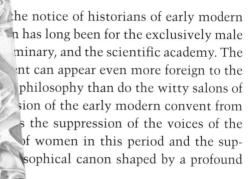

he notice of historians of early modern
n has long been for the exclusively male
minary, and the scientific academy. The
nt can appear even more foreign to the
philosophy than do the witty salons of
ion of the early modern convent from
s the suppression of the voices of the
f women in this period and the sup-
sophical canon shaped by a profound

lso obscured the philosophical con-
ns. As the sanctions of exile and ex-
onvent, sympathizers often defended
nuns could not even understand the
and theological controversies that had provoked the
campaign against them. On occasion even the embattled nuns themselves argued that they simply ignored the complex quarrels over
grace and freedom that had enraged their opponents. If such a claim
were true, which I will deny in this study, then the writings of the
nuns could be dismissed as simple works of piety. While the ancient
charges of coyness and stubbornness against the Port-Royal nuns
may well be justified, the charges of theological and philosophical
ignorance against these erudite Augustinians clearly are not.

Another political factor has turned the writings of the nuns into
an invisible canon. Quite simply, they lost the battle. After a century of heroic resistance, the French throne destroyed the Port-Royal
community and razed the convent buildings to the ground. A literary elite has long savored the nuns' manuscripts, preserved in obscure archives and carefully guarded attics. But the Jesuits' muscular
Christianity, with its emphasis on good works and individual merit,
decisively molded a modern Catholicism that could barely comprehend the old Augustinian categories of predestination, election, concupiscence, and efficacious grace. The devotion of a small circle of
literary critics and historians to the works of the nuns has not yet
succeeded in creating a broader philosophical and theological public
for these works.[4] Tellingly, we do not yet have a complete, let alone
a critical, edition of the works of Mère Angélique, Mère Agnès, or

Mère Angélique de Saint-Jean in the French original. Translations into foreign languages are virtually nonexistent.

Given our virtual ignorance of the nun philosophers of Port-Royal, much of this monograph presents translations of and commentaries on the writings of the three Arnauld abbesses. To assess the philosophical pertinence of their work, their long-silenced arguments must first be heard. Like their combative lives, the arguments of the Port-Royal abbesses revolve around conflict, polemic, defense, and resistance. But these martial arguments also constitute a complex philosophical brief on the attributes of the hidden God, the primacy of charity in monastic virtue, and the ethical limits of cooperation with an oppressive political regime. Knowing intimately the Augustinian philosophical tradition, the Arnauld nuns transform this tradition in light of the gendered concerns of a persecuted community of women religious. It is the philosophical tale of the Port-Royal nuns that remains to be told.

CONVENTUAL PHILOSOPHY

To understand the philosophy developed by Mères Angélique, Agnès, and Angélique de Saint-Jean, it is necessary to understand the history of the convent they governed.[5] The century of the reformed Port-Royal (1609–1709) constitutes the last and the most visible era of the convent, but the reforms engineered by Mère Angélique, her sister, and her niece are inexplicable independently of Port-Royal's struggle during five centuries to embody the Benedictine and Cistercian ideals of monasticism.

Located in the valley of the Chevreuse in the southwestern Parisian region, the abbey of Port-Royal was founded by Mathilde de Garlande in 1204 as a cenacle of intercessory prayer for her husband, Mathieu de Marly, who had left France to fight in the Fourth Crusade. Approved by Eudes de Sully, the bishop of Paris, the convent drew its first nuns from neighboring Benedictine convents. Placed under the jurisdiction of the abbot of Cîteaux, the general superior of the Cistercian order, in 1225, the abbey adopted the austere, secluded ethos of the Cistercian order.

During the thirteenth, fourteenth, and fifteenth centuries, Port-Royal led an observant monastic life. Abbesses were drawn from leading French noble families: Montfort, Villeneuve, and Dreux. In recognition of the convent's good reputation, church authorities granted the convent a series of privileges. The abbesses were to be elected by the nuns themselves rather than being appointed by secular or episcopal powers. The convent could conduct a boarding school for girls; the laity could spend periods of retreat at the convent guest house. Accountable to the abbot of Cîteaux, Port-Royal was exempted from the jurisdiction of the diocese of Paris.

In the sixteenth century Port-Royal underwent a steep decline. The Concordat of Bologna (1516) between Pope Leo X and King Francis I had given the French monarch the right to nominate abbesses at Benedictine and Cistercian convents on French soil. The post of abbess at Port-Royal quickly became an object of simony, coveted by affluent aristocratic families as a sinecure for their daughters. The convent was governed by a series of absentee abbesses, who drained the abbey's material resources but ignored its spiritual needs. The personal lives of the nuns became increasingly decadent. The vow of poverty collapsed as nuns used gifts from family and friends to decorate their rooms, enhance their wardrobes, and fund personal allowances. Cloister disappeared as nuns freely visited farms and inns in the region and entertained guests in their apartments. The nuns' masquerade balls during Carnival became a fashionable social event. Religious offices languished. During the last three decades of the sixteenth century, sermons were preached only on formal social occasions, such as a profession of vows. Barely literate confessors and chaplains demonstrated a greater taste for hunting than for spiritual ministry. During their official visitations to the convent, delegates of the abbot of Cîteaux admonished the abbesses concerning the multiple abuses present in the convent. But the exhortations remained a dead letter in a Port-Royal that had abandoned its Cistercian fervor and had become a worldly refuge for the younger daughters of the nobility.

In 1602 the eleven-year-old Mère Angélique Arnauld was inaugurated as the abbess of Port-Royal. Her appointment reflected typical abuses of the period. Her nomination was granted by King Henri IV as a recompense for the Arnauld family's services to the crown; the Vatican's ratification of the nomination was obtained through the use of fraudulent documents falsifying the age of the nominee. The desultory governance of the convent suddenly began to change in 1608, when the young abbess underwent a religious conversion. During the next five years Mère Angélique introduced a series of reforms to conform Port-Royal's practices with the Cistercian interpretation of the Rule of Saint Benedict: common property, with abolition of all personal possessions; restoration of the night office; manual labor; strict rules of silence, with the restoration of sign language; perpetual abstinence from the use of meat. With the assistance of her sister Mère Agnès, Mère Angélique quickly transformed a decadent convent into a model of the reforms mandated by the Council of Trent.

Due to the insalubrious climate of the valley of the Chevreuse and the expansion of community membership to approximately eighty nuns, Mère Angélique transferred the convent to the Parisian neighborhood of Saint-Jacques, adjacent to the Sorbonne, in 1625. Dissatisifed with the direction of the Cistercian order, now headed by an opponent of reform, Dom Nivelle, the abbess placed the convent under the jurisdiction of the archdiocese of Paris in 1627. In 1629 King Louis XIII abandoned the royal prerogative to name Port-Royal's abbess and permitted the nuns to elect their own abbess for a three-year term. Ending her thirty-year abbacy in 1630, Mère Angélique was replaced as abbess upon the election of Mère Marie-Geneviève de Saint-Augustin Le Tardif, who reigned for two terms (1630–36).

The Angelican reform not only altered the spiritual and moral atmosphere of Port-Royal; it fostered the development of a theological culture in a convent that in 1600 was barely cognizant of the rudiments of the Catholic faith. Eminent theologians like Benoît de Canfield, Archange de Pembroke, and François de Sales became spiritual directors and lecturers at the convent. During the period 1626–33, the Oratorians became especially influential in shaping the spirituality of the convent. Pierre de Bérulle emphasized an apophatic theology focused on the incomprehensibility of the divine attributes, while Charles de Condren stressed the annihilation of the self that should characterize the soul of the disciple truly abandoned to the divine will.[6] Both emphases would durably mark the spiritual practices and the religious philosophy pursued by the Port-Royal nuns. Under the direction of Sébastien Zamet, bishop of Langres and an episcopal overseer of Port-Royal, Mère Angélique participated in the ill-fated venture to found a new religious community devoted to adoration of the Blessed Sacrament (1633–36). After the collapse of the experiment, she returned to Port-Royal, now governed by her sister, Mère Agnès, who ruled for two terms (1636–42). Despite the failure of the Institut du Saint-Sacrement, perpetual adoration of the Eucharist would remain one of the central devotional practices of Port-Royal and one of its most palpably Tridentine characteristics.

During the 1630s Port-Royal became intertwined with what would later be labeled the Jansenist movement. In 1633 Jean du Vergier de Hauranne, abbé de Saint-Cyran, became the spiritual director of Mère Angélique. He became the spiritual director of Port-Royal in 1634 and had his protégé Antoine Singlin appointed as the convent's chaplain in 1636. A disciple of Bérulle, Saint-Cyran reinforced the Oratorian stress on an apophatic theology that underscored God's incomprehensibility. A close friend of Cornelius Jansen, bishop of Ypres and professor of theology at Louvain, Saint-Cyran championed Jansen's radical Augustinian theology. This neo-Augustinianism stressed the depth of human concupiscence, the complete dependence on grace for salvation, and the role of divine sovereignty in predestination and election. Reflecting the long-simmering quarrel over grace, Jansen's Augustinianism denounced the theology of the Jesuits, in particular the disciples of Molina,[7] for exaggerating the role of human freedom in the act of salvation and for destroying the role of divine sovereignty and grace in the formation of the elect.

To Jansen's variant of Augustinianism Saint-Cyran brought his own controversial views on sacramental practice. Claiming to follow the tradition of the primitive Church, Saint-Cyran argued that Holy Communion should be infrequent, preceded by careful spiritual preparation and followed by a visible increase in virtue. Similarly, sacramental absolution from sin should be granted only if the penitent exhibited perfect contrition, sorrow because one had offended God, after a thorough examination of conscience. Once again, the Jesuits, with their campaign for frequent Communion and their doctrine of imperfect contrition, sorrow for sin due to fear of spiritual and temporal punishments, became the target of criticism.

In 1637 a group of clerics and laymen commonly called *les solitaires* began to live at the abandoned buildings of Port-Royal des

Champs. Including many male members of the Arnauld family, the *solitaires* quickly extended the influence of Port-Royal and Saint-Cyran's theology through the *petites écoles* they established for boys and their translations of patristic and monastic texts into French. The nuns' revived convent school and the growing number of cultivated laity, such as Blaise and Jacqueline Pascal, attending sermons at the Port-Royal de Paris convent further amplified the prominence of the convent as a model of religious reform and as a fortress of neo-Augustinian thought.

Political conflict soon followed. In 1638 Cardinal Richelieu arrested Saint-Cyran and imprisoned him in the Chateau de Vincennes. No charges were ever filed. Richelieu considered Saint-Cyran a dangerous political dissident. The priest had openly criticized the annulment of the marriage of Gaston d'Orléans, the brother of Louis XIII, as an abuse of political power; his moral rigorism was seen as a stinging critique of the lax morals of the court. The prime minister had not forgotten *Mars Gallicus* (1635), the pamphlet of Saint-Cyran's mentor, Cornelius Jansen, which had condemned French foreign policy for attacking Catholic nations and for forming cynical alliances with heretical and schismatic powers. The imprisonment only heightened Saint-Cyran's influence, exercised through an extensive correspondence. Released in 1643 upon the death of Richelieu, a weakened and sickly Saint-Cyran had acquired the status of a martyr for the Augustinian cause.

Published posthumously in 1640, Jansen's *Augustinus* ignited what would become the quarrel over Jansenism. In this dense thirteen-hundred-page Latin tome, Jansen argued that the church's doctrine on grace must follow the teaching on grace developed by Saint Augustine, acclaimed by numerous popes and church councils as "the doctor of grace." The Augustinian doctrine of grace emphasized the depth of human sinfulness, the gratuity of predestination, the small number of the elect, and complete human dependence on divine grace for salvation. According to Jansen's doctrine of efficacious grace, only God could free a human being from his or her slavery to sin in order to do good; only God's grace could maintain the saved human being in the posture of charity toward God and neighbor. For Jansen, modern theologians, especially the Jesuit disciples of Molina, had resurrected the heresy of Pelagianism, the belief that one is saved by one's own moral effort, which Augustine had combated. For Jansen's opponents, his theories effectively destroyed human freedom and introduced a concept of predestination suspiciously close to that of Calvin. Jesuits pressed church officials for a condemnation of the book.

The Holy Office of the Inquisition censured the *Augustinus* in 1641, followed by Pope Urban VIII's bull *In eminenti* in 1642. But the terms of the condemnation were murky. The Vatican appeared to be condemning the relaunching of the old *querelle de la grâce* by both the radical Augustinians and their Jesuit critics.[8] For good measure, the Holy Office condemned the writings attacking the *Augustinus* as well as those defending it. The concern for church unity and the desire to foreclose a new irresolvable dispute on the relationship between divine and human will appeared to trump any concern over heresy.

During the new abbacy of Mère Angélique (1642–54), the convent strengthened its fidelity to the Augustinian theology of Jansen as interpreted by Saint-Cyran. The letters and conferences of Mère Angélique defended the controversial theory of sin and grace maintained by the Jansenist circle and condemned the more humanistic theology advanced by the Jesuits. Saint-Cyran's *Simple Theology* served as the central catechetical text used in the convent school and novitiate. The posthumously published *Christian and Spiritual Letters* of Saint-Cyran (1645–47) became a staple of the convent's devotional literature. The brother of Mères Angélique and Agnès, Antoine Arnauld, emerged as the leading theologian of the movement after the death of Saint-Cyran in 1643. A skilled polemicist, he defended the theology of Jansen in two *Apologies for Jansenius* (1643, 1645) and used abundant biblical and patristic documentation to justify Saint-Cyran's controversial sacramental theology in his *Of Frequent Communion* (1643). Coauthored with François Hallier, his *Moral Theology of the Jesuits* (1643) denounced the alleged laxism practiced by Jesuit casuists in their moral theories and confessional practice.

Supported by the writings of the *solitaires* and by the approval of sympathetic aristocrats, the convent of Port-Royal continued to expand. Enclosing over one hundred nuns, Port-Royal in 1648 sent a group of nuns to reoccupy the buildings of Port-Royal des Champs, rehabilitated by the manual labor of the *solitaires*. With the approval of the archbishop of Paris, Port-Royal would henceforth include a rural and an urban house, each governed by a prioress subordinate to Port-Royal's one abbess.

The enhanced prominence of Port-Royal's convents, schools, and publications intensified the political and ecclesiastical opposition to the Jansenist movement. The Cathedral of Notre Dame theologian Isaac Habert delivered a series of sermons denouncing the Jansenist theory of grace as heretical. Earlier sympathizers with Port-Royal, notably Vincent de Paul, turned against the movement. De Paul argued that the moral and sacramental rigorism of Arnauld would only discourage Catholics from frequenting the sacraments. Prime minister during the regency of Anne of Austria, Cardinal Mazarin solicited condemnations of Jansenist teaching during various assemblies of French bishops. Although bitterly divided between advocates and opponents of Jansen, the Sorbonne became the central theater of the campaign against the movement. In 1649 the syndic Nicolas Cornet asked the theology faculty to condemn seven propositions concerning grace and freedom as heretical. Although Cornet declined to name the source of these alleged errors, they closely echoed the text of the *Augustinus*. Despite its Gallican tendencies, the faculty voted to forward the controversial propositions to Rome for a final adjudication of their orthodoxy.

Under the abbacy of Mère Marie des Anges Suireau (1654–58) and the new abbacy of Mère Agnès (1658–61), opposition to the doctrine of Port-Royal became the official policy of the church. In 1653 Pope Innocent X's bull *Cum occasione* condemned five propositions drawn from Cornet's list as heretical. The censured propositions were as follows: "1) It is impossible for the just to keep some of God's commandments, even when they desire and try to follow them, if they are lacking the grace necessary to keep them. 2) In our state of fallen nature, it is impossible to resist interior grace. 3) In our state of fallen nature, we must be free from external constraints, but not from internal necessity, in order to gain merit. 4) The Semi-Pelagians rightly admitted the necessity of grace for all good acts, even for the first stirrings of faith; however, they became heretical when they argue that this grace can be either accepted or rebuffed by human beings. 5) It is a Semi-Pelagian heresy to claim that Christ died or shed his blood for all human beings."[9] *Cum occasione* cited the *Augustinus*, but the loose phrasing of the document cast doubt on the relationship between the censured theories and Jansen's book. In 1656 Pope Alexander VII published *Ad sacram* to remove any ambiguity in the dispute. He declared that the condemned heretical propositions had been drawn from the *Augustinus* and that the church was condemning them precisely in the sense Jansen had given them.

As the fortunes of the Jansenist party declined, Antoine Arnauld devised an ingenious theological distinction that would permit the Port-Royal circle both to accept the church's condemnation and to maintain its allegiance to the Augustinian theology of Jansen. According to Arnauld's *droit/fait* distinction, church authorities had the right and duty to bind the conscience of the faithful on matters of *droit* (the law of faith and morals), since right belief and right conduct were essential to salvation. In such declarations of *droit*, the church enjoyed the infallible assistance of the Holy Spirit. On matters of *fait* (empirical fact), however, the church did not enjoy such supernatural authority. Church authorities were free to make such judgments of *fait*, such as the determination that a particular book or movement is heretical, but they could not demand more of the faithful than an attitude of respectful silence. Since such empirical judgments were fallible, only as credible as the evidence presented and the interpretation of the evidence, such judgments remained open to subsequent alteration or even reversal. The application to the papal declarations was clear. The Jansenists accepted that the five censured propositions were heretical; at least in certain contexts, they could bear a heretical meaning. The Jansenists could not accept, however, the claim that Jansen himself had defended these heretical theories. Submitting to the church in its judgment of dogmatic *droit*, they would withhold assent to what they believed to be its erroneous judgment of *fait*.

Critics immediately denounced Arnauld's distinction as destructive of ecclesiastical authority; stripped of its disciplinary authority to condemn particular persons or books, the church would be confined to nebulous declarations concerning dogmatic or moral truth. Once again the forum of anti-Jansenist agitation, the theology faculty of the Sorbonne voted to condemn Arnauld for what they believed to be his own mistaken judgments of *droit* and *fait* in his polemical *Second Letter to a Duke and Peer* (1655). By a narrow majority, they censured Arnauld for claiming that *Cum occasione* had not clearly condemned the *Augustinus* (an error of *fait*). Even more adamantly they condemned what they considered an error of *droit*: Arnauld's contention that Saint Peter's denial of Christ indicated that he had lacked the grace to perform the right act at this moment. For his critics, such a refusal to place moral responsibility on Saint Peter's own misuse of his freedom revealed the grave moral errors present in the Jansenist doctrine of efficacious grace. In 1656 the Sorbonne annulled Arnauld's doctorate in theology and excluded him from the faculty.

Even outside the Port-Royal circle, the *droit/fait* distinction received substantial support. Sympathetic bishops defended the theological soundness and patristic pedigree of the distinction. Priests of Gallican sympathies applauded a distinction that clipped the power of the Vatican to intervene in theological disputes. Critical of growing royal absolutism, parliamentarians in Paris and the provinces championed a theory that blunted the throne's anti-Jansenist campaign conducted by Mazarin.

The tenuous effort of Arnauld to ward off the condemnation of the Port-Royal movement soon received literary and supernatural reinforcement. In January 1656 Blaise Pascal pseudonymously began to publish the *Provincial Letters*, a series of public letters that defended Jansen's theory of grace, the *droit/fait* limitation on church authority, and the doctrinal and moral integrity of the Port-Royal convent. The most celebrated letters attacked the alleged moral laxism of Jesuit casuists. An immediate literary success, the polemical *Letters* placed the opponents of the Jansenist party on the defensive. The convent itself became the scene of a more spectacular intervention. On March 24, 1656, Marguerite Périer, the niece of Blaise Pascal and a boarding pupil at Port-Royal, underwent a sudden healing of a chronic lachrymal fistula of the eye after the application of a relic of the crown of thorns in the convent chapel. Jesuit pamphleteers denounced the miracle as a fraud and illusion, but after careful investigation a reluctant archdiocese of Paris officially declared the miracle worthy of belief. Jansenists insisted that divine intervention had underscored the righteousness of their cause.

Once Louis XIV assumed personal governance of France in 1661, the quarrel over the papal condemnation turned into outright persecution of Port-Royal. With the support of the French Assembly of Bishops, the king promulgated a formulary of assent to the bulls of Popes Innocent X and Alexander VII. All priests, nuns, and teachers were to sign the formulary under oath. Even before the nuns could resolve their position on "the crisis of the signature," Louis XIV proceeded to attack the convent. On April 23, 1661, royal emissaries dismissed the pupils from the convent school and expelled the postulants from the convent. Royal *lettres de cachet* ordered the exile or imprisonment of the convent's chaplain and confessors. Archdiocesan delegates conducted an investigation on the grounds of Port-Royal which attempted to find evidence of heresy among the nuns.

The motives for Louis XIV's assault on Port-Royal were mixed. As France's anointed defender of the faith, he sincerely attempted to crush a movement condemned as heretical by several popes. Like Richelieu and Mazarin, he despised the moral rigorism of the Jansenists, which clearly opposed the loose morals of the court and the *raison d'état* ethics of French foreign policy. The king's primary motive, however, appears to have been political. Not without justification, he saw the Jansenist movement as the religious counterpart of the Fronde (1648–52), the loose coalition of aristocrats and parliamentarians that had plunged France into civil war in its effort to arrest royal absolutism and to restore the ancient rights of local nobles and parliaments. Numerous prominent lay associates of Port-Royal had in fact participated in the Fronde, most notably Madame de Longueville, the cousin of Louis XIV. The entire ethos of Port-Royal, not least the convent's insistence on the chapter election rather than royal appointment of its abbess, seemed to breathe a democratic, antimonarchical spirit. Interpreting religious dissidence as an inevitable source of political dissidence that would threaten the throne, Louis XIV considered the destruction of the Jansenist party, in particular its citadel in the Port-Royal convent, as a principal objective of his reign.

The long crisis of the signature indicated that the royal destruction of the Port-Royal movement would not be a simple affair. When the Parisian archdiocesan vicars Contes and Hodencq prefaced the controversial formulary with an irenic pastoral letter explicitly admitting the legitimacy of the *droit/fait* distinction, Antoine Arnauld counseled the nuns to sign the formulary without any further reservation. Led by Soeurs Angélique de Saint-Jean Arnauld d'Andilly and Jacqueline de Sainte-Euphémie Pascal, the nuns opposed Arnauld's position as deceptive. The formulary clearly indicated that the signatories were condemning the five propositions in the sense that Jansen had allegedly given them in the *Augustinus*. Under pressure from their exiled confessors, the nuns signed the formulary in June 1661, but against the advice of Arnauld each nun added next to her signature a phrase indicating the strictly qualified nature of her assent. Infuriated, the throne annulled the reserved signature and the vicars' pastoral letter on July 9; the Vatican confirmed the annulment on August 1. Faced with a new demand for an unreserved signature, the nuns adroitly added their own preface, stipulating the qualified nature of their assent, to the copy of the formulary which they signed without additions to their signatures on November 28, 1661. Subsequent efforts to elicit an unamended assent to the formulary were resisted by the nuns.

The incapacity of the state and the church to force the doctrinal surrender of Port-Royal led to more forceful measures. In August 1664 the new archbishop of Paris, Hardouin de Péréfixe, personally confronted the nuns at Port-Royal and condemned them for their disobedience. He placed the convent under interdict, sentenced a dozen of the prominent opponents of the formulary to house arrest in distant convents, and imposed anti-Jansenist Visitation nuns as superiors of the convent. Traumatized by the new campaign of coercion, a small minority of nuns gave an unreserved assent to the formulary and resumed religious life at Port-Royal de Paris. In 1665 the *nonsigneuses* were regrouped at Port-Royal des Champs, where they continued to lead a minimal religious life under armed guard and deprived of the sacraments. In 1666 the king declared the definitive separation of Port-Royal into two communities: Port-Royal de Paris, a small community of *signeuses* under the direction of the royally appointed abbess, Mère Dorothée Perdeau; and Port-Royal des Champs, the larger community of *nonsigneuses* still nominally under the abbacy of Mère Madeleine de Sainte-Agnès de Ligny

(1661–69) but in fact under the strict governance of the archbishop of Paris and the military representatives of the crown lodged at the convent. At the moment of the division of the convents, Louis XIV also imposed an inequitable division of the material goods of Port-Royal, with the bulk of the wealth given to the *signeuse* minority in Paris and only a small pittance provided for the *nonsigneuse* majority at Champs.

Despite the apparent victory of the throne in crushing the convent and the broader Jansenist movement, the punitive measures had not resolved the crisis. The published writings of the nuns themselves, notably Mère Agnès's *Image of a Perfect and of an Imperfect Nun* (1665) and the *Constitutions of Port-Royal* (1665), presented the public with the portrait of a convent that appeared to correspond perfectly to the Council of Trent's ideal of reformed religious life.[10] Reports of the appalling treatment of the nuns at the militarized Port-Royal des Champs perturbed a public opinion baffled at the severity of the measures taken against the *nonsigneuses*. Headed by the theologically distinguished Nicolas Pavillon, bishop of Alet, a quartet of French bishops intervened in the dispute to defend the *droit/fait* distinction and to defend the nuns' refusal to sign the unamended formulary because they sincerely believed its judgment of fact concerning Jansen was erroneous. When the Vatican and French throne maladroitly attempted to depose the four bishops on the grounds of disobedience, the effort only aroused opposition from other Gallican bishops who had little sympathy for Jansenist theology but who defended the rights of a French bishop to make theological declarations for the members of his own diocese.

Elected in 1667, Pope Clement IX saw the resolution of the Jansenist crisis as a priority for his pontificate. He believed that this division within Catholicism was destroying its capacity to face its external enemies and that the brutal treatment of the resistant nuns was scandalous. An irenic diplomat, he pursed negotiations to surmount the crisis and to restore the quarreling parties to amity in the church. Preoccupied by foreign affairs, especially his impending war with Holland, even Louis XIV favored a negotiated solution to the festering internal trauma over the crisis of the signature. Clement IX's "Peace of the Church" took effect in early 1669 when the nuns reluctantly signed a new formulary in which they promised to condemn the five censured propositions "wherever they are to be found, even in the works of Jansenius." The ambiguous phrasing seemed to offer more than the "respectful silence" defended years ago by Arnauld but in fact did not provide the clear condemnation of Jansen's alleged errors that the opponents of Port-Royal had long demanded. On February 18, 1669, the Vatican lifted the sanctions against the convent and declared the nuns innocent of the charges and calumnies against them.

Despite its fragility, the Peace of the Church brought a decade of unaccustomed serenity to Port-Royal. Under the abbacy of Mère Marie de Sainte-Madeleine du Fargis (1669–78), the convent entered what Sainte-Beuve describes as its "beautiful autumn." Replenished by new novices and postulants, the Port-Royal des Champs convent grew in numbers. Prominent aristocratic and bourgeois families enrolled their children in the reopened convent school for girls and the *petites écoles* for boys conducted by the returned *solitaires*. Following Clement IX's injunction to avoid polemics concerning the theology of grace, Arnauld concentrated on anti-Protestant polemics. The Port-Royal *solitaires* produced a flood of pedagogical works and scholarly translations, the most notable being their monumental translation of the Bible, spearheaded by Isaac Le Maître de Saci. In manuscript and in print, the works of the Port-Royal nuns found a broad European theological public. The letters and conferences of Mères Angélique and Agnès propagated their theories of monastic virtue and their concept of religious reform. Soeur Jacqueline de Sainte-Euphémie Pascal's treatise on education, *A Rule for Children,* offered the Port-Royal convent school as a model for emulation by other academies for girls. Especially influential were the biographies, autobiographies, eulogies, and legal depositions that defended the doctrinal orthodoxy and moral probity of the nuns and which detailed the measures of persecution taken against the *non-signeuses*.

The tranquil autumn of Port-Royal ended abruptly under the abbacy of Mère Angélique de Saint-Jean Arnauld d'Andilly (1678–84). In 1679 Harlay de Champvallon, the new archbishop of Paris, informed the new abbess that the king had ordered the closure of the Port-Royal school and had banned the admission of new novices to the convent. With the peace treaties of Nijmegen (1678–79) sealing

France's hegemony in Europe, Louis XIV was now free to focus on eliminating religious dissidents, notably the Jansenists and the Huguenots, he deemed a threat to civic unity. The measures of the crown assured a slow but certain death for the community. Dispersed and threatened with imprisonment, the *solitaires* fled into exile, many like Arnauld and Nicole finding refuge in the Lowlands. Personally sympathetic to the convent, Pope Innocent XI, already embroiled with Louis XIV over the rights of the French crown in disposing of church revenues, risked no public gesture of displeasure. The most erudite of the Port-Royal abbesses, Mère Angélique de Saint-Jean presented numerous lectures on the Scriptures, the Rule of Saint Benedict, and the Constitutions of Port-Royal to reinforce the courage of the doomed community. But neither they nor her repeated appeals to the king and ecclesiastical authorities could arrest the decline of the convent.

Under the abbacies of Mère Marie de Sainte-Madeleine du Fargis (1684–89), Mère Agnès de Sainte-Thècle Racine (1689–1700), and Mère Élisabeth de Sainte-Anne Boulart de Ninvilliers (1700–1706), the impoverished convent continued to decline in numbers and advance in average age. A new crisis of the signature provided the pretext for the demise of the convent. In 1705 Pope Clement XI promulgated the bull *Vineam Domini Sabaoth*, which condemned the resolution of a "case of conscience" endorsed by the majority of the Sorbonne theological faculty in 1701. The case of conscience concerned confessional practice: Could a priest absolve from sin and censures a sympathizer with the Jansenists who maintained only a "respectful silence" and not a clear assent concerning the Church's findings of *fait* about Jansen? The Sorbonne had responded in the affirmative, but the Vatican condemned its verdict, since the refusal to accept the church's judgment of *fait* courted as grave a risk of heresy as did the refusal to accept the church's judgment of *droit*. Once again the government of Louis XIV ordered a submissive formulary to be signed by all priests, nuns, and teachers. In 1706 the Port-Royal nuns signed the formulary assenting to the judgment of *Vineam*, but they added a restrictive clause stipulating that they accepted *Vineam*'s judgment only on condition that it did not impinge on any of the concessions granted by Pope Clement IX at the time of the Peace of the Church.

Infuriated by the new expression of resistance by the nuns, the throne quickly retaliated. When Abbess Boulart de Ninvilliers died later in the year, the nuns were denied the right to elect a new abbess. In 1709 armed guards, bearing royal *lettres de cachet,* escorted the remaining nuns to exile and house arrest at distant convents. In 1710 Louis XIV personally ordered the destruction of the buildings of Port-Royal des Champs and even the dynamiting of the convent cemetery to avoid the possibility that the abandoned convent would become a scene of pilgrimage. As Sainte-Beuve dryly notes, Louis XIV had punished the recalcitrant nuns with the sanctions usually reserved for assassins of a king.

The convent is not only the site for the philosophical reflection developed by Mères Angélique, Agnès, and Angélique de Saint-Jean; it shapes the very form and content of this philosophy. The genres employed by the abbesses reflect the culture of a cloistered convent and the particular culture of a Jansenizing convent wracked by persecution. The letters of the abbesses are predominantly letters of spiritual direction, counseling perplexed souls along an ascetical itinerary, or letters of appeal to ecclesiastical and political authorities to justify the positions of Port-Royal. The abbatial conferences treat the monastic vows at length and privilege distinctively monastic virtues, such as silence, rarely practicable for a laywoman. Many of the more original arguments concerning the virtues surface in the abbesses' austere commentaries on biblical and monastic texts. As Catherine Villanueva Gardner argues, the contributions of early modern women to the philosophical canon are often ignored because their philosophical arguments are pursued in literary genres foreign to the dominant philosophical genre of the discursive treatise.[11] To engage the philosophical arguments concerning God's attributes, the moral virtues, or human freedom embedded in these conventual works, one must brook monastic genres and technical doctrinal disputes that even the sympathetic contemporary Christian may find forbidding.

Accentuating the monastic character of Port-Royal's philosophy can also avoid the narrowness of an earlier historiography that reduced the history of the convent to the quarrel over Jansenism and which treated the nuns as naïve disciples of Saint-Cyran. As F. Ellen Weaver contends in her revisionist histories of the convent, the primary preoccupation of the Arnauld abbesses was to create a reformed convent that would embody the ethos of primitive Cistercianism, itself a reform of the earlier and broader Benedictine tradition.[12] This monastic reference to the Benedictine-Cistercian tradition deeply shapes the philosophical concerns of the nuns, especially in the theory of virtue defended by the Arnauld abbesses.

FAMILIAL PHILOSOPHY

The century-long history of the reformed Port-Royal is simultaneously the history of one remarkable family: the Arnaulds.[13] Providing three of the abbey's most influential abbesses (Mères Angélique, Agnès, and Angélique de Saint-Jean), the Arnauld family provided many other nuns for the convent and many of the *solitaires* renowned for their scholarly work as associates of the convent. The family nurtured the Jansenist movement's foremost theologian (Antoine Arnauld), its preeminent biblicist (Isaac Le Maître de Saci), and one of its most learned bishops (Henry Arnauld, bishop of Angers). The family not only dominated the convent and the broader Jansenist movement through the intellectual and religious achievements of its members; it imparted a distinctive coloration to the philosophical perspectives of its literary abbesses. The family's Protestant origins influenced its sympathy for religious tolerance and possibly the Calvinizing tendencies of Port-Royal's theology. Its early quarrel with the Jesuits set the stage for a bitter dispute between the convent and this powerful religious order over issues of grace, moral theology, and church authority. Its sociological status as a prominent member of the *noblesse de robe,* the aristocratic class of lawyers who dominated the French parliaments and judiciary, shaped the juridical quality of the philosophical arguments used by the Arnauld abbesses in their disputes with civil and ecclesiastic authorities.

Originally from the Auvergne, the Arnauld family distinguished itself by its service to the French crown. A lawyer who defended the financial interests of the court before the Parlement of Paris, Antoine de la Mothe–Arnauld (1490–1585) held the lucrative post of general procurator to Catherine de Medici, the queen of France. A

Huguenot, La Mothe–Arnauld was personally protected from harm during the Saint Bartholomew's Day Massacre in 1572 by the order of the queen. Shortly after surviving the massacre, La Mothe–Arnauld converted to Catholicism, but his wife, Anne Farget, remained a practicing Huguenot, and only a minority of his children would abandon the Protestantism in which they had been baptized. Well into the seventeenth century, members of the Arnauld family would remain prominent congregants of the Huguenot church in Charenton, adjacent to Paris. Many would figure among the Huguenot exiles who fled France after the Revocation of the Edict of Nantes in 1685.

During the theological wars of the 1660s, critics of Port-Royal would cite the Protestant pedigree of the Arnauld family as the source of the reheated Calvinism (*calvinisme reboulli*) they claimed to be the convent's operative theology. Defensive about their indisputable Protestant connections, the Catholic Arnaulds of Port-Royal often emphasized the specifically Catholic and anti-Protestant nature of their beliefs. As the persecution against the convent intensified, Mère Angélique repeatedly cited the impeccable orthodoxy of her former spiritual director, Saint François de Sales, as evidence of her Catholic good faith. The nuns often argued that their practice of perpetual adoration of the Blessed Sacrament, a devotion anathema to Calvinists, proved their Catholic allegiance. During the Peace of the Church, Antoine Arnauld devoted considerable time to anti-Protestant polemics, of which the massive *Perpetual Faith of the Church in the Eucharist* is the most visible testament.

The son of Antoine de la Mothe–Arnauld, Antoine Arnauld the Elder (1560–1619), like his father a convert to Catholicism, inherited the position of general procurator to Catherine de Medici, a post he held until the queen's death in 1589. In the same year he opened his full-time practice as a lawyer, serving such prominent clients as the duc de Guise. Beneficiary of a humanist education in the classics at the Collège de Navarre, Arnauld the Elder soon distinguished himself as an orator in the Parlement of Paris, the prestigious corps of jurists that functioned as the ultimate court of appeals for a quarter of French territory and as the jealous interpreter of the laws, customs, and precedents collectively known as the French constitution. Using his juridical and oratorical skills to support the claims of the

French throne, Arnauld the Elder received several pensions from Henri IV in recognition of services rendered.

During the reign of Henri IV, Arnauld the Elder also distinguished himself by the vehemence of his opposition to the Jesuits, whom he considered lethal ultramontane enemies of the French throne. When in 1589 the combined forces of Spain and the Catholic Ligue threatened to destroy the army of the then-Protestant Henry IV, Arnauld's pamphlet *Against Spain, or Philippics concerning the Intrigue and Deceptions used by Philip, king of Spain, to seize the French Crown,* denounced the Jesuits as agents of Spain and the Vatican seeking to destroy the legitimate claimant to the French monarchy. After a failed assassination attempt on Henri IV in 1593, Arnauld publicly demanded the expulsion of the Jesuits from the kingdom on the pretext that some of their theologians had openly supported the practice of regicide in cases where a ruler was attempting to impose heresy on a Catholic nation. On behalf of the Sorbonne, a bastion of anti-Jesuit sentiment, the lawyer denounced the Jesuits for the threat their colleges posed to the rights and privileges of the French university and for the dangers their ultramontane ecclesiology posed for the traditional prerogatives of the French throne concerning religious matters. After 1610, when Henri IV was assassinated by a religious fanatic, Arnauld's imprecations against the Jesuits as traitors and corrupters of morals became even more embittered.

Commentators have often described Arnauld the Elder's anti-Jesuit campaign as the "original sin" of the Arnaulds, an attack on the Counter-Reformation's most powerful elite which would precipitate the Jesuits' vengeful campaign against the Arnauld family's most visible creation, Port-Royal. Throughout the seventeenth century scarcely a theological or political controversy erupted that did not feature an Arnauld and a Jesuit on opposing ends of the dispute. The venomous rhetoric used by both sides in the recurrent pamphlet wars indicated that the differences of opinion were rooted in a personal antipathy between two prominent Catholic families as well as in two antithetical visions of the proper path for a reformed Catholicism.

If Arnauld the Elder exalted the powers of the French throne, he counseled it to adhere to a policy of religious toleration in the treatment of its Protestant minority. A staunch supporter of the Edict of Nantes, he warned Louis XIII of the moral and political dangers of a reprise of the anti-Huguenot campaign. As the crisis of Jansenism deepened, later generations of the Arnauld family would turn against the royal absolutism of Arnauld the Elder; opposition to royal interference in theological controversies and more broadly to civil interference in matters of conscience would render the old absolutist claims untenable and even injurious. The family patriarch's defense of religious tolerance, however, would endure as one of the family's tenacious beliefs. The bitter experience of persecution endured by Arnaulds associated with Port-Royal only deepened their sensitivity to the moral peril of civil coercion in the area of religious conviction.

Using his excellent court connections, Arnauld the Elder inadvertently helped to create the reformed Port-Royal by obtaining Henri IV's nomination of his daughter Jacqueline (1591–1661), later known as Mère Angélique, as abbess of Port-Royal. After the inauguration of her reform campaign in 1609, Mère Angélique attracted her other sisters to the convent. Originally named the abbess of Saint-Cyr, her sister Jeanne (1593–1671), known in religion as Mère Agnès, was professed as a Port-Royal nun in 1614. Anne-Eugénie (1592–1653), Marie-Claire (1600–1642), and Madeleine (1608–49) soon followed. Even the oldest sister, Catherine Arnauld Le Maître (1590–1651), legally separated from her adulterous husband, entered the convent. When their widowed mother, Catherine Marion Arnauld, entered the convent, she used a substantial part of the family fortune to purchase a property for the new Parisian location of Port-Royal.

Mère Angélique exercised the same ascendancy over her nieces that she had over her own sisters and mother. An alumna of the Port-Royal convent school, Angélique Arnauld d'Andilly (1624–84), known in religion as Mère Angélique de Saint-Jean, would acquire renown as the most intellectually accomplished of the Port-Royal nuns. Her sisters soon followed her into the convent. The abbacies of Mères Angélique (1602–30, 1642–52), Agnès (1636–42, 1658–61), and Angélique de Saint-Jean (1678–84) constitute the most influential and, from a literary perspective, the most productive periods of a reformed convent that had become an Arnauld familial enterprise.

No less substantial were the contributions of the male members of the Arnauld family to the bourgeoning Port-Royal. The *solitaires* living in the environs of Port-Royal and conducting their *petites écoles* included many male descendants of Antoine Arnauld the Elder. His eldest son, Robert Arnauld d'Andilly (1589–74), lived in the environs of Port-Royal des Champs after the death of his wife, Catherine Le Fèvre de la Broderie, in 1637. An indefatigable scholar, Arnauld d'Andilly translated over thirty philosophical and theological works into French. His versions of Augustine, Teresa of Avila, and the desert fathers are still considered a consummate achievement in neoclassical French prose. The youngest son, Antoine Arnauld the Younger (1612–94), emerged as the most distinguished theologian of the Jansenist movement. He defended the doctrinal orthodoxy and moral integrity of the Port-Royal nuns in a flood of pamphlets. In his celebrated controversies with Descartes and Malebranche, as well as in his own treatises on logic and epistemology, Antoine Arnauld infused the radical Augustinian theology of the convent into the philosophical disputes of the period.

The next generation of the Arnauld family expanded the circle of *solitaires*. The son of Robert Arnauld d'Andilly, Henri-Charles de Luzancy (1624–88) was a priest who served the ministerial needs of the Port-Royal nuns during the periods of persecution. Through her unhappy marriage with Isaac Le Maître, Catherine Arnauld Le Maître produced three sons who became distinguished members of the *solitaires* community. Abandoning a brilliant career as a lawyer and Parlement orator in 1637, Antoine Le Maître (1608–58) became the first of the *solitaires* and a patristic scholar of distinction. An outstanding biblicist, Isaac Le Maître de Saci (1608–58) was the principal architect of a new translation of the Bible, whose first major achievement was the controversial Mons New Testament (1667). After a military career, their brother, Simon Le Maître de Sérincourt (1611–60), joined them in their retreat in the shadow of Port-Royal.

Outside the circle of the *solitaires*, male members of the Arnauld family played a signal role in defending the Port-Royal convent during its years of persecution. The son of Antoine Arnauld the Elder, Henry Arnauld (1597–1692), bishop of Angers, was an ardent member of the quartet of bishops who defended the *droit/fait* distinction, championed neo-Augustinian theology, and insisted on the right of a bishop to guide his own diocesan flock on matters of theological doctrine. The son of Robert Arnauld d'Andilly, Henri-Charles Arnauld de Pomponne (1618–99), rose in diplomatic circles to become Louis XIV's secretary of state for foreign affairs. The victim of two public disgraces, Pomponne was a mercurial defender of Port-Royal. He stoutly defended the innocence of his cousin Isaac Le Maître de Saci during the latter's captivity in the Bastille, but he criticized his sister Mère Angélique de Saint-Jean for her intransigence against compromise solutions to the crisis of the signature.

In their works, the Arnauld abbesses defend positions already fixed in the jeremiads of Arnauld the Elder: opposition to Jesuit casuistry; the moral imperatives of religious tolerance; the respect of the traditional rights of the French episcopate; certain theological and moral theses similar to those held by Calvinism. But it is in form rather than substance that the philosophy developed by the Port-Royal nuns reveals its distinctive Arnauld pedigree. Daughters of the *noblesse de robe,* the nuns often employ a highly juridical form of argument to prove the truth of their position. Their lengthy justifications cite precedents in the Bible, the church fathers, church councils, and earlier papal declarations. They employ a lawyer's skill to expose the contradictions in the arguments of their opponents and to adduce in church history evidence that contradicts their opponents' claims. Daughters and sisters of parliamentary debaters, they often use the oratorical techniques of hyperbole, irony, and rhetorical questions to underscore the perfidy of their persecutors. Whether they are explaining the virtue of humility or questioning the *droit/fait* distinction, the Port-Royal abbesses ably use the Arnauld family's cherished literary genre of the legal brief embellished by flights of Ciceronian indignation.

The debt of the Port-Royal nuns to the Arnauld family's *noblesse de robe* status can be easily exaggerated. In his celebrated sociological study of the Jansenists, *The Hidden God,* Lucien Goldmann argued that the distinctive apophatic theology of Port-Royal sprang from the disempowerment the social class of jurists and parliamentarians had undergone under the absolutist policies of Henri IV, Louis XIII, and Louis XIV.[14] As these *noblesse de robe* families experienced the anomie of losing their ancestral privileges and social authority, they increasingly worshipped a "hidden God" notable by his absence, obscurity, and arbitrariness. As many critics have argued, the thesis of Goldmann is unconvincing. Many religious orders of the period drew disproportionately from the *noblesse de robe* for the simple reason that this educated class of French subjects, schooled in an ethics of sacrifice for the common good, made natural candidates for the priesthood and sisterhood. The Jesuits themselves were examples of such disproportionate recruitment, but their robust theology of God's positive attributes showed little trace of the *via negativa* that characterized Port-Royal. If the *noblesse de robe* status of the Arnauld family cannot be isolated as a sociological cause of the convent's operative theology, the legal methods of disputation typical of this class clearly shaped the juridical cast of the abbesses' arguments on the divine attributes, the moral virtues, and human freedom.

The distinctive familial pedigree of the texts written by the Arnauld abbesses explains an obvious omission in this monograph: Jacqueline Pascal, known in religion as Soeur Jacqueline de Sainte-Euphémie. Incontestably Soeur Jacqueline is one of the leading philosophers of the Port-Royal convent. Her *Rule for Children* has long been acclaimed as a key treatise in the philosophy of education for women. In the nineteenth century Victor Cousin and M. P. Faugère published separate scholarly editions of her works; recently Jean Mesnard has provided critical editions of her works in his monumental but as yet unfinished collection of the works of the Pascal family.[15] Contemporary studies in French, German, and English analyze her thought.[16] Her writings and philosophical concerns, however, diverge sharply from those of the Arnauld abbesses. A poet prodigy who published her first book of verse at the age of twelve, she never abandoned the literary genres she mastered in the salons and courts of her adolescence. Her *On the Mystery of the Passion of Our Lord Jesus Christ* bears the mark of the *maxime,* and her biographical sketch of Mère Angélique uses the techniques of the *portrait moral.*[17] Whereas Mères Angélique, Agnès, and Angélique de Saint-Jean entered the convent as children, Soeur Jacqueline entered the convent as an adult who had worked closely with her brother Blaise on his scientific and philosophical projects. Descartes was a personal acquaintance, lambasted in one of Jacqueline Pascal's letters.[18] Soeur Jacqueline's background, literary style, and

philosophical preoccupations differ so clearly from those of the Arnauld abbesses that she has been accorded only a minor place in this
study of the convent's dominant philosophy.

The juridical temperament of the reformed Port-Royal was not
limited to the members of the Arnauld family who served as the
convent's officers and advisers; it also reflected the social background of the nuns who entered the convent during the Angelican
reform. As William Ritchey Newton notes in his sociological study
of Port-Royal, the demographic composition of the convent changed
dramatically through the course of the seventeenth century.[19] In
1610, at the beginning of the Angelican reform, the majority of nuns
were drawn from the provincial aristocracy; by 1640 the majority of
nuns entering the convent came from families in the legal profession; by 1660 a majority of nuns had fathers who served the crown
as administrators or as members of Parliament. This entry of a legal
elite into the reformed Port-Royal not only created strong court and
parliamentary connections to sustain the convent during its persecution by the throne; it created an unusually literate body of nuns,
avid for the theological culture promoted by the Angelican reform
and capable of defending the embattled convent through their own
written juridical arguments. This *noblesse de robe* literacy, forced
to hone and express itself in a flood of memorials and letters, explains in part the immense corpus of work left by the reformed Port-
Royal to posterity. In his eighteenth-century study of the writings
produced by the convent, Dom Charles Clémencet identifies fifty-
four nuns as authors of surviving works; most were the authors of
multiple works.[20] Thomas M. Carr notes that the massive corpus of
writings left by the Arnauld abbesses has no counterpart in the literary remains of other seventeenth-century convents.[21] Like other abbesses in reformed convents, the Arnauld abbesses delivered a large
number of addresses in the convent: formal commentaries on sacred
texts in chapter; informal admonitions at the daily assembly; responses to nuns' questions at the informal "conferences" that replaced recreation at Port-Royal. Unlike those at other convents,
however, the Port-Royal nuns carefully transcribed the abbatial addresses for circulation among the nuns and lay allies of the convent.
The early esteem for the convent as a model of reform in the 1620s
and the later scandalous reputation of the convent as a fortress of

heresy in the 1660s created a broader public for these works. Like the Arnauld family itself, the new *noblesse de robe* Port-Royal featured a juridical literacy that throve on the volleys of theological disputation.

DISCIPLES OF AUGUSTINE

No one would contest the designation of Mères Angélique, Agnès, and Angélique de Saint-Jean as spiritual writers or even as theologians dealing with ascetical matters. In fact, the term *théologienne* was used derisively by Port-Royal's opponents to mock the nuns dabbling in doctrinal issues believed to lie beyond the competence of women. The designation of these authors as philosophers, however, is more controversial. None of the authors received a formal philosophical education. Their writings ignore certain prominent philosophical disputes of the period, notably those concerning modern science and the rise of a mechanistic physics. Given their Augustinian theology of concupiscence, the nuns are skeptical of the capacity of reason alone to prove God's existence. They are hostile to the efforts of Christian humanists, especially the Jesuits, to construct a natural-law ethics based on generic human nature and its alleged capacity to cultivate natural virtues. Such characteristics of the writings and mentality of the Port-Royal nuns pose serious obstacles to a properly philosophical analysis of their arguments concerning the virtues and freedom.

Despite these reservations, a solid case can be made for considering these nuns as philosophers and for analyzing their works in terms of the categories proper to the discipline of philosophy. The works meet several criteria for classification as a philosophical and not only as a literary canon.

First, the texts deal extensively with issues long considered to be the province of philosophy. Three in particular receive substantial treatment. The nuns often discuss the difficulty of arriving at a positive knowledge of God's attributes and, following the tradition of apophatic theology, tend to name God in terms of negative attributes. In the area of ethics, the authors develop a virtue theory adapted to the context of the convent and defend a neo-Augustinian position on the illusion of moral virtue existing independently of the theological virtues of faith, hope, and charity. Under the duress of the sanctions imposed during the crisis of the signature, the nuns elaborate a theory of human freedom related to the right and the duty to contest abuses of power by political and ecclesiastical authorities. The fact that these concerns arise within a theological dispute does not lessen the philosophical quality of concerns long considered central in the philosophical disciplines of natural theology, ethics, and anthropology.

Second, the Port-Royal nuns not only consider perennial philosophical issues, they propose a sustained argument to justify the position they are advancing on a given issue. Many convent writings praise the attributes of God or exhort nuns to cultivate a set of moral virtues. But such expressions of devotion or moral earnestness do not in and of themselves constitute a philosophical argument. The Port-Royal nuns studied in this monograph, however, often provide a carefully reasoned justification of the claim they are making regarding a divine attribute, a moral virtue, or an alleged violation of a right of conscience. As Bernard Chédozeau argues in his study of the intellectual culture of Port-Royal, the nuns distinguished themselves not only by the theological culture they acquired, but also by the elaborate explanations (*explications*) they often gave on ascetical and doctrinal questions troubling the convent. These lengthy explanations are often characterized by "impressive intellectual efforts paying homage to reason and logic—and sometimes to paradox."[22]

The abbatial conferences in particular show this concern to develop a prolonged argument on contested issues; the persistent concern to fix these arguments in written form that could be read by a broader public suspicious of Port-Royal's beliefs increased the precision and rigor of the arguments themselves. Mère Angélique not only exhorts the nuns to practice moral virtues; she explains why the pretension to possess such moral virtues as justice in the absence of such theological virtues as humility is illusory. In her mystical evocation of God's negative attributes, Mère Agnès clarifies why the Godhead is properly considered infinite, inaccessible, and unlimited. When she exhorts her subjects to remain steadfast in their fidelity to the Augustinian account of grace, Mère Angélique de Saint-Jean analyzes how the exercise of doubt operates in a network of power where the majority incessantly pressures dissenting minorities to abandon their convictions. One often has the impression that the philosophical argumentation offered by the Port-Royal nuns represents a conversation they have overheard; the technical categories are often lacking and the argument often ends more abruptly than a professional philosopher's would. But as they construct their justifications of God's alterity or the ethical limits of political power, the nuns employ the tools of philosophical logic and construct their own metaphysics of necessity and freedom.

Finally, the Port-Royal nuns pursue these philosophical issues within a distinctive intellectual tradition: the Augustinian tradition, a community of thought that is simultaneously philosophical and theological. As Philippe Sellier argues in his magisterial study of French seventeenth-century literature, the entire seventeenth century can be classified as "the century of Augustine," so influential are the works and theories of Augustine of Hippo.[23] Port-Royal's works have long been labeled "Augustinian," as have the works of the era's leading philosophers: Descartes, Pascal, and Malebranche. Such a ubiquitous classification, however, tends to provide only the vaguest indications of the specific philosophical traits of the theories advanced by the Port-Royal nuns. Specifying the various strands of the Augustinian tradition embedded in the theological culture of the nuns can clarify the distinctive philosophical perspective brought by the nuns to questions of ethics and natural theology. It can also indicate where the nuns develop their own original variations on that tradition, often shaped by concerns of gender, and where the nuns develop arguments that transcend the Augustinian heritage, notably in their distinctively modern arguments on the rights of conscience.

The complexity of the Augustinian philosophy developed by the Port-Royal nuns can manifest itself only once a certain legend concerning the nuns' intellectual culture has been challenged. Both ancient and modern defenders of the nuns under persecution have claimed that the pious nuns simply ignored the terms of the theological controversy swelling around them. According to this version of events, the nuns were naïve victims of calumnies initiated by the Jesuits and their allies to destroy the visible center of the Jansenist movement; strictly cloistered from the world and ignorant of the

Augustinus, the nuns refused to sign statements condemning a book they had never read and treating technical issues of grace they could not fathom. At the height of the crisis of the signature in the 1660s, Madame de Sablé defended the nuns along these lines of theological ignorance. "You will not find it odd if I tell you that in the convent there were one hundred and twenty nuns outstanding in piety. They took away eighty nuns who, because of their tender consciences, feared to offend the truth by saying that these propositions [the five condemned theological propositions] are in a book they had not even read because it is in a different language than theirs."[24] In her chronicle of the convent, the twentieth-century historian Cécile Gazier offers a similar defense of the nuns based on their ignorance of the contested literature and theories in the radical Augustinian movement. "The *Augustinus* never penetrated the walls of the monastery; neither did the *Provincial Letters.* Even *Of Frequent Communion* does not appear to have been found there."[25]

This image of the theologically unsophisticated Port-Royal nun is impossible to square with the massive documentary evidence provided by the nuns themselves on their theological and philosophical culture. Few if any of the nuns had actually read the *Augustinus;* the turgid Latin alone of this massive theological tome denied access to all but the most erudite specialists. But the letters, autobiographies, and transcripts of interrogations indicate the extensive knowledge possessed by the Port-Royal nuns, especially their abbesses, of the issues tormenting the Church during the quarrel over the *Augustinus.* Other works of Jansen were widely read in the convent; his *Reform of the Interior Man,* translated by Robert Arnauld d'Andilly, was a staple of public reading in the refectory.[26] The works of Saint-Cyran, popularizing Jansen's theory of grace and presenting his own controversial sacramental theories, were assiduously studied. Edited by Port-Royal's *solitaires,* his *Letters* were frequently recommended for spiritual reading.[27] His *Simple Theology,* used as a catechetical text in the convent school and novitiate, clearly defended Jansen's controversial theory of efficacious grace. "Question 3: Can we merit this grace? We can do nothing at all to merit this initial grace, by which we enter into God's service. It is necessary for it to come to us through God's pure mercy, through which he predisposes and attracts all those who draw close to him. Question 4: Is it sufficient to have this initial grace? No, because after we have entered through it into God's service, we can do nothing unless we are somehow able to advance forward. This can only happen if God predisposes us at every stage and sends new grace and new assistance."[28] The disproportion between divine grace and human freedom in the act of salvation could not be more plain.

The letters of the abbesses, especially those of Mère Angélique, manifest their intimate knowledge of their relative Antoine Arnauld's *Of Frequent Communion*, with its extensive discussion of the quarrel over grace and its defense of Jansen's position. Blaise Pascal's *Provincial Letters*, with its criticism of the papal censures of Jansen, are quoted by his sister Soeur Jacqueline de Sainte-Euphémie in her celebrated letter defending the right of the nuns to refuse to assent to the formulary's censures.[29] Even beyond explicit textual citation, the nuns' discussions of the doctrine of grace and the legal arguments against the sanctions imposed on them manifest a sophisticated grasp of the theological disputes and the controversy over church authority that wracked the French Augustinian party in the middle of the seventeenth century.

Throughout their writings, the Port-Royal nuns declare themselves to be "disciples of Saint Augustine." In part this self-designation is a rejection of the term "Jansenist." Like Antoine Arnauld and Pierre Nicole,[30] the nuns considered the sobriquet "Jansenist" to be an invention of the Jesuits, who sought to create a phantom heresy in order to destroy an Augustinian movement holding perfectly traditional views of grace. But this self-designation also manifests the Augustinian pedigree of the convent's philosophical perspective. If this Augustinian orientation includes Jansen's account of divine causation and human freedom, it represents a far more complex ensemble of broadly Augustinian traditions.

The first and most obvious component of the convent's Augustinian philosophy consists of the works and theories of Saint Augustine himself. All these abbesses cite the text of Augustine's works. His *Confessions, Treatise on Virginity*, and later writings on grace are the most frequent object of the nuns' commentary. Their arguments on the necessity of grace to cultivate the moral virtues and on the nature of the virtues central to the state of consecrated virginity often rest on passages of Augustine. The most erudite of the abbesses, Mère Angélique de Saint-Jean also quotes Augustine's *City of God*, drawing from it a dualistic anthropology sharply opposing the soul to the body and a dualistic philosophy of history, where the diametrically opposed City of God and City of Man are engaged in an apocalyptic struggle over humanity's salvation.

In his sympathetic study of Jansenism, Leszeck Kolakowski insists that the Port-Royal nuns and their allies were simply defending Augustine's actual views on such controversial issues as the damnation of unbaptized infants, views repeatedly endorsed by the popes and councils of medieval Christendom.[31] It was only in the atmosphere of the more humanistic Catholicism of the late Renaissance that such Augustinian views suddenly appeared erroneous or even pernicious. The accuracy of the portrait of Augustine etched by the nuns in their quotations and commentary, however, is a more complex subject of controversy. Isaac Habert, an early critic of the *Augustinus*, developed some of the standard charges against Port-Royal's use of Augustine.[32] He claimed that the Jansenist party quoted Augustine selectively, focusing almost exclusively on his later works when he was waging a doctrinal battle against the Pelagians and their heretical theory of the ability of humans to save themselves by their own meritorious works. In the heat of the polemic against the Pelagians, Augustine did indeed denigrate the role of human freedom in salvation and exalt the role of grace. But in many other works, notably the early treatise *On Free Will*, Augustine presented a more positive philosophy of human freedom and of the moral responsibility of the human agent concerning his or her salvation. Habert claimed that in its truncated version of Augustine, Port-Royal ignores the more libertarian side of the "doctor of grace," just as it ignores the doctrine of grace proposed by other fathers of the church, notably the Greek Fathers, who held a more optimistic view of postlapsarian humanity, especially in its capacity to choose the good through the personal exercise of freedom. Accurate or distorted, it is this late, anti-Pelagian Augustine who shapes the convent's philosophical outlook.

A second Augustinian or more broadly Neoplatonic strand in the abbesses' philosophical perspective resides in the medieval monastic authors they favored for instruction and personal meditation. The Rule of Saint Benedict, the object of extensive commentary by

Mères Agnès and Angélique de Saint-Jean, explicitly builds on the ascetical theory proposed by Saint Augustine in a group of writings collectively called the Rule of Saint Augustine.[33] Especially influential in the nuns' account of the virtues is Augustine's theory of the virtue of poverty, as quoted and interpreted by Benedict. Composed for the monks and hermits on Mount Sinai, Saint John Climacus's *Ladder of Perfection* provides a precise definition of each of the virtues he considers essential for monastic perfection.[34] Widely used in the Port-Royal school and refectory, the treatise's analysis of distinctively monastic virtues, such as obedience and silence, finds a clear echo in the virtue theory elaborated in the nuns' own writings. Climacus also places this account of virtue into a Neoplatonic framework of the gradual ascent of the soul from corporal concerns to a purely spiritual union with God. The cofounder of the Cistercian order, Saint Bernard of Clairvaux figures as a major reference in the philosophical reflection of the nuns.[35] Their lengthy considerations on the virtue of humility in the cloistered life rest squarely on the different types of humility identified by Bernard in his *Steps of Humility*. Like his treatise *Of the Love of God*, Bernard's treatise on humility rests on a Neoplatonic schema of the gradual purification of the soul from material to exclusively spiritual concerns. His doctrinal work *Of Grace and Free Will* explicitly uses Augustine's texts to explain the church's teaching on this perplexing relationship. Under the influence of these and similar monastic treatises of Augustinian provenance, the nuns constructed a hierarchy of virtues built on the conviction that salvation consists in a strict liberation of the soul from the flesh.

A third component of the convent's Augustinian tradition derives from the broadly Augustinian perspectives of two preeminent authors of the Catholic Reformation: Saint François de Sales and Saint Teresa of Avila. As in most French religious houses of the period, de Sales's *Introduction to the Devout Life* was the favored spiritual book of the nuns and lay associates of Port-Royal.[36] De Sales's personal role as the spiritual director of Mère Angélique and early defender of the Angelican reform of the convent enhanced the authority of his arguments on the virtues essential to the Christian life and the necessity to implore the assistance of grace in one's moral struggles. With their insistence on the necessity to annihilate self-will in order to find union with God, the abbesses naturally fastened on de Sales's concept of abandonment to divine providence in their commentaries. In many of her works, Teresa of Avila employs a Neoplatonic framework to describe the various states of the soul as it moves through the stages of purification, illumination, and union with God.[37] In offering counsel to perplexed souls in letters of spiritual direction, the nuns occasionally invoke Teresa's itinerary of the ascent of the soul, with its diagnosis of typical problems at various stages of ascent. Since Teresa was a female reformer canonized by the church, her authority is cited on questions of gender and authority in the convent. A reformer who insisted on the prerogatives of Carmelite prioresses against the claims of chaplains and even bishops, Teresa is often invoked as a church-approved precedent for the efforts of Port-Royal's embattled abbesses to maintain the authority of the abbatial office and the convent chapter during times of persecution.

As with their portrait of Augustine himself, the Port-Royal nuns' interpretation of such modern Augustinian spiritual writers as François de Sales and Teresa of Avila bears a distinctive slant. The moral rigorism of the convent, due in part to Saint-Cyran's influence, ignores the counsels of moderation offered by both authors in their discussions of the virtues. The Port-Royal abbesses could not accept the many concessions to one's "state in life" that de Sales was willing to grant laywomen from aristocratic and bourgeois backgrounds. His willingness to countenance attendance at balls or careful attention to properly ornamented dress contradicted the strict separation from the world's vanities enjoined by the nuns on the pupils of the convent school. Tellingly, one of the disputes between Port-Royal and the new French Carmelite convents following the Teresian reform concerned the practice of poverty. The Carmelite taste for a certain sumptuousness in liturgical music and church decoration is condemned by Mère Angélique as a dangerous concession to the world. Just as Port-Royal's theological doctrine of *sola gratia* tended to excise the more libertarian passages from Augustine's canon, the convent's moral rigorism tended to venerate a François de Sales and a Teresa of Avila shorn of their aesthetic exuberance and their prudential concern for human weakness.

More central to the Augustinian philosophy of the convent is the Oratorian school's highly Platonized version of Augustine. Dominating the spiritual direction of Port-Royal from 1626 to 1633, the Oratorians Pierre de Bérulle and Charles de Condren strengthened the influence of the *école française* on the convent's spirituality. An ardent defender of Augustine's theology against the revived Scholasticism of the Jesuits, Bérulle also championed the retrieval of the Neoplatonic philosopher Pseudo-Dionysius. A master of apophatic theology, this obscure patristic philosopher had insisted that God can be named only by negative attributes. Incapable of knowing what God is, we can affirm only what God is not. As Jean Orcibal notes in his study of philosophical Bérullism,[38] Bérulle became the master of a new piety and religious philosophy that stressed God's incomprehensibility, God's radical difference with creatures, and our incapacity to form adequate concepts corresponding to the divine essence.

A close friend and disciple of Bérulle, Saint-Cyran reinforced this vein of apophatic theology in the convent's common philosophy. Widely studied by the Port-Royal nuns and their pupils, his *Simple Theology* opens with an initiation into the *via negativa:* "Question 2: What is God? This is a question we will only be able to answer well in Paradise, where we will see God clearly. Then can't we know God in this life? We can, but imperfectly and by a dark and coarse knowledge. This is similar to the knowledge nursing infants have of their father."[39] Later in the catechism he defines God as "an incomprehensible spirit." Mère Agnès's *Private Chaplet of the Blessed Sacrament* is only the most celebrated of the Port-Royal texts stressing the divine incomprehensibility, a position deriving in large part from the mystical Platonism of Bérulle.

Saint-Cyran's propagation of an apophatic view of God's attributes among the nuns is not limited to his reinforcement of Bérulle's Platonized *via negativa*. In his study of Port-Royal's philosophy, Antony McKenna underlines Saint-Cyran's early sympathy for fideism. "In the field of philosophy, Port-Royal was first characterized by the intervention in 1626 of Saint-Cyran in defense of Charron, the disciple of Montaigne, against the attack of the Jesuit Carasse. This can be interpreted as an alliance of Augustinian theology with

Christian Pyrrhonism, and heralded the subsequent quarrels between rationalists and Pyrrhonists after the publication of Descartes's *Discours de la méthode*."[40] What unaided reason fails to
affirm with certitude can be demonstrated by reason illuminated by
faith in God's revelation as authentically interpreted by the Catholic
Church. The frequent references to "the hidden God" are an affirmation of the incapacity of reason alone to provide a plausible portrait of God. Only faith, granted by a decree of God's grace, can
permit the human person to glimpse the living God, radically other
than the creature. In this apophatic perspective, the effort of philosophical theology to demonstrate God's existence and attributes
from a scrutiny of nature fails because both nature and the human
mind contemplating it have been radically corrupted by the effects
of sin.

Finally, the most obvious and most studied component of the
convent's Augustinian philosophy derives from the theology of the
Jansenist circle: the dogmatic theology of Jansen himself, especially
his theory of radical depravity and total dependence on grace, and
the complementary theology of Saint-Cyran, with its moral and sacramental rigorism. The works of Saint-Cyran and Antoine Arnauld
permitted the nuns to grasp Jansen's controversial theory of grace,
with its ancillary philosophy of freedom and determination. Circulated within the convent, Saint-Cyran's *Of the Grace of Jesus Christ,
Of Christian Liberty, and Of Justification* offers as stark a portrait
of human concupiscence as any radical Augustinian could offer. "It
is necessary to know that the first man and all human beings in him
have fallen through sin not only into an abyss of mud that has dirt-
ied them and blackened them in all their bodily parts and in all of
their souls, but also onto sharp stony points that have broken and
wounded their entire bodies and their entire souls."[41] Antoine Arnauld's *Of Frequent Communion* and other polemical tracts clari-
fied the theological controversies over necessity and freedom. Avidly
read by his sisters and nieces in the convent, these treatises helped
the nuns to grasp the canonical nuances of the *droit/fait* distinction,
an early variant of the fact/value distinction. As Louis Cognet argues in his sketch of Jansenism, the heart of the Jansenist controversy was the quarrel over grace.[42] The Arnauld abbesses clearly
comprehended this sophisticated dispute over freedom and deter-

minism in a theological context. They also advanced detailed positions on the attendant moral and political issues surrounding the long-standing *querelle* during the various crises of the signature.

Supported by the biblical, patristic, and theological culture of the Port-Royal nuns, the Augustinian philosophy of the convent cannot be reduced to a series of intellectual currents conveyed by books used for instruction or meditation in the cloister. Much of the sophistication and vivacity of the philosophical argument developed by the Port-Royal abbesses springs from the personal contact the nuns enjoyed with a constellation of outstanding philosophers. Among the closest associates of the nuns are three philosophers of the first rank: Antoine Arnauld,[43] Blaise Pascal,[44] and Pierre Nicole.[45] In addition to their seminal books, this trio of preeminent philosophers profoundly shaped the philosophical culture of the convent by their sermons, lectures, parlor conversations, and letters to the nuns. Even many Port-Royal associates of lesser philosophical stature still maintain a minor position in the philosophical history of the period: Saint-Cyran, Bérulle, de Sales, Lancelot,[46] and Fontaine.[47] The distinctive Augustinian culture of Port-Royal was further strengthened by the circle of scholarly *solitaires* who translated key Augustinian authors into French and by the broader network of vaguely Augustinian writers frequenting the convent: Racine, La Rochefoucauld, Boileau, Madame de Sévigné, and Madame de Sablé.

If Port-Royal's Augustinian philosophy emerged from various ancient and modern sources, the nuns transformed the Augustinian tradition they inherited. Their gendered concerns as women, especially as vowed religious in a convent, altered the received Augustinian and Neoplatonic theories. Their apophatic approach to God's attributes, for example, is deeply tied to the convent's practice of perpetual eucharistic adoration. As the vowed bride of the absent bridegroom, the nun-adorer has particular reasons to dwell upon God in terms of absence and negation. Leaning on a predominantly male monastic literature of the virtues, the nuns often stress the gendered contours of the virtues the nun must cultivate, such as the dangers of the virtue of humility for a nun when it is manipulated into blind obedience by a hostile confessor. When during the crises of the signature the abbesses censure an unreserved or even partial assent to certain ecclesiastical declarations, they must set aside the guidance of Augustinian precedent and forge a new theory of the limits of political and ecclesiastical authority. The rights of that most modern human faculty, the conscience (*la conscience morale*), become central to their argument; it is specifically the right of women to participate critically in theological controversies that fuels their account of the embattled conscience. The nuns grasp the subtle *droit/fait* distinction crafted by Arnauld, but they challenge it as a jesuitical evasion of one's moral duty to refuse to give even the appearance of submission to falsehood. An ethics of militant resistance replaces the ethics of prudence embraced by the leading clerics of the Augustinian party. Part of the complexity and the paradox of the philosophy developed by the Port-Royal nuns under the blow of persecution is the simultaneous affirmation of a radically Augustinian theory of grace, which offers scant space to the exercise of free will, and a social philosophy of limited civil power, which defends the right of dissent as an expression and guarantor of human freedom.

METHODS OF INTERPRETATION

The philosophical analysis of the writings of the Port-Royal abbesses requires the use of several concurrent methods to excavate and critique the philosophical argument embedded in their texts. Literary analysis can situate the argument of the nuns within the context of literary genres proper to monastic life and to Port-Royal in particular. A theological interpretation of the texts is crucial because the primary purpose of the works is to stake a position on ascetical questions proper to nuns and on the theological disputes wracking the convent and the broader church. Certain passages are simply unintelligible apart from the quarrel over grace, the dispute over the *droit/fait* distinction, and the crusade against Jesuit casuistry. The central method of analysis is properly philosophical. Descriptively, it studies the writings of the nuns in terms of perennial philosophical categories of ethics, anthropology, metaphysics, and philosophical theology. Normatively, it critiques the philosophical positions advanced by the nuns in terms of logical consistency and sufficient justification. Finally, this analysis of the Port-Royal canon

examines the role of gender in the arguments defended by the abbesses, especially on structural questions of authority and the virtue
of obedience.

Since the writings of the Arnauld abbesses are virtually unknown to an Anglophone public, the first literary task of this monograph is to offer translations of the more philosophical passages in
their work. The copious translations risk at times turning the book
into a *florilège* of convent maxims, but the philosophical argument
cannot be grasped independently of the ascetical prose in which
the nuns frame their considerations on the divine attributes, the
moral virtues, and the rights of resistance. To foster greater clarity
in the translation, I have often broken the long periodic sentences
of the nuns into smaller, simpler sentences. In translating horizon-
tal gendered universal terms, such as *l'homme*, I have generally
used gender-neutral terms, such as *humanity* or *the human person*.
In translating vertical gendered references to God, however, I have
maintained the masculine nouns and pronouns used by the nuns
themselves. Their Trinitarian theology and their spousal metaphors
for the life of the nun would only be betrayed by a gender-neutral
deism. To permit the reader to consult the French original of the
nuns' works, I have included as appendices the integral French
original of three of their more philosophical writings.[48]

Complementing the work of translation is analysis of the literary genres in which the nuns presented their arguments. The contemporary Anglophone reader is not accustomed to finding philosophical discussions encased in letters of spiritual direction, biblical
commentaries, or devotional treatises. It is the monastic genre of
Port-Royal's literature that easily renders the philosophical concerns
of the nuns inaccessible. It is difficult to grasp the abbesses' arguments on the moral virtues, for example, without explaining the institution of the abbatial conference and the various forms the conference took under the different abbesses. The letters of spiritual
direction by the abbesses to nuns and laity outside the cloister contain substantial reflections on God's attributes, but these letters of
ascetical counsel have a different finality than do the more academic
epistolary exchanges between a Descartes and a Princess Elisabeth.

Equally important is a theological analysis of the works of the
nuns. The abbesses' treatment of philosophical issues is usually

embedded within texts with a clear religious purpose and a primarily theological structure of argumentation. Considerations of the perennial philosophical issue of necessity and free will are lodged in the interior of discussions of the relationship between divine grace and voluntary cooperation in the act of salvation. Mère Agnès's controversial exploration of God's negative attributes surfaces in a devotional treatise employing the traditional Catholic prayer form of the litany. The dismissal of the classical moral virtues as illusory follows a logic different from that of the libertine salon; it draws its warrant from the broader neo-Augustinian critique of all claims of human moral merit independent of God's grace as blasphemous. Like the philosophy of the mature Augustine himself, the Port-Royal nuns paradoxically situate philosophical questions of knowledge, right action, and freedom at the interior of a theological anthropology proclaiming the radical concupiscence of postlapsarian humanity, the defectiveness of its reason, and its incapacity to pursue the good.

The primary method used for the interpretation of the nuns' writings is philosophical. I have found three areas where the Arnauld abbesses develop a sustained philosophical argument: ethics, philosophical theology, and theories of personal freedom. The most extensive of the ethical reflection concerns the moral virtues to be pursued by cloistered nuns. In philosophical theology, the apophatic account of the divine attributes is striking in its complexity. The nuns' efforts to justify their right to refuse ecclesiastical and political judgments they believe to be erroneous constitute the most original part of their reflections on freedom. In detailing these philosophical arguments, I have attempted to situate them in an Augustinian philosophical tradition that is broader than earlier commentators have suggested. I have also combated the widespread tendency to characterize the Port-Royal philosophy as Cartesian, since their theories are often foreign to, if not in some cases hostile to, those of Descartes.[49] The philosophical argument of the nuns also undergoes critical analysis. Not surprisingly, their attempt to justify the right of conscience to refuse to assent to apparent falsehood rests uneasily on a metaphysics strongly marked by determinism.

A properly philosophical analysis of these conventual texts can reveal a canon different from that habitually presented by literary critics and historians. Literary critics have long emphasized the works reflecting the convent's unusual literary genres: the narratives of captivity, the hagiographic necrologies, and the unusual eulogies praising deceased Port-Royal members called *miséricordes*. Historians have typically focused on the convent's extensive memoirs, with their apologetic chronicles of major Port-Royal personalities and events. I have given such works only cursory treatment in this philosophical study of the theories of the Arnauld abbesses. Certain long-forgotten works, notably Mère Angélique de Saint-Jean's epistemological treatise *On the Danger of Hesitation Once One's Duty Is Known*, receive extensive analysis. The letters of Mère Angélique are studied for their treatment of salient monastic virtues, such as silence and poverty, rather than for their historical information on the courts of France and Poland. Long studied by theologians and literary critics, Mère Agnès's *Private Chaplet of the Blessed Sacrament* is studied here for its arguments concerning the incomprehensibility of God. Obviously the philosophical theses developed by the nuns cannot be severed from their theological framework. The Augustinian tradition refuses on principle the sharp distinction between philosophy and theology championed by neo-Scholastic and rationalist schools of the period. Highlighting the ethical and epistemological arguments of the nuns, however, can reveal a philosophically significant canon sensibly different from the devotional or autobiographical one routinely privileged by the literary or historical exegete.

Finally, the analysis of the writings of the Port-Royal nuns requires attention to the gendered nature of their argumentation. Their ethical theory is not only written by women; it privileges a set of virtues believed to be central to vowed women committed to an austere life of contemplation. The apophatic portrait of God points to an ungendered Godhead, since God can be named only by what God is not. In the rhetoric of negation, God is neither male nor female. Like the male *solitaires*, the nuns defend a space for the right of conscience in the crisis of the signature, but their defense is specifically an apology for the right of women to engage in critical discussions of religious issues and of questions of the limits of authority. In her recent study of Port-Royal, Daniella Kostroun argues that the nuns make specifically feminist claims in their defenses of the right of nuns to exercise authority and of the convent to enjoy a certain autonomy. "The Port Royal women were feminists, therefore, not just because they believed in the equal value of men and women, but because they believed that, as women, they could make a special contribution towards a radical reform of their society that would improve the condition of all French subjects."[50] This classification of the nuns as feminist may be forced. One searches in vain for an argument by the nuns that women should have access to the same social positions and educational opportunities enjoyed by men. In their philosophical reflection, however, the nuns develop a moral philosophy and a theory of freedom shaped by the gender-specific experiences of women in the setting of a besieged convent.

CHAPTER 2

MÈRE ANGÉLIQUE ARNAULD

Virtue and Grace

Architect of the reform of Port-Royal, Mère Angélique Arnauld (1591–1661) might appear an odd candidate for the title of philosopher. Her rudimentary education provided little access to the philosophical canon. As abbess she repeatedly warned her nuns about the danger of vanity in theological speculation. In her voluminous correspondence and conferences, however, Mère Angélique constructs a detailed Augustinian philosophy concerning God, the virtues, and freedom. Sympathetic to apophatic theology, she prizes the attribute of incomprehensibility in the Godhead. Distinguishing authentic virtues from their counterfeits, she dwells on those virtues, such as poverty and penance, proper to the life of vowed religious. She explores the paradoxes of human freedom. On the practical level she provides moral norms for the exercise of religious and political authority by women; on the theological level she argues that all meritorious action is rooted in God's grace.

A REFORMER'S VOCATION

Born on September 8, 1591, Jacqueline-Marie Arnauld was the second daughter of the lawyer Antoine Arnauld and

Catherine Marion Arnauld.[1] Both members of prominent families renowned for their judicial achievements, the parents had early designated their second daughter for the convent. Madame Arnauld's father, Simon Marion, personally handled the political and ecclesiastical negotiations to provide his granddaughter with a favorable position as abbess in conformity with the family's social status and ambition.

A close friend of Henri IV, who held the power to nominate the majority of abbots and abbesses in France, Marion convinced the king to appoint Jacqueline-Marie as the future abbess of Port-Royal. On June 23, 1599, the king named her to the position. In the papers forwarded to the Vatican for confirmation of the nomination, the Arnauld family falsified the age of the seven-year-old novice, who was far too young to meet the minimum canonical requirements for a religious superior. Rome initially rejected the nomination, arguing that someone who had not even pronounced her vows as a nun could not be installed as the superior of a convent. Only in 1602, after negotiations with the then current abbess of Port-Royal and new overtures to the Vatican, which again falsified the age of the candidate, did Rome send the necessary confirmation of the office. The fraud employed to obtain the abbacy would haunt the older Mère Angélique and fuel her critics on the legitimacy of her position. Her childhood experience of forced vocations, political interference in religious affairs, and the trafficking in religious benefices would strengthen her resolve to combat precisely these vices in her reform of Port-Royal.

The early formation of the future abbess acquainted her with a French convent culture that had grown decadent. On September 1, 1599, she was clothed in the habit of a novice at the Abbey of Saint-Antoine-des-Champs. She then joined her sister Jeanne (the future Mère Agnès) at the Abbey of Saint-Cyr, where her sister had just been appointed abbess, although the six-year-old girl could not exercise the office until she had reached the age of twenty. In 1600 Jacqueline-Marie was sent to the Cistercian Abbey of Maubuisson to acquire the rudiments of an education. Governed by Angélique d'Estrées, the sister of the mistress of Henri IV, Maubuisson had become notorious as the least reformed convent in the kingdom. The mother of at least twelve illegitimate children, apparently sired by twelve different men, Abbess d'Estrées openly used the convent's luxurious apartments as a refuge for trysts by the king and other members of the court. Banquets, masquerade balls, parties with the local gentry, and dances with monks from a nearby abbey dotted the social calendar of a convent where the obligation of the divine office had been largely abandoned.

In this lax atmosphere Jacqueline-Marie developed a rudimentary literacy, nourished by the romantic tales that were the favored reading of the Maubuisson nuns. She also developed an interest in ancient history through the reading of Plutarch's *Lives*.[2] The study of Plutarch's edifying narratives introduced her to the philosophical Stoicism that was enjoying a particular vogue in French intellectual circles of the period. Religious instruction was virtually nonexistent. On September 29, 1600, she received the sacrament of confirmation and adopted the name of Angélique. At her profession of monastic vows on October 29, 1603, she added an invocation to Saint Mary Magdalene. Henceforth, she would be known as Mère Marie-Angélique de Sainte-Magdeleine, popularly called Mère Angélique.

On April 10, 1602, Mère Angélique was solemnly installed as the coadjutor abbess of Port-Royal with right of succession. The sudden death of the Port-Royal abbess, Dame Jeanne Boulehart, on July 3, 1602, propelled the ten-year-old nun into the office of abbess. On July 5, 1602, Mère Angélique formally took possession of Port-Royal as its abbess.

Ably assisted by her parents, the infant abbess quickly placed a semblance of order into the demoralized convent of a dozen lax and impoverished nuns. Chosen as prioress, an older nun guided her on the rituals and daily governance of the convent. Monsieur Arnauld launched litigation that successfully secured contested properties for the convent. Lay superintendents who had pillaged the convent's ample resources in orchards and livestock were dismissed. Madame Arnauld personally supervised the rehabilitation of the dilapidated convent buildings. Although far from reformed, the nuns led more respectable lives as they recited a truncated office and accompanied their abbess on leisurely walks through the convent grounds. They praised their new superior for their improved material circumstances. In later autobiographical statements Mère Angélique admitted that she still disdained the vocation of a nun, which she neither understood nor liked. But from a secular perspective, her early abbacy (in fact the abbacy of her parents) had profited both her family and the grateful nuns. On December 17, 1604, the general superior of the Cistercian order left a favorable report on the state of the convent, requesting only efforts for a modest increase in the number of nuns to sixteen.

According to Mère Angélique the first stirring of religious reform occurred on March 25, 1608, as the abbess listened to a sermon by an itinerant Capuchin preacher, Père Basile. For the first time the abbess accepted with happiness her vocation as a nun. She asked her father to petition the Vatican to provide a bull of absolution for the deceit employed to obtain her post and for permission publicly to repronounce her vows, which she had earlier pronounced out of ignorance and under duress. She proposed to her skeptical subjects the project of reforming Port-Royal by returning the convent to strict observance of the Cistercian rule, itself a reformist revival of the primitive rule of Saint Benedict. On March 21, 1609, the chapter of the convent voted to endorse the reform, immediately made operative by the abolition of the nuns' private property and the placing of all the nuns' property and funds in common.

The most dramatic reform involved the restoration of the convent's cloister, banning the laity from entry into the internal spaces of the convent. On September 25, 1609, occurred the celebrated *journée du guichet,* on which Mère Angélique refused her own family entrance to the convent and demanded that they meet her behind the grille of the visitors' parlor. An enraged Monsieur Arnauld denounced his daughter's actions, but the family soon resigned itself to supporting the work of a daughter who had suddenly asserted her adulthood as an authentic nun committed to reform. Other changes followed: the imposition of silence and the use of Cistercian hand-language; the proper recitation of the divine office; rising at two o'clock in the morning to chant the office of matins; the imposition of rigorous periods of fast; the restoration of the chapter of faults, where nuns publicly accused themselves of their transgressions and received a penance from the abbess. In 1614 she instituted the last of the major public reforms: the return of year-round abstinence by the adoption of a strict vegetarian diet. Focusing on her own reformation, she expressed sorrow for past deceptions and infidelities as she repronounced her vows on May 7, 1610, in the presence of Dom Largentier, the abbot of Clairvaux.

The early years of reform also permitted Mère Angélique to shape a new theological culture for Port-Royal. Theologically distinguished preachers, such as the Capuchin Archange de Pembroke, provided conferences on Christian doctrine for religiously ignorant nuns. Sermons and lectures helped the nuns to develop a biblical and patristic culture that would complement the texts they chanted during the divine office. Reading at table featured the writings of the desert fathers, Saint Augustine, and other patristic authors; the "modern" devotional literature championed by the Jesuits was tellingly absent from the new intellectual culture fostered by the reform. The abbess also promoted an austere aesthetic culture shaped by primitive Cistercian spirituality; plainchant was preferred to polyphony, functional architecture to decorative, devotional paintings to statuary.

Now a revered architect of monastic reform, Mère Angélique was commissioned by Dom Boucherat, the abbot-general of the Cistercian order, to undertake a perilous mission: the reform of the notorious abbey of Maubuisson. On February 5, 1618, the abbot-general sent a troop of archers to arrest and incarcerate the scandalous Angélique d'Estrées. Facing a recalcitrant group of lax nuns hostile to any reform initiative, Mère Angélique decided to reform the abbey by personally choosing and forming twenty novices for the convent. Her decision to accept undowered candidates and to reject affluent candidates she considered without vocation shocked aristocratic opinion, long accustomed to using convents like Maubuisson as an asylum for surplus daughters. One of the principles of Mère Angélique's concept of reform, the personal freedom of vocation, had become a practical policy.

The stormy reform of Maubuisson followed an uneven course. An enraged Angélique d'Estrées, escaped from the convent of the Filles Pénitentes, expelled Mère Angélique and her disciples from the convent. Only a new military occupation of the convent definitively removed d'Estrées and permitted Mère Angélique to resume governance. In the midst of the turmoil Mère Angélique made the acquaintance of François de Sales, bishop of Geneva, and placed herself under his spiritual direction until his death in 1622. In 1620 she befriended Jeanne de Chantal, the cofounder of the Visitation order with de Sales, with whom she corresponded over a period of twenty years. The Salesian emphasis on abandonment of the will to divine providence palpably influenced the spirituality of Mère Angélique, although her later moral rigorism diverged from the spirit of moral moderation typical of Salesian theology. In 1623 the abbess left a semireformed Maubuisson to return to Port-Royal with an entourage of young novices she had personally recruited for a reformed monastic life.

On March 3, 1623, Mère Angélique resumed personal governance of Port-Royal, ably assisted by her sister Mère Agnès, who had renounced the abbacy of Saint-Cyr and had become the co-adjutor abbess of Port-Royal in 1619. Enlarged by new vocations and the transfer of nuns seeking a reformed convent, the community of eighty had outgrown the antiquated and insalubrious buildings of the old convent. Mère Angélique decided to open a Parisian branch of Port-Royal on the grounds of the Hôtel de Clagny in the Faubourg Saint-Jacques, a neighborhood adjacent to the Sorbonne which already housed a series of new monasteries. Dom Boucherat, the head of the Cistercian order, consented to the move in 1624; Jean-François de Gondi, the archbishop of Paris, approved in 1625, but only on condition that the entire community move from the valley of the Chevreuse to the new Parisian location and that the convent accept supervision by the archdiocese of Paris over its affairs. By the summer of 1626 the entire community had transferred to the new Port-Royal de Paris. Thanks to the generosity of lay benefactors, construction began on a church and cloister marked by Mère Angélique's Cistercian taste for architectural sobriety.

Following her reform of Port-Royal, Mère Angélique now attempted to enhance the autonomy of the convent vis-à-vis external religious and political authorities. In 1628 she received permission from Pope Urban VIII to transfer direction of the convent from the Cistercian abbot-general, residing at the abbey of Cîteaux, to the archbishop of Paris. This jurisdictional change was occasioned by the abbess's long-standing dissatisfaction with the chaplains and confessors appointed by Cîteaux for Port-Royal; it was also precipitated by the 1625 election of Dom Nivelle, an opponent of monastic reform, as the order's abbot-general. Even more audacious was the successful effort to change the governance of the convent by abolishing royal appointment of the abbess and instituting election of the abbess by the Port-Royal chapter of nuns for a three-year term.

In 1629 Louis XIII approved the change, setting the stage for Mère Angélique's resignation as abbess in 1630, followed by the election of Mère Geneviève de Saint-Augustin Le Tardif, who served as abbess until 1636.

During this transition Mère Angélique increasingly relied on the counsel of Sébastien Zamet, bishop of Langres. Presenting himself as a champion of religious reform, evidenced by his personal efforts to reform the Cistercian convent of Tard in his diocese, Zamet supported the legal changes effected by the abbess in the statutes of Port-Royal. Confidant and adviser of the new abbess, Mère Geneviève, Zamet interested Mère Angélique in his new project: the establishment of a new religious order, the Institut du Saint-Sacrement, to be devoted to perpetual adoration of the Eucharist. Since Port-Royal had already established the practice of perpetual adoration in its own convent and since Zamet appeared to promise patronage for a reformed convent free of compromise with unreformed monastic authorities, Mère Angélique at first enthusiastically joined the bishop in the new enterprise. The consequences for Port-Royal and for the ephemeral Institut would soon prove disastrous.

Under the tutelage of Zamet, the ethos of Port-Royal de Paris quickly changed. The once sober convent chapel was now filled with elaborate bouquets, exotic incense, and glittering embroidery as the liturgical offices became more theatrical. Spiced dishes on pewter plates replaced the old plain food on earthenware vessels. Each nun was provided with an inkwell and writing stand to record her latest mystical inspirations so that she could share them with distinguished visitors in the convent parlor. Even convent punishments took a more dramatic turn. New confessors ordered nuns to whip each other for perceived transgressions. Suspect as a silent opponent of the new regime, Mère Angélique herself became a victim of the ascetical pageant. Wearing a sign stating I AM A PIECE OF TRASH, she was ordered one evening to circulate among the nuns in the refectory as she carried a box of refuse in front of her.

In 1633 the long-planned Institut du Saint-Sacrement was finally launched in the fashionable neighborhood adjacent to the Louvre. The general direction of the new religious order was confided to a troika of authorities: Bishop Zamet; Jean-François de Gondi, archbishop of Paris; and Olivier de Bellegarde, archbishop of

Sens. Although opposed by Zamet, Mère Angélique found herself named the superior of the fledgling community, due to the insistence of Gondi. Zamet's influence permeated the new convent. Located near the palace, the convent was to accept as novices only well-bred daughters of the aristocracy. The theatrical liturgies and luxuriously appointed chapel quickly attracted a court clientele avid for spiritual exhilaration. Rather than keeping silence, the nuns were urged to master the art of polite conversation so that they could share their spiritual insights with the cultivated courtiers who crowded the convent parlors. Amateur couturier, Zamet even designed the fashionable scarlet-and-white habit to be worn by the nuns as they chanted their elaborate offices.

The tension between Zamet and Mère Angélique, completely opposed on the proper path of reform in the religious life, quickly became a bitter quarrel among the three canonical directors of the order. In 1633 Archbishop de Bellegarde attempted to humiliate Zamet by delating the *Private Chaplet,* a brief devotional work by Mère Agnès, to a theological committee of the Sorbonne for condemnation. Written in a luxuriant lyrical style, the work was widely considered a specimen of the mystically exalted literature inspired by Zamet and his Oratorian allies at Port-Royal and now at the Institut du Saint-Sacrement. The Sorbonne committee promptly condemned the text as riddled with theological errors. Outraged, Zamet turned to a theologian friend, Jean du Vergier de Hauranne, the abbot of Saint-Cyran, to defend the work against its critics. Saint-Cyran not only ably defended the work in a popular pamphlet; he solicited the approbation of Cornelius Jansen and other Louvain theologians for the orthodoxy of the contested treatise. When Rome finally intervened in the squabble in 1634, it diplomatically ordered the text withdrawn from circulation but refused to condemn the work itself.

Riven by financial problems, philosophical disagreements, and jurisdictional disputes, the Institut languished. In 1636 Mère Angélique received permission from the archbishop of Paris to return to Port-Royal, still under the authority of the archdiocese. The ascendancy of Zamet had collapsed. The Institut du Saint-Sacrement survived until 1638, when the last nuns returned to Port-Royal. The only trace of the failed experiment remained in the convent's new name, Port-Royal du Saint-Sacrement, and in the new white scapular emblazoned with a scarlet cross, symbolizing the bread and wine of the Eucharist, added to Port-Royal's Cistercian habit.

Port-Royal quickly returned to the austere path of reform originally championed by Mère Angélique. On September 19, 1636, the convent chapter elected Mère Agnès as abbess; she served two terms until 1642. Mère Angélique was immediately appointed novice mistress, responsible for the formation of young nuns. Gently contested by her sister, who was still sympathetic to the more mystical piety of Zamet, Mère Angélique introduced Saint-Cyran, her spiritual director from the Institut du Saint-Sacrement, as the new director of Port-Royal. In his conferences and sermons Saint-Cyran reinforced the sober, practical piety advocated by Mère Angélique and introduced his own particular theology of the spiritual life.

Condemning the alleged laxism of the Jesuits, Saint-Cyran insisted on a rigorist sacramental practice. Sacramental absolution in confession was valid only if the penitent expressed perfect contrition (sorrow for sin due to the offense caused God) rather than imperfect contrition (sorrow for sin due to fear of spiritual or temporal punishment). The risk of sacrilege in the reception of Holy Communion was so great that the Sacrament should be approached rarely, only after the most scrupulous preparation. "Retreats" from eucharistic reception were recommended as an aid to arouse a deeper sense of one's sinfulness and unworthiness before God. Stressing the Augustinian theology of grace defended by his longtime friend Cornelius Jansen, Saint-Cyran underscored the radical concupiscence of the human person and the central role of predestination in a salvation rooted in grace. In addition to daily biblical meditation, the reading of the church fathers, especially Saint Augustine, was to nourish the intellectual and spiritual lives of the nuns.

The treatises, manuals, letters, and sermons of Saint-Cyran quickly became staples for personal devotion, the formation of young nuns, and the catechesis of laywomen in the convent's school. The imprisonment of Saint-Cyran by Richelieu's order in the Chateau de Vincennes (1638–43) only glorified him as a martyr for Port-Royal. The influence of Saint-Cyran on the theological personality of Port-Royal should not be exaggerated. His work largely confirmed the ascetical practices, the theological intuitions, and the Salesian spirituality Mère Angélique had long embodied in her reform of the abbey. But Saint-Cyran provided Mère Angélique and her colleagues with a precise neo-Augustinian philosophy with which they could express their ideal of religious reform and which would set the terms of their conflict with Jesuits and other critics.

During the 1640s the abbey of Port-Royal became the center of a broader movement clearly associated with the works and theories of Cornelius Jansen, as interpreted by Saint-Cyran. In 1642 Mère Angélique was elected abbess, a position she held until 1654. In 1637 a group of devout laymen and clerics, popularly known as the *solitaires*, had begun to rehabilitate the abandoned buildings of Port-Royal des Champs. Their *petites écoles* for boys, conducted at various locations, introduced pedagogical innovations that influenced French education far beyond Jansenist circles. In 1648 Port-Royal nuns began to occupy the restored Champs convent, since the Parisian convent could no longer house the more than one hundred nuns who had flocked to Port-Royal. Henceforth the abbess of Port-Royal would govern both locations as branches of the same convent, assisted by a prioress resident at each site. In 1648 a new, larger church at Port-Royal de Paris opened to accommodate the crowds attending the sermons and conferences of convent chaplain Antoine Singlin, a protégé of Saint-Cyran who perpetuated the latter's controversial teaching on grace, the sacraments, and morality. Aristocratic families in the Paris area vied to place their daughters in Port-Royal's bourgeoning convent school.

The triumph of Mère Angélique's reform only sharpened the opposition of critics. When her brother Antoine Arnauld published *Of Frequent Communion* (1644), defending Saint-Cyran's controversial sacramental theology, he was forced into hiding by the virulence of Jesuit criticism. Brother Robert Arnauld d'Andilly's translation of Jansen's *Reform of the Interior Man* (1645) reinforced the association of Port-Royal with a moral rigorism opposed by the court and the Jesuits. In 1651 a fiery pamphlet by the Jesuit theologian Jean de Brisacier denounced the Port-Royal nuns as "impenitent women, desperadoes, opponents of the sacraments, fanatics, and foolish virgins."[3] Although Mère Angélique publicly cautioned her nuns to avoid participation in the theological controversies, her private correspondence indicates detailed knowledge of the works and theories under dispute. In numerous letters she intervened with prominent religious and political authorities to defend Port-Royal against its critics.

During the Fronde (1648–52), the intermittent civil war that ravaged Paris and its countryside, Mère Angélique distinguished herself by her charitable work for the starving poor and by her welcoming of more than four hundred nuns traumatized by the pillage and rape practiced by marauding troops. As François Boulêtreau argues, the heroic charity of the abbess during this period of terror consecrated her popular image as a living saint among many of the peasantry in the Parisian region.[4]

In 1654 Mère Marie Suireau was elected abbess, a position she held until her death in 1658. She was succeeded by Mère Agnès, who served as abbess until 1661. Even out of office Mère Angélique continued to guide Port-Royal as the persecution of it and the broader Jansenist movement intensified. Antoine Arnauld's controversial works defending the orthodoxy of the *Augustinus* and condemning the denial of sacramental absolution to lay sympathizers of Port-Royal once again forced him into hiding and ultimately caused his condemnation by the theological faculty of the Sorbonne in 1656. In 1656 Blaise Pascal anonymously published the first of his *Provincial Letters,* attacking Jesuit casuistry and defending the neo-Augustinian party's theory of grace. In her correspondence Mère Angélique indicated her support for the philosophical positions defended in these controversial works, but she showed increasing alarm at the violent rhetoric overtaking the theological champions of Port-Royal.

As the crisis of the *Augustinus* reached its denouement, the persecution of Port-Royal hardened. In 1660 the government ordered the closure of the *petites écoles* and the dispersion of the *solitaires.* In 1661 the Assembly of the Clergy ordered that clergy, religious, and teachers sign a new formulary clearly indicating submission to the church's condemnation of the five controversial theological propositions on grace and to the church's judgment that Jansen had defended these propositions in the *Augustinus.* On April 23, 1661, civil authorities decreed the expulsion of the boarding pupils, the closure of the convent school, and the expulsion of postulants, thus appearing to compromise the very future of the order. On June

23–24, 1661, the nuns of Port-Royal reluctantly gave qualified signatures to the formulary, indicating that they accepted only the judgments of *droit* (the condemnation of the five propositions as heretical) but that they refused any assent to judgments of *fait* (that Jansen had in fact advocated such positions). Few were surprised that this awkward compromise was promptly denounced by both religious and political authorities. As the crisis of the signature continued, the nuns were forced to choose between unqualified submission to the condemnation of Jansen or the gradual destruction of the convent.

As the fortunes of the convent quickly declined, a sickly Mère Angélique intensified her intercession with civil and religious authorities on behalf of the embattled community. Addressed to the queen-mother Anne of Austria, her last major letter (May 25, 1661) defended the orthodoxy of the Port-Royal nuns. "We have never desired anything other than to live in Christian simplicity as humble daughters of the church, having no other faith than its own, revering the pope as the church's head and the vicar of Jesus Christ and holding as condemned all the errors and heresies he has condemned."[5] Even the phrasing of her defense subtly suggests that the nuns were bound to accept only church judgments that were clearly condemnations of theological error, not empirical statements of fact. She justified her boldness in addressing the queen in this controversy by citing the precedent of Teresa of Avila: "Madame, I believe that God will use the piety of Your Majesty and the wisdom of the king, as he used Phillip II, ancestor of Your Majesty, in the past, to save Saint Teresa [of Avila] from the greatest persecution she ever knew. We see in her writings that even the pope had been wrongly informed about her and the nuns of her order and that his nuncio had been prejudiced against her, thus pushing this controversy, according to her own words, to the last level of violence. When everything seemed lost, God revealed to her that she should present herself to her king and that he would treat them as a true father."[6] The flattering historical reference subtly indicates that misjudgments of fact were neither rare nor recent at the papal court. The abbess blamed the long-standing Jesuit caricature of Port-Royal for the opprobrium the nuns were currently enduring. Even on her deathbed, she embodied the militant suffering for the truth she had long enjoined on her subjects and correspondents.

Mére Angélique died on August 6, 1661.

WORKS

Accustomed to writing occasional works, Mère Angélique composed no treatises of systematic philosophy and theology. She left behind three major literary works: her autobiographical *Report*, her massive correspondence, and the spiritual conferences she delivered to the Port-Royal nuns. In the latter works, she developed her own Augustinian theology with philosophical excurses on the divine attributes, the moral virtues, spiritual freedom, and the exercise of authority by women.

Composed at the command of Abbé Singlin in 1655, the *Report Written by Mère Angélique Arnauld Concerning the Major Occurrences at Port-Royal* recounts her life from her unhappy childhood until her return to Port-Royal in 1636. More than a narrative, the autobiography is a pointed apology for the abbess's policies of reform. Saint François de Sales is lauded as the inspiration behind the reform; Zamet is condemned for his worldly, theatrical spirituality; Saint-Cyran is exalted as the model of ascetical wisdom. The narrative permits Mère Angélique to defend her actions in the controversies surrounding the imposition of cloister, the conflicts at Maubuisson, the quarrel over the *Private Chaplet*, and the fiasco of the Institut du Saint-Sacrement.

The *Report* is one of the apologetic works cultivated by Mère Angélique's nephew the *solitaire* Antoine Le Maître, starting in 1648, and her niece Mère Angélique de Saint-Jean, starting in 1651. As the persecution against Port-Royal intensified, the scholarly couple encouraged the nuns to write memoirs that would explain the history of the controversial reform of the convent, highlighting both its theological orthodoxy and its moral probity. Jean Lesaulnier's recent critical edition of the *Report* (1992)[7] provides a more accurate version of the autobiography than did the earlier Cognet critical edition (1949),[8] inasmuch as it is based on the earliest extant manuscript version of the text (BNF Ms. Ffr. 17795). If the *Report*

provides a gripping chronicle of the vagaries of Mère Angélique's reform campaign until its triumph in the late 1630s, the polemical
and hagiographical tone of the document indicates its limits as a
historical narrative.

Her massive correspondence constitutes Mère Angélique's major
literary monument.[9] Published in three volumes in 1742–44 by Jansenist exiles at Utrecht, her collected letters contain more than thir-
teen hundred letters addressed to more than one hundred correspondents. As Jean Mesnard notes, the presence of hundreds of other
unpublished letters of the abbess residing in French, Belgian, and
Dutch archives indicates that a definitive edition of the abbess's
complete extant correspondence would be even more extensive.[10]
Starting in 1620, the surviving letters of Mère Angélique were addressed to several groups of correspondents: members of the Arnauld family; other nuns, especially fellow superiors; laywomen
who sought her spiritual counsel and who often served as benefactors of the convent; clerics and laymen, many of them *solitaires*,
prominent in theological controversies; ecclesiastical and political
dignitaries whose intercession was sought to protect Port-Royal
against its critics. A special place is occupied by Marie-Louise de
Gonzague, queen of Poland, with whom the abbess frequently corresponded over the course of decades.

Among her familial correspondents, Mère Angélique's older
brother Robert Arnauld d'Andilly and younger brother Antoine Arnauld hold a central position. The letters with two scholars well-
versed in theology permitted the abbess to discuss the controversies
surrounding grace, free will, and casuistry. Her later correspondence
with her nephew Antoine Le Maître and her niece Soeur Angélique
de Saint-Jean Arnauld d'Andilly offered her the occasion to state her
position on the rights of conscience during the persecution of the
convent and to specify the virtues necessary to endure the opposition of the throne.

In her correspondence with other nuns, the abbess often provides spiritual direction for the exercise of certain virtues. She also
offers practical advice for the resolution of typical convent conflicts.
Numerous letters defend the right of the superior to exercise authority in the governance and reform of her convent. Significant in
this regard are the lengthy missives to Mère Catherine Morant, ab-

bess of the Benedictine abbey of Gif. She also supports efforts at the constitutional reform of convents that will enhance the power of convent chapters to elect their own superior and to defend their own customs.

More worldly in tone, the correspondence with prominent lay-women supporting Port-Royal permits Mère Angélique to offer spiritual direction to women remaining in the world. In fostering a deeper abandonment to God and detachment from the world, the abbess often functions as a moralist criticizing the vices typical of the aristocracy: vanity, concern for reputation, and spiritual sentimentality. Her voluntarist emphasis on the primacy of will over emotion in the spiritual life flavors much of her ascetical advice. Moral rigorism emerges in her critique of the education favored by these aristocratic women, an education privileging artistic achievement and the acquisition of social graces. The letters to the Princesse Guéménée, Madame de Sablé, and Madame de Longueville typify the sympathetic but critical attitude adopted by the abbess toward the host of aristocratic women who stoutly defended Port-Royal but who never quite overcame their worldly fascination with a convent that had become fashionable by its very austerity and refusal to compromise.

With the priests and laymen attracted to Port-Royal as the quarrel over Jansenism intensified, Mère Angélique adopts a more intellectual tone. With the theologian Jacques de Sainte-Beuve, the humanist Claude Lancelot, and the medical doctor Jean Hamon, the abbess shares her positions on the latest chapter of the struggle between the Jesuits and the Jansenists; she seeks counsel on strategies to protect the embattled convent. Always the spiritual director, she repeatedly reminds her interlocutors of the specific moral and theological virtues they need to balance their tendency to rely on rhetorical skill and political calculation in the midst of persecution.

In her correspondence with ecclesiastical and political dignitaries, such as Archbishop Paul de Gondi of Paris and Queen-Mother Anne of Austria, the lawyer Arnauld dominates Mère Angélique's voice. Her defense of Port-Royal carefully weaves together pertinent documents, historical precedent, and logical argument to prove the convent's innocence and to unmask the perfidy of its opponents.

Her apology for the orthodoxy and integrity of the convent often tackles larger questions concerning the moral limits of authority.

The extensive correspondence with Marie-Louise de Gonzague, the queen of Poland, reveals another facet of Mère Angélique. Before her departure for Warsaw in 1646, Gonzague had been a fervent partisan of Port-Royal, participating in several retreats at the convent. For more than fifteen years Mère Angélique exchanged weekly letters with the lonely Polish queen and her French entourage: her confessor, François Fleury, and her companions, Marguerite Josse and Madame des Esserts. The normally taciturn abbess becomes affectionate. Staunch proponent of detachment from worldly possessions, she dwells on her sentimental attachment to Gonzague's presence. "I can tell Your Majesty that you are as present to us as you were when we had the honor of seeing you. Your little cell here is often discussed. It will carry the name of Your Majesty forever. Your rosary, a picture of you—in a word, everything is precious to us."[11] Opponent of expressions of emotion, she freely confesses her grief at the death of her sister Catherine de Saint-Jean Le Maître. "Your Majesty is aware of the death of my sister Catherine de Saint-Jean Le Maître. . . . Madame, I confess to you that I am still so human that my feelings suffer terribly from her absence, even though my spirit is greatly consoled by my hope that God, having provided her with so many graces by his pure mercy, has received her into his bosom."[12]

The correspondence with the queen also provided the occasion for Mère Angélique to explore the proper exercise of political authority by women and to criticize the vices typical of a royal court. As Poland is devastated by war and Port-Royal is paralyzed by persecution, the correspondence explores the weight of social evil and the difficulty of detecting divine providence in the midst of oppression.

Throughout the correspondence the extensive theological culture of the abbess is evident. An avid reader, her theological and philosophical interests appear in her commentaries on the books she cites. It is sacred Scripture itself that is the most cited work in her letters; the Psalms and the Epistles of Saint Paul are frequent objects of exegesis. Among patristic authors Saint Augustine holds pride of place, with the *Confessions* being his most cited work.

Other patristic works include *The Lives of the Desert Fathers,* Saint John Climacus's *Ladder of Perfection,* Saint Bernard's *Steps of Humility,* and the *Rule of Saint Benedict.* Hagiographies include *The Life of Saint Bernard,* by Antoine Le Maître. The works of Saint François de Sales, especially his *Introduction to the Devout Life,* dominate the modern French works of spirituality she recommends to her addressees. Among modern Spanish works of theology, she frequently cites the writings of Saint Teresa of Avila and of Venerable Louis of Grenada. On several occasions the abbess confesses her particular enthusiasm for the treatises of Saint Teresa, first published in French in 1602.

The correspondence indicates a detailed knowledge of the works that figured prominently in the Jansenist controversies: Jansen's *Reform of the Interior Man;* Saint-Cyran's *Simple Theology* and *Collected Letters;* Antoine Singlin's *Collected Sermons;* Antoine Arnauld's *Of Frequent Communion, Apologies for Jansenius,* and *Letters to a Duke and Peer;* Blaise Pascal's *Provincial Letters;* Mère Agnès's *Private Chaplet of the Blessed Sacrament;* Jean de Brisacier's *Jansenism Confounded;* Étienne Binet's *Summary Discussion of a Booklet Entitled "Private Chaplet of the Blessed Sacrament."* She recommends the use of Antoine Le Maître's *Office of the Blessed Sacrament,* a controversial effort to translate the Latin hymns and psalms of the liturgy into the French vernacular. In several letters she declares her general philosophical orientation by declaring herself a "disciple of Saint Augustine,"[13] but this is clearly an Augustinianism deeply shaped by the neo-Augustinian theology of Jansen and his Port-Royal disciples.

Mère Angélique was well aware that her letters had quickly acquired a semipublic status. Sympathetic convents and aristocratic houses freely circulated the missives received from a hero of religious reform. Letters dealing with religious and political controversies swirling around Port-Royal were often treated as "open letters," apologies for the convent that were to be used in the pamphlet wars of the period. In vain the abbess complained that admiring Port-Royal nuns would surreptitiously copy her letters before they were dispatched to her addressees. Shortly after the abbess's death in 1661, her niece Soeur Angèlique de Saint-Jean Arnauld d'Andilly copied and collated the extant letters in the convent. This collection constituted the core of the manuscripts preserved by generations of Jansenists and finally published by Jansenist exiles in the 1742–44 Utrecht edition.

The third major work of Mère Angélique consists of transcriptions of spiritual conferences presented by the abbess at Port-Royal in the 1650s.[14] These informal conferences (*conférences familières*) took place during the convent's recreation period. Nuns would pose questions to the abbess, who would then attempt to resolve the problems raised. Delivered in 1652, 1654, 1655, and 1659, the conferences were transcribed by Soeur Angélique de Saint-Jean Arnauld d'Andilly, who did not hesitate to add her own editorial comments, praising the wisdom of her aunt. Published at Brussels in 1757, the conferences provided Mère Angélique with a forum to present her solutions to typical moral dilemmas in a cloistered convent.

Primarily practical in orientation, the conferences also permitted the abbess to develop certain philosophical positions. Her moral voluntarism controls her argument that intention rather than act or even virtue constitutes the center of moral value. In her pointed criticisms of superstitious practices and sentimental piety, a determined rationalism appears. The unvarnished Gospel, made manifest in practical gestures of justice and mercy, is to be preferred to a piety vitiated by abstract metaphysics or by uncritical emotion.

Also of philosophical interest are various unpublished abbatial addresses of Mère Angélique that remain in manuscript form at the Bibliothèque Nationale de France (BNF Ms. Ffr. 17794, vols. 5–6). As Thomas M. Carr remarks, this collection of abbatial addresses is remarkable for its variety: addresses on the Rule of Saint Benedict, practical instructions for the maintenance of the convent, reprimands and assignment of penances for infractions of the Rule, occasional addresses at the moment of a vow ceremony or the election of an abbess.[15] The major manuscript work is her commentary on the Rule of Saint Benedict, in which Mère Angélique shows the patent Oratorian influence of Condren in her treatment of the virtue of humility as a species of annihilation. "We are obliged to be in a continual state of annihilation in order to honor the state of Jesus Christ in this mystery [his passion] and to correspond to the plan he has for us to merit grace by rendering to God this perfect homage of our annihilation before him."[16]

LETTERS

Negative Theology

All of Mère Angélique's letters concern religious questions. Only a handful, however, focus on the attributes of God. Faithful to the *via negativa,* the abbess returns repeatedly to the incomprehensibility of God, whose ways defy human understanding and desire. Tied to this incomprehensibility is divine sovereignty. It is the will of God, ordering human history according to his hidden designs, that resides at the heart of the divine mystery and which constitutes the object of Christian adoration. Allied to this philosophy of divine attributes is a religious epistemology. The recognition of God's obscure sovereignty is the product neither of logical deduction nor of generic grace; it emerges as the fruit of certain spiritual practices, such as habitual meditation on one's personal death or a synoptic grasp of the finitude of the world.

Several letters address the inscrutability of God. To Soeur Anne de Sainte-Magdeleine Halley, a nun shaken by calumnious charges against the convent, Mère Angélique insists that unexpected turns of fate reveal the inscrutability of God himself.

> Remember that his [God's] goodness effects the salvation of his elect by different tribulations and that his ways are inscrutable. . . . You know, Sister, that through his mercy we have tried to walk in truth and simplicity before him. What they accuse us of is false. Aren't we happy enough to suffer through the witness of our conscience? There are no accidents in God. None of the strange incidents in this affair were unknown to him. If he didn't want all of them, he at least permitted them. It will end as it pleases him. Whatever human beings may do, he will not do anything other than what he has commanded from all eternity. Since this is infallible, Sister, what could disturb us about it?[17]

To explain the enigma of moral evil in the calumnies, the abbess employs the neo-Scholastic distinction between God's concurring will and tolerating will. But the passage's emphasis on God's perfect will governing the world, buttressed by its opening theology of election, minimizes human freedom. The vicissitudes of human history indicate the presence of a sovereign will directing events, but the baffling moral pattern of this history, where the innocent suffer alongside the sinful, veils this divine will in obscurity.

So impenetrable is God's will that one can easily misread history when one attempts to interpret God's actions in the world. In a letter to the prioress of the abbey of Gif, Mère Angélique explains how the effort to pinpoint God's intentions can lead to serious error. "The judgments and ways of God are admirable. Often it happens that he seems to want to destroy when he wants to build up. What appears to be a result of his anger and justice is actually a result of his mercy. Blessed are the souls who see in every event only his holy will in order to submit to it in the certitude that it will always be favorable to them."[18] The refusal to respect the inscrutability of God's will not only misconstrues history by substituting human projections for God's impenetrable wisdom; it easily induces a distorted perception of God's other attributes, such as a mistaken substitution of divine anger for divine mercy.

This passage also indicates the rupture between Creator and creature in the abbess's theology. While the believer may recognize and adore the divine will operative in the events of history, the morally and semiotically ambiguous sequence of these events does not permit the believer to affirm the specific divine intention behind a particular occurrence.

Narrowly tied to divine inscrutability is the sovereignty of God. God alone directs history by his eternal decrees, especially in the salvation of the elect. In a letter to her brother Robert Arnauld d'Andilly, Mère Angélique laments the forgetting of God's sovereign majesty that characterizes convent life as well as the libertine society of the broader French world. "I see the sins, the irreligion, and the libertinism of the world, as well as the nonchalance and the inattentiveness of those who are happy to be withdrawn from it, not only by their body but also by their heart. They possess the fear of God in the world without being of it. Still, they do not truly pay attention to honor God and to make reparation for the many outrages he receives at the hands of the evil. As a result, the majesty of God is not truly honored. It is practically forgotten by everyone, in first place by me."[19] This passage underscores the voluntarist cast of the abbess's theory of the divine attributes. The widespread contemporary forgetting of God, operative in the cloister as well as in the salon, is more precisely the forgetting of God's sovereignty as Creator and Savior of the world. It is God's majestic will that has been eclipsed in religious piety as well as in skeptical arguments.

Mère Angélique's insistence that the inscrutable sovereignty of God should prevent the enlightened believer from quickly interpreting the work of God in history emerges with particular force in her analysis of the celebrated miracle of the holy thorn in 1656. Whereas many sympathizers of Port-Royal, notably Blaise Pascal,[20] had interpreted the miracle as a divine confirmation of the convent's sanctity, the abbess treats the event with cool indifference.

> I am astonished that the world talks so much about the miracle that has happened and even more that it claims that more of them will happen. I couldn't believe anything less. If I had to hope for and ask for something from God, it would not concern the corporeal; it would concern so many unfortunate souls who languish in miseries a hundred times worse than the evils of the body, where health and strength often only serve to kill the soul. Dear Sister, do not desire that God should assert his truth by visible miracles, but by the invisible one of conversion of hearts, which is done without clamor or noise.[21]

As the abbess argues in other letters on the topic, the miraculous healing of Marguerite Périer must be received with humility, since the divine intention behind the apparent miracle remains obscure.

The miracle should also be placed at a distance because the goods of the body are far inferior to those of the soul. The evangelical experience of conversion, effected by the sovereign work of God's grace, presents greater characteristics of the miraculous than does any physical healing. Just as God's sovereign will remains veiled in obscurity, the most important work of God, namely eternal salvation, occurs in the invisible realm of the soul. Furthermore, it is a work operated according to the inscrutable logic of God's choice of the elect.

The proper recognition of God's attributes, especially God's incomprehensibility, does not emerge as the conclusion of discursive reason; it is the work of grace. Mère Angélique insists that authentic knowledge of God arises as the result of engaging in certain grace-inspired practices. Many of these practices pivot around meditation on the finitude of oneself and of the world. The abbess counsels many of her correspondents to meditate on their own mortality in order to face God's sovereign will in a posture of truth. Her advice to the queen of Poland is typical.

> The life of this world is only a succession of perpetual miseries that follow each other and end in death. This is the greatest of evils for the impious and the consummation of the penance of the servants of God. These final sufferings are for both kinds, but the most terrible of these sufferings endured by the first kind at this moment are only a tiny beginning of those into which they will be plunged for all eternity; for the last kind, this is the end of suffering and what places them in the possession of every good. These thoughts console me and I pray God that his Holy Spirit will engrave them in the heart of Your Majesty and make you firm and unmovable in every kind of event. May you fear to lose only God, love only God, desire only God. Everything will then serve you—evils as well as goods—to advance in his love and to merit his kingdom.[22]

By meditating on one's mortality, and in particular on the divine judgment that awaits us at the moment of death, the believer can awaken to a new recognition of God's majestic sovereignty, no longer encumbered by the concerns of everyday life. Not confined to the intellectual affirmation of God's existence, this recognition manifests itself in a new theocentric disposition of the believer. The love of God alone, not the love of God conditioned on the reception of past or future benefits, becomes the mark of a believer adoring God's absolute mystery.

Not confined to a negative theology, Mère Angélique's philosophy of God's attributes recognizes certain positive qualities of God accessible to human reflection. The correspondence repeatedly cites the goodness, providence, justice, and mercy of God. The discussion of the positive attributes, however, occurs against the backdrop of God's impenetrable mystery. For the abbess, the positive affirmation of God's qualities is subordinate to the affirmation of

God's inscrutable will. The rupture between divine and human natures trumps the similarity between the two in certain moral attributes. The recognition of this obscure divine sovereignty cannot surface in a syllogistic exercise of rational reflection on the conditions for the existence of the cosmos. It emerges only in the assiduous practice of meditation on the mortality of oneself and of the universe one briefly inhabits. The truths concerning God's attributes are progressively disclosed in an ascetical itinerary sustained by God's grace.

Theocentric Virtue

Often composed as moral exhortations, the letters of Mère Angélique frequently urge her correspondents to advance in the course of virtue. The cardinal virtues of prudence, temperance, fortitude, and justice receive only minor attention. In the Augustinian perspective these virtues are customarily treated with suspicion as the masks of neopagan pride. From the monastic viewpoint these virtues primarily concern those who still live in the world, struggling to develop a minimum of discipline over their sensual appetites. In the theocentric universe of the abbess, the theological virtues of faith, hope, and charity hold central place. Strikingly, Mère Angélique provides a theocentric account of less explicitly religious virtues, such as patience and self-knowledge. The convent is not simply the site for the exercise and perfection of these generic Christian virtues; it constitutes a distinctive way of life whose vowed commitments foster the cultivation of such monastic virtues as poverty, obedience, and contempt of the world. Transposed into a theological key, the virtues emerge as a cluster of intellectual and volitional habits uniting the soul to God, even to the point of annihilation of the human subject.

At the center of Mère Angélique's edifice of virtue stands the virtue of piety. Fostering reverence before the mystery of God, piety consists in the filial recognition of and submission to God as the origin and end of every creature. Several letters to the queen of Poland clarify the abbess's conception of piety.

Piety not only focuses on the mystery of God; it abolishes any trace of preoccupation with oneself or the world. In contemplating the eternity of God, for example, the pious person abandons concern for the world. "The sufferings and all the evils of this world, which lasts so little, are nothing in comparison with eternity . . . We have the same God as good and powerful as the God of Daniel, who preferred to risk death than to fail to pray to God and destroy the lie of false divinities."[23] Rather than a simple reverence for God and respect for sacred things, authentic piety fosters a sentiment of adoration so pure that other considerations, even concern for one's life, disappear.

Any adulteration of piety by attachment to the world constitutes a diabolic ruse. "This enemy of our salvation has little concern about who possesses the kingdoms of the world; all his rage is directed against God. His principal purpose is to rip out the hearts of love we owe God and to make them attached to creatures, giving them the place of God, who alone merits to be loved and who has given everything to humanity so that it will sacrifice everything to him. By this sacrifice it obtains from his divine goodness the grace to possess him and to reign with him forever."[24] In this account of piety, the characteristic dualism of Mère Angélique appears. The choice of God inevitably involves a firm rejection of the world. Creator opposes creature; eternity opposes temporality. A capacious piety engendering a simultaneous reverence toward God and the world rests on a spiritual illusion. As the abbess insists in numerous letters of spiritual direction, this astringent piety of adoration can be sustained only through daily meditation on God's attributes and an ascetical program that firmly limits access to worldly diversions.

This rigorist concept of piety governs Mère Angélique's treatment of the theological virtues, specifically hope and charity. In numerous passages she provides a standard Christian definition of hope as the aspiration to eternal life with God, rooted in the resurrection of Christ. Typically, however, the abbess's concept of hope accents the opposition between the desired heaven and the corrupt world we must currently traverse. A letter to the queen of Poland explicates this dualism operative within authentic hope.

> Madame, I hope that by the mercy of God we will see Your
> Majesty one day in an eternal kingdom to reign with God. The
> peace and joy there will never be perturbed by some disturbing

news or some negative event. Then we will see all the grandeurs of the world as nothings and all the pleasures as misfortunes, since we will see clearly that they were obstacles to our true happiness and that they placed us in jeopardy of not attaining it. On the contrary, all the afflictions helped us to experience the sorrow we should have for not having loved and served God with the ardor we should have. This sadness is actually a kind of happiness, since it makes reparation for our greatest unhappiness, which is our sins.[25]

The virtue of hope, which permits the Christian to face death and judgment without despair, reinterprets one's personal history. The terrestrial sources of happiness are unmasked as diversions from the ascetical path to heaven, which can easily lead the moral agent to damnation through sin. The terrestrial occasions of sadness, objects scorned by a worldly perspective, are now revealed as stimulants to the repentance that is the sign of the elect summoned to eternal bliss. Earnest of a paradisial future, the virtue of hope permits the Christian to arrive at a paradoxical evaluation of the authentic sources of joy and sadness in the past and to identify correctly the occult moral forces operative in the spiritual combat of the present.

Focused on the afterlife, the virtue of hope also strengthens the believer to negotiate the vicissitudes of everyday life with serenity. In the daily life of the Christian, hope manifests itself as confidence in God's providence, especially in the midst of adversity. In a letter to Madame de Sablé, Mère Angélique describes the nature of this persevering hope as she struggles against illness.

We don't know when it will please God to stop the course of this evil [a fever]. We are using several medications they have given us. Dear sister, the best medicine is confidence in God and the strong conviction that nothing will happen to us except what he desires. As for myself, I am convinced that so many of the worries we develop in trying to avoid evils do greater evil than the evils themselves. Blessed are those who, according to the word of Our Lord, have no concern about tomorrow. This does not prevent a reasonable prudence that avoids anxiety and that does everything under the guidance of God's spirit, leaning only on God and the promises he has made to us to help us in every need.[26]

Although hope centers the believer on God's eternity and the desire to share this eternity in heaven, the virtue simultaneously fortifies him or her in serenely accepting the contradictions of daily history. Unrooted in personal courage, this confidence flows from a recognition of and abandonment to the divine providence secretly guiding personal and collective history to its consummation.

One of the distinctive traits of Mère Angélique's philosophy of hope consists in the alliance she forges between the virtue and a theology of election. The abbess supports the controversial Jansenist thesis on the small number of the elect and the even more controversial thesis that divine initiative alone, rather than personal merit, bears the responsibility for one's membership in the elect. The hopeful endurance of the contradictions of life is a probable indication that one has been called to the elect.

> We must invoke the divine Spirit to remain steadfast in the midst of these storms that God stirs up and calms according to his pleasure and always for his glory and the benefit of his elect. I don't consider any evil in the world greater than the incertitude we have as to whether we are part of this small and blessed number, but one of the greatest assurances we can have that we are part of the elect is to accept affliction patiently through a true submission to God and not through a human courage. I cherish the afflictions that give rise to the holy hope of our election.[27]

The passage's treatment of election retains the traditional Catholic reservation on certitude regarding one's salvation. In the Catholic perspective certitude on such a question smacked of presumption. This treatment of hope, nonetheless, transforms the exercise of the virtue of hope in the midst of tribulation into a public sign of election. In divorcing the virtue from courage and allying it to submission to God's will, the abbess heightens the chasm between hope and the moral virtues. She also accentuates the strictly theocentric origin and nature of the virtue.

Like hope, the theological virtue of charity is given a rigorist treatment by Mère Angélique. Authentic charity is not a general love of God and neighbor. Several letters insist that true charity exists only when the love of God and neighbor has abandoned the least trace of attachment to the world.

Many charitable people commit the fault of not applying themselves enough to continually directing their intentions toward the
good of those for whom they have undertaken these works. They
think that these are works of superrogation that only oblige them
to the degree that their pity, their mood, and their inclinations
carry them. True charity clearly has other rules but they are little
known. As a result, certain actions we believe to be guided by this
divine virtue are in fact guided by cupidity. . . . It is this light of
grace that gives you other eyes for the world than you had before
and that makes you recognize its corruption.[28]

This astringent criterion for the identification of authentic charity
indicates that the virtue is rarer than most Christians believe. Authentic charity must be motivated uniquely by a concern for the
other; the presence of self-interest corrodes it. Charity is strictly
governed by the will; the admixture of emotions, moods, and idio-
syncratic desires distorts it. The fruit of the exercise of true charity
is a clearer perception of the corruption of the world and a firmer
distance from it. The abbess's insistence on the purity of intention
and of consequences surrounding the exercise of charity provides a
severe ascetical framework for this conception of the virtue.

The ascetical cast of this theory of charity does not prevent
Mère Angélique from locating the proper exercise of charity in one
traditional site: almsgiving to the poor. In many letters the abbess
exhorts her correspondents to give generously to the poor, especially
in times of epidemic and famine. She frequently reminds them that
the divine judgment at the moment of death involves a strict scrutiny of our generosity toward the poor. Typically, however, she
stresses that this scrutiny focuses primarily on the intentions behind the public act of almsgiving rather than on the act itself.

Theological Reconstruction

Mère Angélique's theocentric recasting of virtue appears even more
strongly in her treatment of moral virtues that do not appear exclusively or predominantly religious in nature. In her reinterpretation,
the abbess exposes the theological infrastructure of these virtues
when they are properly exercised and manifests the dependence of
these moral habits on God's providence. Three virtues illustrate her

methods of theological revision of moral habits: humility, patience, and self-knowledge.

Several letters allude to the standard Christian conception of humility as the just and moderate estimation of one's value in comparison with others. Mère Angélique's conception of humility, however, transcends a concern for modesty. Authentic humility entails the recognition of one's radical sinfulness in the light of God. A letter to a boarding student at Port-Royal exemplifies this humility allied to peccancy.

> My beloved sister, begin by humbling yourself infinitely if it is possible for you to do so. Consider the greatness of God and your smallness. Admire the graces he has given you. Perhaps you have never paid them real attention. Pray God that he will pardon you this ingratitude and that he cause it to cease by the omnipotence of his grace, making you begin to recognize what you owe him. Now what we owe him in the first and most important place is to humble ourselves in the knowledge of our inclination to evil and our inability to do good.[29]

The humility championed in this passage is neither demure nor modest. Rooted in a radically Augustinian account of human concupiscence, it stresses the sinful depravity that constitutes the heart of human shame. Based on our utter inability to effect our own salvation, this humility plunges the moral agent into anguish and confusion at the consideration of God's unrequited goodness.

The virtue of patience also receives a theological reconstruction. The difficulty of cultivating patience is explained by an anthropology focused on human concupiscence. The ingrained sinfulness of humanity, ceaselessly preferring self-interest to the common good, frequently renders social life unbearable. In a letter to Madame Allen, Mère Angélique admonishes her correspondent for a naïve perfectionism that refuses to see the necessity of patience in a sinful world.

> You imagine that she [the person criticized by Allen] must be perfect? Aren't you afraid that by showing disapproval you might find yourself with the same fault? My dear sister, to avoid falling, we

must humbly suffer the faults of others and of ourselves. We are born in sin and we will be completely freed from it at the moment of death. Still, we must weep before God to obtain his grace to destroy our corruption little by little. That is the main reason why the world is called "the valley of tears." All the other evils it produces cannot be compared to this one.[30]

Patience is not required simply to negotiate the frustrated hopes of everyday life; it entails a sympathetic tolerance of the imperfection that makes human life a perpetual conflict. The patient disciple is summoned to participate in the cross of Christ, where the tenacious sinfulness of humanity is lovingly borne, rather than denied or instantly abolished.

Especially original is the abbess's concept of the patience appropriate for the politically powerful. Patience permits the Christian monarch to grasp that God's assistance cannot be manipulated by human desire, even of the most pious sort. Seasons of apparently unanswered prayers, resulting in suffering for an entire kingdom, can open the powerful both to the exercise of patience and to a renewed reverence for God's absolute sovereignty.

> If Your Majesty [the queen of Poland] did not immediately submit to God's will and surrendered to some movement of anger [at the moment of a diplomatic failure], there is still time to make satisfaction. God will be pleased by it. His goodness always receives us when we return wholeheartedly to him. It is a mercy of God for kings who are truly Christian when God lets them discern the true intention behind the contradictions he permits to happen to them. In fact these rulers depend on his omnipotence, of which he gives them only a small portion to make them his images and subdue the nations by a visible power taken from his invisible one. It is necessary for their good and for their humility that they experience they have no power other than what God gives them and what he takes away when it pleases him.[31]

Like individuals, entire nations endure the Job-like experience of the just who suffer prolonged injustice and who find their prayers unanswered. The governors of these nations in times of spiritual disappointment face an opportunity to accept the temporary triumphs of evil in a fallen world. They are also freed in this practice of patience to recognize more deeply the utter independence of the will of God, who makes and unmakes as he desires, and the stark omnipotence of God, whose power cannot be manipulated by human command. Tempered by personal and communal suffering, authentic patience is allied to the disclosure of God's absolute sovereignty.

Even the Socratic virtue of self-knowledge undergoes substantial theological revision. Authentic self-knowledge springs neither from introspection nor from social interaction. It emerges only through the agency of God's grace when the depth of our sinfulness is revealed and when we experience God's work of personal conversion. A letter to Princesse Guéménée, a prominent laywoman preparing to make a general confession of her sins, explains why the experience of conversion and the concomitant desire for repentance represents a privileged moment in the acquisition of self-knowledge.

> Madame, I humbly ask you to have no anxiety concerning what you have to do [confession of sins] and to believe that you need neither an examination of conscience nor any other preparation for it other than the real desire God has given you to live for him alone and to follow all the counsels that will be given to you so that you may follow this holy desire. This presupposes a true hatred of all that is opposed to God. You see that by a completely exceptional grace, he gives you every day greater light to know him and strengthens your will to follow him, leaving or embracing everything he shows you to oppose or to be necessary for the project he has shown you. A sick man who has an ardent desire to be healed has no difficulty in telling what is troubling him. His suffering makes him state his problem clearly and he easily explains his illness to the doctor. If you had spent an entire year examining your conscience with the most careful attentiveness, before God had touched your heart, you could not have been as prepared and, I would even say, you would not have known your faults as well as you do at this moment without any personal examination of conscience. It is grace alone that can give us such knowledge.[32]

Following Saint-Cyran's controversial theology of conversion, the abbess locates authentic self-knowledge—that is, the knowledge of our sinful selves in the light of a merciful God—in the operation of grace alone. Opposing Jesuit spirituality, with its confidence in personally initiated techniques of examination of conscience, the abbess insists that the immediate experience of graced conversion is the only authentic site for the individual to grasp his or her personal history of creation, fall, and redemption. Only in the reception of God's grace, not in introspective analysis, can the individual face his or her fundamental identity as a grave sinner meriting damnation but drawn to salvation by the unfathomable mercy of God.

Monastic Virtue

More than a theological ethics, Mère Angélique's philosophy of virtue constitutes a monastic ethics. Many of the moral habits commended by the abbess are rooted in the monastic vows of poverty, chastity, and obedience. They reflect the strict flight from the world that constitutes one of the pillars of the monastic ethos. The correspondence's monastic revision of moral dispositions emerges clearly in the treatment of three virtues: poverty, obedience, and contempt of the world.

If Mère Angélique considers poverty a spiritual disposition of dependence on God, she frequently argues that material austerity must express and stimulate this interior virtue. For those called to monastic life, the strict practice of material poverty constitutes a guarantee of the community's religious vitality. Chiding her sister Mère Agnès for overestimating the aesthetic quality of liturgical offices as a criterion of monastic vigor, Mère Angèlique insists that strict material poverty is the salient indicator of a successful vocation.

> I am certain that a girl who truly loves poverty in everything will make a good nun and that whoever loves all the other things of religious life without poverty will be a very imperfect nun. In fact, she will scarcely be a nun at all. . . . If we must always deprive ourselves of everything that is only for the pleasure of the senses, in this matter [of poverty] we must deprive ourselves of everything

that is not necessary to sustain life and to give the strength to observe the rule and to provide the services we owe to religious life. As for other accommodations, I think it's necessary to give up as much as is possible for us and have a constant concern to save what we can for the poor.[33]

The passage's concern to maintain a strict interpretation of the practice of poverty reflects the abbess's long-standing conviction, rooted in her personal experience of decadent convents, that relaxation of the vow of poverty constitutes the principal cause of the dissolution of monastic houses. The concern for the poor in this letter is not rhetorical. To underscore her point, Mère Angélique sent Mère Agnès a piece of stale bread recently used by a beggar at the convent door to show the desperate state of the poor and to dramatize the solidarity with the destitute which authentic Christian poverty must cultivate.

Nothing better illustrates the abbess's rigorist interpretation of the virtue of poverty and its material accoutrements than her charming letter to Monsieur de Sévigné, a benefactor of Port-Royal, when she returns his gift of a lamp.[34] She remarks that she was delighted to keep her old, "ten *sous*" lamp, which she happily lights with cheap, synthetic oil. On the virtue of poverty the abbess underlines the necessity of strict material scrutiny to avoid spiritual illusion.

The correspondence often places the virtue of poverty within a Christological framework. It is the life of Christ, especially his impoverished birth, itinerant ministry, and humiliating death on the cross, which provides the principal inspiration to the Christian for the proper exercise of poverty. "Our Lord prefers to have poor housing with nuns who love or at least tolerate poverty than to live with nuns possessed by cupidity and vanity. He only showed his glory once. That was on Mount Tabor. But in his birth, in his death, and in the entire course of life, he always appeared as a poor man."[35] The hidden stimulant of asceticism, the virtue of poverty serves as an evangelical witness to the impoverished person of Christ. It is the desire to follow Christ in his physical and spiritual poverty that constitutes the primary Christian motive for the renunciation of material goods.

The correspondence often praises the virtue of obedience as a central disposition in the Christian life. Through the vow of obedience the nun experiences the general providence of God through the particular direction of her superiors. Mère Angélique insists, however, that behind the external practice of obedience must reside a complete abandonment of one's soul to the direction of the Holy Spirit. "I pray God with all my heart . . . that he will give you the grace to act no longer according to the inclinations of your own soul. . . . If you performed miracles by some natural action of your own, it would only serve to lead you into error. As long as it did not serve the cause of your salvation, it would only be destructive for you."[36] Beyond the legal practice of obedience to one's legitimate superior lies the broader virtue of obedience, construed as a complete docility to the guidance of the Holy Spirit upon the soul. In numerous letters to lay correspondents, notably the queen of Poland[37] and Monsieur de Sévigné,[38] the abbess commends this spiritual obedience, wherein the soul annihilates its personal desires in complete abandonment to the designs of God.

The monastic cast of Mère Angélique's philosophy of virtue clearly emerges in her praise of contempt of the world as a key spiritual disposition. A letter to her niece Mademoiselle de Luzanci explains the necessity of this contempt for laity as well as for vowed religious.

> I admit, my dear niece, that many graces of God are necessary to disdain the world and to suffer its disdain for us; however, it is impossible to please God without this grace. My dear friend, that is why we must constantly ask God for it, because it is necessary for our salvation. My dear niece, remember that the apostle Saint John says that whoever loves the world does not possess the charity of God and that whoever lacks charity, according to the same apostle, remains in the state of death. Now it is impossible to hate the world without the world hating us, despising us, and taking us for fools, just as it did the Son of God and all the saints.[39]

Fidelity to Christ tolerates no compromise with the world. Although created by God, the world experienced by the Christian is a cosmos and a society penetrated by sin and bitterly opposed to the kingdom

of God. In the spiritual dualism typical of Mère Angélique's theology, the choice for God simultaneously entails a decisive choice
against the world, properly characterized as an attitude of contempt,
disdain, and hatred.

Writing to the queen of Poland, the abbess describes the earnestness with which this contempt of the world must be sustained.

> By your actions and by your true will, recognize that you must live
> entirely for God and must condemn everything that opposes his
> glory and that refers to the world, if you have any hope of being
> among the happy number of his elect. If you cannot remain satis-
> fied with the frequent recourse to this self-examination, do not
> lose heart. Correct yourself and, wholeheartedly imploring the
> divine mercy, make right what you know to be wrong. Enter into
> yourself and hold yourself firmly in the path that leads to the truth
> that is narrow and difficult for the senses. There at least God will
> console you and give you more real joy than the world can provide
> in all its deceptive and bitter delights.[40]

Although not all are summoned to flee the world for the cloister, all
Christians are called to assume an attitude of contempt for the
world that characterizes mature spiritual combat.

This encomium of contempt for the world as an essential virtue
reflects the sectarian cast of Mère Angélique's moral philosophy.[41]
In her perspective, the Church, construed as a small band of the
elect, must firmly combat a world perpetually anointing itself as the
replacement of God. Reciprocal antagonism between the redeemed
self and the world is the inevitable outcome of authentic fidelity
to God's grace. Rather than constituting a violation of charity, contempt for the world springs from a purified charity, focused on God's
incomparable goodness and on the need of souls to be freed from en-
slavement to the world's illusions.

Submission of the soul to God through poverty and obedience is
insufficient to achieve complete unity with God. The subject itself
must be abolished. A letter to her niece Soeur Angélique de Sainte-
Thérèse details the abbess's vision of this virtue of spiritual annihilation: "Nature's sentiments and human interests cast such great
shadows in our minds that they obscure the lights of faith and of

right reason. To remedy this misfortune, let yourself collapse into God, my dear Sister. Do not try to attract his grace toward you by your reasoning and speeches; rather, forget every such design. Let yourself be engulfed in him—in the ocean of his mercy."[42] Echoing Bérulle's spirituality of annihilation, the passage insists that the summit of the spiritual life consists of a union with God so intense that the soul loses its differentiating identity as a self over and against God. The vagaries of the efforts to be united with God through the ascetical virtues recede as the soul merges with the sovereign Godhead.

Given her concern for practical virtues and her suspicion of mystical illusion, this rhetoric of abolition of the self holds a secondary place in Mère Angélique's philosophy of virtue. Even in the tempered psychological theory of the abbess, however, the perfection of the moral agent resides in the contemplative virtue of annihilation, wherein the emotional and intellectual operations of the differentiated self are silenced and overcome. No longer simply the author and object of virtue, God becomes its sole content. The human self has vanished.

Suffering for the Truth

As the persecution against Port-Royal intensified, the correspondence stressed one particular virtue: suffering for the truth. Especially in the letters to her brother Antoine Arnauld, Mère Angélique underscores the necessity to defend religious truth, specifically the embattled truth concerning grace, against political and ecclesiastic pressures to submission. As the opposition to the Jansenist movement stiffened, the letters analyze strategies of resistance that would permit the persecuted to uphold their doctrinal convictions while maintaining communion with the Catholic Church and their fealty to the French throne.

Far from being a naïve observer, the abbess limns the virtues of the persecuted with detailed knowledge of the background theological disputes. Her correspondence manifests her knowledge of patristic literature, notably Saint Augustine, whose position on grace she champions. She comments on the controversial authors of the Jansenist circle: Saint-Cyran, Arnauld, Pascal, and Jansen himself. She criticizes the polemical anti-Jansenist literature produced by the Jesuits, especially by Jean de Brisacier, an intemperate critic of the convent. Although Mère Angélique argues in several passages that neither she nor her nuns comprehend the doctrinal controversies agitating French Catholicism, the bulk of the correspondence challenges such a claim. The abbess's survey of the controversial literature is not a cursory one; in several letters she elaborates her own position on the nature of grace and the proper exercise of Church authority in doctrinal matters. If the correspondence praises the virtues of humility and obedience, the letters on resistance to persecution argue that authentic submission to God can never deteriorate into blind surrender to religious and political powers. A properly theocentric exercise of the virtues must lead the Christian to resist assaults on the fundamental truths concerning God in the economy of salvation.

Many letters explore the traditional Christian themes of the uses of adversity and the ascetical value of suffering. But the campaign launched against her brother Antoine Arnauld in 1643 leads Mère Angélique to develop one of her most distinctive themes: the virtue of suffering on behalf of the truth. In consoling her brother, hidden from the police, the abbess declares persecution for the sake of religious truth a grace.

> Although I am not without great feelings of tenderness and sorrow because of our separation, it is nonetheless true that the vision I have of the great and singular grace God has granted us to suffer for the truth, trying to serve the souls he has redeemed by his blood, overcomes all my feelings. As a result I can only think spontaneously about the extreme and ardent desire I have that you endure this temptation in a Christian and holy way. By enduring persecution in this manner, you will teach the faithful the practice of penance more effectively than you would have taught them its theory by your book [*Of Frequent Communion*].[43]

In the case of Antoine Arnauld, the persecution endured for suffering for the truth is not a generic example of courage. Suffering for the truth here is a signal grace precisely because Arnauld is attacked for his defense of our complete dependence on grace for salvation and for his warning on the danger of sacrilegious Communion when we are not in the state of grace. His witness as a hunted fugitive from the law is an existential witness to the necessity of serious penance precisely because his proscribed works had defended the need of perfect contrition and strict separation from our sins for a worthy practice of sacramental confession. The truth governing his exercise of the virtue of suffering for the truth is the specific truth concerning the grace of Jesus Christ, proclaimed by Saint Paul, explained by Saint Augustine, and now defended by the persecuted disciples of Jansen.

Central to evangelical witness, the virtue of suffering for the truth is not immune from moral distortion. Mère Angélique emphasizes that the manner of accepting persecution for the truth must be as pure as the doctrinal content of one's witness. In a typical letter she warns her brother Antoine Arnauld that charity must characterize his response to his critics.

> All I desire is that it may please God to fill you more and more, not only with the knowledge of the truth, but with a perfect love that you faithfully practice and that gives you a humble patience toward everything. This impassioned applause from so many people disturbs me. Although I know that, thank God, you are not sidetracked by this and that you know as well as anyone the truth that there is nothing but sin and weakness in us and our actions, I still experience every day that our corrupt nature never ceases to take some secret satisfaction in this, stealing what we clearly know does not belong to us.[44]

This admonition reflects the abbess's growing concern over the polemical tone taken by the writings of the Jansenist party. Later remarks on Arnauld's *Apologies for Jansenius* and Pascal's *Provincial Letters* censure the sarcasm that characterized the Jansenist arguments in the pamphlet wars.

Her counsel of charity also unmasks the pride that can easily poison the virtue of witness to the truth. The applause of the world, turning Arnauld and his companions into celebrity prisoners of conscience, indicates that something has gone awry in the movement's witness, since the world will always oppose the truth of Christ's grace championed by the movement's leaders. It is not tenacity in the witness to any truth that the abbess praises; it is only the witness to the Gospel's truth concerning sin, repentance, and redemption— a truth dreaded by the complacent majority—which constitutes religious virtue.

Written as the French government intensified its measures against Port-Royal in 1661, the last letters of Mère Angélique attempt to discern the theological meaning of the persecution and to explain the spiritual attitude to be adopted by the besieged nuns. Several letters interpret the stiffened persecution as divine punishment for the convent's spiritual complacency.

> On condition that all these misfortunes separate us from everything of the world that amuses us and diverts us from him [God], they will be beneficial. Up until now we have only had prosperity and the result was complacency. This has undoubtedly delighted us and diverted us from the subjection of spirit in which we are obliged to live. All the holy instructions we have received have made a greater impression on our minds, giving them light, than on our hearts to increase the fire of holy charity.[45]

In this perspective the persecution is to be accepted as a pedagogical grace, permitting the nuns to experience the love of Christ crucified with an intensity unavailable in a fashionable convent admired by the world for its external austerity.

Enduring persecution is not a generic exercise in courage. For Mère Angélique this virtue must be allied to a concern for religious truth, specifically the doctrinal truths concerning the grace of Christ. The abbess herself often asserts that she and her nuns ignore the theological disputes that initiated the disciplinary measures against the convent. In one of her letters, a plea to Queen-Mother Anne of Austria to intervene on behalf of the beleaguered Port-Royal, the abbess makes a typical declaration of innocence:

> Madame, concerning the errors against faith with which some say the convent has been infected for some time, I declare before God to Your Majesty that our spiritual directors have had on the contrary such a particular concern to never discuss these issues with

us. They never allowed us to discuss these technical issues, which are far above the capacity of our sex and our status. Rather than giving us the least knowledge of these questions, they always kept us at a distance from anything that had an appearance of controversy. For this reason alone they never had us read any of the contested books, even those with the most edifying subject matter, such as *Frequent Communion* among others.[46]

It is difficult to square such declarations of theological ignorance with the rest of the abbess's correspondence. In addition to manifesting a broad biblical and patristic culture, the letters attest to the abbess's detailed knowledge of key works in the quarrel over grace and moral casuistry, a quarrel in which she is never indifferent.

Her early letters reveal a knowledge of and adhesion to the theological views of the two architects of the Jansenist movement: Jansen himself and Saint-Cyran. The abbess defends Jansen against Jesuit attacks. "The Jesuit priests shout in the pulpit in a strange way against the bishop of Ypres [Jansenius] to the point of calling him a reheated Calvin and denouncing his doctrine as the most pernicious heresy ever taught."[47] On several occasions she quotes Saint-Cyran's *Simple Theology*, a catechism synthesizing the controversial theological and moral positions of the Jansenist party. "He [Saint-Cyran] does not stop having enemies who snarl at him. They made a great effort to condemn the small book [*Simple Theology*] I sent you, but in the end the objections they made against the book were found to be ridiculous."[48] In the abbess's defense, it is clear that she had not actually read the *Augustinus*, since she could not read Latin, and it is probable that the priests at Port-Royal refrained from discussing technical details of the dispute in the pulpit and the confessional. But the abbess read numerous French works defending the controversial doctrinal and moral theories of the Jansenist circle. She clearly grasped the specific religious theses whose defense she prized as a virtue.

Her letters manifest an especially intimate knowledge of the controversial works authored by her brother Antoine Arnauld. She expresses agreement with the theological theories expressed on the sacraments in *Of Frequent Communion* and on grace in *Second Apology for Jansenius*.[49] The abbess expresses similar sympathy for

the critique of Jesuit casuistry in Pascal's *Provincial Letters* and re-
vulsion at the swift condemnation of this work by political authorities.[50]

If her letters champion and propagate the Jansenist school of
authors, Mère Angélique also engages in detailed criticism of the
movement's opponents. Especially pointed is her critique of a pamphlet attacking Port-Royal by the Jesuit Jean de Brisacier. "Under
the persuasion of Madame d'Aumont, I read some passages from the
book by Father Brisacier. I was shocked and disturbed more than I
can say to see a religious and a priest publish such horrific falsehoods and such bizarre libels."[51] Although the abbess concludes that
Brisacier's libels should be answered quietly by the nuns' irreproach-
able conduct, she conducted an epistolary campaign to obtain the
book's suppression. A letter of December 17, 1651, asks Jean-
François de Gondi, archbishop of Paris, to condemn the book; after
the archbishop promptly does so, the abbess thanks him for his swift
censure in a letter of January 1652.[52]

Nor is the papacy spared in Mère Angélique's theological criticism. When Innocent X's bull *Cum occasione* (1653) condemned the
five propositions on grace and appeared to condemn Jansen as a defender of these heretical doctrines, the abbess wrote a series of letters offering her own restrictive interpretation of the text. To the
abbess of Gif, she dismisses the document as a temporary political
triumph of the Jesuits that in no way diminishes the authority of
Saint Augustine and his disciples on the doctrine of grace.[53] To the
queen of Poland, she argues that the apparent condemnation of
Jansen must be read contextually. She claims that the pope warmly
praised the theologians who had defended the Jansenist doctrine of
efficacious grace in his presence and that the pope in no way in-
tended to weaken the Augustinian school of theology from which
this doctrine proceeded.[54] The abbess's hermeneutic of context and
intention transforms an apparent defeat for the radical Augustinians
into a modest victory. When she encourages members of the Jansenist circle to accept the teaching of the bull, the highly reserved
nature of this assent is transparent.

Not confined to critical remarks on the works of others, Mère
Angélique often engages in personal speculation on doctrinal con-

troversies. In a letter to the chaplain of the queen of Poland, she subtly mixes a declaration of ignorance on the quarrel of grace with a clear statement of her own position.

> As for myself I must confess that I do not understand these propositions [the five propositions condemned by Innocent X] at all. I am happy to stay with what the Lord tells us when he says that without him we can do nothing and with what his Apostle tells us when he says that we can do nothing by ourselves, that by ourselves we cannot even pronounce the name of Jesus. That is enough to make me believe that I need the grace of Our Lord for every good work and that I am obliged to ask for this grace. I think it is a great misfortune that the pride and presumption of human beings has forced the saints to convince them by so many arguments and disputes to hold fast to the truth that will always be victorious regardless of what malice might do.[55]

This brief, pious argument is hardly neutral. By stressing the complete dependence of human beings on God's grace for their salvation and their capacity to perform good works, the abbess eliminates the role of human freedom as a contributor, even on a secondary level, to salvation. Behind the position of the champions of a greater emphasis on free will (frequently referred to as *Molinistes* by the abbess) lies more than a theological error; it is moral vice ("pride and presumption") that motivates the refusal to recognize the actual extent of God's grace. While declaring ignorance of the current ecclesiastical dispute over grace and free will, she firmly endorses the neo-Augustinian position in the quarrel.

The virtue of suffering for the truth emerges in Mère Angélique's correspondence as a moral habit with precise noetic boundaries. The truth at stake is the truth concerning the nature of our redemption, specifically the nature of the grace by which Christ saves us. Any minimization of this truth reflects human pride and endangers the very salvation of the members of the church. The suffering endured by fidelity to the truth of grace involves a humble recognition of one's own sinfulness, but this humility can never be degraded into a craven acceptance of doctrinal error due to deference to political or religious authorities. As the abbess indicates in her subtle interpretation of Innocent X's teaching, resistance to apparent error concerning this truth must be carefully calibrated, but it clearly remains resistance to worldly church members intoxicated by their own power and blind to the very grace that has founded their community and their authority.

Grace and Causation

More than an object of doctrinal reverence, grace constitutes the necessary condition for the exercise of all human virtues. Denouncing contemporary tendencies toward a neo-Pelagian account of virtue, which exaggerates the power of human freedom, Mère Angélique defends the necessity of grace in the first stirring, let alone the maturation, of moral as well as theological virtues.

> I can assure you that I never even imagined that I could do anything without grace. I almost wish to send you a book called *The Paradise of Prayers* by the good father Grenada; in chapter XIV, which is full of prayers to request virtues, the first concerns asking for God's grace. I recited it many times in my youth with a great devotion that came, I believe, from the same grace. I think it would be appropriate if you would discuss in front of several reliable people this strange saying that we should not ask for grace. . . . Every Christian must certainly oppose such a blasphemy. Today I learned that even Pelagius never dared to say this, although this pernicious consequence could be inferred from his unfortunate maxims.[56]

Such passages abolish the distinction between the theological virtues, dependent on the supernatural intervention of grace, and the moral virtues, founded on the natural freedom of the human person. Given the radically fallen state of humanity, whose concupiscence vitiates every exercise of freedom, any virtuous movement toward the good requires the agency of grace. The cultivation of the virtues can never be a self-cultivation, given the self's obdurate slavery to pride. It is only in an itinerary of grace that authentic justice and courage, let alone hope and charity, can emerge and reveal their true authorship.

In her letters of spiritual counsel Mère Angélique admonishes her correspondents to rely on God's grace rather than on their own illusory merit. A letter to Soeur Angélique de Sainte-Agnès de Marle de la Falaise warns the nun to substitute solicitation of grace for her current self-reliance.

> When our lights and our perspectives on virtue and on our own perfection exist only in our minds and when we do not try to make them enter our heart, by a true desire to use them by practicing them, they certainly offer us no help in our moment of need. On the contrary, having only inflated our pride and self-worth, when we think we are what we should be, they gravely damage us and ruin us entirely in the sight of God. My dear Sister, that is why we should place our confidence in God alone and pray to him without ceasing in all our miseries, our weaknesses, our imperfections, and our repugnance. If we were faithful in doing this, we would be all too happy. It is the perfect remedy. When we persevere in seeking, knocking, and asking, we infallibly find and receive the good spirit that is grace.[57]

Only grace, communicated in a serious life of prayer, can inaugurate the reign of virtues in the human soul. Efforts to cultivate the virtues on the basis of personal initiative are doomed to failure since the initiative itself is rooted in pride. This illusion has an intellectual component since it springs from a confusion between a mental desire for virtue with the actual practice of the virtues by a soul transformed by the redeeming grace of Christ.

In the primacy accorded grace in her philosophy of virtue, the Augustinianism of Mère Angélique is clearly affirmed. Grace cannot build on nature, since the corruption of postlapsarian humanity is so thorough. The Christian Aristotelianism of the Jesuits is an illusion. True justice flourishes only in the shadow of justification in Christ; true courage takes root in the pneumatological gifts of fortitude and fear of the Lord. The theology of grace and the philosophy of virtue become one, since the virtues alleged to flourish outside the realm of grace, such as the courage of the Stoics, are only counterfeits of the authentic virtues caused by God's wisdom.

Educational Philosophy

One of the signal contributions of Port-Royal to the development of women was its convent school. Devoted to boarding pupils and a small number of orphans, the school provided an education mirroring the austere contemplative ethos of the convent itself. In several letters Mère Angélique sketches her philosophy of education for women. Since the cultivation of the theological and moral virtues is considered the primary objective of this education, the abbess underscores the suitable ascetical means to achieve this end. The personalism of her educational philosophy emerges in her insistence that it is the quality of the teacher, rather than the quality of the curriculum, that governs the success of pedagogical endeavors. The abbess's moral rigorism appears in her criticism of alternative contemporary approaches to the education of women, especially programs that emphasize artistic formation.

For Mère Angélique the one indispensable monastic practice to be used in the education of girls is the rule of silence. An atmosphere of silence encourages the development of serious prayer and reverence for God, key goals of Christian education. In a letter to her brother Antoine Arnauld, the abbess details the specifically educational benefits derived from a strict regime of silence: reduction of the commission of faults and of the necessity of correction; greater attention of the pupils to their needlework; greater joy when the hour of recreation arrives; less jealousy among the pupils; a better humored faculty, easily irritated by noise.[58] Through the asceticism of silence the pupils are gradually drawn into the virtues of monastic life. It is the central physical and psychological condition for the contemplative apprehension of God.

Addressing the Ursulines, a modern order explicitly founded for the education of women, Mère Angélique clarifies the nature of the religious virtues to be cultivated in sound education. The fear of God is the principal virtue, but given the mercurial temperament of children, it proves a difficult one to nurture. "Dear mother superiors, it is a great work to raise children in the fear of God and true piety. It is very difficult and thorny. It often leads to discouragement when we are truly zealous and when we see so much corruption in nature and so much craft of the demon to rip out goodness and sow evil."[59] The solution to this pedagogical problem lies in the identification and formation of schoolmistresses capable of understanding the psychology of children and guiding them in this complicated apprenticeship in religious virtue. The abbess cautions the Ursulines that in her experience few people are capable of such work; once nuns have been found with such capacities, they should be retained and supported in their taxing mission. More than the content of catechism classes or the order of school prayer, the personal witness and psychological finesse of the teacher constitute the pivot of successful initiation of the pupils into piety and analogous virtues.

Supportive of a strictly monastic model of education, Mère Angélique firmly opposes any approach to education of women she considers worldly. In a letter to Madame de Bellisi, the abbess criticizes the proposed curriculum for the education of Bellisi's daughter. Prospective courses in Latin, geography, and writing are tolerated, but the courses in singing and dancing are censured as incompatible with Christian education. "Singing, however innocent people like to find it, is very corrupt in its charming words, which are full of poison beneath their decent appearance. The same problem exists in simple airs where a false joy and foolishness are found. As for dancing, beyond its evil there is madness. Finally, my dear sister, according to the laws of the gospel, the morals of Christians must be as pure as they were at the beginning of the church."[60] The condemnation of singing and dancing reflects the moral rigorism of the abbess. All attendance at balls and theatrical performances, not only attendance at those that are clearly licentious, constitutes a danger to the salvation of the Christian. Instruction in such arts serves as a propaedeutic to a future fall into libertinism. The reference to the early church reflects the primitivism inherited from Saint-Cyran. The ascetical opposition to the world typified by the desert monks and nuns of the early church must once again become the norm for Christian conduct and education. Such a severe ascetical norm underscores by contrast the moral decadence of contemporary Christian schools, such as the academies directed by the Jesuits, whose use of theater, music, and ballet represents a scandalous compromise with the world.

At first glance the correspondence's philosophy of education does little to empower women. It sharply limits access to the arts and sciences. Its focus on submission to God's will, accomplished in silence as students pursue their sewing, appears an icon for the passivity of women. In several respects, however, this rigorist monastic model of education promotes a certain spiritual empowerment. The emphasis on the right and duty of all pupils to acquire a theological culture and a personal set of religious virtues minimizes the distinction between the nun and the laywoman. In this educational model all are called to meditate on the Bible, to engage in informed theological conversation with a spiritual director, and to pursue a personal experience of the sovereign mystery of God. Furthermore, one of the major goals of this ascetical education is to permit each pupil to discover her personal vocation from God. Mère Angélique emphasizes that one of the conditions for admittance to the convent school is parental respect for the freedom of each pupil to choose to enter the convent or contract a marriage when she reached maturity. In an era when the *paterfamilias* usually determined the destiny of his daughter at a young age, such an accent on vocational liberty provoked opposition. At Port-Royal the ascetical discipline of prayer and mortification becomes the path to vocational freedom for women.

Gender and Authority

One of the characteristics of the reform engineered by Mère Angélique at Port-Royal was its enhancement of the spiritual authority of women. The Angelican reform defended the following gender-related principles: the election of the abbess by the convent chapter rather than by royal appointment; the right of the abbess to approve the chaplains, confessors, and preachers assigned to the convent; the right of the abbess to function as the principal spiritual director of her nuns; the right of the nuns in chapter to approve their constitution and regulations; the right of the nuns to pursue biblical and patristic study; the right of laywomen to be educated, to receive spiritual direction, to audit sermons, and to undertake retreats at the convent.

Acting as a spiritual director to perplexed nuns and laywomen, Mère Angélique often counseled her correspondents on the appropriate exercise of authority. Her numerous letters to superiors in other convents specify how authority should be asserted in the cause of religious reform as decreed by the Council of Trent and modeled by Port-Royal itself. They also provide advice on the typical pitfalls faced by women who by office must govern other women. Her letters to secular rulers, especially Marie-Louise de Gonzague, queen of Poland, examine the Christian use of civil power. The treatment of the poor and of one's enemies receives particular attention.

Defending the right and duty of women to exercise authority, the correspondence elaborates an ethics of power. It examines the use and abuse of authority in various circumstances. It describes the spiritual character necessary for the one exercising power and judges the value of the constitutions proposed to organize women's power within convents. The letters also sketch a theology of power, rooting the finite authority of the abbess and queen in the omnipotence of God.

Despite her moral rigorism, Mère Angélique's counsels on good governance by religious superiors return repeatedly to the necessity of flexibility. Writing to the superior of the Annonciades in Boulogne, the abbess argues that a sound superior must adapt her directives to the temperament of each nun subject to her.

> Superiors must be extremely reserved in all their words and must weigh all of them according to the golden measure of holy charity. Whether they are exhorting, correcting, or consoling, they must proportion themselves according to the capacity of each soul. They should be neither too strong nor too soft. Not only must they avoid treating each soul like the others; they must also treat the same soul in different ways according to the underlying disposition they detect and that vigilant charity makes them carefully hide. They must effectively apply themselves to the service of their sisters and be capable of doing for them what is always necessary: to destroy, to uproot, to plant, and to build up.[61]

The letter later argues that the work of spiritual edification, which necessarily involves moments of critique and rebuke, is an immensely delicate task. Many nuns will disguise their weaknesses in the presence of a superior too ardently committed to swift reform; others will simply resist the superior, stubbornly satisfied with their counterfeit of religious life. The progress of convent reform pivots around the capacity of the superior to engage in authentic spiritual governance, which entails a personal knowledge of each nun's moral personality and a prudent ability to guide each nun to greater spiritual perfection within the limits of her moral capacity.

This insistence on the paramount role of personal governance appears in the correspondence's critique of constitutions and legislation concerning convents. Although she recognizes the necessity of carefully enforced laws to reform religious life, Mère Angélique criticizes reformers whose reliance on rules suffocates the charismatic governance of a convent by a woman superior. A 1635 letter criticizing a proposed constitution for the Annonciades of Boulogne illustrates her opposition to a purely legalistic reform. The abbess objects to the proposed method of punishing transgressions, wherein the superior holds the convent's rulebook in hand as she corrects each nun according to the letter of the law. "I should tell you that in the area of penances, it seems to me that one should usually grant freedom to a superior to act according to her own inclinations. She must try to take into account the spirit of God and the different circumstances, and not try to regulate the nuns all in the same way. The letter kills and the spirit gives life."[62] Legislative regimentation ignores the different temperaments of the nuns to be governed. A severe public penance that could crush a sensitive soul might easily be accepted by a more resilient one. Authentic spiritual governance respects the freedom of the superior to consult her charismatic experience of the Holy Spirit as she judges the unique circumstances of each case she must adjudicate.

Other criticisms of the proposed Annonciade constitutions enhance the authority of the superior and the freedom of the nuns.[63] The terms of the superior and the identity of the nuns eligible to elect the superior should be specified. The loose phrasing of this question in the draft constitutions easily places the governance of the convents into the hands of external authorities. The role of the confessor should be reduced. The convent should be able to set expectations for the confessor, if he is a diocesan priest; the nuns should not be forced to confess to an extraordinary confessor; spiritual conferences with the confessor should not be a regular part of the convent schedule, since such lectures easily cause boredom. The proposed rules of prayer and recreation are too constrictive. Rather than prescribing that the subject for daily meditation should always be drawn from the Passion of Christ, the rules should permit the nuns to follows the broader range of Christological mysteries celebrated by the church in the course of the liturgical year. The recreation period should involve spontaneous group discussions rather than the structured spiritual dialogues proposed in the draft constitutions.

In defending the authority of women superiors, Mère Angélique recognizes that she is operating out of a particular vein of reform Catholicism. She confides in the abbess of Gif that the writings of Saint Teresa of Avila have inspired her own views on convent governance. "I have been reading Saint Teresa since my return. I find in her a number of admirable and instructive things, especially her incessant instance on the necessity of meditation. The unfortunate part of holding office is to have so little time for seclusion, reading, and prayer."[64] Although Port-Royal and the Teresian-reformed Carmelite houses became rival models of reformed convents in France, the abbess recognizes the parallel of her reform with the older Spanish initiatives. In both reforms the personal authority of the female superior was defended against attempted encroachments by the male figures of the chaplain, the confessor, the bishop, or the king. In both reforms the ultimate guidance for the superior and the nuns composing the convent chapter was found in the promptings of the Holy Spirit discerned in personal meditation.

The political exercise of authority by women also receives ample treatment in the letters. In her extensive correspondence with the queen of Poland, Mère Angélique specifies the interior virtues that should characterize the soul of the monarch. The abbess also sketches certain policies that should accompany an authentically Christian exercise of civil power.

On one level the virtues necessary for the Christian monarch are the same as those essential for all Christians committed to a serious spiritual life. The abbess exhorts the queen to humble herself before God and to attach herself to God alone.[65] The queen should cultivate patience and complete submission to the will of God.[66] Like a cloistered nun she should treat the world with contempt and exercise special care to distance herself from its enticements.[67]

Using Bérullian language of annihilation, Mère Angélique insists that authentic piety recognizes the nothingness of the self. "Madame, he [God] will treat you in his judgment just as you have treated him here, because he will honor those who have honored him as their sovereign lord, considering themselves nothing at all before his divine majesty."[68] The asceticism, spiritual demands, and abnegation of self required of the Christian woman exercising civil authority still pass by the narrow gate.

On another level the woman exercising political power requires certain spiritual dispositions proper to her state in life. Mère Angélique often analyzes the proper use of adversity by the queen. For the queen of Poland, the adversity was rarely personal; it consisted in the specter of war that periodically devoured her kingdom, with the attendant demons of plague, famine, and diplomatic betrayal. The abbess counsels the shattered queen how to face such reversal. Political devastation should draw her closer to the impoverished reign of Christ. "Since the king of kings made himself, for the salvation of kings as well as of others, so poor that he wanted to be born in a manger, he has not permitted kings to love magnificent things and he has made such things contemptible to all those he wanted to make holy."[69] Not only should the queen identify with the humble Christ the king; she should interpret her political adversity as a sign of divine friendship in the tradition of the paradigmatic monarch saint, the crusader Saint Louis. "See what he [God] made your ancestor Saint Louis suffer, not for his sins, but as an apparent reward for his good works. He leaves his flourishing kingdom to undertake a great and painful and expensive journey not to conquer kingdoms but to deliver the church and poor Christians from the oppression of barbarians. Instead of granting a happy ending to such a holy war, God sanctifies this incomparable king by destroying his army and by making him the captive of the miserable captives of demons."[70] The crucified kingdom of Christ and the failed crusade of Saint Louis provide a spiritual typology for the contemporary queen devastated by the invasions of Poland. The political failure of God's representatives provides the spiritual opportunity for a deeper reliance on God alone. These passages of spiritual analogy with the kingly Christ and the warrior saint legitimize the governmental authority of women inasmuch as women exercising civil power are assimilated to the religiously normative (Christ) and politically normative (Saint Louis) exemplars of regal authority.

Not confined to the interior realm, the virtues of the Christian queen must manifest themselves in public political action. The correspondence frequently underscores the necessity of solicitude toward the poor as an earnest of Christian charity.[71] The divine judgment on the monarch at the moment of death will focus on the generosity shown toward her destitute subjects. Mère Angélique also stresses the necessity of loving one's enemy, to manifest a promptness to pardon transgressions. Christ's forgiveness of his enemies from the cross should inspire the queen's pardon of her enemies currently besieging Cracow.

> Madame, your soul should often ponder these words of Our Lord Jesus Christ, nailed to the cross and reduced to the last extremity by the most horrible malice and cruelty that could ever be imagined: "Father, pardon them; they do not know what they do." Madame, it was not only those who crucified the Son of God who did not know what they did, because they did not know he was the king of glory; it is also those who make war on you and those who help them, because they are not attacking you alone— although that in and of itself is a terrible cruelty—but they are also crucifying Jesus Christ himself.[72]

Although the charity inhabiting the soul of the Christian queen is a sovereign gift of God's grace, it must express itself in a polity visibly shaped by that love. The fate of the poor, the criminal, and the foreign aggressor in this polity determines to what extent the exercise of civil power by a female ruler is an authentically Christian one.

CONFERENCES

Divine Incomprehensibility

Informal talks presented to the nuns during recreation periods, the conferences (*entretiens*) of Mère Angélique explore a variety of religious topics. Responding to questions raised by the nuns themselves, the conferences easily shift their focus from the banal to the

sublime. Certain talks deal with minor conflicts within the convent: What are we going to do with the nuns who snore? Others
treat perennial conundrums in speculative theology: Why does God
permit so much suffering by the innocent? Many simply encourage
the nuns to cultivate the interior dispositions considered ideal for
the Port-Royal nun. Several conferences treat philosophical issues.
These talks ally discussions about divine attributes, especially the
incomprehensibility of God, with a concept of human nature stressing the depth of concupiscence. The virtue theory developed in the
conferences defends charity and humility as the paramount virtues
and condemns pride as the principal vice. The conferences also provide the occasion for Mère Angélique the rationalist to emerge.
Pointed critiques of superstition and mysticism underscore the sobriety of authentic faith. Furthermore, the conferences offer the abbess the opportunity to defend a theology of grace that brooks no
concessions to the alleged contributions of human merit to salvation.

Among the attributes of God, central place is again accorded divine incomprehensibility. Several conferences evoke the chasm between God and the human person, a chasm that blocks the human
person from penetrating the qualities or purposes of the Godhead.

> Everything he [God] does is above human ability. It is incompre-
> hensible to our minds. If we exist before God as if we were tiny
> ants, is it odd that we can neither know him nor grasp the great-
> ness of his intentions? Ants can neither know the thoughts of
> human beings nor judge their actions. Now there is far less simi-
> larity between God and us than there is between us and ants.
> Although they are below human beings, they have in common
> with us the fact that they are creatures. But between human beings
> and God there is no proportion. They must recognize that God is
> a being infinitely above them. Consequently it is impossible for
> them to know his ways.[73]

Between divine and human natures there is only opposition. Analogy collapses in the recognition of strict alterity.

Other passages explicate the implications of this divine incomprehensibility. The nuns should be skeptical about philosophical

speculation on divine purposes; conclusions concerning God's nature independent of God's self-revelation in Scripture are suspect. The virtue of humility is noetic as well as moral. Positive affirmations about God's attributes must be qualified by the recognition of the radical limits of such affirmations and of the persistent danger of projection of human qualities into the essence of God. Just as the recognition of divine incomprehensibility should lead the believer to accept the infinite distance between Creator and creature, this recognition should assist the believer to reverence the absolute sovereignty of God, who disposes of individual and collective history in ways unfathomable to the human mind.

Conjoined to this philosophy of divine incomprehensibility is a peccatory anthropology— that is, a philosophy of human nature that stresses the depth of human sinfulness and the continuing distortion exercised by concupiscence on the human person. It is sin and not only finitude that makes it impossible for the human person to grasp God's attributes and designs. This emphasis on human sinfulness clearly emerges in Mère Angélique's response to a nun's query on the suffering of the innocent. The abbess replies that the alleged innocence is an illusion, since sin radically marks all human beings. "We should not call them innocent. No one is innocent before God. He even found corruption in the angels. The least venial sin merits more than all the evils of the earth. . . . A theologian once preached here that committing one venial sin voluntarily was as if one saw Our Lord and then mocked him."[74] This passage expresses the moral rigorism of the abbess inasmuch as minor sin is assimilated to sacrilege. It also evokes the intensity of the corruption that the Fall continues to inflict on humanity. Not only does the human person find it impossible to choose the good or union with God by his or her own strength; the corruption of the soul distorts the human intellect as it attempts to formulate an accurate concept of God. In such a perspective, it is not the alleged scandal of evil that is inexplicable; it is God.

Authentic piety permits the human soul to approach the incomprehensible God when the speculative intellect proves incapable of it. For Mère Angélique, it is the spiritual act of adoration that allows us simultaneously to recognize the impenetrable mystery of God and to affirm our own sinful nothingness before God. In response to

a nun's question on the convent's practice of adoration of the Blessed
Sacrament, the abbess analyzes the primacy of the broader spiritual
attitude of adoration. "The greatest need we have is to adore God.
The greatest fault we commit is not doing so. If we ask God to give
us the grace to adore him, we remedy our greatest need and by adoring him we make reparation for our greatest faults."[75] More clearly
than intercessory prayer, the act of adoration recognizes the absolute mystery of God, which eludes adequate expression through
human concepts or linguistic formulas. In the silence of adoration,
the one praying also faces her radical creatureliness, distorted by the
ravages of sin. At Port-Royal, adoration is not simply a favored devotional practice; it is the necessary and unique spiritual attitude in
which both God's infinite mystery and finite human misery are
wordlessly affirmed.

Augustinian Virtue

Many of the conferences exhort the assembled nuns to a more perfect practice of the virtues. Within an Augustinian framework Mère
Angélique sharply separates the natural from the supernatural virtues. Critical of the neoclassical exaltation of pagan virtues, the abbess argues that the alleged natural virtues, such as courage, are
illusory. Their benign external appearances mask various species of
human selfishness. Rooted in grace, the theological virtues of faith,
hope, and charity alone constitute a habitual attachment to the
good, freed from the self's calculation. Concerned with the broad
spectrum of Christian virtues, the conferences also clarify the nature of the monastic virtues proper to conventual life.

Suspicious of the Renaissance veneration of the Greco-Roman
classics, Mère Angélique attacks the authenticity of the virtues
based on nature alone. For Christian humanists of the period, notably the Jesuits, the theological virtues crowned the cardinal virtues
of temperance, fortitude, prudence, and justice. In principle these
generic moral virtues could be acquired by any human being through
the proper exercise of intellect and will. Like other Jansenists, Mère
Angélique objected to such an irenic account of virtue. The distortion of intellect and will by sin and concupiscence foreclosed any
exercise of virtue; free will might survive, but it survived as a slave

to the passions opposed to the moral order. Outside the realm of grace, alleged moral virtues are only counterfeits of authentic inclinations toward the good.

The conferences unmask several of the standard moral virtues to expose the immoral selfishness that animates them. Typical is the dissection of courage and generosity. "For the love of Jesus Christ we must renounce everything that gives us some satisfaction. There is nothing more pleasant for a generous person than the act of giving. People who possess courage according to the world's perspective fear nothing so much as asking for something. It is characteristic of the rich to give and it is the duty of the poor to ask."[76] The altruism of generosity and courage is only apparent. The gift of alms to the poor satisfies the benefactor; the public figure courageously opposing enemies is only too happy with the public acclaim it attracts. The heart of virtue, sacrifice of self, is absent in a sequence of gestures shaped by self-glorification.

The passage also suggests a class structure undergirding the deceptive edifice of neoclassical virtues. In a society divided between rich and poor, it is only natural for the rich to give and the poor to beg; it is necessary for the courageous, empowered by civil society, to defend the powerless. Rather than transcending nature and self, such generous and courageous actions comfort them. The deceptive virtues are only the functional habits of agents blithely pursuing their expected roles in a society whose power imbalances reflect the grip of concupiscence.

Following Saint Paul, the conferences insist on the primacy of the theological virtues: faith, hope, and charity. Bestowed by God's grace, the theological virtues unite the soul with God and constitute the source of authentic moral virtue. Linking the theological virtues to the spiritual combat of the Christian ascetic, the abbess imputes to each of the theological virtues her characteristic militancy.

Faith is no longer the simple assent to the truths revealed by God; it is an assent that frees the believer to combat the disorder of evil. Faith is defined as "the belief we have in the truths of the gospel; it makes us conquer the flesh, the world, and the devil."[77] Grounded in God's evangelical revelation, this militant faith manifests itself in the moral conquest of the typical evils threatening the human person.

The conferences clarify the nature of this militant faith. Authentic faith verifies itself through moral warfare against the world. Those who claim to possess faith but do not conduct themselves according to the principles of evangelical combat harbor an illusion. "In this sense we overcome the world by faith, since it is the certain belief we have of these truths that makes us do what is good. From this it is easy to see that those who do not live a life in conformity with the gospel do not have a living faith. They do not overcome the world; they are overcome by it."[78] In her defense of living faith, the abbess endorses the Catholic side of a simmering Reformation quarrel. Most Protestant theologians had defended the thesis that salvation rests on faith alone (*foi seule*), an adherence to Christ independent of personal works or merit. Catholic theologians had countered by defending the thesis of salvation by living faith (*foi vivante*), a belief in Christ manifesting itself in works of justice and charity.

In the conferences, true faith reveals itself publicly by a series of actions characterized by the evangelical virtues. The believer is not saved by her moral conduct, but the authentic believer receives a saving faith that validates itself by a pattern of moral conduct stamped by the Gospel's war against the deceits of the world.

In one of their most original passages, the conferences contrast the Christian virtue of hope with its counterfeits in contemporary court society. Focused on heaven, authentic hope rests on Christ's promise of eternal life. By contrast the terrestrial hope of the courtier dissipates itself in anxiety over a cherished political or economic goal. "Worldly people, especially the great and powerful, find it practically impossible to exercise this holy waiting. This is because they nearly always are waiting for something else: the conclusion to a business affair or some plan for their benefit. In addition the burdens of different pressing concerns powerfully distract them from this disposition, which can only be authentic in those who are truly voyagers in this world, loving nothing in it and desiring nothing from it."[79] The passage subtly analyzes the religious skepticism that has invaded a faction of French polite society. Rather than outright atheism, it is a religious insouciance that suffocates authentic hope by transferring the virtue to the purely secular drama of the next promotion or the next profit. The passage also exalts the cloistered vocation as one of the few contemporary sites propitious to the "holy waiting" that is the corollary of true Christian hope.

Charity emerges as the paramount theological virtue in the conferences, but Mère Angélique qualifies its preeminence by claiming
that humility is just as central. Part of the originality of the abbess's
concept of charity is how tightly she conjoins it to humility and
how this tempered charity is yoked to a spirituality of annihilation.

> Charity is nothing other than the love of God and the love of God
> is an authentic desire that he reign in everything and by every-
> thing and that all creatures annihilate themselves and recognize
> his supreme greatness and infinite majesty. It contains everything
> and cannot be fathomed. He is the only being worthy of existence;
> in comparison everything else is nothingness. Humility is an
> abasement of oneself and a true knowledge of one's nothingness.
> It is a total emptying of everything one possesses in order to take
> it all in God.[80]

This interpretation of charity typifies the abbess's approach to the
entire spectrum of virtue. Charity is radically theocentric, a love of
God oblivious to the world. It operates an abolition of the self, which
cannot sustain any claims of merit or even of existence before the
grandeur of God. Rather than humanitarian action, authentic charity
is a stark abandonment to God that annihilates the self.

Despite its militantly theocentric focus, charity inevitably manifests itself in the social sphere. The loving service of the poor and
the sick constitutes an outward sign of a moral agent animated by
true charity. Mère Angélique counsels her nuns to focus their charity
in a particular way on their sister nuns who are mentally infirm.
"Just as we should not deal with them as a source of amusement or
of mockery, we should not say that we should not speak to them at
all or that we should not listen to them. That would smack of contempt. Just as charity makes us speak, charity should make us silent
and appear to be attentive to them, as the affection and the compassion we owe them grow."[81] For all the sternness of her moral counsels, the love of the disabled remains a central preoccupation of the
abbess. Unsentimental, the respect of the mentally ill emerges as
the visible sign of a charity removed from self-love or the adulation
of the powerful.

Many conferences treat the ascetical virtues characteristic of
monastic life. This asceticism often emerges as an amalgam of three

moral dispositions: penance, mortification, and poverty. "Religious life is a life of penance and true penance is only accomplished by true poverty, mortification, work and the renunciation of our selves and our inclinations; without this mortification, there is no true penance. That is why all the good works animated by self-will are only an empty image of piety and penance that is good for nothing."[82] Like the theological virtues, the monastic virtues are not moderating habits that purify the inclinations of the self. They spiritually abolish the self in a complete renunciation of one's personal desires. Rather than fortifying the will, they dissolve the human will in total abandonment to the divine will.

Among the ascetical virtues of the nun, poverty holds the primary place. The conferences repeatedly warn the nuns that relaxation in the practice of poverty is the principal cause of decadence in religious orders. Monastic poverty is more than personal austerity or the renunciation of personal possessions; it involves a sobriety in the architecture, decoration, clothing, and food that characterizes an entire convent. In a needling passage on the taste for liturgical pomp in Carmelite convents, Mère Angélique (paraphrased by Mère Angélique de Saint-Jean) sketches this aesthetics of poverty: "As someone was speaking about the Carmelites, Mother [Angélique] said that she very much respected them as being good nuns. She said we should not criticize the sumptuousness of their buildings and the gold decorations in their convents and their church, because they have counselors who advise them that these things destined for God's service and piety should be called 'the spoils of Egypt.' If we had the same counselors, we would also like such things."[83] Echoing the traditional Cistercian penchant for plain architecture and furnishings, the passage presents true religious poverty as the taste for a cloistered material culture marked by restraint and austerity.

Anatomy of Vice

If the spectrum of virtue includes a wide variety of moral habits, vice can be reduced to one basic disposition: pride. Pride masks the internal substitution of the self for God. As a disguised interior disposition, pride is more dangerous for the soul than are immoral public actions that quickly provoke censure. "This pride, which we count as nothing, is so abominable before God that he despises it more than anything that is obviously horrific. This is because pride places the soul in a worse state than does something that appalls sensitive souls. Ordinarily visible events humble us, while we are not alarmed about these sins that hide in the recesses of the heart. We are not even aware of them."[84] Pride can manifest itself publicly in contempt for others, but its unique destructive power lies in its capacity to remain hidden, even from the view of the moral agent poisoned by it.

One of the palpable psychological effects of pride is the disordering of desires within the moral agent. No longer directed by the desire for God, the person possessing disordered desires experiences anguish in the pursuit of temporal objects that cannot satisfy and that torment with the prospect of damnation. "There is nothing that so torments or so damages a soul as any kind of disordered desire. It treats the soul as a torturer who makes it suffer incessantly in every imaginable manner, because everything that opposes this desire is a torment, which inflames the passions to the most extreme limits."[85] Nor is the torment confined to earthly life. The abbess depicts the despair of the damned as an eternal rage due to the utter incapacity to fulfill the destructive desires that now permanently disfigure their souls.

Like other Augustinian philosophers, Mère Angélique conceives the moral life as a series of variations on love. For the redeemed, the virtue of charity frees them to an ecstatic love of God that abolishes the claims of the world and the self. For the sinful, the paralyzing vice of pride distorts love into a violent, pervasive attraction toward the perishable goods of the world. In their affective slavery, the quarreling desires become a parody of charity. For the damned, pride freezes their desires for all eternity. The angry, insatiable desire for one more affair or one more act of revenge closes the forsaken soul to the serene vision of God.

Rationalism

The conferences' treatment of religious faith is marked by a certain rationalism. Convinced of the corruption of human reason due to the effects of original sin, Mère Angélique opposes a rationalism that would claim that reason alone can give us an adequate portrait of God's attributes or the basic principles of moral conduct. She opposes even more strongly a rationalism that would dismiss appeals to divine revelation. In her counsels on religious practice, nonetheless, the abbess criticizes certain tendencies that taint the Christian faith with the irrational. This spiritual rationalism characterizes her attacks on superstition and mysticism.

In several passages the conferences censure the tendency to substitute superstitious practices for the solid acquisition of virtue. A conference on All Souls' Day in 1653 laments the practices of popular piety that routinely deform the recollection appropriate for this liturgical day of prayer for the dead.[86] Condemned practices include worldly visits to graves, vulgar songs sung by gangs of boys, and playhouses filled with grotesque images of the souls in purgatory. The use of the latter practices to raise money adds a whiff of simony to the pious customs. The abbess laments that such excesses of popular piety only encourage Protestant criticism of the orthodox doctrines and practices that the excesses obscure.

Not confined to the religion of the masses, superstition also blights the piety of the nuns themselves. One conference criticizes a nun who asked to see the relic of a saint reported to work miracles. Mère Angélique insists that participation in the virtue of saints is far preferable to a desire for physical contact. She holds suspect a faith that privileges the miraculous over the ethical. "We must desire to find the humility and patience of the saints. We must ask God for this grace. If he grants it, we will see truly helpful miracles, ones that are as great in dignity as the soul is in terms of the body."[87] The abbess never denies the miracles in the Bible or in the lives of canonized saints. On the contrary, she praises them and alludes to them in her instructions. But her suspicion of a faith built too enthusiastically on the miraculous and her defense of a faith that verifies itself in strict moral conduct introduces a note of rationalism into her account of right piety.

The conferences also provide a frosty treatment of mysticism. Mère Angélique criticizes a nun who desired to receive personal revelations. She warns her listeners that the revelation of Jesus Christ himself should be sufficient for any soul committed to serious discipleship. "What beautiful visions could we desire other than the Incarnation of Jesus Christ? What revelations could be more certain than what God has revealed to his church? For myself I am committed only to these because they are infallible, while there is often fraud in the others."[88] This critique of the taste for mystical visions reflects the abbess's broader skepticism of the work of the imagination; it easily deludes the believer and diverts her from the cultivation of virtue. The criticism also indicates the danger of obscurantism in the life of faith. The mysteries on which the Christian stakes his or her life are those revealed by Christ, proclaimed by the Bible, and properly interpreted by the authority of the church. It is this public revelation, not private revelation based on subjective experience and possibly fantasy, which is the sole object of genuine faith.

Not surprisingly, such criticisms of superstition and mysticism elicited charges that the Port-Royal nuns were crypto-Calvinists. The censure of puerile superstitions seemed close to a dismissal of popular devotions. The warnings on an excessive cult of relics appeared akin to a condemnation of the veneration of saints. The dismissal of mysticism in favor of a biblical piety had a disturbing Protestant echo. Port-Royal easily refuted the charges. Mère Angélique repeatedly invokes the Blessed Virgin Mary, cites the church fathers, and praises church councils, especially the reforming Council of Trent. What Calvinist community would take perpetual monastic vows, let alone devote itself to adoration of the Eucharist? This Catholic apologetic, however, does not quite suffocate the rationalist strain of piety supported by the abbess in her conferences. Opposed to the opulent piety of baroque Catholicism and disdainful of the exuberant piety of popular Catholicism, Port-Royal fostered a spirituality that was sober, learned, restrained—in short, reasonable. In its minimization of the miraculous and its emphasis on moral endeavor, the abbess's rationalist spirituality presages the more skeptical, political Jansenism of the following century.

Grace and Freedom

Throughout the conferences Mère Angélique defends one central theological thesis: our complete dependence on God's grace for the capacity to perform a single virtuous act as well as for our salvation.

She contests any claim that salvation is built on the cooperation between human freedom and divine grace; it is grace alone, granted by
a decree of God's inscrutable sovereignty, which frees the elect for
union with God. Although she avoids the citation of her theological
sources, the abbess clearly endorses the interpretation of Saint Augustine's doctrine of grace developed by Jansenius and Saint-Cyran.
Her impassioned rhetoric and her categorical refusal to concede
human freedom a role in the act of salvation indicate her militant
attachment to the radical Augustinian position in the quarrel over
grace.

Mère Angélique's theology of grace clearly appears in her discussion of the growth of Port-Royal. The abbess had opened the conference by claiming that the reform and expansion of the convent
were due to God's power alone. When a nun in the assembly responded that human beings had cooperated with God on this project,
the abbess corrected her. In this as in all other projects for the good,
God alone is the cause; grace cannot share its initiative with corrupt
human nature. "This nun responded that the creature cooperated
with him [God]. Mother [Angélique] told her that the creature could
never cooperate with the grace of God, that it would lose infinitely
more than it would keep for good use. God's grace always suffered
some loss when it came to us. If we were capable of receiving one
single drop of this celestial water of grace, we would be holy and
perfect. But the creature is incapable due to sin, which is infinitely
opposed to this grace."[89] Crippled by concupiscence, human nature
cannot redeem itself. In the act of salvation, it cannot truly cooperate with God's initiative of grace because the weakened free
will it maintains can only guide it to evil. Similarly, in any moral
endeavor, it is God's grace that stimulates the human will to embrace the good. To describe such a properly divine initiative as a
partnership between Creator and creature is to endorse an illusion
fabricated by human pride.

This emphasis on the omnipotence of grace governs Mère Angélique's exegesis of biblical accounts of conversion. She interprets
Jesus' pardon of the good thief as a sovereign exercise of God's freedom to save as he wills. "God grants his grace to whomever he
pleases. This is seen in the prayer of the thief he touched and converted in the very act of sinning. At first he blasphemed just like the

other thief; nonetheless, one is taken and the other left behind. Jesus Christ looks at the former with his great mercy to save him and he leaves the latter by an effect of his justice that condemns him."[90] The salvation of the good thief has no relationship to merit on his part, since he is clearly a sinner. He is saved by the decision of Christ to free him through grace, a decision that is accountable to nothing other than God's inscrutable wisdom. The fact that one thief remains damned in his sins while the other finds paradise through grace starkly underscores the freedom of God to redeem as he wills.

Mère Angélique's gloss on the Lucan pericope on the good thief (Luke 23:39–43) reflects her adherence to the distinctively Jansenist doctrine of efficacious grace. According to this theory, the saving liberation of a human person from sin, a liberation that simultaneously confers the capacity to perform good works, is accomplished by God's grace alone. Unmerited, this grace cannot be resisted by the person thus saved. The authorship of the salvation of the human person remains uniquely divine. Other interpretations of the salvation of the good thief have explained his salvation as an effect, at least in part, of his good works. Whereas the bad thief cursed Christ during the crucifixion, the good thief recognized the innocence of Christ and denounced the injustice of the crucifixion. Christ's subsequent promise of paradise for the thief could be construed as a reward for this act of justice. For the abbess, however, it is God's grace alone that directs the entire scenario of salvation. The thief's act of justice, as well as his justification for eternity, springs uniquely from divine causality.

Similarly Mère Angélique analyzes the conversion of the Gentile centurion Cornelius (Acts 10:1–31) as a pure effect of God's grace. Both Cornelius's stature as a righteous Gentile and his subsequent conversion to the early church represents the work of God's grace rather than his personal initiative. "Cornelius was a Gentile and did not belong to the People of God. At the very least he was most pleasing to God. We cannot give any reason for this other than the fact that the spirit of God is not bound and that he blows where he will. When it pleases God to convert someone, the desire the person has to belong to him is pleasing to him because God himself gave it to the person."[91] This passage refuses to interpret the conversion of Cornelius as a cooperative effort between God's offer of grace and the centurion's free acceptance of it. In the abbess's perspective, the entire drama of the centurion's conversion has a unique cause: God's grace. It is grace that inspires the preliminary moral earnestness of Cornelius and his acceptance of grace, as well as the gift of grace itself.

This radically Augustinian theory of grace does not go unchallenged by the nuns auditing the conferences. One nun objects that if all our actions are caused by grace, we could easily excuse moral transgressions since the moral agent no longer seems to enjoy any authentic freedom or responsibility. A nun, for example, could excuse her absence from chanting the divine office by claiming that she had lacked God's grace to do so. The abbess violently condemns such a hypothetical argument. "If someone gave me such an answer, I would pay her back with several good slaps. I would not fear to offend God by becoming angry. There are moments when we should not pardon and when we cannot punish severely enough. This would be such a time, since this attitude borders on contempt of God."[92] The abbess's inflamed reply does not constitute an argument. She might have claimed that God's grace causes us to perform only good works, such as prayer; it is concupiscence, rather than grace, that would prompt a nun to neglect her most sacred duty. The difficulties encountered by Mère Angélique in convincing her own nuns of the correctness of this doctrine of grace indicate the depth of the ecclesial suspicion that this theology of grace had effectively eviscerated human freedom.

CONCLUSION

From a philosophical perspective the letters and conferences of Mère Angélique constitute an original chapter in the Augustinian revival of seventeenth-century France. Primarily works of practical advice, the writings develop a sustained argument on the divine attributes, the nature of virtue, and the relationship between divine causation and human freedom. If the abbess's philosophy draws largely on the radical Augustinian theology defended by Jansen and his allies, it maintains its own originality. It uses the materials of the *Augustinus* controversy to fashion a philosophy of resistance to abuses of civil and ecclesiastic authority. Gendered, her philosophy recon-figures the moral and theological virtues according to the ethos of convent life; it justifies the exercise of authority by women in the religious and political spheres.

In her discussion of the divine attributes, Mère Angélique uses negative theology to limn the *Deus absconditus*. What God is not trumps the attributes indicating what God is. Enlightened reflection concerning God privileges the attribute of incomprehensibility. Her apophatic philosophy of divine attributes underscores the rupture between God and humanity. Efforts to conceive God analogously through the use of moral attributes drawn from nature end in illu-sion because of the constitutional difference between the infinite Creator and the finite creature, a difference radicalized by the cor-ruption introduced by original sin and its sequel in concupiscence. Throughout her works the abbess emphasizes the alterity of God, ir-reducible to the anthropomorphic spiritual attributes fabricated by human wish and projection. Her militant theocentrism insists that truthful discourse concerning God begins and ends in the recogni-tion of God's impenetrable mystery.

This recognition of God's absolute otherness is not the conclu-sion of syllogistic argument on the nature of God. Mère Angélique studies the spiritual site from which this recognition of divine in-comprehensibility arises. The framework for the acknowledgment of God's utter mystery is broadly fideistic. In the grace-inspired vi-sion of the invisible God who creates the world from nothing and saves the elect by an inscrutable eternal decree, the soul glimpses the incomprehensible essence of the Godhead. But the abbess speci-fies the spiritual site for this acknowledgment of God's alterity in one particular practice: adoration, the loving contemplation of God's unimaginable grandeur which is simultaneously a recognition of one's utter fragility, even one's nonexistence as an annihilated self. Part of the originality of her apophatic philosophy of the divine at-tributes lies in her designation of the spiritual posture of adoration as a necessary condition for the existential recognition of God's stark otherness. Discerning the places and practices propitious for the disclosure of God's alterity becomes as central as the affirma-tion of that alterity through the use of negative attributes to desig-nate the Godhead.

Mère Angélique's moral philosophy uses the traditional Augustinian account of virtue. According to this perspective, the natural virtues championed by classical antiquity and contemporary Christian humanists are only masks of the vice of pride. Courage, temperance, and justice are vitiated by the self-interest that motivates their exercise. Inaugurated by grace, only the theological virtues of faith, hope, and charity are truly virtuous, since they alone are grounded in the pure love of God.

The originality of the abbess's moral philosophy resides in her distinctive revision of the general Augustinian approach. Student of Saint-Cyran, she interprets the virtues with a blunt moral rigorism. True poverty eliminates the slightest desire for aesthetic consolation; authentic obedience annihilates the least expression of self-will. Traditional theological and moral virtues are given a radically theocentric focus, tinged by a Jansenist theology of election. Hope thus emerges as the perfect abandonment to divine providence, patience as abandonment of personal desires and acceptance of any divine alteration of the present. Not only does the abbess transpose the definition of the virtues under the influence of her anthropology of abandonment of the will; a personal witness to persecution, she imbues her moral philosophy with a combative militancy by privileging the virtue of suffering for the truth. This new virtue is neither generic courage nor simple fidelity to one's conscience. It is a suffering in and through the church done by an elect minority whose doctrinal intransigence on grace witnesses to the supremacy of grace in the very act of redemption that has founded the church.

Suffering for the truth grounds Mère Angélique's ethics of resistance to abuses of power. The abbess develops her own casuistry on the action to adopt by the Christian when faced by an ecclesiastic judgment that appears to contradict the truth. The Christian must always embrace the judgments of the church concerning faith and morals; in the face of erroneous judgments concerning matters of fact, however, the conscientious Christian must adopt a posture of respectful silence or even, when someone's reputation is unfairly damaged, outright opposition. The abbess's epistolary campaign with Parisian archbishop Jean-François de Gondi, demanding official censure of the allegedly libelous pamphlet of Jean de Brisacier against the nuns of Port-Royal, is a vivid application of the ethical duty to resist defamation of character and to effect a restoration of the order of justice. To accomplish her goal, she uses a detailed, documented narrative of the orthodoxy and moral integrity of the aggrieved party, complemented by a careful unmasking of the techniques and motivations of the politics of calumny.

Mère Angélique's philosophy of resistance entails more than a casuistry of appropriate or inappropriate defenses of an imperiled truth; it promotes certain virtues, such as patience and love of one's enemy, which permit the unjustly persecuted to endure opprobrium with sufficient grace. On a more metaphysical level the ethics of resistance discerns the role of persecution in the mystery of divine providence, especially in God's apparent abandonment of the elect to the violent opposition to the world. In a theological register this philosophy of resistance relates the contemporary persecution of the neo-Augustinian party to Christ himself, contemned by a world he must redeem through his passion and mocked by the jealousy and calumny of his opponents.

If power can be abused in the persecution of the elect, it can be properly used in the governance of religious and civic communities. The abbess's philosophy of power is a gendered one inasmuch as it justifies the exercise of authority by women and specifies its proper use by the abbess or the queen. Mère Angélique's reform of Port-Royal and of other convents is tied to her advocacy of the right of religious women to exercise authority. The female religious superior is to serve as a spiritual director, theological instructor, and disciplinarian for her nuns. Respectful of the priesthood, the abbess is still the one who designates the convent chaplains, confessors, and preachers. Rather than being subordinate to the male cleric, the abbess is to appoint and dismiss the clerical assistants necessary to maintain the sacramental life of the convent. This empowerment of women is not limited to the religious superior alone. Assembled in chapter, the community of professed nuns is to exercise its corporate authority by the election of its superior, adoption of its constitutions and laws, and approval of measures to resolve specific conventual problems.

In the civic arena, women are charged by Mère Angélique to exercise authority in an evangelical manner, ever vigilant to succor the poor in the periodic outbreaks of war, pestilence, and famine.

Justifying the right of women to exercise political authority, the abbess also admonishes women rulers to acquire a spiritual wisdom
that will permit them to exercise patience, hope, and charity in periods of civic tribulation when God appears to have abandoned the
cause of the just. If the classification of Mère Angélique as feminist
would obviously be anachronistic, her apology for the exercise of
authority by women and her deontology for the proper use of that
authority clearly constitute a gendered philosophy of power.

The original contributions of Mère Angélique to the era's Augustinian revival cannot obscure the limitations of her philosophical
reflection. Written as practical directives to reformers stymied by
persecution, the abbess's claims concerning divine attributes or
theocentric virtues are often more of a sketch than a discursive
proof. The fideistic framework of the abbess's arguments further
limits the philosophical quality of the positions she defends. Controversies concerning the nature of virtue or the limits of political
authority are often resolved by appeals to Scripture, to the doctrine
of patristic authors (especially Saint Augustine), to precedents established by church councils, or to the example of canonized saints.
The abbess often ably harmonizes these sources to develop an original argument on controversial issues, but the argument routinely
remains within an epistemology that circumscribes the truth within
the virtue of faith and within the divinely inspired sources of revelation illuminating that faith. The abbess's philosophical arguments
usually emerge as the by-product of a more central theological conversation on the nature and implications of redemptive grace. Her
radical Augustinian creed, simultaneously stressing divine inscrutability and human concupiscence, heightens the fideistic atmosphere
in which her philosophical considerations emerge.

Another substantial limitation in Mère Angélique's philosophy
resides in her frequent recourse to negation in the treatment of theological and anthropological questions. The God known by faith is a
divinity who cannot be known by the scrutiny of nature or history.
Authentic philosophy can designate God only by what God is not.
The knowledge of the God whose primary attribute is incomprehensibility is a nonknowledge. In the abbess's philosophy, reflection on
the essence of God quickly terminates in surrender to absolute mystery. The obscure knowledge of the devout resembles the indecisive
opinion of the agnostic.

The abbess's Augustinian theory of concupiscence governs a similar negation concerning human nature. Brutally disfigured by sin, human reason is unreliable since it is the toy of passion, ignorance, and prejudice. Claims to truth, even with elaborate logical justification, are invariably tainted by pride and self-interest. Even the self-knowledge acquired by introspection consists of illusions wrought by personal vanity. The most authentic knowledge of the human self frankly acknowledges its nothingness, tied both to the original finitude of the human creature and to the depravity inaugurated by the Fall. Such negative theology and negative anthropology ably unmask the pretensions of human reason, the illusions fabricated by a disordered will, and the fragility of human knowledge. But the conceptual portraits of God and humanity generated by the systematic recourse to negation bear an emptiness and a redundancy tied to the method of the *via negativa*.

Finally, the philosophy of Mère Angélique develops a contradictory account of human freedom. On the speculative level she so emphasizes an Augustinian theory of divine sovereignty, predestination, election, and utter dependence on grace for moral action that human agency seems to disappear. Only divine causation appears to enjoy true freedom. On the practical level, however, the abbess insists on the moral duty to resist efforts to destroy one's conscientious allegiance to the Paulinian, Augustinian, and Jansenist doctrine of grace. A substantial part of her canon details the actions, virtues, and spiritual practices necessary for effective combat against attempted coercion. But how this human moral agency exists in such a deterministic cosmos governed by an absolutely sovereign deity remains an enigma. In her conferences the abbess admits she would slap a nun who claimed she had neglected the divine office because God had so determined her behavior. The abbess's outrage is clear but its justification is not. It is difficult to discern the origin and consistency of human responsibility in a history ruled by a deity who saves and infuses moral virtue according to his inscrutable wisdom.

Mère Angélique's struggle to reconcile divine causation with human moral freedom reflects the paradoxical position of many architects of the era's Augustinian philosophy. Numerous neo-Augustinian moralists conjoined defenses of predestination with admonitions to follow the strictest moral conduct. The abbess's quandary over the status of human moral responsibility also reflects the impasse over the nature of human freedom evidenced by several rationalist metaphysicians of the period. Occasionalists like Malebranche and monists like Spinoza struggled to defend a human freedom that was more than nominal. A deterministic metaphysics rested uneasily with moral exhortations to cultivate personal virtue or political tolerance. The abbess's vigorous juxtaposition of God's omnipotence with the moral duty to resist oppression cannot eliminate the paradox of a human freedom that is exalted in the practical arena but which appears to vanish in the forum of theological speculation.

CHAPTER 3

MÈRE AGNÈS ARNAULD

Adoration and Right

A younger sister of Mère Angélique, Mère Agnès Arnauld
(1593–1671) has long suffered oblivion in the shadow of the
illustrious reforming abbess. Commentators have routinely
contrasted the personalities of the sister abbesses: Angélique
the entrepreneur, Agnès the mystic; Angélique the intransigent, Agnès the indulgent; Angélique the rationalist, Agnès
the emotivist. In this perduring stereotype the philosophical
contributions of Mère Agnès have all but vanished. Her voluminous writings, however, provide a signal contribution
to the philosophy of God's attributes, virtue theory in the
context of the convent, and the concept of freedom as resistance to abusive authority.

In *Private Chaplet of the Blessed Sacrament*, Mère
Agnès analyzes the essence of God in terms of rupture and
distance. Her *Image of a Perfect and an Imperfect Nun* details the virtues central to the convent's way of life and criticizes the subtle counterfeits of virtue present in the cloister.
Her *Spirit of Port-Royal* studies the virtues, particularly the
virtues of annihilation, central to the convent's moral character. As principal author of the *Constitutions of Port-Royal*,
the abbess presents the rights and duties of the nun in a legal

framework that defends the spiritual authority of women. In her *Counsels on the Conduct Nuns Should Maintain,* she specifies the actions and attitudes to be adopted by the nun facing violations of conscience by political and ecclesiastical authorities. The extensive correspondence of the abbess clarifies the theological, ethical, and political theses defended in her spiritual treatises.

A CONTEMPLATIVE'S LIFE

Born on December 31, 1593, Jeanne Arnauld was the third daughter of Antoine Arnauld and Catherine Marion Arnauld.[1] Like her elder sister Jacqueline (the future Mére Angèlique), Jeanne was destined by her family for the convent. After negotiations conducted by her maternal grandfather, Simon Marion, Jeanne Arnauld was appointed the abbess of the Benedictine Abbey of Saint-Cyr by Henri IV in 1599. To govern on behalf of the five-year-old abbess, whose age had been falsified to meet canonical requirements, a mature Benedictine nun was appointed as the regent of Saint-Cyr until the infant abbess reached the age of twenty. Unlike her older sister, who chafed for a decade against her imposed vocation and the constraints of convent life, Jeanne Arnauld cheerfully accepted the traditions of monastic life from the moment she took the veil as a Benedictine nun on June 24, 1600, and assumed her name in religion, Mère Catherine-Agnès de Saint-Paul, popularly known as Mère Agnès. The child abbess conscientiously attended all the liturgical offices celebrated in the convent, edifying others by the obvious consolation she enjoyed in executing her monastic duties. According to Mère Angélique, Mère Agnès had memorized the entire Latin psalter and the hymns of the Catholic liturgy by the age of nine.[2]

Mère Agnès's presidency of Saint-Cyr was interrupted by the unexpected turn in the career of Mère Angélique, summoned to become the abbess of Port-Royal after the sudden death of Madame de Boulehart in 1602. Terrified of a charge she found repugnant, Mère Angélique asked her more pious sister to assist her and their parents in improving the conditions of a dilapidated convent that had drifted away from monastic observances. Mère Agnès stoutly defended her sister in her subsequent reform initiatives; morally and physically she stood at the side of her sister during the decisive *journée du guichet* (1609), in which Mère Angélique refused her parents permission to penetrate the strict cloister she had imposed on the convent. Committed to the Port-Royal model of monastic reform, Mère Agnès renounced her abbacy at Saint-Cyr in 1610. On January 28, 1611, she was clothed in the Cistercian habit as a nun of Port-Royal. She pronounced her vows as a Cistercian nun on May 1, 1612. The close association between the sisters in the reform of Port-Royal was now legally sealed.

Mère Agnès quickly assumed positions of authority within Port-Royal. Even before her formal profession as a Cistercian nun, she was appointed novice mistress. This position in the formation of candidates for the sisterhood permitted the adolescent Mère Agnès to manifest her unusual qualities as a spiritual director. During the perilous reform mission of Mère Angélique at Maubuisson (1618–23), Mère Agnès functioned as a vicar for her sister, being named sub-prioress in 1618 and coadjutor abbess in 1619.

During her first decades at Port-Royal, Mère Agnès developed an eclectic monastic spirituality that drew from different currents of the Catholic reform in France. The Jesuit Jean Suffren served as her spiritual director from 1614 to 1626. The Capuchin Archange de Pembroke and the Feuillant Eustache de Saint-Paul Asseline, erudite preachers at the convent, also served as spiritual advisers. The works of Saint François de Sales served as a literary guide for Mère Agnès, who often commended the writings of the bishop of Geneva to her spiritual directees. She also studied and recommended the works of Saint Teresa of Avila, in particular the *Autobiography, The Path of Perfection,* and *The Interior Castle.*

With the transition of the convent from the old location in the valley of the Chevreuse to its new Parisian site in 1625, Port-Royal underwent the influence of the Oratory, a congregation of priests founded by Pierre de Bérulle in 1611. Architect of the *école française* of spirituality, Bérulle and a host of Oratorian colleagues became the preferred preachers, lecturers, and confessors at the convent until the decline of their influence in 1633. Typified by Bérulle's massive spiritual treatise, *The Grandeurs of Jesus* (1623), Oratorian theology stressed the Incarnation as the focal point of the Christian faith, the primacy of adoration in prayer, and the annihilation of the self as the fundamental response of the believer in the face of the mystery of God. Sympathetic to speculative mysticism, it encouraged the mature believer to meditate on the various states of existence found in Christ, the angels, and the saints. Communication of these insights in lyrical language through letters, prayers, and spiritual conversation was considered an essential part of Christian witness. Among the Oratorians serving Port-Royal de Paris during this period the most influential was Charles de Condren. A respected scholar who held a doctorate in theology from the Sorbonne and counted Descartes among his personal friends, Condren provided the convent with a sophisticated theological framework for the Oratorian themes of adoration, annihilation, and speculative reflection on the states of Christ. Becoming an avid disciple of Condren, Mère Agnès quickly adopted his spirituality of annihilation and the Oratory's taste for speculative mysticism.

The new political direction of Port-Royal accentuated the ascendancy of the Oratory. In 1625 Sébastien Zamet, bishop of Langres, befriended Mères Angélique and Agnès, sharing with them his projects for convent reform in his own diocese and his dream of the foundation of a new religious order devoted to the adoration of the Blessed Sacrament. In 1625 Zamet was appointed the clerical supervisor of Port-Royal des Champs. A close friend of the Oratory, he supported the apostolate of the Oratorian priests in the convent and the adoption of Oratorian theological theories and devotional practices by the nuns. In 1629 Zamet sent Mère Agnès to reform the Cistercian monastery of Tard in Dijon along semi-Oratorian lines. In 1630 the chapter of Port-Royal elected as abbess Mère Geneviève de Saint-Augustin Le Tardif, a protégée of Zamet originally from the Tard convent. Re-elected in 1633, Mère Geneviève continued to stress Oratorian spirituality, flavored by the theatrical piety increasingly favored by Zamet. In 1633 a disillusioned Mère Angélique and a handful of nuns began the disastrous experiment of the Institut du Saint-Sacrement on the Rue de la Coquillière. When Mère Agnès returned to Port-Royal from Tard in 1635, she encountered a community bitterly divided over Zamet's direction and her elder sister embroiled in an ecclesiastical fiasco.

In 1636 the chapter of Port-Royal elected Mère Agnès as abbess. Having abandoned the Institut, Mère Angélique was quickly appointed novice mistress. Mère Geneviève was dispatched on a vain mission to save the floundering Institut. Banning Zamet from returning to the convent, Mère Agnès promptly returned the convent to the austere reform regime championed by her sister two decades before. But unlike her sister, who rejected the Oratorian ascendancy as a deviation from true reform, Mère Agnès continued to privilege the Oratorian theology of mystical annihilation in her abbatial conferences and in her epistolary direction of perplexed souls.

During the Oratorian ascendancy, Mère Agnès found herself at the center of the first major conflict between Port-Royal and its ecclesiastical and political opponents: the affair of the *Private Chaplet*. A brief devotional treatise praising sixteen attributes of Christ in the Eucharist, corresponding to the sixteen centuries elapsed since the institution of the Eucharist at the Last Supper, *Private Chaplet of the Blessed Sacrament* was written by Mère Agnès in 1626.[3] She wrote an early draft of the work in response to an earlier chaplet of praises of Jesus composed by Soeur Geneviève Le Tardif, the future abbess. Mère Agnès provided a longer list of praises, now focused more narrowly on the attributes of Jesus within the eucharistic species. Aflame with his project for founding a religious order devoted to eucharistic adoration, Zamet heartily approved the litany and ordered its publication for private use in the convent.

Impressed by Mère Agnès's litany of invocations, Charles de Condren asked his spiritual directee to explain at greater length how she understood each of these attributes of Christ. Claiming that she could express herself more easily in writing than orally, she wrote down her reflections in a single session and presented them to the Oratorian. In subsequent accounts she insisted that she wrote the meditations spontaneously, as if guided by another spirit, and that she was moved by sentiments of annihilation and abasement when she pondered these attributes.

Condren lauded this expanded *Chaplet*, enriched by theological speculation on the positive and negative attributes of the divinity present in the eucharistic Christ. The praise was unsurprising since Mère Agnès's treatise had incorporated the major themes of Oratorian spirituality: the contemplation of the divine essence made manifest by various states of Christ; the primacy of the virtue of humility, radicalized as a species of abasement; the mystical experience of the annihilation of the self; the search for spontaneous divine inspiration during speculation on the divine attributes. With his customary dramatic flair, Zamet declared that the reflections on the Eucharist emanated not from the nun herself but from the very thoughts of Jesus Christ within her. Endorsed by the convent's clerical authorities, the *Private Chaplet* quietly circulated among the nuns of Port-Royal. It slowly acquired a larger audience among Condren's fellow Oratorians, Claude Séguenot and René Barrême; among other reform-minded nuns, such as Marguerite-Marie de La Trémoïlle, the abbess of Lys; and among lay allies of the convent, notably Madame de Longueville.

Leading an obscure existence as a devotional pamphlet, the *Private Chaplet* suddenly became the center of an international controversy in 1633 when Octave de Bellegarde, archbishop of Sens and one of the episcopal supervisors of Port-Royal, submitted the text to a committee of Sorbonne theologians headed by André Duval, once an ally of the convent but now an opponent of its direction under Zamet. On June 18, 1633, the committee delivered a stinging censure of the treatise's "extravagances, impertinences, errors, blasphemies, and impieties, which tend to turn souls away from the practice of the virtues of faith, hope, and charity."[4] In her autobiographical *Report*, Mère Angélique recounts how the Port-Royal nuns, heretofore esteemed as models of reformed monasticism, suddenly found themselves accused of heresy and even witchcraft in the gossip of the salons and court.[5]

Apologists for Port-Royal have long argued that Bellegarde's instigation of the condemnation of the *Private Chaplet* was inspired by personal jealousy against the increasing influence of Zamet in the governance of the convent.[6] To humiliate his rival, Bellegarde publicly attacked the orthodoxy of one of his leading protégées, whose devotional treatise so perfectly expressed the mystical theology of Zamet's Oratorian allies. In this apologetic version of the controversy, Mère Agnès is a hapless victim of personal jealousies that used theological quibbles as a cover. But Bellegarde's campaign against the *Private Chaplet* also represented an opposition in principle to the new spiritual currents nurtured by Zamet in the convent. For the archbishop of Sens and his Jesuit allies, this new taste for speculative mysticism had dangerously confused the properly divine inspiration behind the Scriptures with the sentimental musings of nuns in an isolated cloister. The Sorbonne condemnation also took pointed aim at the apophatic theology of Mère Agnès herself, since the committee strongly objected to a theology so stressing divine transcendence that cultivation of the moral virtues appeared to be undercut.

Buoyed by the Sorbonne condemnation, Bellegarde intensified the campaign against the *Private Chaplet* by commissioning the Jesuit theologian Étienne Binet to write his *Remarks,* which circulated in manuscript form among critics of Port-Royal and which amplified the charges of heresy against the author of the text. The archbishop of Sens asked the Vatican to condemn the opuscule formally, a request seconded by Cardinal Richelieu, who instructed the French ambassador in Rome to pressure the papacy to condemn a new heresy spreading in Paris. Port-Royal quickly counterattacked. The besieged Zamet commissioned Jean du Vergier, abbot of Saint-Cyran, to defend the orthodoxy of the contested treatise. Saint-Cyran countered the Sorbonne committee by obtaining formal approval of the book by two leading Louvain theologians, Cornelius Jansen and Liber Froidmont, in July 1633. Delighted at the eruption of a new religious dispute in France, the Spanish throne, ruling Belgium as part of the Spanish Lowlands, quietly encouraged the Louvain defense of Mère Agnès. By October 1633 Saint-Cyran was circulating his own book, *Apology Made to Defend a Small Book Entitled "Private Chaplet of the Blessed Sacrament,"*[7] a carefully argued theological treatise that defended the nun's work by showing the orthodox roots of her controversial phrases in the Scriptures, patristic writings, and the decrees of Church councils. The publication of a new book, *Elevation of Spirit to Our Lord Jesus Christ,*[8] which juxtaposed in parallel columns the text of the *Private Chaplet* with the text of Oratorian Claude Séguenot's larger theological commentary on the *Chaplet,* bolstered the defense of the work's orthodoxy.

Attempting to palliate feelings on both sides, the Vatican ordered the withdrawal of the *Private Chaplet* from circulation but pointedly refused to condemn its theology or to place it on the *Index of Forbidden Books.* To suffocate the quarrel, it demanded the suppression of works attacking or defending the treatise. A decade before the tempest over the *Augustinus,* Mère Agnès's *Chaplet* had drawn together the future antagonists over Jansenism into a quarrel over the nature of authentic adoration.

During her first abbacy at Port-Royal (1636–42), Mère Agnès guided the convent, enlarged by the arrival of nuns from the Institut du Saint-Sacrement and from the abbess's previous abbey of Tard, back to the monastic reforms introduced by Mère Angélique. As Mère Angélique candidly admits in her memoirs, however, the relationship between the two reunited sisters was initially cool.[9] The ascendancy of Saint-Cyran in the convent's spiritual life divided them. A close friend and spiritual director of Mère Angélique from her anguished days at the Institut, Saint-Cyran had begun to preach regularly at Port-Royal in 1635. By the next year he had become the undisputed spiritual guide of the community, mesmerizing the nuns by the theological erudition he displayed in his sermons, lectures, and sessions of spiritual direction. His austere moral and sacramental doctrine appeared the perfect antidote to the lyrical, ostentatious piety of Zamet, which had nearly destroyed the reform ethos of the convent. Saint-Cyran's practical and antimystical piety, however, had a tone different from the expansive speculative spirituality of Mère Agnès.

Despite her temperamental differences, Mère Agnès ultimately rallied to the support of Saint-Cyran, even defending his controversial views on the sacraments, where he argues that authentic confession and absolution of sins require perfect contrition and that one should periodically abstain from reception of Holy Communion out of fear of sacrilege and out of need for greater conversion. During Saint-Cyran's captivity at the Chateau of Vincennes (1638–43), Mère Agnès strengthened his authority over the community by circulating the letters he wrote regularly from prison, by ordering his works to be read at table and in the convent school, and by repeatedly citing him as a prominent spiritual authority in her conferences and letters. The living martyrdom of Saint-Cyran, victim of the political cynicism of Richelieu, enhanced his sway over the bourgeoning convent and its abbess.

Mère Agnès's first abbacy also witnessed the consolidation of the abbey's reform and the extension of its influence in the French church. Starting in 1637, Mère Agnès began to write the constitutions for Port-Royal. An attempt to codify the practices of the Angelican reform, the legal document drew upon the Rule of Saint Benedict, earlier Cistercian constitutions, and the decrees of the

Council of Trent. In the long gestation of the document, Mère Agnès drew upon the practices and counsels of others. F. Ellen Weaver details the particular contributions of Mère Angélique, Saint-Cyran, Antoine Arnauld, and Antoine Singlin to various drafts of the document.[10] But the rhetoric and the mystical impulse of the text remain Mère Agnès's own. The *Constitutions* enshrined key principles of the Angelican reform: the election of the abbess for a three-year term; the legislative authority of the convent chapter; the insistence on the vocational freedom of candidates for the novitiate or for enrollment in the convent school; the abolition of the dowry requirement; strict prescriptions on poverty, cloister, and silence. The sections on prayer proper to Port-Royal nuns, especially on the freedom and spontaneity to be enjoyed in personal meditation, bear the personal stamp of Mère Agnès.

The influence of Port-Royal increased through several educational initiatives. The convent school of Port-Royal gradually increased its number of pupils, as the devout Parisian aristocracy and bourgeoisie vied to place their daughters in a school celebrated for its moral discipline as well as its academic rigor. In 1637 the first *solitaires*, led by Mère Agnès's nephew Antoine Le Maître, began to live in the abandoned buildings of Port-Royal des Champs. At the instigation of Saint-Cyran, they started to conduct their *petites écoles*, renowned for their new tutorial methods of teaching and their modernist pedagogy, stressing the French vernacular over Latin and scientific experimentation over lecture and memorization. The flood of textbooks, translations, and treatises produced by the *solitaire* schoolmasters, complemented by Jacqueline Pascal's *Rule for Children* describing the methods and spirit of the convent school, exported Port-Royal's philosophy of education to a broader European public. The use of the Parisian church for public sermons, especially the spiritual conferences of the convent chaplain, Antoine Singlin, attracted a cultured public to Port-Royal, many of whom chose the clergy affiliated with the convent as their confessors. The long-standing privilege of Port-Royal in permitting laywomen to board on the convent grounds for brief periods turned the convent into a popular retreat for devout aristocratic women.

At the election of Mère Angélique as the new abbess in 1642, Mère Agnès was once again appointed as novice mistress. Matured by the conflicts and theological lessons of the 1630s, Mère Agnès excelled in a post of religious formation that drew upon her skill as a spiritual director. Numerous memoirs from former novices at Port-Royal attest to her shrewd psychological insight, her compassion, and her theological erudition in guiding worldly candidates to contemplative depth as cloistered nuns. Not limited to the novices of the convent, Mère Agnès's preeminence as a spiritual director acquired a large lay audience, primarily through her extensive correspondence. Distinguished directees included her theologian brother Antoine Arnauld; her scholarly cousin Antoine Le Maître, who renounced his political career and marriage plans at the urging of the abbess; Anne Herrault de Cheverny, marquise d'Aumont, a Port-Royal benefactor seeking counsel on education; Madame de Sablé, hostess of a prominent literary salon; and the poet Jacqueline Pascal, the sister of Blaise Pascal.

The series of letters to Jacqueline Pascal, who ultimately entered Port-Royal in 1652, illustrates the psychological insight and theological culture Mère Agnès brought to her apostolate as spiritual director. When Pascal complains about the delay imposed on her entry into the convent by her father's opposition, Mère Agnès explains the theological reasons for the delay. "Our Lord wants to purify you by this delay because you have not always desired it. It is necessary to have a hunger and thirst for justice to expiate the disgust one had for it at other times. Saint Augustine . . . wonderfully expresses this delay of God in souls, who desire the abundance of God's grace, which God has postponed."[11] The anxiety of Pascal to discover quickly God's will is countered by the exhortation to seek spiritual tranquility. "This desire must possess the nature of its principle. As the Holy Spirit, who is its author, is a spirit of peace and sweetness, it is necessary that you maintain this will in the tranquility of your soul by repressing its emotional movements."[12] In praising Pascal's growing renunciation of her earlier intellectual vanity, Mère Agnès ties spiritual poverty to an Augustinian anthropology of concupiscence. "You also possess the happiness of the poor in spirit. In a sermon Monsieur Singlin told us that it consisted in recognizing that we are only lies and sin. The lies are the shadows in the mind, the sins the shadows in the heart."[13] In delicately guiding the prickly Jacqueline Pascal to spiritual freedom, Mère Agnès alludes to the sources of her operative Augustinian philosophy: the works of Augustine himself, the Augustinian monastic theology of Saint Bernard, and the Jansenist gloss on the Augustinian tradition by Saint-Cyran and his disciple, Singlin.

Mère Agnès's influence was not confined to the rarified ministry of spiritual direction. In 1647 she finished the first version of Port-Royal's constitutions, which received the approbation of the archbishop of Paris in 1648. When the expanding Port-Royal community reoccupied the Champs buildings in the valley of the Chevreuse in 1648, she was named the prioress of Port-Royal des Champs. During the Fronde (1648–52), she assisted her sister in maintaining the beleaguered convent and succoring the poor in an atmosphere of pestilence and famine.

Complementing her administrative work, she used her correspondence as an armament in the growing theological controversy surrounding the convent and the broader Jansenist movement. She defended her brother Antoine Arnauld in the quarrel provoked by the publication of his *Of Frequent Communion* and during his disgrace when the Sorbonne condemned his theological theories. In a 1644 letter to Antoine Arnauld, she wryly declared herself an *Arnauldiste* because of her support for her brother's controversial theology of grace. "Apparently God's grace and mercy will follow us in the future, as it has saved us and accompanied us in the past. It is necessary to conclude that we have only been taught good doctrine, since they cannot find any bad doctrine here. Consequently it must be permitted to be an *Arnauldiste,* since we all here are and since it seems that it has made us such good women."[14] In 1652 she published a public defense of her *Private Chaplet* against the allegations of heresy by the Jesuit Jean de Brisacier. "Some people wanted to find impieties and blasphemies in this writing because they are convinced that it will only have the result of ruining the effects of love God has shown to us, especially in the sacrament of the Eucharist and the mystery of the Incarnation. I declare that such things have always been and still are, by God's grace, far removed from my sentiments, my intentions, and my mind."[15] Other letters indicate her personal involvement in other theological controversies concerning the Jansenist circle: the publication of the collected letters of Saint-Cyran;[16] Claude de Sainte-Marthe's *Defense of the Nuns of Port-Royal*;[17] and the defense of the imprisoned *solitaire* theologian Isaac Le Maître de Saci.[18]

In her study of the abbess's relationship to theological controversy, Linda Timmermans claims that "nothing indicates that Mère
Agnès (unlike [her niece] Angélique de Saint-Jean and other nuns)
was truly knowledgeable about the questions concerning grace. If it
is easy to point out contradictory passages in some nuns who, on
the one hand, protest that they are ignorant and, on the other hand,
sometimes on the same page, give incontestable proof of extensive
theological knowledge, it is impossible to discover such contradictions in the correspondence . . . of Mère Agnès."[19] Such an affirmation of the abbess's lack of theological knowledge is difficult to
reconcile with the many discussions of controversial theological
works concerning grace which fill her letters. It is certainly true
that Mère Agnès did not read the *Augustinus* and that she relied on
the advice of her brother Antoine Arnauld and other clerics to comprehend the technical, canonical language in which the papal bulls
and formularies condemning Jansen were framed. Like her sister
Mère Angélique, nonetheless, Mère Agnès acquired an extensive
knowledge of the theories on grace, morals, and the sacraments
which characterized the Jansenist movement.

During her second period as abbess (1658–61), Mère Agnès confronted the growing persecution of Port-Royal, rooted in the increasingly bitter quarrel over the *Augustinus*. The condemnations by
Innocent X (1653) and Alexander VII (1656) of the five propositions
as Jansen had allegedly defended them set the stage for the royal and
episcopal demands for French subjects to sign a formulary of submission to the church's judgment. Sympathetic to Arnauld's *fait/
droit* distinction, if strictly interpreted, the abbess was adamant in
her communications with her subjects and her external correspondents that she could not sign any statement affirming that Jansen
had upheld the condemned propositions.

> The church is attacked in truth and in charity, the two columns
> that support it. This is what they are trying to destroy by this un-
> fortunate signature, by which we would offer witness against the
> truth and destroy the charity we should have for the dead as well as
> the living. We would be subscribing to the condemnation of a holy
> bishop who never taught the heresies they impute to him. . . .
> When God is found on one side and something else on the other,
> there should be no doubt as to what we should conclude. Jesus

Christ stated it clearly when he said, "Whoever loves his father or his mother more than me is not worthy of me."[20]

Tellingly, the abbess justifies the refusal to give an unqualified signature to the formulary in terms of charity toward Jansen, not only in terms of truth and integrity. She pointedly refuses to use the argument that she and the other nuns do not understand the scholarly controversy over the doctrine of grace; on the contrary, she insists that the fact that Jansen never defended these propositions is clear to those who examine the facts of the case.

Mère Agnès's psychological and theological skill also governs her argument on the crisis of the signature. The perplexed nuns rightly experience a painful tension between loyalty to the truth represented by Jansen's theology and loyalty to the ecclesiastical and political authorities they serve. The deft reference to Christ's apothegm on the choice between love for one's parents and love for Christ himself reveals not only the correct solution to this conflict of conscience; it evokes the depth of the anguish provoked by the very existence of such a disturbing choice.

In 1661, after royal emissaries had closed the convent school and dismissed its novices, the counsels of resistance became cries of protest. As the convent faced virtual destruction, Mère Agnès protested to Louis XIV himself.

> We received this new order to send away our postulants and novices and to receive no more in the future, which in effect would represent nothing else than the desire to extinguish one of the most ancient abbeys of your kingdom, and to completely abolish our congregation . . . Sire, your piety and respect for the church should help you judge easily that one of the areas where secular authority should have a lesser role and where even the church's authority should make a decision only after a solemn, canonical judgment is the question of suppressing a monastery and an order legally entitled to provide servants for Jesus Christ over the course of centuries.[21]

More than a protest over the strangulation of Port-Royal's future, Mère Agnès's letter to Louis XIV boldly limits the scope of the authority of the throne and even of the ecclesiastical hierarchy in the treatment of a religious order. The divine foundation of both the church and the French monarchy cannot justify the deterioration of their supervision of monastic life into a raw abuse of authority to eliminate perceived theological dissidents in an obscure theological quarrel.

Even after the end of her abbacy, Mère Agnès remained the moral center of the nuns, the object of intensified persecution. In 1664 the persecution of Port-Royal took the form Mère Agnès had earlier predicted: denial of the sacraments through a sentence of interdict; placement of the convent under the governance of a foreign nun imposed by the archbishop of Paris; dispersal of nuns refusing an unqualified signature to house arrest in foreign convents. Mère Agnès herself was exiled to the Visitation convent in Faubourg Saint-Jacques. Attempts to persuade her to sign the formulary failed, but she tactfully endured the painful incident of witnessing two of her nieces at Port-Royal, Marie-Angélique Arnauld d'Andilly and Marie-Charlotte Arnauld d'Andilly, sign a slightly revised formulary at the personal urging of the bishop of Meaux, Jacques-Bénigne Bossuet. While Soeur Angélique de Saint-Jean Arnauld d'Andilly, Mère Agnès's combative niece who had become the leader of the *nonsigneuses* grouped at Port Royal des Champs, denounced the cowardice of the *signeuses*, Mère Agnès refused to condemn the nuns who had rejected her counsel. As in her spiritual direction, she recognized the complexity of the moral and legal issues involved in the case, the fact that well-intentioned Christians could arrive at different solutions, and the role that the passions aroused by the controversy could play in determining whether to sign the formulary or not. As Jean Mesnard argues, the restraint exercised by Mère Agnès in judging the minority who signed the formulary indicates the extent of the nun's opposition to coercion in questions of conscience.[22]

The persecution, interdict, and exile of the nuns did not diminish the external influence of Port-Royal. On the contrary, new publications carried the theology of the convent to a wider European audience. Mère Agnès's *Image of a Perfect and an Imperfect Nun*, a treatise on the virtues essential to the cloistered vocation, was published in Paris in 1665, ironically with the approval of the same king who was orchestrating the destruction of the convent. In the same year her *Constitutions of Port-Royal* was published by a sympathetic Amsterdam publishing firm. As persecution engulfed the convent, Antoine Arnauld spirited several trunks of Port-Royal papers across the border to exile in the Lowlands. Memorials praising Mère Agnès's courage under persecution as well as theological works by the abbess herself found a sympathetic Protestant as well as Catholic public.

Before and after the inauguration of the "Peace of the Church" (1669), Mère Agnès attempted to save Port-Royal through a letter-writing campaign to a large circle of religious and political dignitaries. Prominent ecclesiastic addressees included Hardouin de Péréfixe de Beaumont, archbishop of Paris; Jacques-Bénigne Bossuet, bishop of Meaux; Nicolas Pavillon, bishop of Alet; her brother Henry Arnauld, bishop of Angers; and Madame Françoise III de Foix, abbess of the Abbey aux Dames. Major political interlocutors included Marie-Louise de Gonzague, queen of Poland; Michel Le Tellier, chancellor of France; and Jean-Baptiste Colbert, minister of finance. Longtime lay allies of the convent such as Madame de Sablé, Madame de Longueville, Blaise Pascal, and his sister Gilberte Pascal Périer were also petitioned by the nun to assist in the convent's defense. In her epistolary apology for Port-Royal's position during the crisis of the signature, Mère Agnès communicated to her correspondents the philosophy of authority, rights, and resistance she had developed in response to the perceived abuse of power.

After six tumultuous decades, the last years of Mère Agnès's life were relatively tranquil. Orchestrated by Clement IX, the Peace of the Church permitted the recalcitrant nuns at Port-Royal des Champs to sign a modified formulary and church authorities to remove the sanctions imposed on the convent. A rejuvenated Port-Royal, its prestige enhanced by the aura of persecution, quickly reestablished itself as a center of reformed monastic life. The reopened novitiate could barely accommodate the many worthy candidates; the convent school was filled with the daughters of a sympathetic aristocracy; the coaches of devout laity once again made their way to sermons and retreats at the convent in the valley of the Chevreuse. Sympathetic presses published a flood of theological treatises, translations, hagiographies, devotional works, sermons, conferences, and letters written by the nuns and *solitaires* of Port-Royal. The convent had entered its brilliant but brief autumn as a free religious community.

Mère Agnès died on February 19, 1671.

WORKS

A prolific author, Mère Agnès was one of the few Port-Royal nuns to see her works published during her lifetime. Three works in particular attracted a wide public and became the object of controversy.

Written in 1626, *Private Chaplet of the Blessed Sacrament* is a devotional treatise presenting an apophatic theology of God's attributes and an anthropology of annihilation strongly influenced by the Bérullian spirituality of the Oratory.[23] Only when a Sorbonne committee condemned the work in 1633 did the treatise attract public attention. Reprinted by both supporters and critics, the *Private Chaplet* became the occasion for Mère Agnès to enter public controversies concerning the nature of prayer and the sacraments.

Published in 1665, *The Image of a Perfect and an Imperfect Nun* revealed Mère Agnès's skill as a moralist.[24] In her study of monastic ethics, she argues that the difference between religious perfection and imperfection is not the stark opposition between virtue and vice; rather, it consists in the subtle distinction between theocentric virtue, characterized by absolute abandonment to God, and anthropocentric virtue, tainted by the presence of self-interest. As Bernard Chédozeau notes, the *Image* ignited a rarified theological controversy over the role of the intellect in prayer.[25] Both Jean Desmarets de Saint-Sorlin in *The Path of Peace and the Path of Inquietude* and Martin de Barcos in *Sentiments of Abbé Philérème on Mental Prayer* criticized the nun for the role accorded to intellectual speculation in the methods of prayer proposed by the *Image* and its companion treatises.[26] In his *Treatise on Prayer* (1679) Pierre Nicole defended the intellectualist strand of Mère Agnès's spirituality against the critique of those who advocated a more affective style of meditation.[27]

Also published in 1665, *The Constitutions of the Monastery of Port-Royal of the Blessed Sacrament* demonstrated Mère Agnès's juridical capacity in her sketch of the laws, attitudes, and virtues essential for the life of a reformed contemplative order.[28] Her model constitution is also an apology for the religious rights of women, since it defends the authority of the abbess and the chapter in the governance of the convent. An essay published as an appendix to the *Constitutions, The Spirit of Port-Royal* is a particularly important speculative work by Mère Agnès because its philosophy of adoration synthesizes an apophatic account of God's attributes with a psychology of annihilation of the subject.[29]

Numerous writings by Mère Agnès appeared long after her death. Like similar Port-Royal texts, these posthumous publications survived due to the heroic work of Jansenists like Antoine Arnauld and Marie-Scolastique Le Sesne de Théméricourt, an alumna of Port-Royal's convent school who clandestinely copied convent documents, storing them in safe havens and circulating them among Jansenists in exile. A refuge for many exiled French Jansenists, the Dutch town of Utrecht became a center for the conservation and publication of these texts in the early eighteenth century.

Among the posthumous publications, two works hold particular interest. First published in 1718, *Counsels on the Conduct Which the Nuns Should Maintain in the Event of a Change in the Government of the Convent* is Mère Agnès's admonition to the Port-Royal nuns as the convent sank more deeply into the persecution of the 1660s.[30] A work of casuistry, the *Counsels* draws careful lines between permissible and impermissible cooperation with evil as the nuns face the dilemmas of exile, interdict, and commands to obedience by foreign religious superiors. An exercise in speculative as well as practical theology, the treatise probes the origin of and moral significance of the oppression visited upon the beleaguered disciples of Saint Augustine by the French throne.

A literary monument of nineteenth-century scholarship, the two-volume edition of the *Letters of Mère Agnès Arnauld, Abbess of Port-Royal* (1858) is a critical edition of more than seven hundred letters written by the abbess.[31] Although the edition is signed by Armand-Prosper Faugère, a prominent literary critic and editor of Pascal, the painstaking work of transcription, collation, and annotation of the collection was done principally by Rachel Gillet, a librarian at the Bibliothèque de la Société de Port-Royal. The correspondence reflects the broad biblical, patristic, and ascetical culture the abbess brought to her ministry of spiritual direction. The complex Augustinian philosophy of the abbess emerges in her letters. Positions on prayer or politics are justified by appeals to the work of

Augustine himself, to the Augustinian theology of Cistercian co-founder Saint Bernard of Clairvaux, and to the theories of modern Augustinians, such as François de Sales, Teresa of Avila, Cornelius Jansen, Saint-Cyran, and Antoine Arnauld.

The long correspondence, begun in 1626 and ended in 1671, also indicates the major changes in Mère Agnès's religious philosophy. The earlier emphasis on mystical abandonment becomes a martial call to resist abuses of power. The original lyrical depiction of God's attributes becomes a more sober meditation on the absence of God in a violent world where the just seem abandoned. The casuistic stress on precise rules of action to defend theological truth replaces the more diffuse speculation on the divine essence.

Other minor treatises have survived the death of Mère Agnès. Among the printed works, her *Of the Love One Must Have for the Cross of Jesus Christ*, published in Jean Hamon's anthology of spiritual treatises on love (1675), uses a Paulinian and Augustinian framework to describe the self-annihilating charity one must bear toward Christ crucified.[32] The treatise also presents a militantly Augustinian account of the concupiscence caused by the fall of Adam. Still in manuscript form at the Bibliothèque Nationale de France, Mère Agnès's *Explanation of the Rule of Saint Benedict* justifies the Angelican reform of Port-Royal by showing how its principles correspond to the stipulations of the Benedictine Rule.[33] Even in this commentary, the abbess's distinctive themes of adoration and annihilation color her interpretation of the legal prescriptions of primitive monasticism.

Divine Alterity

A devotional treatise, *Private Chaplet of the Blessed Sacrament* possesses a simple surface structure. Each of the sixteen paragraphs celebrates a particular attribute of Christ in the Eucharist. The first sentence of each paragraph praises Christ for the possession of a particular divine attribute, prominently displayed by his presence in the Eucharist preserved in the tabernacle. The body of each paragraph clarifies the nature of this attribute, systematically highlighting the differences between the divine nature of Christ and the finite and peccatory nature of humanity. The mystical rhetoric of the

Chaplet, clearly influenced by the sulfurous lyricism of Bérulle and Condren, often veils Mère Agnès's philosophical argument on the nature of the divine attributes. The recurrent use of the subjunctive mood often obscures the difference between the ontological attributes of Christ himself and the attributes the adorer wishes to impute to Christ in the mystery of the Blessed Sacrament. Despite this stylistic density, the *Chaplet* uses the categories of eucharistic piety to evoke the chasm between divine and human natures by analyzing Christ's attributes in terms of a negative theology.

The closing six attributes are the most apophatic in diction and sense: inaccessibility, incomprehensibility, independence, incommunicability, illimitability, and inapplicability. Inaccessible, Christ "remains in himself, letting creatures remain in the incapacity to approach him."[34] Incomprehensible, Christ "alone knows his ways and he justifies to himself alone the plans he has for his creatures."[35] Absolutely independent, Christ "acts as the first cause without any subjection to the ends he has given himself."[36] Incommunicable to others, Christ "does not lower himself to engage in relationships disproportionate to his infinite power."[37] Illimitable, Christ "acts according to the vast extent of the divine; he cares nothing for what comes from the finite."[38] Inapplicable to temporal concerns, Christ "takes cares of himself and does not concern himself with anything that happens outside of himself."[39]

Each negative attribute underlines the rupture between Creator and creature. Divine inaccessibility bars any common meeting point between God and creature. Divine wisdom veils knowledge of the divine essence from the creature. Divine independence blocks any human scrutiny of God's purposes. Divine incommunicability, illimitability, and inapplicability render futile any anthropomorphic conception of the relationship between God and humanity because of the radical disproportion between the two natures. As the believer adores God present in the Eucharist, she faces the unfathomable mystery of God, defined more accurately by what God is not (infinite, incomprehensible, unlimited) than by what God is.

Rooted in the act of adoration, the apophatic recognition of God's negative attributes fosters a series of abandonments in the person of the human adorer. Recognizing God's inaccessibility, "creatures renounce the desire for a meeting with God and accept that he remains in a place proper to the condition of his being."[40] Divine incomprehensibility guides souls to a blessed ignorance. "Souls take account of their ignorance and love the mystery of the counsels of God."[41] Reverence for God's independence leads souls to abandon their power of petitionary prayer in favor of simple adoration of God's will. "When souls are in the state of grace, God has promised to give himself to them. They should not build their hopes on that promise but rather remain in a blessed uncertainty that honors the independence of God."[42] God's incommunicability stimulates a fundamental humility before Christ. "Jesus Christ does not lower himself to relationships disproportionate to his infinite power. Souls should remain in the unworthiness they have for such a relationship."[43] The glimpse of God's illimitability should lead souls to renounce their own limited volitional desires. "They should cherish neither in their thoughts nor in their intentions anything other than a commitment to the vast designs of God."[44] Divine inapplicability encourages the adorer to make God, rather than his or her preoccupations, the center of the soul. "They should prefer to be forgotten by Christ than to be remembered by him, since the latter would give him an occasion to leave his own considerations in order to become preoccupied with creatures."[45]

An apophatic theology shapes an apophatic anthropology. Before the incomprehensible God, the human person can respond only through a sacred ignorance that abandons anthropomorphic projections of God and a silenced will that accepts God's impenetrable will. More than an attitude of reverence, humility emerges as an abandonment of conceptual and volitional claims on God provoked by a sacred awe before God's utter alterity.

On the surface the other divine attributes studied by the *Chaplet* appear more positive in nature: holiness, truth, existence, self-sufficiency, satiety, plenitude, eminence, and rulership. Since each of these traits could be attributed to human beings as well as to God, they would appear to function analogously, evoking certain similarities as well as dissimilarities between the divine and human natures. In Mère Agnès's analysis, however, these attributes acquire a decidedly negative connotation. They also serve to highlight the abyss between God and creatures, an abyss in which apparently analogous terms function almost entirely to express difference rather than resemblance.

In this apophatic recasting of religious terms, the holiness of Christ is a divine trait that categorically separates him from sinful humanity. "Jesus Christ exists in the Most Blessed Sacrament in a way in which he never goes outside of himself. That is to say that the company he wants to have with humanity is separate from it and resides only in himself. It is not reasonable that he should approach us because we are only sin."[46] Existence in Christ is God's perfect existence, whose plenitude overwhelms the comparatively fragile existence of all creatures. Compared with God's essence, which is existence itself, other beings appear nonexistent. "Jesus Christ establishes himself in everything souls are. He is everything he wants to be and makes all other beings disappear. As the sun blots out all other light, he exists simply to exist."[47] The divine eminence of Christ overshadows alleged claims of eminence by any creature. "Jesus Christ enters into all his rights. He rises gloriously in pre-eminence. He makes a separation in greatness between himself and creatures. May souls accept their lowliness in their homage to this greatness."[48] In this apophatic transposition of even positive divine attributes, Mère Agnès underscores the radical dependence of all creatures upon God and the utter dependence of God on nothing other than his own inscrutable essence, that is, a divine existence, knowledge, and will that are wholly other than those of fragile humanity.

The ontological chasm between God and creature disclosed by a proper apophatic affirmation of these divine attributes encourages the adorer to operate his or her own spiritual distance from God the unfathomable. Spiritual concerns for self must yield to simple awe before the perfection of the divine essence. This spiritual abnegation often assumes the form of annihilation of the self. Christ's perfect freedom invites the adorer to complete union with him. "As he [Christ] draws existence from himself, he also wants others to exist for himself. In this vein he rejects all promises that seem to contain a conditional commitment. He wants to receive those who exist as if they sprang from the free movement of Christ himself."[49] In this movement of self-annihilation and union with God, preoccupations with the self's destiny recede. The perfect self-possession of Christ invites the soul to a union so intimate that only God remains. "Jesus Christ appropriates souls to himself. He draws them to himself so that souls rise up to him and take their life from him. All their actions are his inasmuch as they receive their movement from him. Nothing is worthy to exist outside of him. If he so pleases, may they not be concerned as to whether he possesses them or not. Rather, it is enough that he possesses himself."[50] In the act of adoration, the soul contemplating the divine essence recognizes its comparative nonexistence and abandons itself to the mystery it ponders in awe.

Given its militant apophatic theology, the criticism provoked by the *Private Chaplet* is hardly surprising. Jesuit critics like Étienne Binet argued that the meditations had undercut the core of eucharistic piety: the tangible presence of Christ's body and blood under the eucharistic species to console the faithful in their needs.[51] Instead of dwelling on the humanity of Christ, the *Chaplet* depicts only his divinity, a divinity evoked in the frostiest terms. Rather than lauding the compassionate Christ who chose to dwell among humanity, the treatise celebrates a divine Christ aloof from the human condition. Instead of encouraging the faithful to present their petitions to the eucharistic Christ, the *Chaplet* urges them to abandon all self-concern and to focus on the unfathomable divinity within Christ. As Mère Agnès gazes at Christ in the Eucharist, she perceives only the paradoxical presence of the divinity that is other than matter, other than the creature, and other than need or lack. It is not only Counter-Reformation Jesuits who contested this glacial eucharistic theology; recent scholars of Port-Royal such as Louis Cognet have also expressed their reservations at this presentation of the eucharistic Christ which seems to bracket the Incarnation itself.[52] In meditating on the most carnal of Christian mysteries, Mère Agnès evokes only divine distance where most Catholic theologians underscore divine-human communion. The *via negativa* has invaded the sacraments.

Port-Royal's subsequent lack of enthusiasm for the *Chaplet* is also comprehensible. As Jean-Robert Armogathe notes, later publicists of Port-Royal did not attempt to republish the controversial work and routinely dismissed it as a spiritual trifle given importance only by the jealousies of the convent's early episcopal overseers.[53] In fact, the *Chaplet*'s speculative mysticism differed in tone and substance from the more practical theology, skeptical of mystical effusion, which became the mainstream of the convent's spirituality. Mère Agnès's meditations on the attributes of God import the highly Platonized theology of the Oratory into Port-Royal's signature activity of eucharistic adoration. The apophatic theology advanced by the treatise transcends the simple recognition of God's incomprehensibility; it grounds a metaphysical argument on how God is other than all creatures. In the abbess's hands the *via negativa* becomes an attribute-by-attribute analysis of the irreducible alterity of God's essence.

Despite its problematic sacramental theology, the *Chaplet* retains its pertinence as an exercise in philosophical speculation. Mère Agnès does not simply praise the eucharistic Christ; she constructs an argument on the otherness of God, as manifest in the divine attributes of Christ. Her analysis of the sixteen attributes demonstrates how God's truth and freedom are radically other than our own. It explains why the incomprehensible God cannot be grasped and why the inaccessible God cannot be localized in our time and space. Within the framework of apophatic theology, the *Chaplet* critiques too anthropomorphic a conception of prayer, which substitutes self-centered petition for adoration, and the concomitant anthropomorphic conception of God, which reduces God's essence to a projection of our own fragile virtues. A treatise of negative theology, the *Chaplet* paradoxically celebrates and analyzes the utter alterity of God in a sacramental site where God's presence would appear to be the most palpable.

Conventual Virtue

The *Image of a Perfect and an Imperfect Nun* provides a complex account of the virtues proper to the nun. It structures its analysis of monastic perfection in terms of fundamental relationships of the nun: to God, to herself, to her superiors, to her subordinates, and to the basic duties of religious life. The contrast between the perfect and the imperfect nun is not a simple binary opposition between virtue and vice; the traits of the imperfect nun are subtle counterfeits of the virtues of the perfect. In this contextualized study of the moral habits central to the conventual way of life, Mère Agnès repeatedly identifies authentic virtue as theocentric, an abandonment to God alone, and corroded virtue as anthropocentric, centered ever so subtly on the human self.

In the relationship to God, the moral status of the nun manifests itself through the quality of four dispositions: reverence for God, submission to God's direction, religious zeal, and repentance for sin. While the perfect nun centers these dispositions on an undivided dedication to God, the imperfect nun subverts these religious virtues by alloying them to nonreligious concerns rooted in the unredeemed self.

The reverence of the perfect esteems God alone, ignoring creatures "as if they did not exist."[54] In the practices of the convent, the nun extends a similar reverence toward the rule of her order and the commands of her superiors since both represent God's particular will for her. The imperfect, on the other hand, corrupt their reverence for God by the existence of a divided heart that "desires something other than God or that fears the loss of something other than God that pleases them."[55] Although the imperfect faithfully participate in the external religious rituals of the convent, their heterogeneous reverence has diminished the internal fervor necessary for proper reception of the sacraments. The result is an unbecoming familiarity with God; its outward sign, according to Mère Agnès in a typically Saint-Cyranian analysis, is too frequent reception of Holy Communion.

The treatment of the virtue of submission to God is clearly influenced by Mère Agnès's apophatic theology. The perfect nun's total submission to God's will fosters a state of indifference in which she gladly accepts privations of God's palpable presence. The abbess establishes a parallel between "the divine perfections that are hidden"[56] and the graces hidden in the soul of the perfect, who accept the night of God's sensible absence rather than cling to sensible consolations in religious exercises. The imperfect, however, can only endure the performance of religious duties when sensible consolations abound. When spiritual aridity emerges, they flee in confusion, unable to accept the darker and more volitional attachment to God that characterizes the mature souls. Mère Agnès condemns in particular an aesthetic attitude that corrupts the imperfect's relationship to theology. "[The imperfect nun] attaches herself to the knowledge of these [religious] truths, which benefit others who use them with simplicity. But they damage the imperfect, because she loves them on account of their beauty rather than on account of their usefulness."[57]

In Mère Agnès's analysis, religious zeal becomes a paradoxically passive virtue. The zeal of the perfect for the honor of God leads them to lament how deeply the world contemns God's benefits. Her own infidelity in honoring God plunges the nun into a state of remorse. So great is her compunction that the zealous nun "stands trembling before God, fearing with Job that God will question her, making her give an account of her actions before God's judgment."[58] For the imperfect, zeal for oneself has simply suffocated any genuine concern for God. The flurry of activity, often stamped with religious externals, scarcely masks a self-interested search for comfort, praise, and power.

In her study of the virtue of repentance, Mère Agnès stresses the posture of the will. The perfect nun accepts all punishments from God for her sins as if she had already entered the flames of purgatory. This authentic repentance requires the abandonment of one's own will. "One must be dead to sin, to one's own will, and to all the attachments it provides in order to enter this place that must purify us."[59] True renunciation of sin also requires radical solitude, a deliberate separation from a sinful world. "A soul faithful to its purgatory retires from everything. It seeks solitude and silence; it desires to be forgotten and to ignore everything that happens, since it exists outside the world."[60] For the imperfect, the desire to end sin vacillates. The imperfect nun continues the practices of repentance, but the desire to renounce sin alternates with the desire to avoid change. Self-will blocks any durable reformation of life. "Not having enough resolution to accept all the things that arise to contradict her and to accept all the occasions for mortification God sends her, she chooses certain things that are good in themselves but for which she feels less repugnance. This only helps to fool her, because she thinks she is doing much when in fact her self-indulgence, in not wanting to contradict her inclinations in everything, is the reason why she makes no progress."[61] Behind the difference between heroic and mediocre repentance lies the opposition between a will abandoned to God to the point of annihilation and a pusillanimous will paralyzed by contradictory desires.

The second relationship analyzed by the *Image* concerns the disposition of the nun toward herself. The relationship to the soul, the body, and one's reputation is highlighted. The moral attitudes isolated by Mère Agnès are simple variations of love and hatred. Part of the philosophical interest in this study of the nun's relationship to herself resides in the starkly dualistic anthropology that undergirds the theory of virtue. The degree of proper dispositions toward oneself reflects the degree of proper balance between the opposed substances of body and soul.

The perfect nun loves her soul as a possession destined for eternity. The abbess analyzes the various qualities of the love borne by the perfect toward their souls. Compassionate, this love must treat the soul as a vulnerable combatant locked in civil war with its body. Vigilant, this love must carefully attend to the least moral danger threatening the soul. Reverential, this love must venerate the soul's authority as a mistress appointed by God to govern the person's actions. Contrasting with Mère Agnès's customary dismissal of the peccatory self, this encomium of love for the soul manifests a more humanistic side to her anthropology. The perfect nun recognizes the honor of "possessing in herself the image of God and knowing that the one who has created us reposes in us as in his dwelling place."[62] The soul's ascendancy in the human person renders it similar in authority to "this angel that God makes walk before his people and whose voice we must listen to and follow, so that he may guide us on our path."[63] Rather than loving the soul, the imperfect simply neglect it. In permitting their body to rule the soul, the imperfect have destroyed the order of subordination established by God. Using a gendered metaphor of mistress (*maîtresse*) and female servant (*servante*), the abbess condemns the anthropological reversal effected by the imperfect nun. "She reverses the order established by God by placing the servant above the mistress, that is to say, concupiscence above the soul. God, on the other hand, wanted the soul to be the mistress and wanted us to chase away the servant."[64] Echoing Augustinian theology, Mère Agnès simply assimilates the body to the sinful forces of concupiscence that threaten the salvation of the soul.

If love constitutes the proper disposition toward the soul, hatred is the appropriate attitude toward the body. The perfect nun treats her body with "aversion and hatred," attentive to counter the recurrent "revolt of the flesh against the spirit."[65] Although the struggle against the body must be conducted with moderation, since even the body should be used to glorify God, as a center of vice and passion the body must be firmly subordinated to the direction of the soul. The imperfect nun, on the contrary, treats the body with indulgence. The imperfect are once more characterized by the vacillation with which they approach spiritual combat. Periods of mortification, often pursued with ardor, alternate with periods of surrender to the body's inclination toward comfort. In a Pascalian metaphor, Mère Agnès describes the vacillating mind directing the uncertain attack against the body. "Her mind is like a reed shaken by the winds, which make it bend sometimes one way and sometimes another."[66]

In her analysis of the relationship of the nun to her reputation, the abbess emphasizes a more social anthropology and contests the pervasive respect for social rank in the French culture of the period. The tendency of the human person to base his or her sense of worth on the comparative prestige of family origin or social position must be uprooted. The perfect nun reverses the code of social eminence by willingly refusing honors that others wish to accord her. She is especially vigilant on the pride that might arise from the prominence of her family of origin. If she comes from a prominent family, "she never speaks about it except in cases of necessity; she desires others to forget these details no less than she does."[67] If she comes from low birth, "she is not ashamed that others know it and that they treat her with humiliation."[68] In its treatment of reputation, the *Image* underscores the subversive social ethics of the convent. In an aristocratic society defined by social rank, the nuns construct an egalitarian society that suppresses an identity based on family prominence. In a culture avid for social honors, the nuns prize an asceticism that actively embraces what a stratified society despises.

The third set of relationships concerns the nun's conduct toward members of her conventual community. Power differences structure the link to superiors, peers, and subordinates. Although the *Image* specifies different virtues corresponding to the different power relationship between the nun and her colleagues, the entire analysis stresses the reverence for the other that constitutes the cornerstone of the conventual ethos. Specifically, this reverence consists in the recognition of the presence of God in the person of each nun to whom one is related by various types of duties.

Toward her superiors the perfect nun practices complete obedience. She opens her spiritual life in frank conversation and willingly accepts the commands of the superior. Her obedience is not based on sensible consolation derived from the superior's human qualities. Rather, it is grounded in the recognition of God's presence in the superior. "She esteems the superior and listens to her as she would to God. . . . A nun obeys her superiors not only with joy, but even more with glory, knowing she honors God by honoring them."[69] Toward her peers the perfect nun practices the virtue of humility. She habitually esteems others as greater than herself and willingly assists them out of this humble estimate. This humble attitude toward self and others, however, springs from a recognition of God's graces at work in her peers rather than an admiration of their personal merits. "In considering the grace of God in them [her peers], the nun does not stop to consider their faults."[70] Toward her subordinates the perfect nun exhibits the virtue of charity. Acknowledging the inevitable imperfections of those who have just begun religious life, the perfect nun tolerates faults with patience and attempts to assist others to grow in perfection. Her response of charitable assistance rather than severe judgment arises from the recognition of God's spirit already at work even in the most immature souls. "She believes herself obligated to strengthen the good which God has placed in these persons not only by her example, but even more by her prayers."[71] Behind the specific virtues of obedience, humility, and charity stands a global attitude of reverence for the other nun as a unique image of God.

The imperfect nun distorts her relationship to members of the community by the mixture of virtues and vices she exhibits. The obedience she offers her superiors vacillates according to her estimate of the human qualities of the nun who seeks to command her. Rather than humility, the imperfect nun manifests resentment and envy toward her peers. Her pride prevents her from considering her colleagues as equals, let alone superiors, in virtue. Rather than exhibiting charity, the imperfect nun disdains her subordinates and magnifies their defects in a spirit of acerbic criticism. Her air of authoritative judgment only masks a pride that refuses to welcome the premises of perfection in younger nuns. Instead of recognizing the trace of God's presence in her sister nuns, the imperfect, imprisoned by vanity, can only dismiss them as inferior images of herself.

The fourth network of relations concerns the nun's tie to the principal virtues of religion. Three of these virtues rest on the essential vows of monastic life: poverty, chastity, and obedience. In her treatment of these religious virtues, Mère Agnès appeals to an anthropology of annihilation, clearly influenced by the Oratorian theology of Bérulle and Condren. Her analysis of these virtues also manifests the theocentric, specifically Christocentric, framework in which the abbess conceives all authentic moral virtue.

The virtues of humility and poverty illustrate the annihilation of self that constitutes the grandeur of the perfect nun. Humility transcends simple modesty toward oneself and generosity toward others. It is the recognition of one's complete dependence on God for any good action, a dependence that has become abject since the Fall. "It is on this knowledge of oneself and on this incapacity in which we are to accomplish the least good and avoid the least evil without God's help that the true nun establishes an unshakable humility."[72] Religious poverty exceeds the renunciation of personal possessions and the communitarian sharing of material goods. It is a spiritual attitude that avows one's utter nothingness before the omnipotence of God. Poverty follows "the knowledge she [the perfect nun] has that nothing was hers before she was made out of nothing; she herself was only nothing, especially since the sin of Adam, who made all humanity worthy of losing not only all the goods of heaven but also those of the earth. We were incapable of possessing them without danger of abusing them and losing ourselves by possessing them."[73] In both sentiment and action the virtuous nun annihilates herself before the mystery of God, who alone creates and redeems. Not surprisingly the imperfect nun manifests herself as the moral agent who maintains an illusion of personal merit based on her own will and who thus proves herself incapable of the self-surrender of the truly humble and poor nun.

Mère Agnès's analysis excavates the theological and Christological foundations of several key conventual virtues. Authentic charity does not consist in the love of neighbor alone; rather, it consists in the capacity to see and serve God in the neighbor. "This pure motive of loving only God in creatures makes her see God in all the people who present themselves to her. She does not stop loving the neighbor regardless of how the neighbor treats her."[74] Christ himself serves as the model and source of this supernatural charity.

"The obligation to love the neighbor is a commandment from the Son of God, not only because she [the nun] received it from him but because he practiced it himself. He loved all humanity with such excess. He gave his life for them, which should reduce her to embarrassment if she failed to show charity toward those who disturbed her. She sees that the Son of God has not only suffered for humanity and its salvation but that on the cross he prayed for his enemies."[75] Similarly it is Christ who provides the perfect model of the annihilation of the self that constitutes the spiritual core of authentic poverty. "So that this necessary annihilation might become voluntary and profitable to souls, he [God] wanted to give them an object full of sweetness and charity by proposing to them the example of Jesus Christ, who chose to live and die in an extreme poverty, by which he was deprived of all the goods of the earth."[76] In Mère Agnès's edifice of the religious virtues, the virtue of the perfect identifies itself by its strict focus on God, rather than the self, and its perfect solidarity with the crucified Christ.

The vacillating imperfect nun, on the other hand, reverses the theocentric structure of virtue. Her alleged charity esteems the neighbor only to the extent that the neighbor can benefit her; a sentimental affection for certain friends has displaced the authentic love of the neighbor in God. A calculus of self-interest has deposed the ecstatic love of God for God's own sake and the reverential love of all creatures for the sake of the Creator.

The final set of relationships concerns the link between the nun and the basic duties of religious life. In this deontology Mère Agnès studies numerous obligations found in any generic religious order: respect for tenets of the order's rule, performance of penance, and maintenance of the external decorum proper to a vowed religious. Two of these obligations, however, reflect more specifically the deontology of the Port-Royal nun. They are the duty to maintain solitude and the duty to assist in the conventual adoration of the Blessed Sacrament.

Affirming Mère Angélique's reform of Port-Royal through strict rules of cloister and silence, Mère Agnès emphasizes the total solitude to be practiced by the perfect nun. This solitude consists in the desire to maintain a strict vigilance over one's soul and to accept prominent convent offices only under reluctant obedience. Despite its interiority, this solitude retains its communal character; the perfect nun gladly accepts manual chores that quietly maintain the conventual life. At its fine point, where the nun experiences her uselessness due to illness or lack of skill, monastic solitude can lead the virtuous nun to recognize God's utter independence of our efforts. "God reduces us to be totally useless in order to learn by our own experience what the Prophet says, 'Since the Lord is God, he has no need of our goods.' That is to say that no matter how excellent our works may be, they provide no benefit whatsoever to him; they are only advantageous to us."[77] Incapable of this spiritual annihilation of self before God, the imperfect nun periodically flees the yoke of solitude. Prolonged parlor visits impress the memories of the world on her soul; admiration for the services she performs prolongs the illusion of her own merit. Perfunctory external observance of cloister and silence only masks a spiritually dissipated self, terrified of solitary abandonment to God.

In her treatment of the duty to assist in adoration of the Blessed Sacrament, Mère Agnès studies one of the most distinctive and Tridentine of Port-Royal's practices. Since the ill-fated effort to establish the Institut du Saint-Sacrement in the 1630s, perpetual adoration of the eucharistic Christ by successive teams of nuns had rivaled the chanting of the divine office as the devotional center of the convent. In her analysis of this duty the abbess emphasizes the spirit of adoration that must animate it. Using the Oratorian rhetoric of annihilation and spousal union, she evokes the mystical core of the obligation.

At the heart of adoration lies a mutual annihilation between Christ and the soul of the nun contemplating the Blessed Sacrament. The gift of the Eucharist "excites her to self-immolation without ceasing to this divine Savior, who shows her the example of the sacrifice she must make of herself to God, by the continual immolation he makes of his entire being to his eternal Father in this august sacrament."[78] The adoration of the perfect does not consist in sentiments of religious awe or praise; it consists specifically in a sacrificial destruction of the self initiated by and mirroring the redemptive sacrifice of Christ present in the Eucharist.

This self-annihilation in adoration leads the perfect nun to the experience of mystical death. Through the graced abnegation of self,

the soul of the mature contemplative is transformed into the crucified Christ she ponders.

> She hears the voice of her Savior, who commands her to announce
> his death by her voluntary death to all visible things and to herself
> until he comes, that is to say, until she dies in her body. He further
> tells her to find her rest and her glory only in the cross, in humili-
> ation and privation of what she loves. She should do this out of
> love for the one who dispossessed himself of his own glory, who
> annihilated himself, and who died for her salvation. It is necessary
> for her to clothe herself with these sentiments and with himself
> through imitation of his virtues in order to merit a place among
> the company of his spouses.[79]

Paradoxically, the spousal union with Christ only emerges at the
end of an itinerary of moral death of the self rooted in the double annihilation of Christ: the Incarnation, by which Christ abandons the
trappings of divinity to assume human form, and the Passion, in
which Christ redeems humanity through the immolation of the
cross. The union between Christ and the soul in the act of adoration
arises in the abyss of mutual self-emptying.

Incapable of this interior adoration, the imperfect nun can only
go through the motions of external assistance at eucharistic adoration. "She reads her rules, but she does not devour them like the
prophet Ezechiel devoured the book God showed him. That is why
the virtue of what is there written does not penetrate her soul."[80]
Tepid and aloof from internal adoration, the imperfect nun simply
ignores the summons to self-annihilation and union with God which
lies hidden in Christ's presence in the Eucharist.

In its constellation of virtues for the nun, the *Image* reveals its
Augustinian pedigree. Dismissing the natural virtues as masks of
pride, Mère Agnès designates as virtuous only those habits of soul
fashioned by God's grace. The cardinal virtues make no appearance;
prudence, fortitude, temperance, and justice impress by their absence. In the abbess's moral universe, grace cannot build on a nature
ravaged by concupiscence. The virtues analyzed by the treatise constitute variations on the theological virtues of faith and charity.
Within a theology that exalts God's sovereignty and contests native

human merit, even the most heroic virtue is unmasked as the shadow of God's grace.

In this fundamentally Augustinian account of virtue, Mère Agnès maintains her own originality. The nun's relationship to God, to herself, and to her conventual sisters determines the particular type of virtues she must cultivate. The requirements for moral flourishing within this specific way of life indicate the identity of the virtues necessary for the nun's perfection. In the *Image*, the proper analysis of the moral traits necessary for the nun cannot be deduced from considering human nature in general or even from pondering the generic essence of the nun. It can emerge only through careful consideration of the basic relations by which a nun constitutes herself: how she prays, how she treats her body, how she performs manual labor, how she obeys her superiors. In this use of a relational rather than essentialist anthropology to support her philosophy of virtue, Mère Agnès develops a contextualist account of virtue that links the necessary moral and intellectual habits of an individual to her particular vocational and social setting.

The *Image* also provides a distinctively contemplative account of virtue. The apex of virtue is the habit of adoration, a loving gaze on God in which the self disappears. This contemplative perspective suffuses the entire edifice of the virtues analyzed by Mère Agnès. Self-respect consists in reverence for the soul destined for eternal union with God. Proper conduct with superiors and subordinates flows from recognition of the presence of God within them. The abbess repeatedly redefines the moral and theological virtues in light of this contemplative vision. Humility emerges as a recognition of one's utter dependence on God, charity for neighbors as the capacity to recognize God's indwelling within them. Several commentators have contended that the youthful, mystical perspective of Mère Agnès in the *Private Chaplet* was abandoned in her more pragmatic works of maturity.[81] The *Image*'s account of virtue, however, argues otherwise. Authentic virtue is rooted in a vision of God not only in God's self but also in the creatures made by God. Behind the disparate spiritual habits constituting conventual virtue lies a single posture of reverence toward God and God's image in the human person. Reflecting Mère Agnès's mystical impulse, the *Image* designates religious illumination and contemplative vision as the sources of authentic virtue.

Communitarian Character

A synthetic essay on the philosophy of the reformed Port-Royal, *The Spirit of the Monastery of Port-Royal* provides a portrait of the characteristic traits of the convent community, much as *Image of a Perfect and an Imperfect Nun* had offered a portrait of the ideal individual nun. This brief treatise presents the religious purpose and the chief moral virtues of the convent in an analysis that employs the tool of apophatic theology and of an Augustinian account of virtue. Its philosophical significance lies in the militancy with which Mère Agnès insists on the incomprehensibility of God and on the opposition between virtue and passion.

According to Mère Agnès, the foundational characteristic of the convent is its religious spirit, its effort to "seek God and follow him in all things."[82] The key attribute of the God pursued by Port-Royal is incomprehensibility. "This spirit learns to conceive of God in an inconceivable manner, not only because he is incomprehensible in his infinite grandeur, but also because we are not capable by ourselves of forming any thought to raise us to him and even less of forming a single thought that would be worthy of him."[83] The emphasis on the chasm between divine reality (the attributes of God) and human capacity (the power to form concepts) abolishes the possibility of a natural theology. Limited by its finitude and further weakened by concupiscence, the human mind cannot move from a comprehension of nature to a comprehension of God. The concepts used to grasp the material and psychological world falter in the presence of the purely spiritual being, God. Unaided by grace, the human intellect can posit only the most obscure of divine attributes, namely incomprehensibility. Paradoxically the only authentic knowledge concerning God constructed by human agency is an acknowledgment of God's unknowability.

In the abbess's analysis of religious knowledge, only faith can provide an idea of God that can free the human person for religious commitment, in the form of spiritual abandonment to God. "The single thought given by faith, namely that God exists, is enough for souls to give them the impression of a reverence that makes them entirely dependent on his divine majesty and that leads them to expect all things from him, according to the order of his providence and not of their desires."[84] This fideistic view of religious knowledge claims that the most minimal truths of revelation, such as the simple affirmation that God exists, can transform the human person. Acknowledging God's existence, the believer not only acquires a more positive knowledge of God's attributes; she begins to recognize her entire dependence on God, manifest in the workings of divine providence. Even this more detailed knowledge of God unveiled through revelation and faith, however, maintains its apophatic note. Mère Agnès's discussion of divine providence insists on the stark opposition between God's will and the human will, evident in the latter's disordered desires. Just as the human intellect fails to grasp God's veiled attributes, the human will fails to fathom God's sovereign will, hidden in the obscure unfolding of divine providence. Rather than abolishing the alterity of God, religious knowledge grounded in faith only underscores it.

This religious devotion to the incomprehensible God fosters the emergence of a series of communitarian virtues in the convent. Mère Agnès focuses on the following traits: piety, charity, equality, force, solitude, humility, gratitude, poverty, industriousness, peace, and compassion. Most of these traits are routine virtues to be found in any Christian catechism or manual of convent life. The abbess provides an original contribution to this theory of conventual virtue by defining several of these virtues according to the distinctive Augustinian theology and practices of Port-Royal. She also adds a characteristic Jansenist note to this philosophy of virtue by her repeated insistence on the opposition between virtue and emotion.

Piety is defined as "remembering God, considering him, and relating all things to him."[85] Authentic piety refuses all inclination to emotional satisfaction, even in mystical form. "The spirit of piety these souls try to follow is neither a sensible favor nor a desire to receive the gift of contemplation."[86] Mère Agnès deepens the intellectualist cast of this version of piety by her emphasis on the biblical culture acquired by the Port-Royal nuns. "They prefer this reading [of the Bible] to all others. Although they do not have a knowledge of most of the mysteries contained therein, they pause over what they understand and leave to God the knowledge of what they do not understand. If they occasionally ask someone to instruct them on the meaning of these words so hidden and mysterious, they do so not out of curiosity but only to profit from the light of others."[87] Despite its gingerly phrasing, this passage ties enlightened piety to theological education. The growth of a biblical piety requires more than prayer and spiritual illumination; it needs formal theological instruction on the mysteries of faith. The abbess here sketches the Port-Royal ideal of a learned piety for women, which formed so visible and so controversial a strand of the convent's spirituality.

Like piety, charity is defined over against human passions. "The mutual charity we desire to establish in these works is not founded on the caresses and the affectionate familiarity people might have for each other."[88] On the contrary, the charity revered in the convent is a purely supernatural virtue, grounded in the initiative of God alone. "This divine virtue is spread through hearts by the Holy Spirit."[89] As such, this theological charity destroys the traces of self-love that stain the exercise of authentic charity. Divorced from sentiment, Port-Royal's charity is strictly a habit of the will transformed by divine initiative.

Just as Mère Agnès conceives the divine attributes according to the categories of negative theology, the virtues she describes as typical of the convent often contain a distinctly negative content. Gratitude, for example, transcends simple thanksgiving for benefits received from God. It initiates a process of radical detachment from creatures. Having freed themselves from attachment to sensate objects, mature grateful nuns progressively detach themselves from religious objects. "They try to have no attachment to the holiest things, such as prayer, Holy Communion, and spiritual conferences . . . they know that they are not our final end, although they lead us to it. That is why they place God above all things."[90] Restored to their theocentric purity, virtues like gratitude free the human person from attachment even to the morally positive creatures and focus the person uniquely on the obscure mystery of God.

Defined with a characteristically libertarian note, the prayerfulness of Port-Royal includes both vocal and mental prayer. Opposed to the elaborate methods of meditation prescribed in many orders during the Counter-Reformation, the convent's approach to prayer leaves each nun substantial freedom to determine the best methods suited to her situation. The fear of a personal mental prayer that deteriorates into mystical self-satisfaction leads Mère Agnès to privilege the public, liturgical prayer of the convent as the surest expression of prayerfulness. "Although mental prayer is made with a more sensible kind of reflection, it is also to be feared that one might seek more of this sensible consolation for oneself, while in vocal prayer, especially in the public prayer in which the church is united to us, the mind is carried toward God without returning on itself."[91] Even in the exercise of monastic prayer, virtue must oppose the corrupting influences of the emotions and of self-will.

One of the most characteristic traits of the convent is its emphasis on equality. The officers of the convent exercise equanimity in the treatment of their subjects. Recognizing the mixture of the strong and weak souls they must govern, they modulate their reactions to avoid unnecessary diversions in the convent. "We do not give praise to members when they have done well and we do not discourage them too much when they have made mistakes. We want to keep their spirit in constant balance, humble in the prosperity of spiritual goods and patient in the privation of the same goods, of which God alone is the master and distributor."[92] This egalitarianism also manifests itself in the convent's practice of admission. Only clear evidence of a God-given vocation, not possession of wealth or social rank or familial prestige, can justify admission to Port-Royal. "The most advantageous human qualities count nothing for them [the candidates for admission] unless it is apparent that grace wants to use them for its ends; outside of this situation they function more as weapons against religious life."[93] Within the convent, differences in rank are minimized. In the area of work, both choir nuns and lay sisters are encouraged to engage in manual labor. "We do not make any difference between the work of the choir nuns and that of the lay sisters. The only exception is that some choir nuns might lack the strength to do this work. We consider this obligation to work as a prolongation of penance and poverty; as a result, the choir nuns are equally obliged to do it."[94] The insistence on the value of manual labor for choir nuns challenged the long-standing practice of Benedictine convents, where choir nuns, drawn largely from the aristocracy, were exempted from manual work. It also challenged a theology of religious life that, considering contemplation superior to work, judged manual chores improper for a choir nun summoned to cloistered contemplation. These various egalitarian practices deepened the suspicion of Louis XIV and his advisers that Port-Royal implicitly subverted the religious and political hierarchies of the period.

One of the more original treatments of virtue in the *Spirit of the Monastery of Port-Royal* emerges in its presentation of the virtue of poverty. Mère Agnès transforms this corporate virtue of common possession of material goods into an aesthetic virtue. The poverty of Port-Royal includes the restraint and austerity with which it expresses itself through artistic forms. This minimalist aesthetic, rooted in Cistercian tradition and opposed to the exuberance of baroque Catholicism, imposes itself especially in Port-Royal's distinctive architecture and music.

The sobriety of the Port-Royal church expresses the strict cloistered solitude as well as the evangelical poverty of the Cistercian nuns.

> The pretext of honoring God by the magnificence of churches
> often causes nuns to lack charity because they never have enough
> to embellish their altars. The nuns [of Port-Royal] try to reduce
> such things to the simplicity typical of their order, at least as much
> as circumstances permit. They are always vigilant to make sure
> that the house of God is clean and proper. This edifies rather than
> scandalizes the world. This modesty is in conformity with their
> church building, which was built very small, because the monas-
> teries of nuns do not exist to attract society toward them.[95]

For the abbess, the church building functions as the external body for the internal spirit of the convent community. Corporate commitment to poverty is symbolically expressed by the plain glass, the simple geometric design, and the sober decoration demanded by Mère Angélique in her revisions of the original architectural plans for the convent church of Port-Royal de Paris.[96] The austere chapel outwardly expresses an uncluttered focus on the mystery of God as well as a communal commitment to material poverty. This passage on architecture also reflects the evangelical concern for the poor that characterized Port-Royal. Too great a taste for ecclesiastical ornamentation cloaks a denial of charity to the poor under the misleading colors of God's glory.

Similarly the liturgical music used at Port-Royal expresses the spiritual poverty of the convent community. Opposed to the elaborate polyphony of the period's ecclesiastical music, the convent uses plainchant for its offices. "This [poverty] is also what moves them to maintain the very simple type of chant prescribed by the church, so that the desire to hear chants pleasing to the ear will draw no one to come listen to them. Moreover, they will not lose so much time and it will not be necessary to have someone from outside to teach them."[97] Reflective of a communal poverty of means, plainchant also strengthens the cloistered solitude prized by Port-Royal as one of the goals of a reformed convent. Its simplicity and uniformity also help to create unity in the convent and reduce the dangers of jealousy based on artistic talent. "Even in this common chant there can still appear some complacency when someone has an excellent voice. Because we love the spiritual good of every soul more than the embellishment of the choir, we forbid these persons to sing solo rather than esteeming and maintaining them for this purpose."[98] Even in the domain of music, the egalitarian ethos of Port-Royal opposes every sign of individual distinction. The corporate poverty of the convent expresses itself in a style and in a taste as much as it does in the personal renunciation of material goods. The neoclassical arches of the convent church and the unadorned Gregorian chant of vespers embody a stark spiritual abandonment to the unembroidered word of God.

In *The Spirit of the Monastery of Port-Royal*, Mère Agnès approaches both divine and human natures from an apophatic perspective. God's fundamental attribute is his incomprehensibility. Speculative efforts to grasp the divine nature never overcome this fundamental obscurity. Even the supernatural knowledge of God disclosed by an act of faith rooted in God's self-revelation only unveils further mystery, as any mature meditant on the Bible knows. Similarly, human nature presents its own opacity. As the human person progresses morally under the conduct of the Holy Spirit, the nature of this redeemed humanity becomes more difficult to grasp. The spiritually mature define themselves by the spiritual as well as the physical consolations they renounce. The authentically humble recognize that they are not the authors of their meritorious works. Only the language of rupture, opposition, and negation can evoke the opacity disclosed at the heart of both divine and human natures.

Both the theology and the anthropology sketched by the treatise manifest the Augustinian framework of Mère Agnès's analysis. The radical concupiscence of human nature prevents it from successfully grasping the nature of God by its own initiative. Grace is not only necessary for salvation; it is necessary for an elementary acknowledgment of God's attributes and providential design. The neo-Scholastic affirmation of God's existence through cosmological analysis and the Cartesian affirmation of God's existence through conceptual analysis are foreclosed by this neo-Augustinian insistence on the radically fallen nature of the human mind, prone to illusion in religious and moral matters.

The abbess's treatment of the virtues similarly reflects an Augustinian cast of analysis. The central virtues of piety, humility, and charity are not only religious in nature; they exist only through the sovereign grace of the Holy Spirit at work in a human nature vitiated by sin. Rather than preparing the human person to receive the theological virtues, traditional natural virtues such as equanimity are the fruits of the redemptive grace of God when they are not simply a moral illusion created by pride. The Augustinian tradition informing Mère Agnès's analysis of the virtues also emerges in her repeated opposition of the virtues, rooted in intellect and will, to the passions of the human agent. Even in the life of the redeemed, modeled by the community of Port-Royal, the external and internal senses, especially those allied to the emotions, must be treated with suspicion.

Mère Agnès's treatise makes a contribution to virtue theory by showing how particular communities, and not only individuals, develop specific moral habits. The virtues displayed by the Port-Royal nuns are not generic Christian virtues; many of them are tied directly to the monastic way of life. The solitude and poverty described by Mère Agnès are difficult to conceive outside the cloister. The convent's egalitarianism contradicts the familial, political, and religious hierarchies of the period. Not content to describe the virtues flowing from the conventual life of Port-Royal, *The Spirit of the Monastery of Port-Royal* praises them as a supreme model of the Christian perfection possible in such a monastic environment.

In part this apology for the moral value of the convent reprises an ancient Catholic polemic on the objective superiority of religious life over lay life and the objective superiority of the contemplative over active religious orders in the constellation of religious life. But the abbess's treatise is also a determined apology for the superiority of Port-Royal over other monastic communities. The poverty of Port-Royal, expressed in its austere architecture and plain liturgical chant, is lauded as evangelically preferable to the more ornate religious art and music employed by other convents. The piety praised in the treatise is not a generic prayerfulness; it the combination of reverence for the incomprehensible God and a sober, learned, biblical culture. Authentic conventual charity is not simple affection between superiors and subjects; it is the egalitarian leveling of social distinctions that characterizes Port-Royal's admission policies and organization of conventual life. As critics have long alleged, the insistence of Port-Royal's apologists on utter humility before an inscrutable God rests on a disturbing paradox since the Port-Royal convent proudly presents itself as a model of this very humility. Faithful to the paradox, Mère Agnès vaunts the humility, solitude, and piety of Port-Royal as a supreme public model of what the virtuous life of God's elect should be.

Gender and Law

The fundamental law for the convent, the *Constitutions of the Monastery of Port-Royal of the Blessed Sacrament* provides elaborate regulations for the officers, worship, and daily order of Port-Royal. So precise are the rules that Mère Agnès details the number of paintings to be displayed on the walls, the type of serge to be used for the habit, and the style of cutlery to be placed on the refectory tables. Of special philosophical interest is the *Constitutions'* treatment of freedom and authority. Contesting a then prevalent view of parental rights, the abbess insists on the vocational freedom of women who seek admission to the convent and of girls who request admission to the convent school. Rejecting elaborate methods of meditation, she defends the freedom of nuns to pursue simple contemplation as the

Holy Spirit directs them. The *Constitutions* also defends the authority of nuns in the governance of the convent. Safeguarding the right of the nuns to elect their own abbess for a fixed term, the *Constitutions* rejects the prevalent method of royal or episcopal appointment of the abbess. The extensive powers of the abbess enhance her spiritual authority in the instruction, spiritual direction, and correction of her subjects. Her right to nominate the convent's preachers, confessors, and delegate of the archbishop minimizes the traditional power of male clerics within the convent. If Mère Agnès's discussion of freedom and authority is limited to the specifics of convent governance, her theses reflect a broader vision of the freedom and authority of women in a Christian context.

Confirming the practice of Mère Angélique, Mère Agnès argues that the convent should accept only women who clearly have a vocation from God and who freely seek admittance. "We should not admit any girl to be a nun if she is not truly called by God. She should show by her life and her actions a true and sincere desire to serve God. Without this we should never admit anyone for any other reason, whether it concerns the intelligence, the nobility, or the wealth she might bring."[99] The principal criterion for admission becomes the free consent of the candidate, verified by a life of prayer and virtue clearly rooted in the Holy Spirit. Questions of parental desire, wealth, and social class are eliminated.

To further purge admission to the convent from any hint of self-interest, the *Constitutions* stipulates that the convent should willingly consider the acceptance of candidates who might appear to be a burden.[100] Women incapable of singing might be admitted, even if they could not contribute to the monastery's major work: chanting the divine office. Such liberality was not self-evident in a period when accomplished choral offices attracted potential benefactors. Women with serious health problems could also be admitted, reasonable adjustments being made to the austere Port-Royal regimen if these infirm candidates showed outstanding virtue. Out of charity the convent should receive women with mental disabilities (*des innocentes*) who would profit from the security and sororal care of the convent. In Mère Agnès's perspective, the reformed convent should not only refuse vocations that are forced or tied to material gain; it should exercise an evangelical preference for the marginal with authentic vocations to the cloistered life.

Mère Agnès's insistence on vocational freedom is especially pronounced in her treatment of the question of the dowry. For centuries
a family had been expected to provide a dowry for a choir nun in a
Benedictine convent. So stringent was the requirement that many
Benedictine abbeys had become asylums for affluent aristocratic
women. Mère Agnès contends, however, that undowered women
with a genuine vocation should be welcomed by the convent. "If
a poor but excellent girl, clearly called by God, presents herself for
admission, we should not refuse her, although the convent could be
heavily burdened. We should hope that God who sent her will feed
her. We should not fear to make such commitments as long as we
choose carefully and we only accept souls rich in virtue in place of
temporal advantages."[101] Conversely she warns that acceptance of
candidates with substantial dowries can easily become the occasion
for professing nuns who lack an authentic vocation to the austere
practices of Port-Royal. Even when a family has substantial resources, all demand for a dowry must be suppressed. Any contribution made by the candidate's family should be treated as voluntary
alms. No bill for the maintenance of a nun should ever be tendered.
If families fail to pay the pension they had promised to provide for
their daughter, their delinquency should be judged liberally, with no
effect on the convent status of the nun concerned. Vocational freedom is tied to a complete dissociation between a candidate's spiritual aptitude and her economic status.

The *Constitutions'* concern for vocational freedom also surfaces
in its treatment of the convent school. The school should admit
only those pupils whose parents are indifferent as to whether their
daughters become nuns or wives. "We will only take those whose
parents . . . offer them to God in indifference as to whether they are
determined to be nuns or to return to the world, as God pleases."[102]
Although this emphasis on the vocational freedom of the child reaf-
firms the Catholic Church's teaching on the freedom of the individual to contract the sacrament of marriage or to profess religious
vows, it opposes the customary power of the *paterfamilias* to determine the future social state of his children. The central purpose of
education at Port-Royal, the gradual awakening of one's personal
vocation through the effusion of grace, counters the patriarchal
claim to determine a daughter's social and religious destiny through
an appeal to filial obedience.

Mère Agnès's emphasis on respect for freedom in education even extends to the decision of parents to place their daughter in the convent school. The *Constitutions* warns the nuns to avoid the slightest pressure in encouraging families to send their daughters to Port-Royal. "The nuns should show no particular desire to receive young pupils. They should use no inducement toward the parents, not even toward their relatives, to offer their daughters for admission; that must come from their own initiative and from a sincere desire for the good education of their children."[103] Destined to discover their vocation in Christ, the Port-Royal students must issue only from families who freely decide to confide them to the convent and who respect the freedom of their mature vocational choices.

Allied to the freedom of the pupils is their equality. The *Constitutions* charges the nuns who serve as schoolmistresses to avoid any partiality in the treatment of the children. Differences in familial background and wealth are to be suppressed. "It is desirable that they [the pupils] all be equal. That is why we should continue as we have done up until now to take care of their upkeep in order to avoid the inequality that happens when some parents generously provide for their daughters while others refrain from providing them with the necessities. Such a state of affairs would exalt the first class and annoy the others. We can remedy this situation by treating all of them as equally as discretion permits."[104] Just as the nuns renounce their divergent family backgrounds to share a common life of radical equality, the convent school pupils distance themselves from social distinctions to form an egalitarian assembly of peers seeking their personal vocations in Christ.

Mère Agnès's emphasis on spiritual freedom governs her discussion of prayer. Opposed to elaborate methods of meditation, she insists that each nun should follow a personal path of prayer during the time allotted for meditation. Charismatic docility to the Holy Spirit trumps reliance on method.

> Private meditations made in common and the other moments of prayer we give the sisters for adoration of the Blessed Sacrament night and day will be used by them according to the grace God gives them. Saint Benedict's intention was that we should give the Holy Spirit room to stir up in us the spirit of meditation, which

consists in a sincere desire to belong to God and to do so in purity and compunction of heart, as it says in the Holy Rule. True meditation is a celestial gift and not a human one; it is the Holy Spirit praying for us when he makes us pray.[105]

Against certain spiritual currents of the Counter-Reformation, which attempted to impose formal methods of meditation and treated spontaneous prayer with a suspicion of illuminism, the abbess defends the mystical freedom of the nun.

Echoing the nun's contemplative freedom, the *Constitutions* evokes her intellectual freedom in the act of reading. Mère Agnès specifies how a nun should transform the reading of religious works into a personal, reflective grasp of theological truths. "[The sisters] should read with the same humility and reverence as if they saw God himself speaking. They should stop at times and interrupt their reading by frequent pauses and intervals so that, holding their spiritual eyes fixed on those things that moved them, they attract the grace by which they might obtain a solid taste of holy things."[106] The act of spiritual reading thus becomes a moment of personal illumination in which grace permits the spiritual senses (*yeux de leur esprit*) to grasp the religious truth embedded within the text. By this patient, grace-inspired penetration of religious texts, the nuns gradually increase their theological knowledge. "They will obtain little by little from God the knowledge of things they did not at first understand."[107]

Mère Agnès's prescription of *lectio divina* is hardly novel in a monastery. The major work of any Benedictine monastery, the divine office chanted at the canonical hours, was composed of biblical and patristic texts that the nuns and monks were urged to study further in private. For centuries Benedictine and Cistercian authors had instructed their colleagues how to turn the act of spiritual reading into a contemplative exercise. The *Constitutions'* instructions on reading, however, provide a distinctive orientation to this ancient monastic practice. As Bernard Chédozeau argues, numerous seventeenth-century French constitutions of women's orders restricted or even discouraged meditation on the Bible.[108] The suspicion that meditation on the vernacular Bible was a Protestant practice still lingered among church authorities. Clerical supervisors of women's convents often attempted to channel the prayer of the nuns into the less intellectual paths of popular piety; biblical and patristic study was censured as a temptation to intellectual pride. Mère Agnès's treatment of reading, however, mandates that each choir nun was to develop a personal biblical and patristic culture. In addition to extensive study of Scripture, evident in the biblical commentaries and epistolary biblical citations produced by Port-Royal, the nuns were expected to develop a command of patristic and contemporary spiritual texts.

The works designated for public recitation in the refectory indicate the theological breadth of this extrabiblical culture: *Lives of the Desert Fathers, Homilies of Saint John Chrysostom, The Spiritual Doctrine* of Saint Dorotheus, the works of Saint Bernard of Clairvaux, the works of Louis of Grenada, and the works of Saint Teresa of Avila. If these texts were chosen primarily to promote personal piety, the abbess's instructions indicate that the nun was expected to develop a substantial knowledge of, and not simply a reverence for, the theological truths presented in these difficult treatises. Her emphasis on the need to seek divine illumination in the act of reading, in order to form a proper judgment on these religious truths, defends the right of the nun to develop a theological knowledge based on primary sources and personal reflection rather than simply on a catechetical synthesis.

Many passages in the *Constitutions* elaborate on the extensive authority of the Port-Royal nun as ruler, teacher, and director of souls. The authority of the abbess emerges clearly in the "chapter of faults," the weekly assembly in which nuns accuse themselves of transgressions in the presence of the abbess.[109] Not only does the abbess assign penances according to the gravity of the faults; she lectures on appropriate passages from the Rule of Saint Benedict and the Port-Royal Constitutions to exhort the community on what she believes to be widespread communal defects. Canonically only the priest can preach and hear confessions, but such conventual customs as the chapter of faults clearly assign to the abbess a spiritual authority analogous to that of preacher and confessor.

Even more striking is the Port-Royal institution of a daily conference, presided over by one of the convent's officers: the abbess, the prioress, the subprioress, or the novice mistress. Informally conducted as the nuns did their needlework, the conference permitted nuns to ask their superior questions on the spiritual life. Mère Agnès stresses the freedom operative in the conference dialogues. "Simplicity consists in proposing frankly our doubts and asking the mother superior questions without reflecting on how the other sisters might judge us. . . . It is an effect of Christian simplicity and liberty to have no secrets and to consider our sisters as ourselves. . . . We must be completely free in this, as in the way we present our words and actions, since we do not do this in front of people we do not love."[110] Although the superior often dealt with light topics and permitted the nuns to chat quietly among themselves, the sophisticated theological content of Mère Angélique's conferences, widely circulated to a lay and clerical public outside the cloister, indicates how this daily recreational hour became a forum for nuns to provide authoritative theological instruction.

Mère Agnès further designates the conference as the place in the daily order where the abbess or prioress can provide a theological commentary on events in the external world. "As for those things that happen in the world, the mother superior will say what she judges appropriate in order to edify the sisters, to make them recognize the advantages of their vocation and the obligation they have toward God, to move them to compassion for the miseries they suffer and to make them understand the obligations nuns have to pray to God for the church and the kingdom."[111] If Tridentine Catholicism banned women from teaching theology, the Port-Royal Constitutions ascribe to the abbess and other convent officials clear occasions and charges for theological instruction.

Allied to the spiritual freedom of the nun is her enhanced authority in the reformed Port-Royal. In its treatment of the role of the abbess, the *Constitutions* details the extensive self-governance to be exercised by the women of the convent. Whereas before the reform the abbess was appointed by the monarch for life, in the reformed convent the abbess is elected by the convent's choir nuns assembled in chapter.[112] A lifetime term is replaced by a three-year term, which can be renewed only twice.[113] Elaborate rules concerning the membership, methods, and rituals of the electoral chapter protect the democratic rights of the nuns in assembly.

Mère Agnès carefully expounds on the spiritual attitudes that must inform this democratic process of election and governance. The nun-electors must seek spiritual freedom. "The Eucharist must purify them from all passion and human respect. It must enlighten and influence them. Being influenced by charity alone, they will merit obtaining from God a mother superior who will guide them by charity alone. The abbess who must govern the house of God should be filled with his holy spirit so that everything she orders will be received not as a command from a creature but as a command from God."[114] Her office of governance requires the exercise of certain virtues appropriate to the political exercise of power. "Because it is very important and very difficult to know when to pardon and when to punish, she will ask God to give her a spirit containing both zeal and mercy, to use each when it is the proper time."[115] Throughout the *Constitutions*, the abbess is seen primarily as a spiritual director who uses her authority to guide her nuns to greater perfection.

To further protect the authority of the abbess and the nuns, the *Constitutions* carefully limits the power of the male cleric within the convent. Although the archbishop of Paris appoints a delegate to oversee the convent on behalf of the archdiocese, it is the abbess who limits the choice of this delegate by presenting the archbishop with a list of three names of priests from which the prelate must choose. Only priests may preach from the pulpit, but the abbess chooses the priests who will serve as the convent preachers. Even the authority of the confessor is subtly undercut by the abbess's typically Saint-Cyranian caution against too frequent a recourse to sacramental confession. "It is better to confess less often when that helps us to confess with greater reverence and circumspection. Having recourse to the remedies of mortification and penance, which are always useful, is sometimes preferable to the sacrament [of penance], which is often useless for those who have not mortified themselves enough and have not corrected themselves enough by doing violence to their nature."[116] Penitential practices undertaken without sacerdotal meditation now rival or on occasion even eclipse the sacramental confession administered by the ordained priest.

On the symbolic as well as the practical level, Mère Agnès exalts the spiritual authority of women. The *Constitutions'* opening treatment of eucharistic adoration depicts the nun and the priest as complementary partners in the mystery of the Eucharist. The nun's act of adoration balances the priest's act of consecration in the one eucharistic sacrifice of Christ. "One of the principal duties of the nuns of this order must be to provide continual adoration of the Blessed Sacrament. By this means they share in the exercises of the priests. The priests place the Blessed Sacrament on the altars; the nuns adore it by a continual adoration night and day, one nun after the other."[117] Through the act of adoration, the nuns transcend the human condition to undertake actions appropriate to angels. "They must forget themselves as much as they can. They must have no other purpose than to imitate what is done in heaven, where the angels who are before the throne of God and of the Lamb prostrate themselves without ceasing to adore the majesty of God."[118] The *Constitutions* even compares the nuns to Christ himself. Adoration should so transform the nun that she becomes in her moral life a living embodiment of Christ.

> Their principal concern must be to become themselves Eucharists, so to speak, by carrying Jesus Christ in their heart and by carrying him as if exposed to the sight of others. They must manifest by their actions the effects of the divine mystery. Although we do not see proofs of the life of Jesus Christ in the ciborium, because he is not visibly acting there, we should clearly be able to see in the nuns the visible signs that he is the living bread by the impression he makes of his virtues in the souls who receive him in a manner worthy of God.[119]

The passive nun transformed by adoration becomes the active embodiment of Christ by the supernatural virtues of Christ she witnesses to others.

Undergirded by a theology of grace, the *Constitutions* repeatedly warns that the virtues, duties, and rights of the nuns and their superiors can be pursued only through the assistance of God. The actions and organization of Port-Royal are merely the external effects of a sovereign grace that God in his inscrutable wisdom has granted the community. In an explicitly Augustinian passage, Mère Agnès underscores the primacy of grace in the work of moral perfection that constitutes the soul of the convent.

It is not enough to know that the efforts of the creature are weak and useless without the assistance of Jesus Christ. Not only in our prayer but also in our actions we should try to observe with humility the different methods God and the saints have brought us to obtain the absolutely necessary assistance from God. As Saint Augustine says, we must work to conquer our vices by continual efforts and ardent prayers, recognizing at the same time that our efforts as well as our prayers, if there is anything good in them, are the effects of grace. We must never focus consideration on ourselves; rather, we must always have our heart elevated on high by giving perpetual thanks to our God and our sovereign master.[120]

The *Constitutions* is not a blueprint for the construction of a moral utopia by the inspiration of the wise and the effort of the virtuous; it is a testimony to the sovereign grace that reformed and refounded a community of women consecrated by Christ to primitive evangelical fervor.

A juridical text, the *Constitutions* makes a contribution to a practical rather than speculative philosophy of human freedom. It is vocational freedom, not a generic freedom of the will, which is the object of its argument. Mère Agnès contends that the human person is not to be defined by the social determinisms of familial origin, rank, or wealth; on the contrary, each person is to be defined according to the vocation that God has clearly granted her. The entrance into religious life and even into school pivots around the exercise of this freedom and is not to be undertaken under duress. In both the cloister and the classroom, the apprenticeship of freedom must continue as the nun exercises her spiritual freedom in prayer and as the pupil slowly discovers her unique vocation in adult life. Paradoxically, the mature exercise of freedom leads both the nun and the pupil to recognize their complete dependence on God's grace. But this recognition of one's utter dependence on God always follows an itinerary that vigilantly safeguards the spiritual freedom of the pilgrim against external constraint and internal routine.

Even more pointedly the *Constitutions* defends the authority with which women must maintain and exercise their spiritual freedom. The authentic exercise of freedom in meditation requires the development of a substantial theological culture. The proper governance of the convent requires an abbess and other officials capable of exercising authority as teacher, spiritual counselor, judge, and ruler. Mature spiritual freedom entails self-governance, as evident in the power of the convent chapter to elect a superior for a fixed term and to legislate on its own behalf. A proper recognition of the dignity of the soul of each sister encourages an egalitarian leveling of the strict social hierarchy that characterized the period's religious and political culture. In her gendered account of authority and freedom, Mère Agnès clearly defends the spiritual rights of women against the demurrals of both church and state.

Ethics of Resistance

As the crisis of the signature deepened in the 1660s, the persecution of Port-Royal intensified. Already in 1661, the government of Louis XIV had closed the convent school, expelled the novices and the postulants, and forbidden the entry of new candidates into the order. Recognizing the probability of greater persecution to come, Mère Agnès composed the treatise *Counsels on the Conduct Which the Nuns Should Maintain in the Event of a Change in the Government of the Convent*, which quietly circulated among the nuns. The treatise presciently envisions two modes of persecution that would shortly descend on Port-Royal: the imposition of external nuns hostile to Jansenism to govern the convent and the exile of recalcitrant nuns to foreign convents where anti-Jansenist nuns and priests would attempt to persuade them to submit to the church's judgment against Jansen. The treatise also accurately envisions the use of interdict, a ban on participation in the church's sacraments, to pressure the nuns to abandon their opposition to an unreserved assent to the church's position on Jansenism.

In the *Counsels* Mère Agnès develops a casuistry of resistance to alleged abuses of authority by ecclesiastical and political authorities in their efforts to subdue the Port-Royal convent. Imagining various scenarios of persecution, the abbess carefully traces distinctions between acceptable and unacceptable types of cooperation with superiors, confessors, and entire communities imposed on the Port-Royal nuns against their will. Not only does Mère Agnès the moralist distinguish moral from immoral actions in the relationship between the Port-Royal nun and oppressive authorities; Mère Agnès the spiritual theologian identifies the moral attitudes that should undergird these actions and the religious purpose of both endurance of and resistance to the attempted oppression of conscience. Exploring the mystery of evil in the form of political persecution, establishing a theoretical demarcation between legitimate and illegitimate cooperation with evil, and presenting casuistic rules for right conduct in an oppressive environment, the *Counsels* proposes an ethics of resistance for the nun to maintain her spiritual integrity.

The primary reason for resistance to exile or to the imposition of foreign superiors springs from the fact that such sanctions constitute a violation of the rights of the community. Since Port-Royal's constitutions enjoy royal and episcopal approval, political and religious authorities cannot arbitrarily use their power to destroy the governance, customs, and spirituality of the convent. Mère Agnès explicitly uses the language of rights to underscore the gravity of the abuse being exercised by the opponents of Port-Royal. "We will indicate how we should act in particular occasions and circumstances to oppose, as much as is necessary, the usurpation of the rights of the community. We must know how to combine the cunning of the serpent with the simplicity of the dove to drag down the lion and the dragon, that is, the violence and the maneuvers they might use against us to rip from our hearts the love of truth and the peace of charity."[121] The "truth" here concerns the Augustinian doctrine of grace as interpreted by Jansen and Saint-Cyran. A false sense of obedience cannot be invoked to force the nuns to commit what they believe to be a falsehood regarding Jansen's position on grace or to become willing participants in the violation of religious rights. For Mère Agnès the moral question concerns not whether but how the conscientious nun should resist a sinful assault on conventual rights.

At the center of this resistance lies the refusal to recognize imposed or foreign superiors as authentic governors of the Port-Royal nuns. The apparent authority of these external nuns is nothing more than a usurpation of power. "They cannot have true authority by usurping a power that does not belong to them. They will be intruders, even when they want to adorn themselves with the obedience due superiors."[122] While pragmatic accommodations might be advisable for the common good or even the spiritual good of the individual nun, the conscientious nun must refuse to recognize the authority of superiors imposed in violation of Port-Royal's law and ethos. Resistance to the oppressive powers seeking to rule the Port-Royal nuns must begin in a lucid analysis of the grave abuse of rights represented by the assault on the convent's legitimate authorities.

As Mère Agnès constructs specific counsels for proper conduct under imposed, hostile superiors, certain general lines of demarcation between moral and immoral cooperation with evil appear. The Port-Royal nuns should cooperate with illegitimate superiors on minor issues, such as performing domestic chores, but must refuse cooperation on certain major ones, such as speaking with imposed spiritual directors. Material cooperation with an illegitimate superior on matters of food, residence, work, and liturgy might be acceptable, but moral assent to the superior's anti-Jansenist views can never be justified.

Virtuous resistance must eschew words of criticism; Mère Agnès champions a strategy of resistance rooted in silence. The Port-Royal nun should refuse to discuss her interior feelings with her imposed superior or confessor, to give her opinion on the sermons she is forced to hear, or to reveal to others her motives for resisting novel practices. The strategy of silent protest includes such simple gestures as the occasional refusal to take bread during a meal to suggest displeasure at the comparative abundance of food. Even in resistance to abuses of power, the contemplative weapon of silence stands paramount.

In the case of government of the convent by nuns imposed from the exterior, Mère Agnès proposes certain rules of action to maintain the integrity of the Port-Royal vocation. In the area of poverty, the upright nun should refuse any introduction of personal property, any assistance from one's relatives, and any complaint about the reduction of the convent's material resources occasioned by persecution.[123] Persecutory impoverishment should prod the nun to increase assistance to the sick members of the community and to welcome any abolition of common property as an opportunity to practice the total poverty exemplified by such mendicant orders as the Poor Clares.[124]

The rules concerning the vow of obedience mix measures of co-operation and resistance. The conscientious nun should obey the imposed superior on minor matters but resist orders on major issues that compromise fidelity to the letter and the spirit of the Port-Royal Constitutions. She should gladly accept orders to assist in manual labor but must refuse tasks that compromise the austere spirit of the order. Strikingly, Mère Agnès forbids any work redolent of frivolous aestheticism. "Not one sister will lift her hand to introduce precious novelties within the monastery, not even into the convent church. Such activity includes placing flowers on the altar or making fancy works of art."[125] The nun should refuse to see unknown people, including foreign spiritual directors, in the convent parlor but she should listen to the sermons given in the chapel, unless they "say something contrary to the truth and defame the people who defend it."[126] If the nun is banned from receiving Holy Communion, she should serenely accept the sanction and limit herself to the practice of spiritual communion.[127]

Throughout her discussion of strategies of resistance to imposed superiors, Mère Agnès stresses the role of language.[128] The nun should avoid all complaints, either orally or by writing. Any communication with relatives should omit discussions of the state of the convent. All conversations with superiors should be brief and succinct. Even the use of coded language is banned. When the nun must in conscience refuse an order, she should refuse to explain the motives behind her refusal. While maintaining respect toward the foreign superiors, the nun must refuse to reveal her interior thoughts and feelings to those who are not her divinely appointed governor. Her systematic reticence and silence in the external forum must be accompanied by an intensified spiritual life grounded in the principles and methods of Port-Royal.

For Mère Agnès the case of exile for Port-Royal nuns posed moral questions of lesser gravity, despite the apparently greater severity of the sanction.[129] Since the superior of a convent should be obeyed in her own house and since any visitor to a convent should respect the particular customs of that convent, the exiled Port-Royal nun should willingly accommodate herself to the new convent's manner of proceeding. She should follow the customs on reception of Holy Communion traditional in the convent. She should confess her sins to the convent confessor but avoid all manifestation of other thoughts and concerns to him. If the convent does not follow the vegetarian regime of the primitive Benedictine Rule, she may occasionally eat the meat offered at meals and should not request a special diet for herself. Manual work should be gladly accepted with the exception of fabricating objects appealing to vanity or fancy. If the Port-Royal nun is ordered to assist at the choral office at the convent, she may safely abandon the use of the Parisian breviary, which had been adopted by Port-Royal for its own use, and employ the liturgical books customary in the new convent.

Despite the willing participation in the external life of the foreign convent, the conscientious nun must refuse all manifestation of her soul to the superior of the new community. "They [the exiled Port-Royal nuns] will show no confidence in the new superiors for what concerns their interior life. They should reserve their souls for those [the legitimate superiors] to whom God has committed them. They will never discuss what they did in their convent and will not speak about it if one asks them."[130] Even in a relatively benign foreign convent, the strategy of passive resistance, especially in self-revelatory discourse, must be maintained.

Mère Agnès does not limit herself to a casuistic presentation of rules of desirable conduct. She explores the theological truths that explain the existence and the intensity of the persecution. The political and ecclesiastical censures represent both a punishment for the vices and a reward for the virtues of the convent. "Although we are justified in believing that God has delivered us into the hands of these hard and merciless people because of our sins, he clearly permits us to be consoled by the thought that we are suffering because we feared to offend him by assenting against our conscience to something we thought impossible to do without attacking the truth and Christian sincerity."[131] The persecution draws the nuns closer to Christ, the supreme object of human contempt. "We follow the path that Jesus Christ himself has marked out. During his entire life he had only enemies and slanderers."[132] To exercise the proper discernment on the correct path of resistant conduct, the nun must grasp the theological causes and ends of the persecution.

An expression of God's providential plan, the persecution of Port-Royal offers the nuns an occasion for spiritual maturation.

Mère Agnès depicts the moral virtues that can be strengthened by persecution, of which patience holds pride of place. Faithful to her Bérullian heritage, she champions several religious virtues that entail the mystical death of the self. Adoration acquires a new urgency. "The first thing we must do is to adore God's action and to avoid losing confidence in his mercy, which draws out some good from the evils that happen to all who love his will and prefer it to their self-interest."[133] The world's contempt fosters a state of spiritual annihilation. "We must humble ourselves under the hand of God and clearly desire him to use what he pleases to destroy the pride that has provoked upon us such a great humiliation. This will not end until we are annihilated before God. He will lift up his servants when it pleases him to visit them."[134] Maintaining her theocentric focus, the abbess insists that the moral and theological virtues purified by the experience of persecution originate in God alone. "God will crown in us the gifts of patience and perseverance which he himself has authored."[135] It is God's sovereign grace rather than human merit that ignites the virtues refined by the world's contempt for evangelical truth.

In the successful endurance of persecution, the nun can acquire a greater spiritual freedom. The deprivation of physical Holy Communion liberates the nun to practice a purely spiritual communion, in which she experiences the interior presence of the risen Christ at the altar of heaven. In a controversial passage, Mère Agnès praises this spiritual communion as superior to the sacramental. "Only too low an idea of this [eucharistic] mystery, which is incomprehensible to the senses, would lead one to believe that it is so dependent on the men who consecrate and distribute it that Jesus Christ can only communicate himself by their ministry to pure souls who were pulled away from this holy and divine table by human injustice."[136] Denial of the sacraments frees the nun toward a more reflective piety, focused on biblical meditation. "Instead of the bread of God, the word of God himself, which must be heard in one's heart, must be read in the [biblical] books with a reverence worthy of he who speaks to us in his gospel."[137] The removal of legitimate superiors, chaplains, and confessors deepens the nun's dependence on the Holy Spirit dwelling in the soul of each member of the elect. In the imposed isolation, "we place our confidence in the promise made to us in Holy Scripture that spiritual anointing, even greater in affliction, will teach us everything."[138] Paradoxically, the phenomenon of persecution, designed to destroy the determination of the Port-Royal resistants, strengthens the nun's freedom to rely more intently on God's internal, purely spiritual presence and to take an even bolder distance from the sacerdotal and sacramental meditation of that presence by the church.

Throughout the *Counsels* Mère Agnès develops a gendered account of freedom and resistance. Her brief against the oppression of Port-Royal is built upon the right of women religious to follow their own constitutions, to elect their own superiors, to maintain their own ascetical practices, and to safeguard their judgment on questions of conscience. Gendered concerns influence many specific parts of the abbess's argument on behalf of conscientious resistance. Recognizing the fallibility and fragility of an individual conscience under duress, she advises persecuted nuns to seek advice on controversial decisions from a small group of nuns distinguished for their prudence. "To avoid acting without direction, they should seek advice from a few nuns of the convent chosen with the counsel and permission of the mother abbess. As a precaution, this should be arranged in advance."[139] Hostile royal or episcopal efforts to manipulate the nuns' consciences are stymied by reliance on the seasoned counsel of female peers appointed by legitimate if silenced female authority.

To illustrate the resistance demanded by persecution, Mère Agnès often cites the example of biblical women. Mary Magdalene's experience of the absent Christ on the morning of the Resurrection can orient the nuns through the experience of the absence of the eucharistic Christ during times of interdict.

> When Magdaelene was looking for Jesus Christ in the tomb, she was full of sorrow. She could not tolerate being deprived of the vision of his body. Since she lacked faith, which made her believe God could not be removed from her, she sank into anguish. But since her charity covered this fault, Jesus Christ did not try to cause and to excite in her soul new desires to find and possess him. In this way his absence produced in her the same effect as if he had

been present. She was attached only to him and was resolved not to leave the spot where he had been placed.[140]

The *Counsels* affirms the normativity of Port-Royal's tradition for the embattled nuns by citing the deceased abbess, Mère Angélique, as a spiritual authority. "Just as our deceased mother abbess told us, perhaps God wants to throw us into the belly of a whale, like Jonah, so that from such a deep and apparently hopeless place, God will hear the shouts and prayers we will offer him as if we were in a holy temple."[141] Even God assumes female form. "It is easy for God to make us strong in the greatest moments after having tried our weaknesses in the least. This is like a mother who lets her infant walk down a very safe path, where she falls without risk, but who holds the infant in her arms on a hard path. Even if the mother herself falls, the infant cannot be hurt."[142] The *Counsels'* repeated use of feminine symbols for God, heroism, and authority underscores the theoretical argument on the right to conscientious resistance by persecuted women.

The *Counsels* represents Mère Agnès's most sustained exercise in applied ethics. Despite her avowed hostility to the virtue of prudence as all too human, the abbess provides a series of prudential rules to govern the conduct of the nun resisting oppression. The resistance is justified by the vocational freedom of women: the right to pursue the vowed life according to constitutions approved by divine authority, rooted in centuries of Benedictine-Cistercian tradition, and founded on the evangelical counsels of Christ himself. The resistance is further justified by the right of women to maintain their judgment on theological controversies when such basic religious truths as the grace of Christ are the object of dispute. Mère Agnès frames the strategy of resistance within a theology of persecution. The passion of Christ, the supernatural virtue of patience, and the mystical posture of self-annihilation assert themselves as the hermeneutical keys to the proper interpretation of the persecution and the spiritual resistance it requires. The elaborate theological architecture of the argument does not efface the palpable modernity of the abbess's theory of the propriety and modalities of conscientious objection to abuses of power. It is in the explicit name of rights (*droits*) and moral conscience (*conscience*) that Mère Agnès devises her code of resistance.

CONCLUSION

Considered as a philosophical corpus, the most striking characteristic of Mère Agnès's works is their militant theocentrism. Her apophatic treatment of the divine attributes depicts a God who is wholly other. God is incomprehensible because God is the inaccessible, the incommunicable, and the illimitable. The mystery of God is betrayed rather than approached in any effort to name God that employs analogies drawn from nature. For all its Tridentine framework of eucharistic adoration, the radically transcendent character of the divinity evoked by the abbess often appears closer to the theology of Barth than to that of Aquinas. The asceticism promoted by her is finally one of the mind, wherein the Christian abandons the attempt to name God through the projection of image and concept; the acceptance of God's sovereign mystery paradoxically brings the believer closer to the truth of what precisely can neither be pictured nor uttered.

Mère Agnès's determined use of the *via negativa* in her philosophy of God, most prominent in her early *Private Chaplet* but still present in her later writings, poses obvious problems. The theoretical portrait of God appears truncated, a pure transcendence that no longer enjoys a complementary immanence. As the critics of the abbess have argued, this imbalance seems especially problematic for a Christian theology, since Christians worship an incarnate deity, revere a Scripture that repeatedly uses analogical parables, and seek union with God through sacraments that are tactile, visual, auditory, even gustatory. If unbalanced and uneasily tethered to the sacramental logic of Catholicism, the apophatic theology of Mère Agnès defends the mystery of God against the tendency of human beings, especially sentimental members of religious orders, to transform the living deity into a projection of purely human love or justice. In its very abrasiveness, the steely mystery of God evoked by the abbess in her philosophy of divine attributes grounds her philosophy of resistance, since the morally upright agent must oppose the most entangling loyalties of family, state, and church in order to give faithful witness to God's obscure sovereignty in the order of grace.

A militant theocentrism also governs Mère Agnès's philosophy of virtue. In her *Image of a Perfect and an Imperfect Nun*, the abbess not only subscribes to a typically Augustinian exaltation of the theological virtues and dismissal of the natural virtues as masks of pride; she conducts a theocentric recasting of the virtues she considers essential for monastic life. Zeal becomes a recognition of one's nothingness without the help of God; spiritual poverty becomes the admission of one's complete dependence on God; humility entails acknowledgment of one's utter misery before God, manifest in the concupiscence of the human condition. In this configuration, all conventual virtues converge as a simultaneous recognition of one's nothingness before the absolute fullness of God's existence, a fullness one can neither depict nor analyze. The abbess deepens this theocentric account of the virtues by the contemplative turn she imparts to them. Charity is no longer the practical service of the neighbor; it is a loving gaze on the image of God, the member of Christ's body, and the temple of the Holy Spirit one perceives in the person of one's neighbor.

Although it unifies the moral virtues by emphasizing their common divine origin and their similar contemplative grain, this theocentric moral philosophy manifests its own contradictions. The emphasis on the complete dependence of these virtues on divine grace, indeed on an inscrutable divine providence, rests uneasily with the repeated exhortation to cultivate these virtues by rejecting any egocentrism that still clings to us. On one level, the difference between moral perfection and imperfection is due solely to the presence or absence of God's grace; on another level, the difference is the result of various responses of human freedom to admonitions to moral repentance. In Mère Agnès's philosophy of moral virtue, the contemplative's account of a moral personality fashioned by grace alone grates against the moralist's account of a moral personality crafted by the free human choice to make God rather than the self one's paramount good.

Mère Agnès's skill as a moral philosopher emerges in her *Counsels* and other writings where she develops her philosophy of resistance. An astute casuist, she carefully distinguishes between the problems posed to nuns in exile and to those governed by imposed superiors at Port-Royal itself. The degree of obedience to the superior shifts according to the different scenarios. The abbess clearly distinguishes between formal and material cooperation with the oppressive evil that is attempting to coerce the conscience of the nuns. The conscientious nun must always refuse formal agreement with the false charge against Jansen and refuse to employ any words or gestures that might suggest assent. Even apparently neutral activities, such as conversations with imposed foreign spiritual directors, must be shunned, since such activities could become the occasion for weakening or even abandoning one's commitment to the truths concerning grace. But material cooperation with the evil of the oppressor poses more subtle problems. The upright nun might follow an order to sweep the hallway or to assist the sick, but she could not accept other commands, such as an order to make silk flowers, which would violate the vows she has pledged to uphold in the spirit of Port-Royal.

Not limited to a subtle set of casuistic rules, Mère Agnès develops a moral psychology and a speculative theology as part of her philosophy of resistance. The persecuted nun can negotiate the actions required to resist oppression only when she cultivates specific virtues, such as patience. Certain basic spiritual attitudes, such as that of adoration, must acquire a new maturity to recognize the providence of God in the midst of apparent abandonment to one's enemies. Proper moral response to persecution also requires a theological grasp of the meaning of the violent opprobrium that has erupted. The enlightened nun must conceive the persecution both as a punishment for personal and collective sins and a graced opportunity to cultivate a more purely spiritual, self-abandoned union with God. The abbess's stress on the primacy of personal abandonment and divine illumination in the genesis of the decision to resist an external authority runs the risk of antinomianism. How the resisting subject can know that her own religious conviction in a controversy is to be preferred to that defended by a superior religious authority remains unclear. Despite this ambiguity, the abbess provides a broad theological framework for the dilemma of conscientious resistance by placing the phenomenon of persecution in the logic of divine opportunity for conversion and moral perfection.

The philosophy developed by Mère Agnès maintains a complex relationship with questions of gender. The gendered nature of her reflection is not limited to the banal fact that the author is a woman writing to and on behalf of a female public. Her apophatic theology, virtue ethics, and theory of personal freedom incorporate gendered concerns into the central themes of her philosophy. The abbess's account of the incomprehensibility of God, manifested through various negative divine attributes, is not a syllogistic conclusion; it arises from the specific experience of adoration undergone by the cloistered nun in vigil before the tabernacle. Her theocentric account of virtue is not a generic theory of the habits necessary for human happiness; it is a contextualized theory of the specific virtues, such as poverty and obedience, pursued by the nun as part of her particular way of life. The convent is more than the site for the elaboration of the abbess's theology and ethics; the nun's mystical experience of annihilation and the nun's struggle to pursue the monastic vows shape the figure of God and the human person at the center of her apophatic theology and philosophy of virtue.

The gendered cast of Mère Agnès's philosophy is even more prominent in her legal texts. Her constitutional design for Port-Royal defends a series of spiritual rights for women. These include the freedom of women to pursue a vocation free of external coercion and even their freedom to pursue an education free of parental pressure to determine one's adult status in childhood. The conventual version of this freedom includes the right of nuns to elect their own superior, to govern themselves through legislation, and to acquire a theological culture appropriate to their vocation. The right of women to govern is translated as the right of the abbess to teach, to provide spiritual direction, to discipline, and to appoint the male clergy who will serve the convent. In her philosophy of resistance, Mère Agnès upholds the most controversial right of the nun: the duty to refuse the demands of political and religious authority when that authority errs in judgment or when it exceeds the legitimate scope of its power. This encomium of the resistant nun rests on the broader right of women to acquire a philosophical and theological culture in order to assert a well-informed assent or dissent on behalf of the truth.

CHAPTER 4

MÈRE ANGÉLIQUE DE SAINT-JEAN ARNAULD D'ANDILLY

Persecution and Resistance

The niece of *Mères Angélique and Agnès*, *Mère Angélique de Saint-Jean Arnauld d'Andilly* (1624–84) dominates the second generation of the reformed Port-Royal. Enclosed within the convent from her entry into the convent school at the age of six until her death as its abbess, Mère Angélique de Saint-Jean became the leader of Port-Royal's intransigents during the convent's persecution. A scholar renowned for her fluency in Latin and Greek, she developed an elaborate theology of the monastic life in her massive conferences and correspondence. Artisan of a philosophy of strict resistance to an allegedly oppressive church and state, she combined the rhetoric of a lawyer, delivering a crisp brief on the rights of nuns, with that of a poet, evoking the apocalyptic signs of God's absence.

Not surprisingly for a second-generation leader called to institutionalize the charisms of the founding generation, Mère Angélique de Saint-Jean develops her philosophy principally through commentaries on the works of others. Her conferences on the Rule of Saint Benedict analyze the virtues proper to monasticism, transposed to reflect the experience of women. Her gloss on the Constitutions of Port-Royal

develops an Augustinian argument on the spiritual war between the two cities which every nun must confront. As the persecution of the convent intensified, her commentary on the *Counsels* of Mère Agnès regarding a hypothetical persecution applies the earlier tract's principles to the concrete moral dilemmas of the nuns actually suffering exile and interdict.

Other more personal treatises complement the philosophy of spiritual combat elaborated in the commentaries. Several devotional works examine how the deprivation of sacramental mediation during persecution paradoxically brings the persecuted to a closer union with God. An epistemological treatise on the danger of doubt in the midst of oppression demonstrates how the virtue of humility can be manipulated by the powerful for immoral purposes. Marshaling the resources of her extensive patristic culture, Mère Angélique de Saint-Jean constructs an ethics of resistance for an embattled Port-Royal destined for destruction.

VOCATION OF A MILITANT

Born on November 28, 1624, at the ancestral estate of Pomponne, Angélique Arnauld d'Andilly was the eldest daughter of Robert Arnauld d'Andilly and Catherine Le Fèvre de la Broderie Arnauld d'Andilly.[1] The daughter of a father from a prominent family of jurists, who at her birth was superintendent of the estate of Gaston d'Orléans, brother of Louis XIII, and of a mother from a prominent diplomatic family, the infant Angélique entered a society dominated by court politics. She also entered a society absorbed by the reform of Port-Royal. Six of her aunts were nuns at Port-Royal: Angélique de Sainte-Magdeleine Arnauld, Agnès de Saint-Paul Arnauld, Madeleine de Sainte-Christine Arnauld, Marie de Sainte-Claire Arnauld, Anne-Eugénie de l'Incarnation Arnauld, and Catherine de Saint-Jean Arnauld Le Maître. In her widowhood, her grandmother Catherine de Sainte-Félicité Marion Arnauld also entered Port-Royal. Four of her sisters followed her to the convent: Anne-Marie, Catherine de Sainte-Agnès, Marie-Charlotte de Sainte-Claire, and Marie-Angélique de Sainte-Thérèse. Her brother Charles-Henri Arnauld de Luzancy became a priest who ministered to both the Port-Royal nuns and to the *solitaires*; her brother Simon Arnauld, marquis de Pomponne, became a minister in Louis XIV's cabinet and a court apologist for the persecuted nuns. Her uncle Antoine Arnauld would emerge as the leading theologian of the Port-Royal circle, while her uncle Henry Arnauld, bishop of Angers, would act as the convent's defender within the French episcopate. Her cousins Antoine Le Maître, Louis-Isaac Le Maître de Saci, and Simon Le Maître de Séricourt would distinguish themselves by their scholarship and their pedagogical skill during their association with the *solitaires*.

A cradle Port-Royalist, Angélique entered the convent's school as a boarder in 1630. From the beginning she showed an ardent attraction for the cloistered life and exhibited a capacity for intellectual work that astonished her contemporaries. Despite the narrowness of the convent curriculum, Angélique became a fluent reader and translator of Latin and Greek. Her biblical and patristic erudition was apparent even before her profession as a nun. The Jesuit scholar René Rapin singled out her sophisticated comprehension of the philosophy of Saint Augustine.[2] The memorialist Thomas du Fossé offered a sexually barbed encomium of her precocious intelligence. "This was a girl who obviously had none of the weaknesses of her sex. Everything was great and male in her. Her mind seemed so superior to the mind of others that even men who are commonly considered the greatest of intellectuals admired her as a prodigy. The excellence of her genius extended to everything."[3] Writing to her daughter, Madame de Sévigné summed up the common estimate of Angélique's intelligence. "All the languages and all the sciences have been infused into her. She is in short a prodigy."[4]

Attracted to the contemplative life and admired for her theological culture, Angélique smoothly made the transition from lay student to cloistered nun. She took the veil as a novice on June 27, 1641, and made her profession of vows as a nun on February 25, 1644. Angélique Arnauld d'Andilly would now be known as Soeur Angélique de Saint-Jean. Recognizing her unusual qualities, the convent quickly assigned her to positions of authority. In 1644 she was appointed headmistress of the lay boarding pupils at the convent. The academic post permitted her to impart her biblical and patristic culture to the students and to experiment with the pedagogical methods borrowed from the *solitaires* conducting the *petites écoles* for boys. Later named novice mistress, she attempted to form the young Port-Royal nuns according to the principles of the Angelican reform and to destroy the last traces of Zamet's influence on the convent's spirituality. Soeur Angélique de Saint-Jean was part of the contingent of nuns who followed Mère Angélique Arnauld in 1648 to reoccupy the convent at Port-Royal des Champs, a move necessitated by the overcrowded conditions at Port-Royal de Paris. She ably assisted her aunts and the terrified refugees housed at the convent during the civil disturbances of the Fronde (1648–52). Once internal peace had returned to France in 1653, Soeur Angélique de Saint-Jean assumed key administrative posts in the rejuvenated Port-Royal des Champs: first as headmistress of the school, then as novice mistress, and finally as subprioress of the convent.

During the 1650s Soeur Angélique de Saint-Jean also began an influential career as a historian of Port-Royal. In 1651 she and her cousin Antoine Le Maître decided to document the life of Mère Angélique and her reform of the convent. The apparent purpose of this historical documentation was to present an accurate portrait of the facts and motives concerning the Angelican reform against distortions created by the convent's enemies, especially during the quarrel over the *Private Chaplet*. Normative in nature, this history would also discourage future generations of Port-Royal nuns from following the directions inaugurated during the Oratorian ascendancy (1625–33) and encourage them to adhere to the original principles of reform, as interpreted through the austere, practical piety of Soeur Angélique de Saint-Jean and Antoine Le Maître themselves. Interviewing Mère Angélique in the parlor numerous times between 1651 and 1654, Le Maître composed several memorials incorporating material on her life which the abbess had given him. In 1654 a reluctant Mère Angélique wrote her own autobiographical narrative, *Report Written by Mère Angélique Arnauld*.[5] Amplifying the original project, Soeur Angélique de Saint-Jean in 1653 began to interview older nuns about their recollections of Mère Angélique and of telling incidents in the early reform. She would finally turn her notes and transcriptions of interviews into her own biography of Mère Angélique, *Report or Documented History of Mère Marie-Angélique*, written between 1671 and 1673.[6]

Soeur Angélique de Saint-Jean also encouraged other nuns to compose their own memorials concerning Mère Angélique and the early, heroic period of the convent's reform. Her own aunt Soeur Anne-Eugénie de l'Incarnation was commissioned to write one of the first memorials. As commentators have long noted, the early histories written and commissioned by Soeur Angélique de Saint-Jean and her colleagues are strongly hagiographic in nature. The purpose, often quite explicit, is to edify the reader by chronicles of the heroic moral virtue of the convent's reformers and the palpable evidence of divine providence in the creation and expansion of this model convent. The perfidy of the convent's critics is underscored. F. Ellen Weaver alludes to the mythological character of these apologetic histories, while Jean Lesaulnier analyzes their literary traits in terms of the genre of legend.[7]

As the opposition to Port-Royal intensified, the historiographical project of Soeur Angélique de Saint-Jean was further amplified. She commissioned nuns to write extensive accounts of their own spiritual experiences, especially their experience of persecution. She assiduously collected letters, memorials, affidavits, transcripts, and eulogies that could document the moral integrity and the doctrinal orthodoxy of the convent. Following Soeur Angélique's literary tastes, many of these chronicles and autobiographies have the ring of tragic theater, wherein innocent victims beg a hidden God to sustain them against the inexplicably sinister forces of civil and ecclesiastical authorities. The immense literary documentation concerning Port-Royal that survived the demise of the convent and which was published in the more tolerant climate of the eighteenth century owes no small debt to the indefatigable historical work of Soeur Angélique de Saint-Jean as author and editor. Her campaign for apologetic documentation permitted the nuns to present their own history in the categories of reform, providence, persecution, and abandonment.

Universally admired for her intellectual prowess and organizational skill, Soeur Angélique de Saint-Jean faced criticism for other personality traits. Her erudition seemed to breed a certain pride in her own opinions and intransigence on what she believed to be matters of right. Combined with a palpable emotional coldness, this intransigence often appeared to others to be a species of arrogance. In his sympathetic portrait of her, Thomas du Fossé attempts to defend the nun against her detractors. "She even affected a certain air of coldness and hardness to keep a certain distance from people who do not know her. But for us who truly know her, there was no one more charming. I can very well speak about this, since I personally experienced this coldness and was not fooled by it any more than others were."[8] In fact, other prominent members of the Port-Royal circle were not so easily convinced.[9] Already in 1641, shortly before her entry into the convent, the imprisoned Saint-Cyran had admonished her for the vanity that seemed to fuel her theological curiosity. Although her aunts Mère Angélique and Mère Agnès warmly praised the niece they believed destined to guide the convent, Mère Angélique periodically confronted what she believed to be intellectual pride in the scholarly nun. Her uncle Antoine Arnauld exhibited the same concern. Their epistolary exchanges indicated profound agreement on the theology of grace that constituted the heart of the *Augustinus* controversy, but in their disagreements over strategy during the crisis of the signature, Arnauld often criticized the haughty tone and the intransigence of the positions advanced by his niece. The convent chaplain Antoine Singlin quickly discovered that accepting spiritual direction at his hands would not be easy for a nun who clearly believed her theological knowledge superior to his own.

The persecution of Port-Royal during the 1660s revealed Soeur Angélique de Saint-Jean's mature vocation as the militant leader of the convent faction opposed to all compromise. Her psychological intransigence had become a collective posture. Like the other nuns, she watched helplessly as royal emissaries exiled the chaplain Singlin and expelled the confessors, lay pupils, postulants, and novices from the convent in the spring of 1661. In the summer of 1661, the crisis of the signature divided the community. On June 8 the vicars of the archdiocese of Paris presented the convent with the formulary each nun must sign. The formulary condemned the five censured propositions and declared that Jansen had defended them; in their pastoral letter accompanying the formulary, however, the vicars explicitly cited the *droit/fait* distinction and stipulated that one could sign the document with this distinction serving as a legitimate qualification of one's signature.

Antoine Arnauld urged the nuns to sign the formulary in such an irenic framework. Allied with Soeur Jacqueline de Sainte-

Euphémie Pascal, Soeur Angélique de Saint-Jean disagreed. She argued that their signatures would still be widely interpreted as assenting to the false statement that Jansen had defended these heretical theories; moreover, signing a statement condemning Jansen, no matter what ingenious reservations the cooperating nun used, would be tantamount to denying the grace of Christ, since the entire controversy concerned the validity of Jansen's neo-Augustinian teaching on efficacious grace. Under pressure from Arnauld's theological circle and from the banished chaplain Singlin, Soeur Angélique de Saint-Jean signed the formularly with the other Port-Royal nuns on June 24–25. Like the other nuns, however, and against the advice of Arnauld, she added a codicil next to her signature, explicitly stating that her signature indicated assent only to issues of *droit* (matters of faith) and that it did not indicate assent to any issues of *fait* (facts) concerning Jansen's book or theology.

Annulling the softened formulary and irenic pastoral letter of June, the Vatican insisted on the unreserved signature of an unamended formulary condemning both the five heretical propositions and Jansen for having defended them. With the untimely death of Soeur Jacqueline de Sainte-Euphémie Pascal on October 4, 1661, Soeur Angélique de Saint-Jean found herself alone at the head of the convent's resistance. When the archdiocesan vicars presented an unvarnished formulary for signature by the nuns on October 31, the novice mistress again counseled resistance to an illegitimate intrusion on conscience. On November 28, 1661, the nuns signed the formulary without writing any qualifications next to their signatures; however, the entire formulary was now prefaced with a paragraph explaining how the uneasy signatures of the nuns were to be interpreted. In a gesture of theological brio, Soeur Angélique de Saint-Jean added a personal postscript to the explanatory paragraph by stating that her own signature "does not in any way attack Saint Augustine's doctrine concerning grace, which is the doctrine of the church."[10] Infuriated by the continuing recalcitrance of the nuns and the subtle legalistic maneuvers of their new strategist, the Vatican promptly rejected the new qualified assent of Port-Royal.

When efforts were made by Jansenist moderates to find an honorable compromise between church authorities and the embattled nuns, Soeur Angélique de Saint-Jean denounced such moves as traitorous to basic religious truth. More than once during this period,

Antoine Arnauld rebuked his niece for an intransigence that un-justly condemned sincere friends of the convent attempting to de-vise a diplomatic solution to the impasse. The ongoing crisis reached its denouement in 1664 with the entry of the new archbishop of Paris, Hardouin de Beaumont de Péréfixe, into the controversy. On April 10, 1664, Péréfixe published the formulary with justificatory bulls; once again the Port-Royal nuns were ordered to sign the for-mulary without amendment. In his own attempt at conciliation, the archbishop informed the nuns that, although the use of the *droit/ fait* distinction was illegitimate in qualifying their signatures, they could use the distinction between divine faith and human faith in distinguishing degrees of assent in their signature. Divine faith re-ferred to an act of assent because God had revealed a certain truth (such as the trinitarian nature of God), whereas human faith referred to an act of assent because trustworthy human evidence supported a certain claim (such as the church's judgment that a particular theo-logian had defended a particular thesis). The Port-Royal nuns and their theological advisers summarily rejected the distinction as in-applicable to their case, since they could not assent in any degree to what they believed to be a malicious falsehood concerning Jansen. Anonymous Jansenist pamphlets soon mocked the confused theo-logical distinction devised by the harried archbishop.

On July 14, 1664, the nuns, at Soeur Angélique de Saint-Jean's urging, once again affixed the *droit/fait* reservation to their signa-tures on the formulary. Outraged at the disobedience of the nuns and the Jansenist campaign of ridicule, Péréfixe arrived in person at Port-Royal de Paris to announce new sanctions against the nuns. A foreign Visitation nun was imposed as superior, assisted by the small group of Port-Royal nuns who had given an unreserved signature to the formulary. Soeur Catherine de Sainte-Flavie Passart, once an ally of the Arnauld nuns during the episode of the miracle of the holy thorn, emerged as the leader of the *signeuses*. To break the re-sistance of the majority, Péréfixe exiled twelve of the most influen-tial dissidents to virtual house arrest in other convents. Soeur Angé-lique de Saint-Jean was among the first of the *nonsigneuses* to be escorted by armed guard to her isolated exile.

Situated next to the Hôtel Carnavalet in the right-bank neigh-borhood of the Marais, the convent of the Annonciade nuns on the

Rue Couture-Sainte-Catherine was to serve as the site of detention for Soeur Angélique de Saint-Jean during the following year. In her *Report on Captivity*, she describes the lively debates she engaged in with her new superior, Mère Marguerite Elisabeth de Rantzau, over the propriety of the formulary and the underlying controversies over the nature of grace.[11] This legalistic disputation, clearly enjoyed by the Port-Royal nun jousting with a superior she believed to be her intellectual inferior, is far from the silence counseled by Mère Agnès in such circumstances. The acerbic rhetoric of the *Report*, written after the nun's return from the Annonciade convent to Port-Royal, alarmed even her allies. Antoine Arnauld admonished his niece on the petulance of her description of the Annonciade convent as a jail (*geôle*) and its nuns as jailers (*geôlières*).

Despite its triumphalistic tenor, the *Report* contains a moving account of the crisis of faith the nun underwent when she heard that several of her own sisters at Port-Royal had signed the formulary without reservation. "A terrible anguish overtook me. . . . I was on the brink of letting my lamp go out because I did not have enough confidence to maintain the fire of my charity and the light of my faith."[12] Although she soon refound her faith after appropriate meditation on the temptation to despair, this evocation of her crisis of faith indicates another side to the spirituality of Soeur Angélique de Saint-Jean. Throughout her writings her evocation of apparent abandonment by God, detected with near-despair by the contemplative heart, provides a counterpoint to the martial arguments of the legal strategist, moving from one battle to another against the enemies of grace.

Released from the Annonciade convent in July 1665, Soeur Angélique de Saint-Jean returned to Port-Royal des Champs, where the archbishop had grouped the *nonsigneuses* of the community. Placed under interdict and then under the ban of excommunication, the nuns were deprived of the sacraments and communication with the external world. Armed guards surrounded the isolated convent on a permanent basis. Proudly bearing the scars of her exile with the Annonciade nuns, Soeur Angélique de Saint-Jean quickly re-established herself as the chief strategist of the convent's resistance. When the archbishop banned the recitation of the divine office in the convent, the intrepid nun devised a new sign language that permitted the nuns to perform a quiet semblance of the office through gesture. She quickly detected the defects in the porous regime of surveillance imposed on the fortress convent; surreptitious letters and even visits began to breach the quarantine.

In 1665 the enterprising subprioress even managed to begin spiritual direction under her cousin Isaac Le Maître de Saci. A distinguished translator of the Scriptures and church fathers, the austere priest proved himself the perfect guide for his embattled cousin. Even when he was imprisoned in 1666, Le Maître de Saci managed to continue his spiritual correspondence with the nun who had deftly circumvented Péréfixe's wall of silence. When Clement IX's Peace of the Church began in 1669, lifting the sanctions against the convent and returning Port-Royal to normal government, Soeur Angélique de Saint-Jean reluctantly signed a newly modified version of the formulary. The nuns' signature now indicated assent to the condemnation of the five propositions "wherever they are to be found, even in the works of Jansenius." The ambiguous formula demanded a greater assent than the nuns' earlier "respectful silence" on matters of fact, but it clearly stopped short of admitting that Jansen had actually defended the heretical propositions or that church authority had properly judged the *Augustinus*. Privately, however, the subprioress admitted that she remained unconvinced by the compromise and presciently predicted that the irenic formulary would bring only temporary respite from Port-Royal's determined enemies.

Her correspondence during the decade exhibits the characteristic intransigence of Soeur Angélique de Saint-Jean. In a 1661 letter to Gabrielle du Gué de Bagnols, a lay pupil at the convent, the subprioress attacks Louis XIV as the principal cause of the onset of persecution.

> I ask and beg him [God] with all my heart that they [the Port-Royal nuns] obtain what they request. This is not vengeance, but a conversion of those who are the primary authors of such an unjust persecution. May God's goodness pardon a prince (who is acting only out of zeal) for doing what others have him do without his thinking about it. I was just struck by the fact that the date on this letter, today, is the very day he begins his reign and the first year he personally begins to apply himself to the governance of the state.

> Make your own judgment about those people who push him to ex-
> ercise such violence as to rip away from the altars the virgins who
> had said farewell to the world, who had enclosed themselves in the
> solitude of the face of God, and who now find themselves engulfed
> in the opprobrium of other people. Aren't these people the greatest
> enemy we could have? They work to provoke against him the anger
> of a jealous God from whom they have abducted his spouses.[13]

The portrait of the king as an enemy of God and as a naïf manipulated by his entourage could easily be denounced as seditious if such
a letter fell into the hands of Port-Royal's critics.

Other epistolary exchanges only sharpened the impassioned critique of Port-Royal's enemies and of the moderates who sought conciliation. A 1661 letter to Antoine Arnauld denounces the grand-
vicars of Paris as cowards for trying to compromise on the formulary
and singles out the Jesuits as the true architects of the nuns' plight.[14]
A 1668 letter to Arnauld bitterly criticizes the Parisian nuns, especially her erstwhile friend Soeur Catherine de Sainte-Flavie Passart,
who had given an unreserved signature. "We would say that Soeur
Dorothée, Soeur Flavie, and the young Soeur Marie Thérèse, each in
her own manner, only followed themselves. They never really entered into the true spirit of the convent, although the second of these
talked about it enough. But that was the very thing she did not understand: the kingdom of God does not consist of words. But that
was all the poor girl had."[15]

The redoubtable subprioress did not hesitate to present in person her stinging rebukes to allies of Port-Royal who had explored
the path of compromise. In a 1669 letter to Madame de Sablé, Soeur
Angélique de Saint-Jean defends herself against criticisms of her personality she believes the marquise had been circulating. The letter
is a blunt criticism of this benefactress's years-long campaign to resolve the crisis of the signature through diplomatic means.

> I believe you have made the most offensive criticisms against me.
> I know no more atrocious offense against friendship, charity, and
> gratitude than the accusation of coldness and arrogance that you
> appear to impute to me. . . . As far as I am concerned, I still find
> some consolation in my [alleged emotional] poverty, because I am

persuaded by my recent experiences that in the area of emotion, firmness is worth more than tenderness. I would go even further by daring to say that I prefer my roughness and dryness to the caresses and softness proffered by certain people you have seen since you saw us.[16]

The inflammatory rhetoric of the letter reflects the nun's conviction that the struggle over the signature is ultimately a war between the friends and enemies of God; the enemies, especially the moderates promoting compromise, must be unmasked by the embattled elect defending the very grace of Christ.

The correspondence from this tormented decade presents a side of Soeur Angélique de Saint-Jean different from that of the strident ideologue. In many letters the nun appears to despair of the inexplicable oppression in which Port-Royal finds itself. Criticizing the attempted compromise of moderates, she detects the presence of the devil. "I am seriously telling you [Antoine Arnauld] that I am aware that the demon has a worse intention in this project [of negotiation] than do human beings. He is only planting snares in the salon of this woman [Madame de Sablé] while she is only trying to keep her head."[17] In numerous letters she interprets the prostrate state of the church and the persecuted state of the elect as a fulfillment of the apocalyptic prophecies of the book of Revelation.[18] Her ardent campaign of protest and resistance coexists uneasily with the melancholy recognition that the plight of the convent revealed a church whose very foundation in the grace of Christ had become an enigma to the majority of its rulers and members.

Soeur Angélique de Saint-Jean also used her correspondence to state her position on the substantive theological issues behind the crisis of the signature. In explaining her opposition to any ambiguous submission to church condemnations, she clearly refuses any acceptance of the church's condemnation of Jansen. "I am willing to subscribe to what is good, namely the condemnation of errors [the five propositions], and I reject what is bad, namely the condemnation of the justice and the innocence of a holy bishop [Jansen]."[19] In her letters she defends Jansen for having upheld Saint Augustine's doctrine of grace, embraced by numerous popes and councils as the church's own. The nun's public statements, however, did not always accord with her epistolary defense of Jansen. When interrogated by the archiepiscopal delegates Bail and Contes in the summer of 1661, she insisted that she was unable to understand the theological issues in the case and that she had never heard such questions discussed in the convent. Even her sympathetic biographer Brigitte Sibertin-Blanc admits that in this testimony "one can detect some knavery and artfulness on the part of the nun, able to affirm without laughing that she understood nothing in the disputed matters and that she had never heard anything about them."[20]

During the Peace of the Church (1669–79), Soeur Angélique de Saint-Jean directed the re-establishment of the convent's religious life, first as prioress of Port-Royal des Champs, then, beginning on August 3, 1678, as its abbess. During these years of peace, the nun devoted much of her time to spiritual direction through letters and parlor interviews. Numerous letters to Mère de Maurisse, prioress of the convent of Saint-Martin, explained how the Angelican principles of convent reform could be implemented in a different convent and order.[21] Letters to her lay directees Mademoiselle de Bagnols and Madame de Fonspertuis insisted on the strict separation from the world required even for a lay Christian.[22] A series of letters in 1671 lamented the appointment of her brother Arnauld de Pomponne as secretary of state; the apparent political triumph will require moral compromises that will lead eventually to sin. When Gilberte Pascal Périer congratulates the nun for the honor brought to her family by this royal appointment, the nun dryly rebukes her: "My beloved sister, I am not happy that you claim to have experienced perfect joy about a piece of news that certainly should have given you a very great fear of the peril one of your true friends is going to be exposed to."[23]

Through this correspondence of spiritual direction, the distinctive theology of Soeur Angélique de Saint-Jean emerges. Her moral rigorism governs the censure of her brother's promotion; fidelity to the Gospel cannot be easily reconciled with such worldly professions as politics, banking, or the military. Her Augustinianism appears in the strict account of concupiscence she offers Mademoiselle de Bagnols: "When a passion . . . manages to possess the heart, it banishes the charity that is its life and makes it fall into death. It makes little difference which of the three concupiscences reigning in the world dominate us; that of the eyes can kill us as easily as that of the first [the flesh]."[24] On an apophatic tone, many letters underscore the alterity of God: "It is necessary to recognize how much the thoughts of God are elevated above our thoughts. We should not imagine that our own views might be as useful as his are."[25] In many apocalyptic passages, the nun warns her directees to recognize the imminent end of the world. In a striking metaphor of the world as a collapsing house, the nun evokes the punishment awaiting the worldly: "Certainly the world is a house that is going to perish. All the lusts that reign in it are a fire that consumes it and all those who are attached to it. But this fire is never extinguished since this will be the same fire that burns in hell for the souls who have been consumed by it in this life."[26]

After her election as abbess in 1678, Mère Angélique de Saint-Jean soon witnessed the collapse of the Peace of the Church. As the shrewd abbess suspected, a hostile Louis XIV, emboldened by the favorable Treaties of Nijmegen (1678–79), now turned his attention to the destruction of his internal enemies. The Port-Royal des Champs convent, once again a flourishing center of Jansenist education and scholarship, became a target for attack. On May 17, 1679, Parisian archbishop François de Harlay de Champvallon arrived at Port-Royal des Champs to decree the expulsion of confessors, postulants, and lay boarding pupils. When challenged as to the motive behind the measures, the archbishop vaguely responded that while no individual person at Port-Royal represented a particular problem for church or throne, the collectivity of the extended Port-Royal community constituted a threat to national unity and religious harmony. On the surface, the sanctions were milder than those imposed during the crisis of the 1660s. The professed nuns and lay sisters could pursue their daily life of prayer and work. In fact, the sanctions constituted a death sentence for the convent. Without candidates for admission, the order would gradually wither. Without the income provided by school tuition, the economic survival of the convent was doubtful. Deprived of resources and personnel, an aging community in the insalubrious climate of the Chevreuse valley seemed doomed for rapid extinction.

Only days after the visitation, the intrepid abbess began her campaign of protest. To her uncle Henry Arnauld, bishop of Angers, she expressed her shock at the sudden and inexplicable imposition of sanctions.

> If Port-Royal were built on a mountain, we would not be surprised that thunderbolts always hit its bell-tower. But there is really something astonishing in the conduct of God and the world here. However hidden we might be in our valley and in our solitude, they seek us and they pursue us everywhere. They make us bear the burden of all the evil they attribute to others. Without accusing us of anything, they condemn us as guilty; while they praise us, they impose punishments on us.[27]

In a series of letters to Pope Innocent XI himself, the abbess insisted that the prejudicial image of the convent, carefully crafted by the enemies of Port-Royal's Augustinian theology, was a tissue of calumnies. The persecution had no basis in fact. "If Your Holiness could for once be informed about all we have suffered, caused by no other human reason than the jealousy and malice of certain people against some very wise and very pious theologians, including some who participated in the direction of this convent, we have no doubt, Holy Father, that the account of our sufferings—which have few parallels in past centuries—would soften the heart of Your Holiness."[28] In the abbess's perspective, the persecution of the convent proceeds from the professional jealousy of the opponents of Saint-Cyran and Antoine Arnauld, not from any legitimate concern over the moral conduct or the theological beliefs of the nuns.

On February 5, 1680, the desperate abbess authored a personal protest to Louis XIV himself. She boldly requests that the reasons for this new persecution be clearly stated. "We have always considered it an obligation to obey His Majesty and to conform to his wishes, as the one who holds the first rank in our duties after what we owe to God. Sire, it is the deepest sorrow for people raised in such sentiments to see that, on the one hand, they are seen as evil in your mind and that, on the other hand, they cannot see any exit to leave this extremely painful state since we are not permitted to know what has put us here and what keeps us here."[29] Clearly the letter is not a plea for clemency. On the contrary, behind the rhetoric of the sorrow of a subject for grieving the monarch lies a steely defense of the right of the imprisoned to know the nature of the charges against them.

The nuns soon learned that the new regime imposed by Archbishop Harlay de Champvallon would entail more than slow asphyxiation of their community. The newly imposed preachers and confessors engaged in pointed critiques of the nuns' orthodoxy. In a letter of April 19, 1680, Mère Angélique de Saint-Jean denounces the outrageous sermon preached by Father Poligné on Good Friday.

> In what manner did Father Poligné make us celebrate the Passion this morning! He didn't preach it; he reenacted it. He chose this day perhaps because he believed we would be better disposed to hear about the opprobrium and ignominy of which Jesus Christ has made his glory today because he glorified his Father by suffering it. During three hours he [Father Poligné] compared us to every kind of heretic through the centuries: to the Arians, to the Donatists, to the Pelagians, to the Novatians, to the Macedonians, to Calvinists. He used all these comparisons to accuse us of disobedience to the chair of Saint Peter and to our pastors, of recognizing only the authority of general councils on matters of faith, of holding private assemblies, of relying on reasoning and not on obedience, of being separated from the society of the faithful, because those who did not obey the church must be considered infidels.[30]

The spiritual aggression committed by the intemperate preacher has only sharpened the campaign of calumny that the enemies of Port-Royal have directed against the convent for decades.

Not confining herself to protests to civic and ecclesiastical authorities, Mère Angélique de Saint-Jean used her correspondence to present a moral and theological justification of her policy of resistance. In a letter to Madame de Fonspertuis, the abbess develops this justification through a distinction between law and freedom. "I hope that you stand for the law of Christian freedom that places the justice of the kingdom of God in the peace and joy of the Holy Spirit and not in these legal observances that smack of the letter that kills when it is separated from the spirit of charity that gives life. This is because it [the law of Christian freedom] makes us love more than anything else the will of God, the source and cause of our happiness."[31] Her argument on the primacy of the spirit over the letter bears a trace of the antinomianism with which the Port-Royal nuns were charged.

Throughout her campaign of protest during her two-term abbacy (1678–84), Mère Angélique de Saint-Jean repeatedly defended the rights of nuns as they are embedded in the Angelican reform. Such rights included the freedom of the chapter to elect its own abbess, the freedom of the community to follow its church-approved constitutions, and the right of the convent to direct a school. The abbess made a particularly ardent defense of the spiritual rights of the abbess. She repeatedly asked the archbishop of Paris to respect the right of the abbess to choose the convent confessors; in 1681 as the new persecution entered full force, she even proposed a list of three possible confessors to the archbishop and urged him to appoint promptly one of her nominees.[32] The defense of the rights of the abbess was not confined to exhortation. Mère Angélique de Saint-Jean's vigorous exercise of the office of abbess indicated her determination to have the abbess accepted as the principal spiritual director, teacher, and theologian of the convent. She exercised this magisterial authority primarily through her prolific conferences on the foundational texts of the monastery. Reflecting the abbess's erudition and her ethics of resistance, the conferences provided detailed commentaries on Scripture, especially the book of Esther, with its apotheosis of the heroic resistant woman; the Rule of Saint Benedict, interpreted according to the principles of the Angelican reform; the Constitutions of Port-Royal, interpreted according to the abbess's moral rigorism; and Mère Agnès's *Counsels,* now applied to the new circumstances of the persecuted convent.

Throughout these abbatial years Mère Angélique de Saint-Jean continued her apostolate of spiritual direction, strongly marked by her neo-Augustinian orientation. The works of Augustine constitute a privileged source of inspiration for the afflicted. "I beg you, my beloved sister [Madame de Fonspertuis], if you have a copy of the book *The City of God,* to read the ninth chapter of its first book. . . . We can find in it lessons for the current moment that will provide edification and consolation in our sufferings."[33] The abbess's philosophy of virtue maintained its Augustinian coloration in its dismissal of natural moral virtues and its exaltation of the theological. In a letter to Mademoiselle de Bagnols, she links a critique of the virtue of prudence to a denunciation of the political considerations

that have reignited the persecution of the convent. "There are circumstances so extraordinary that charity should not take account
of prudence. . . . Politics is so opposed to the gospel that we should
not even pretend to possess it, only because we want to pretend to
offer some incense to it. This is the idol of our time. I detest it with
all my heart."[34] In the abbess's reconfiguration, the Augustinian dismissal of prudence becomes a dismissal of the modern *raison d'état*,
the cynical principle justifying any foreign or domestic aggression
by the state.

Ardent and persistent, Mère Angélique de Saint-Jean's campaign
to recover the freedom of Port-Royal found few echoes in public
opinion. The original reforming generation, especially Mères Angélique and Agnès, had long since died. Prominent lay defenders of the
convent, notably Madame de Longueville, the cousin of Louis XIV,
had also disappeared. Threatened with imprisonment, the *solitaires*
had abandoned the valley of the Chevreuse, many of them carrying
the hidden manuscripts of Mère Angélique de Saint-Jean to their
houses of exile in Belgium and Holland. Still agitating the isolated
community of Port-Royal, the quarrel over grace no longer held the
interest of the broader Catholic world, more focused on moral and
church/state controversies. Pope Innocent XI privately expressed
sympathy for the humiliated nuns, but the Vatican's own struggles
with Louis XIV, especially the bitter quarrel over the *régale*, pre-
vented any public intervention.[35] In her last years, the icy indifference of the religious and political world to the ongoing persecution
of the nuns became the abbess's final cross.

As the isolated convent faded in numbers and vitality, the apocalyptic tone of Mère Angélique de Saint-Jean's estimate of a fallen
world became even more pronounced. "When will we be in the Holy
City in which God himself is the light and where consequently
there are no longer any shadows? This life here below is quite different. Everything casts a shadow. When the day fades, the shadows
become longer. That is where we are now. It is certainly more true
of our time than it was of the time of which Saint John said, 'It is
the last hour.'"[36] The sentinel of the persecuted convent could perceive only a world of obscurity in which the most basic moral and
religious principles had vanished.

Mère Angélique de Saint-Jean died on January 29, 1684.

WORKS

A prolific author, Mère Angélique de Saint-Jean composed numerous works in a wide variety of genres: autobiography, biography, letters, scriptural exegesis, legal commentaries, chronicles, eulogies, and devotional treatises. Many of her works were published in the eighteenth century once the censorship of the French government had relaxed and a diffuse Jansenism had attracted a broad, educated European public. The quarrel caused by Clement XI's anti-Jansenist bull *Unigenitus* (1713) created a widespread curiosity about the ruined convent that had once been the center of the Jansenist movement. The editors of the 1736 edition of her commentary on the Rule of Saint Benedict allude to the literary renown the abbess's previously published works had acquired: "The works of Reverend Mère Angélique de Saint-Jean are quite well known and do not need further praise. Several opuscules of this pious abbess have already been published at different times. They have sufficiently won the approval and the favor of the public to let us hope that the work we are now presenting to the public will find the same reception."[37] Many of the abbess's writings, however, still remain in manuscript form alone. By far the most important of these manuscripts is the multivolume collection of the abbess's letters, housed in the Bibliothèque de la Société de Port-Royal.

From a philosophical perspective the most important works are the conferences delivered to the Port-Royal nuns during Mère Angélique de Saint-Jean's abbacy. Her commentary on the Rule of Saint Benedict, *Discourses on the Rule of Saint Benedict* transforms the early monastic theory of virtue by adding a neo-Augustinian stress on the necessity of grace for the performance of any virtuous action.[38] Her *Conferences on the Constitutions of the Monastery of Port-Royal* defends the rights of nuns, especially of abbesses in the governance and theological formation of their subjects.[39] The accompanying biblical commentaries on the books of 1 Kings and Esther underscore the role of heroic women in opposing oppression and the precedent of a miracle granted by God to those who are persecuted for fidelity to his name. A commentary on the *Counsels in the Event of a Change in the Government of the Convent* of Mère

Agnès, *Reflections to Prepare the Nuns for Persecution* is shaped by Mère Angélique de Saint-Jean's ethics of militant resistance.[40] Mère Agnès's diplomatic casuistry on material cooperation with evil becomes a summons to uncompromising opposition to the counterfeits of grace in an apocalyptic world starkly divided between the elect and the demonic.

Complementing her historiographical works, the abbatial commentaries are designed to instruct the nuns on the true foundations of the community in the biblical canon, the primitive monastic rules, and the doctrine of the two venerable reformers, Mères Angélique and Agnès. The abbess is clearly struggling against three perceived temptations for her subjects: surrender to the court's persecution either by abandoning their convictions or by permitting an imposed regime to alter the ethos of the convent; reversion to the more theatrical piety that had prevailed during the ascendancy of Zamet; simple laxness, as an aging and isolated community drifted away from heroic virtue and settled for a minimal spiritual routine. The commentaries also serve a philosophical purpose by systematizing the Augustinianism of the reformed Port-Royal. Augustine's account of concupiscence, Jansen's concept of election, and Saint-Cyran's moral rigorism find themselves fused in the abbess's ideal of conventual life, couched in her apocalyptic vision of combat. The abbess's firsthand knowledge of the actual texts of Augustine and Augustinian authors provides an erudite framework for this synthetic Augustinian philosophy.

In two other works, Mère Angélique de Saint-Jean writes in distinctively Port-Royalist literary genres. Her *Report of Captivity,* written in 1665 after her return from exile at the Annonciade convent, uses the martyrological hyperbole typical of the Port-Royal captivity narratives.[41] The lengthy debates with the Annonciade superior permit the author to state her neo-Augustinian theory of grace. In the *Miséricordes,* a collection of eulogies, the abbess praises the virtues of recently deceased laity, usually relatives of Port-Royal nuns or benefactors of the convent.[42] Faithful to her Augustinian perspective, the virtues are presented as the work of God's grace, not the fruits of the deceased's personal merits. Echoing the theology of Saint-Cyran, the key event in the deceased's life is often presented as a mature moment of conversion, when the person renounced a life of routine, morally mediocre Christian practice for a vigorous, demanding faith among the elect of Port-Royal.

Several opuscules deal with the problem of persecution and the moral certitude the conscientious nun must conserve in the face of it. Written during her house arrest at the Annonciade convent in 1664–65, *Reflections on the Conformity of the State of the Nuns of Port-Royal with That of Jesus Christ in the Eucharist* dwells on the deeper, more spiritual unity with Christ made possible by the deprivation of the sacraments triggered by the decrees of interdict and excommunication.[43] *Three Conferences on the Necessity to Defend the Church* exhorts her subjects to distinguish between servile and enlightened obedience during the renewed persecution of the convent.[44]

Especially important from a philosophical perspective, *On the Danger of Hesitation and Doubt* summons the nuns to resist the temptation to doubt the justice of their cause under the duress of persecution.[45] More generally, it argues that the action of doubting is never a neutral exercise. To determine whether one should engage in doubt, and if one should, what type of self-scrutiny is appropriate, the conscientious agent must assess the motives and interests of those who are encouraging or even forcing the practice of doubt. Like persecution and declarations of heresy, doubt has its politics.

The historian Mère Angélique de Saint-Jean is responsible as author or editor for dozens of the Port-Royal memorials that appeared in print in the eighteenth century. Among the most important are her *Report or Documented History of Mère Marie-Angélique,*[46] first appearing in 1723, and her biographies of the other members of the Arnauld and Arnauld d'Andilly families who became nuns at Port-Royal, published in 1742.[47] Hagiographic in nature, the memorials idealize the nuns by praising their moral virtues and on more than one occasion by showing the miraculous origin of their actions, especially their triumph over enemies. The memorials also constitute a defense of the convent's neo-Augustinian orientation, both in its intellectual allegiance to Jansen's theory of grace and in its austere moral practices, faithful to the doctrine of Saint-Cyran.

Mère Angélique de Saint-Jean's works were published regularly throughout the eighteenth century. Edited by Pasquier Quesnel,

Report of Captivity appeared in 1711. In the same year, *Reflections on the Conformity of the State of the Nuns of Port-Royal with That of Jesus Christ in the Eucharist* appeared in print. Edited by Dom Rivet de La Grange, the *Necrology of Port-Royal* was published at Amsterdam in 1733.[48] Many of its death notices were written, edited, or commissioned by the abbess. *Discourses of Mère Angélique de Saint-Jean Called "Miséricordes"* appeared at Utrecht in 1735. *Discourses on the Rule of Saint Benedict by Reverend Mère Angélique de Saint-Jean* was published at Paris in 1736. Indicating the changed official French attitude toward the Jansenists and the altered climate of censorship, the monastic commentary appeared with the approval of the faculty of the Sorbonne and the imprimatur of the king. Published at Utrecht in 1742, the three-volume *Memoirs to Be Used for the History of Port-Royal* contains numerous biographies written by the abbess. Printed at Utrecht in 1760, *Conferences on the Constitutions of the Monastery of Port-Royal* contains her commentaries on the Constitutions of Port-Royal, the book of Esther, and the book of 1 Kings. At the moment of its appearance, an editor of *Les nouvelles ecclésiastiques* praised the commentarics' author: "We are astonished at the genius of this incomparable woman. We have difficulty understanding how, given her responsibility for governing a large community in difficult times and passing part of her days and nights in prayer, she was able to give so many conferences, without speaking of the letters she was continually asked to write."[49] Published in 1750, *Interesting and Edifying Lives of the Nuns of Port-Royal* contains several opuscules addressing persecution. *Exercises of Piety for the Use of Port-Royal*, printed in 1787, includes devotional works written by the abbess and her colleagues.[50]

Approximately nine hundred in number, the manuscript letters of Mère Angélique de Saint-Jean are currently archived in the Bibliothèque de la Société de Port-Royal in Paris.[51] Copied and collated by Rachel Gillet, the indefatigable nineteenth-century librarian who also edited the letters of Mère Agnès Arnauld, the letters indicate the broad interests of the abbess. Her wide circle of correspondents included popes, cardinals, bishops, abbots, abbesses, kings, queens, aristocrats, lawyers, artists, and students. Her letters of spiritual direction to laywomen, notably Mademoiselle de Bagnols and Madame de Fonspertuis, underscore the stark opposition between the world and the disciple of Christ. After the abrogation of the Peace of the Church, the abbess's legal skill is expressed in her carefully argued pleas to pope, king, and members of their respective courts. Especially interesting from a philosophical perspective are her many exchanges with her uncle, the philosopher and theologian Antoine Arnauld. These letters permitted the nun to explain her position on the quarrels concerning the Augustinian theory of grace and the related disputes on the limits of civil and ecclesiastical authority.

Among the unpublished manuscripts at the Bibliothèque de la Société de Port-Royal long attributed to Mère Angélique de Saint-Jean, *Of Direction* provides a staunch defense of the spiritual rights of women by insisting that the abbess herself, not the priest chaplain or confessor, is the principal spiritual director of the nuns under her care.[52] "It is certain that the founders of orders argued that the abbots and abbesses should be the spiritual directors of all their monks and nuns. They argued there is no one else except them. I do not know if one could find any example of monks or nuns who had directors outside their monasteries. One can find much truth in the fact that in the seventh and eighth centuries some priests came to hear the confessions of the nuns at certain times of the year, but outside of these times these confessors were rare."[53] Other manuscript works by Mère Angélique de Saint-Jean include *Thoughts on Various Subjects*, a series of liturgical meditations following the feasts of the Church year,[54] and *Faithful Narrative of the Miracles and Visions of Soeur Flavie*, a stinging critique of the *signeuse* who became the superior of the anti-Jansenist minority of nuns grouped at Port-Royal de Paris.[55]

Concupiscence and Virtue

Composed of twelve hundred pages published in two volumes, the *Discourses on the Rule of Saint Benedict* constitutes Mère Angélique de Saint-Jean's most extensive cycle of commentaries. Written by Saint Benedict himself, probably between 530 and 560, the Rule is a brief text of seventy-three chapters, in which Benedict sets forth the basic laws and principles of the cenobitic monasticism he had founded in Italy. The charter of Western monasticism, the Rule of

Saint Benedict reflects earlier monastic rules composed by Saint Pachomius in Egypt, Saint Basil in Asia Minor, Saint Augustine in northern Africa, and Cassian in Marseilles. It closely follows the anonymous *Rule of the Master*, composed at the beginning of the sixth century.[56] Despite its dependence on earlier monastic sources, Benedict's Rule manifests its originality by its emphasis on the communitarian character of the monastery (sealed by a lifelong vow of stability), on the extensive powers of the elected abbot, and on moderation in ascetical practices. The frequent object of commentary by subsequent generations of Benedictine and Cistercian religious, the Rule generated numerous commentaries by distinguished abbesses, such as the medieval Hildegarde of Bingen.[57]

Especially striking is Mère Angélique de Saint-Jean's transformation of the laconic, practical Rule into a treatise of radical Augustinian theology. This transformation emerges most clearly in two sections of the commentary: the discussion of the Rule's prologue and the gloss on the Rule's stipulations on the monastic virtues. In her commentary on the prologue, the abbess defends key neo-Augustinian theses: the depth of human concupiscence, total dependence on God's grace for moral action, the primacy of divine election, and the small number of the elect in the act of salvation. Her commentary on the virtues, especially the elaborate analysis of humility, provides a theocentric account of morality inasmuch as all moral action proceeds from a will unchained by God's grace. Embedded in this discussion of virtue is an anthropological analysis of the nature and inclinations of the human faculty of the will.

A central neo-Augustinian theme recurring in the commentary on the prologue is the insistence on the small number of the elect. Chosen by God out of a sovereign free act, the elect manifest their salvation by their obedience to God's Word in their moral conduct. In various passages this elect is assimilated to members of religious orders or to members of the persecuted Jansenist minority. "Make us remember this great truth Jesus Christ taught us in the gospel: that 'there are many who are called but there are few who are elected.' We see the truth of this every day. Only too often it happens that in a great multitude of people there is only one person who truly shows the quality of being a child of God and who merits this name by the obedience he or she shows him and by the love he or she brings him."[58] Although one's intimate union with God is revealed by habitual acts of obedience and charity, this moral activity is itself a result of God's election of the individual to salvation. Rather than earning one's salvation, the moral actions are the sign of a salvation granted by God alone.

This repeated emphasis on the primacy of election, reinforced by the concomitant stress on divine predestination, provoked the accusations that Calvinism was embedded within Jansenist theology. In the perspective of election, authentic perception of moral truth is not only possible only within the light of faith; the light of faith itself is reserved for a small elect chosen by God's inscrutable wisdom.

Further accentuating the fideist cast of the commentary's moral philosophy is the recurrent emphasis on complete human dependence on grace for the capacity to perform moral actions. The power to embrace the authentic good, as well as the ability to discern the nature of the good, requires divine assistance. "To arrive at this [perfection] we need God to give us his grace and his light. Without this we broaden the path [of salvation] and fall away from it rather than advancing forward. We are only shadows by ourselves. We are mistaken about whatever light we seem to have if it is not God himself who lights our lamp and enlightens us."[59] The necessity of grace for moral enlightenment and action undercuts the traditional Catholic appeal to natural law. Unredeemed, the human person can only surrender to the counterfeits of the good life fabricated by concupiscence. The passage's reference to human nature as a shadow (*ténèbres*) indicates how insubstantial human nature and human moral codes are apart from the grace of salvation.

In her commentary on the monastic virtues of obedience, silence, and humility, Mère Angélique de Saint-Jean stresses the disordered nature of the human will. The virtue of obedience transcends submission to the command of a legitimate superior; it is rooted in the salvific obedience of Christ to his Father in the mystery of the cross. It is the fallen nature of humanity that renders the virtue of obedience so prominent, since the unbridled exercise of freedom can lead humanity only to perdition.

In describing the necessity of the virtue of obedience, the commentary analyzes the distortion of human freedom effected by the

Fall. It focuses in particular on the subordination of the intellect to the will that has turned the exercise of human freedom into the blind pursuit of desire. "In the original state of creation there was a perfect relationship between human reason and will. At the present time, however, this is no longer the case. Reason has become an instrument between the hands of self-will, which uses it in an improper and destructive way by arming itself with the false appearances of reason to find a shadow of justice in injustice itself."[60] In the abbess's perspective the exercise of reason has deteriorated into rationalization. So pervasive has the rationalization become under the weight of concupiscence that even well-intentioned people habitually choose evil disguised as an apparent good. Only obedience to God's will can correct the distortion of freedom as willfulness and inaugurate an authentic freedom that issues in the love of God and neighbor.

For the nun, the generic Christian virtue of obedience is concretized through her vow of obedience. Unmediated obedience to God can easily lead to confusion concerning the precise nature of the divine command; obedience to a visible superior acting on God's authority, however, can focus the practice of the virtue.

> Obedience is further considered as a continual exercise of faith. God is invisible; the senses cannot find him. . . . Only faith can hear him, look at him, and see him in the obedience we offer to the person who holds his place. . . . Faith makes us practice obedience. That is why we exercise it more when we obey persons whose merits seem less. When we happen to have superiors who do not appear worthy of this rank, we are not dispensed from obeying them in everything that is not contrary to God's law and to the rules of the order.[61]

In her encomium of obedience, Mère Angélique de Saint-Jean places clear limits on the extent of its obligations. The nun can never be ordered to violate God's moral law or to violate the constitution and rules of her particular order.

The implications of the limitations are obvious. The nun can never be coerced by an appeal to obedience to affirm a religious judgment she believes to be false. Obedience cannot trump the ethical duty to avoid lying. Similarly the nun cannot accept an order to violate the rule of life she vowed to uphold at the moment of her profession. She could not, for example, be forced to engage in spiritual exercises or types of work that violate the Constitutions of Port-Royal. While the text of the *Discourses* never explicitly cites the larger issue of obedience to distant ecclesiastical and political authorities, the crisis of the signature and its sequel of persecution are never far from the surface.

The commentary on the second virtue, silence, confirms the moral superiority of the monastic way of life. Strictly practiced at Port-Royal, which resurrected the Cistercian sign language of the Middle Ages, silence permits the nun to exercise a continual attentiveness to God which the laywoman plunged into the world's noise can rarely cultivate. Many passages in the conferences develop the obvious argument that religious contemplation, the primary activity of the cloistered nun, requires a regime of silence as one of its necessary conditions. Mère Angélique de Saint-Jean complements this traditional argument by adducing other moral arguments on behalf of the virtue of silence.

Silence helps to suppress the vices that frequently flourish in situations of unbridled speech. Since language is often the vehicle for sinful acts and the expression of vicious dispositions, strict silence stifles the offensive medium in its source. "In maintaining silence we mortify curiosity, vanity, self-love, and all the other poisons that use the tongue to spill outside and to encourage their impetuous, disordered movements. Silence heals the disposition of the soul. It cuts back on the pleasure we take in diversion; it removes the occasion for complaints and grumbling; it prevents us from communicating to others our imperfections and from becoming a subject of scandal."[62] Tellingly this brief for monastic silence assimilates vice to the passions. In giving free rein to the expression of emotion, frequent conversation is already morally suspect.

Internal support of the external practice of silence, humility imposes itself as the paramount monastic virtue. In the seventh chapter of his Rule, Saint Benedict lists twelve types of the virtue of humility. They are: (1) fear of God; (2) suppression of self-will; (3) submission of will to superiors; (4) obedience in especially difficult matters; (5) confession of major faults; (6) recognition of one's unworthiness; (7) preferring others to oneself; (8) avoiding singular conduct; (9) speaking only at the proper time; (10) avoidance of worldly laughter; (11) elimination of pride; (12) proper external expression of humility. In her 224-page commentary on the Rule's sketch of this virtue, Mère Angélique de Saint-Jean transforms this schematic ladder of humility into an elaborate treatise on the human soul, reflecting Port-Royal's neo-Augustinian theology and her own heroic ethics of spiritual combat.

Echoing Port-Royal's Oratorian strain of spirituality, the commentary frequently conceives humility as a species of personal annihilation. The humble nun not only recognizes the truth of her own finitude and sinfulness; in the face of God's majesty, she recognizes her utter nothingness and desires the dissolution of her self into God. In the mystery of the Incarnation Christ himself presents the paradigm of annihilation. "He [Christ] not only lowered himself by clothing himself with the appearance of a servant; he took this very nature upon himself. Since humanity is nothing but a nothingness, God effectively annihilates himself by making himself human. This is our model. If we must judge the humility we should have according to the humility of Jesus Christ, into what type of annihilation should we enter to pay him homage?"[63] The commentary repeatedly describes mature humility in such rhetoric of annihilation.

The analysis of humility also provides an occasion for the abbess to pursue one of her cherished neo-Augustinian themes: the small number of the elect. According to her argument, the palpable lack of humble people in the world and the quasi omnipresence of pride indicate that few are saved. "We must hope in God's mercy, but at the same time we must work to make ourselves worthy by humility. Salvation is only for the humble; consequently, the humble will not be damned. One must be one or the other, saved or damned. It is quite certain that they are few who are saved, since one can only be saved by humility, which consists in the love of humiliation and abasement."[64] Just as the presence of virtue is an earnest of salvation, the presence of vice is a token of the damnation to come. The withering dismissal of the vast majority of humanity manifests the paradox attacked by critics of the Jansenists. Damning the mass of humanity for its pride, the Port-Royal cenacle haughtily presents itself as the vanguard of the humble chosen by God for salvation.

The seat of virtue and vice, the will is the human faculty that must undergo conversion so that humility might flourish in the human person. Humility can emerge only when the will liberates itself from subordination to its own desires and submits itself perfectly to God. "There is something perverted in humanity: its will. Thus, there is nothing more necessary than its being established in a proper order, that is, in the submission it owes to God. Humanity is wounded because it is turned toward itself by acting through its own will. It is not possible for humanity to be healed unless it turns and converts itself to God through the obedience and submission it owes to God."[65] This portrait of the will wounded by concupiscence uses several Augustinian motifs. The weakness of the will is radical, a matter of perversion (*perverti*) rather than of mild infirmity. The spiritual status of the will is determined by the object of its fundamental attraction: sinful toward the self or beatific toward God.

If the human person can detect the slavery of its will to the self, it cannot by its own power free the concupiscent will to a proper love of God. Only grace can heal the perverted will and liberate it to a stance of habitual charity toward God and neighbor. "It is not enough for humanity to know the will of God; it is a grace he grants when he manifests his will, but it is necessary for God to give it another grace above this one to make it accomplish his will."[66] Although the commentary on humility contains several passages insisting on the need of the nun to cooperate with God's grace, it places greater emphasis on the initiative of grace to create the submissive will that humility signifies. God emerges as both the artisan and the measure of the humble moral character.

Despite its traditional association with docility, humility in Mère Angélique de Saint-Jean's account has a martial cast. Precisely because they have submitted themselves to God's will and they constitute a vulnerable minority, the humble can expect the world's opprobrium.

> We are obliged to be in the disposition of suffering martyrdom. This was the situation of the first Christians, whose lives must be imitated by truly religious people. They expected death at any hour. Although they did not know from what torture they would die, there was nothing they were not ready to suffer. We do not know what God will expose us to, but we do know that as

Christians and as nuns, we are called to follow Jesus Christ and Jesus Christ crucified, to carry our cross after him and to renounce ourselves. This cannot be done without suffering.[67]

Although the martyrdom of the humble involves internal, ascetical struggle against willfulness, it also entails violent confrontation with a world determined to crush those who testify to God's grace. The apocalyptic references to the martyrdom that can unfurl at any moment clearly allude to the renewed persecution engulfing Port-Royal.

In an elegiac passage the abbess compares the suffering of the persecuted nuns to the distress of Israel exiled in Babylon. She evokes the lamentation of displaced minorities who earn persecution because of their fidelity to God.

Let us consider the sacred sadness of true Israelites who refused to sing their canticles in a strange land and who wept unceasingly because they saw themselves banished from Jerusalem, which is the object of their desires and their happiness. . . . It is the weeping that the Holy Spirit produces in the heart of the elect. They protest to God that the holy city is the unique object of their joy. Seeing themselves banished, they do not want to seek any pleasure on earth, where they are considered as exiles and strangers.[68]

While the concept of religious fidelity during persecution as a type of exile on earth has universal application, the allusion to the fate of Israel in Babylon has very specific applications to the precarious convent. Three of the punishments inflicted on the nuns recall the Babylonian exile: the physical banishment to other convents for the most intransigent nuns; the imposition of foreign rulers on the Port-Royal convent; the ban on chanting the psalms and canticles of the divine office during the period of interdict. The history of persecuted Israel constitutes a mirror for the hunted nuns to comprehend their own fate as exiles. Far from meek compromise, the humility required of the nuns is the militant refusal of God's earlier elect to accept religious error and their determined embrace of the persecution occasioned by their refusal.

In its analysis of obedience, silence, and humility, the *Discourses* develops a contextualized theory of virtue. The preeminence of the monastic vocation is its capacity to foster the flourishing of such moral habits. The obedience of subject to superior, the external silence of the cloister, and the ascetical practices of humility that punctuate the monastic day provide a material and spiritual culture propitious for the pursuit of these virtues. The virtues analyzed by the abbess are not generic human or even Christian moral dispositions to be cultivated indifferently by all members of the church; they are virtues more proper to religious because they can be more easily and profoundly cultivated within the monastic way of life. They are superior, and not only complementary, to the typical virtues cultivated by the laity inasmuch as they promote a more emphatic union with and submission to God.

Mère Angélique de Saint-Jean also develops a gendered account of virtue. It is specifically the nun, and not vowed religious in general, who is the moral agent called to practice these virtues. Obedience is to be exercised through execution of the commands of an abbess; silence is to be practiced through the simple prayer of adoration typical of Port-Royal; humility is to be exhibited through resistance to the opponents of religious truth, the tormentors of the convent. Rather than advocating the submission of women, the abbess uses the apparently passive virtues of traditional monasticism to justify the religious authority of women and the duty to accept the martyrdom provoked by the convent's witness to the gospel of grace.

Dualistic Metaphysics

Primarily devoted to practical applications, Mère Angélique de Saint-Jean's *Conferences on the Constitutions of the Monastery of Port-Royal* contains numerous passages illustrating the abbess's neo-Augustinian philosophy. The commentaries return repeatedly to a metaphysics inspired by Augustinian dualism, especially Saint Augustine's theory of the two opposed loves that animate history and society. The concept of liberty championed by the work is a graced liberation from sin rather than the exercise of free will. In her rigorist interpretation of Mère Agnès's earlier rules on the reception of Holy Communion and sacramental confession, Mère Angélique de Saint-Jean shows herself a strict disciple of the Augustinian Saint-Cyran, with his controversial theses on the necessity of periodic abstention from the church's sacraments.

Reverently quoting Mère Agnès's legal stipulations and acclaiming them as a divinely inspired code for the convent, Mère Angélique de Saint-Jean provides an Augustinian framework for understanding the Constitutions' rules. Citing Saint Augustine's *City of God*,[69] the abbess argues that the life of virtue proposed by the rule of Port-Royal and the spiritual combat required to attain such a life must be interpreted in terms of the conflict between two contradictory loves that divides every nun as well as every society. "Saint Augustine says that the love of God and cupidity build two completely opposed cities. One is the celestial Jerusalem, that is, charity that goes right up to contempt for ourselves. The other is the earthly Babylon, that is to say, cupidity that enkindles in us a love for ourselves. . . . The liberty we give ourselves to follow our own inclinations is the source of many evils. Only the sword of the fear and love of God can remove this false freedom and destroy it."[70] In this perspective moral progress requires an authentic love of God, verified by the presence of the virtue of charity, and the suppression of the corrosive love of the world, signaled by preoccupation with the self.

This Augustinian emphasis on the fundamental metaphysical conflict between the two cities also reflects the dualistic moral vision of the abbess. Throughout her analysis of the Constitutions and in her other writings, she stresses the need to choose between the divine and the diabolic. The effort of the diplomatic to find a third way in the conflicts roiling the convent is invariably dismissed as a failure to exercise heroic charity.

Sustained by the principles of the Port-Royal constitutions, the earnest nun can make spiritual progress only by substituting authentic love for its counterfeits. The entire spiritual history of the individual can be understood by an accurate analysis of which kind of love predominates in the soul at a given moment. "To renew the heart, one must destroy one love by another. We must always arrive at the principle of Saint Augustine: two loves have built two cities and we are necessarily citizens of one or the other. The love of God right up to contempt of ourselves constitutes the City of

God and the kingdom of Jesus Christ; the love of ourselves right up to the contempt of God builds Babylon, which is the kingdom of the demon."[71] Following Augustine the abbess develops an anthropology that stresses the primacy of the will. In this voluntaristic approach to human nature the amatory posture of the will is not one moral trait among others; it is the key determinant of the ensemble of virtues and vices possessed by a moral agent fundamentally turned toward God or toward the demonic.

In Augustinian fashion Mère Angélique de Saint-Jean underscores that Christ provides the grace and not only the paradigm for the development of charity, the key to a sanctified moral character. "My sisters, Jesus Christ is not only our model; in order to become a source of grace for us, he annihilated himself. As Saint Paul says, he shed his blood to purify us from our dead works."[72] It is grace rather than human merit that permits the Christian to cultivate authentic charity and to claim citizenship in the kingdom of God. Opposing the humanist insistence on personal endeavor and the Jesuit emphasis on the power of human beings to cooperate freely with God's grace, the abbess identifies God's grace as the sole cause of the charity that characterizes the soul of the redeemed.

This insistence on the primacy of grace does not prevent Mère Angélique de Saint-Jean from defending a certain moral pragmatism in her interpretation of the Constitutions. Suspicious of mysticism, she often argues that the rule-bound activities of the nun should lead to a palpable improvement in her moral character. Her treatment of the activity of reading the Scriptures typifies her emphasis on the priority of practical moral growth over speculative curiosity.

> There is a difference between really receiving the truth as the word of God and simply receiving it as the word of a man sent on God's behalf and who speaks by God's spirit. This latter mode suffices to give us a sense of reverence and attention to what they tell us. But we must receive the truth in the former mode so that it might bring about a change in our heart. This is what makes the real distinction between the word of God and the word of a messenger from God. This is what God points out through his prophet: "My word will not return unfaithful to me; it will produce all the effects for which I sent it."[73]

Although she praises Mère Agnès's phrases in the Constitutions, Mère Angélique de Saint-Jean's insistence on the primacy of moral improvement differentiates her from the more speculative, mystical emphasis of the earlier abbess. It is practical conduct rather than illuminative insight that provides the truest test of God's authentic presence in typical conventual activities, such as daily biblical meditation.

In her treatment of the sacraments, Mère Angélique de Saint-Jean reflects another strain of Augustinian theology: the rigorism of Saint-Cyran. Although Saint Augustine himself provided few indications on the dispositions necessary for the worthy reception of the sacraments, Saint-Cyran used the Augustinian doctrines of concupiscence and election to construct a theology that warned of the dangers of frequent sacramental reception. According to this position, the sinfulness of humanity and the comparatively few members of the elect indicated that many Christians who routinely received sacramental absolution and Holy Communion were courting sacrilege, since they were frequenting the sacraments in a state of grave sin. Saint-Cyran argues that a confession can be made worthily only when the penitent's motive is one of perfect contrition, one of sorrow for having offended God, rather than imperfect contrition, one of fear of punishment for sin. Similarly one can receive Holy Communion worthily only in a state of grace after a thorough confession; an increase in moral virtue should be tangible after each reception of the Eucharist. Going beyond the actual text of the Constitutions, the abbess clearly follows Saint-Cyran in presenting her subjects with a rigorist set of counsels on sacramental practice.

In her treatment of the sacrament of penance, Mère Angélique de Saint-Jean dwells on the long and rigorous process of repentance and self-examination which should precede the sacramental act of confessing one's sins and receiving absolution. The Council of Trent had insisted on the integral confession of one's sins, preceded by a thorough examination of conscience guided by such standard biblical texts as the Decalogue. But the spiritual preparation envisaged by the abbess obeys more severe criteria.

> We should not reduce all of repentance to confession and absolution by the priest. On the contrary, this is where it should end. It is

like a reward and a last kind of assistance given by God to souls who are really touched by his love. Having a great sorrow for their sins and having used all the means they could in satisfaction for their sins, they fear not being able to return to the state of grace with him unless he himself opens this mysterious bath for them and unless he reassures them through the mouth of his ministers and their pardon.[74]

This insistence on a long and detailed period of preparation for the sacrament of confession subtly undercuts the primacy of this sacrament in the spiritual life. The major work of repentance (arousal of sorrow for sins, use of means of penance, reparation for sins) appears to occur independently of the sacramental arena. Only coming at the end of a long penitential process, the sacramental absolution seems to ratify the forgiveness of sin rather than effect it.

Similarly the treatment of the Holy Eucharist clearly discourages frequent reception of Holy Communion. According to the Council of Trent those in a state of mortal sin should abstain from presenting themselves for Communion. But the abbess extends the concept of grave sin to the vaguest and most hidden of spiritual imperfections: "Coldness of heart, the bitter taste one has for holy things, the slight impression that Holy Communion has made in us of the life of Jesus Christ and of charity can very well be as serious a reason to remove ourselves from receiving the Eucharist as are our external faults."[75] Far from constituting transgressions against the Ten Commandments, such sketchy interior faults would appear to bar even the most virtuous Christian from the altar during extended periods of time. Like sacramental confession, eucharistic Communion finds itself decentered in the Christian life of piety.

The *Discourses on the Constitutions* are suffused with the radical Augustinian philosophy defended by Mère Angélique de Saint-Jean as head of the intransigent faction at Port-Royal. On several levels the philosophy of the *Discourses* illustrates the junction between Augustine's theology and moral rigorism which characterized Port-Royal after the ascendancy of Saint-Cyran. The Augustinian concept of the two opposed cities illuminates the personal combat between virtue and vice that tolerates no compromise and disdains human prudence. The misery of concupiscent humanity and its utter dependence on grace for any good work grounds a philosophy of virtue that exalts divine election and abases human merit. To justify periodic abstention from the sacraments, the Augustinian armory of concupiscence, the *massa damnata,* and the irresistibility of grace is deployed to demonstrate the sinfulness of even the most virtuous moral agent. In her legal commentary on Port-Royal's rule, the abbess uses key theological categories of ancient and modern Augustinianism to construct a stark ethical dualism where only a blessed minority understands and embraces a spiritual war opposing the splendor of the heavenly city to the squalor of the demonic earthly one.

Deontology of Resistance

A cycle of abbatial conferences, *Reflections to Prepare the Nuns for Persecution, in Conformity with the "Counsels" Mère Agnès Left on This Matter to the Nuns of This Monastery* is ostensibly a commentary on the *Counsels on the Conduct Which the Nuns Should Maintain in the Event of a Change in the Government of the Convent,* written by Mère Agnès in the environs of 1664. Substantial parts of the conference are verbatim citations of Mère Agnès's earlier work, followed by a gloss of the passage that the assembled nuns had just heard. Mère Angélique de Saint-Jean exalts the authority of Mère Agnès as if she were an inspired author akin to Moses. The *Constitutions* and the *Counsels* assume the aura of Holy Writ. "As God used her [Mère Agnès] to give us his laws and to let us know the path by which we must arrive at the perfection of the religious life to which he has called us, it seems we could say that he wanted to continue to do in these counsels what she had already begun: to teach us just how far patience and religious mortification must go in the events where we will have to practice the poverty we vowed."[76] But in tone and thesis the *Reflections* develop a moral theology markedly different from the diplomatic casuistry practiced by her aunt. Whereas Mère Agnès speaks prudently about alternative strategies in the hypothetical event of persecution, Mère Angélique de Saint-Jean speaks ardently as a living survivor of the exile and interdict of the 1660s and as an anxious witness to the new persecutory campaign against Port-Royal. Her *Reflections* uses an apocalyptic rhetoric and a moral argument against compromise to address a community where persecution had become a normal state of affairs.

An early passage of the *Reflections* artfully describes the reality of a convent that had become synonymous with the experience of persecution.

> For my part I do not see why someone would say that it is dangerous to commit oneself to be a nun in a convent like this, which is so often exposed to persecution and affliction. I would rather say that it would be better to complain that this is an odd view of religious commitment, since it does not clearly understand that in giving ourselves to God, we were supposed to leave ourselves and abandon ourselves to follow him everywhere he leads us. If someone says that given our weakness we will possibly lack the strength to resist persecution, how would we have enough strength to pray or to have a single good thought?[77]

Mère Agnès's prudent counsels, alternating submission with refusal, could not survive intact in the atmosphere of religious warfare that had engulfed Mère Angélique de Saint-Jean's community. As the passage indicates, this is a persecution that the abbess of Port-Royal accepts with relish and a resistance she directs with martial determination.

The *Reflections* makes three notable philosophical contributions. First, it redefines the theological virtues of faith and hope so that they constitute a global spiritual vision of events rather than a more narrow assent to religious truths or confidence in divine promises. Second, it develops a philosophy of resistance to oppression, with particular attention to the spiritual resources necessary for minorities to maintain this resistance. Finally, it provides a new framework for the apophatic theology of Port-Royal by exploring how the suffering of persecution makes the distance of the hidden God even more acute in personal experience and in theory.

In developing its philosophy of resistance, the *Reflections* recasts the virtues of faith, hope, and charity. Its treatment of the theological virtues is shaped by the context of combat against perceived oppression. Faith involves a tenacious assent to God's providence in the midst of an apparently apostate world, and hope invokes providence in the solitude of an apparently successful persecution.

The *Reflections* also recasts theological vice. It is fear rather than pride that now constitutes the principal obstacle to the fidelity of the minority defending religious truth. Cowardice emerges as the fatal opponent of a faith that must manifest itself as theological courage.

To grasp the *Reflections'* reinterpretation of the theological virtues, it is important to recognize the primacy accorded the theological virtues by Mère Angélique de Saint-Jean's moral philosophy. Like other neo-Augustinians, the nun denies that the natural moral virtues, such as justice and temperance, possess any intrinsic worth. Divorced from grace such apparent virtues are only masks of the vice of pride.

> All virtues, no matter how great they seem, are worthless if they are separated from charity, which makes us practice them out of a spirit of piety and in view of God alone. The least things done out of this spirit become great before God and the greatest become less than nothing if they are not so motivated. We see this in the pagans, where we sometimes see quite great qualities that have made them practice the most basic virtues, but this effort is worthless for them. Because they did not know God, everything they did was only done out of vanity; it vanished like smoke.[78]

This dismissal of the alleged virtue of the pagan reflects the anti-humanist polemic of Port-Royal. Authentic moral virtue can arise only from the theological virtues, preeminently charity, lodged in the soul of the moral agent redeemed by grace. This passage also indicates that the criterion of moral value resides neither in the act itself nor in its effects, but in the posture of the will of the moral agent.

In the midst of persecution faith permits the believer to maintain her confidence in God's mercy. The virtue sustains the suppliant against the temptation to despair. "It is faith that supports us in our afflictions and we can lean only on faith for the hope of our salvation. It obliges us to believe always in the mercy of God and to have recourse to this mercy in all our difficulties."[79] More than an assent to revealed truths about God, faith emerges as an adherence to the providential mercy of God at the center of salvation.

Faith illuminates the mind of the believer, permitting her to interpret the events of everyday life, especially those involving persecution. Opposing the impressions of common sense, faith reveals the positive ascetical meaning of apparent failure. "The grand merit of faith consists in not judging things according to the senses and in recognizing that goods are often hidden in evils and that tears are the sources of joy and consolation for people who love God and who are saddened for having offended him and having brought down his anger upon them. They rejoice to find in their suffering something to satisfy God's justice."[80] A heuristic tool, faith guides the believer in decoding the theological drama of salvation and atonement hidden in the external phenomena of oppression and reversal.

With clear Neoplatonic and neo-Augustinian echoes, the *Reflections* often opposes the virtue of faith to the senses. The knowledge of God and of the world's spiritual war gained through the illumination of faith contradicts the evidence of the senses. Just as the believer perceives the body and blood of Christ beneath the eucharistic veil of bread and wine, she must penetrate the spiritual realities hidden beneath the surface drama of conflict and persecution. "We are everywhere in our senses; if we are not careful, we follow their judgment rather than that of faith. . . . Our faith should penetrate all the veils that seem to fall in front of our eyes."[81] While the senses disclose the world as a material reality where the just perish, faith unveils it as a spiritual reality where a just minority manifests the grace of its election through virtuous suffering.

As it counters the senses, faith also contests the passions. The passions are treated with suspicion since they frequently exhibit a force rooted in concupiscent self-love. "Faith lifts us up and makes us masters of all our passions, while love for ourselves makes us slaves of an infinity of masters, under whose domination we lose, if we are not careful, the true freedom of the children of God."[82] The freedom wrought by faith is not free will, present in the actions of both the virtuous and the vicious; it is the freedom from domination by the passions that characterizes the virtuous moral agent in her habitual adherence to the good. Not a fruit of personal effort, this moral freedom is the offspring of faith rooted in grace.

Not only does faith oppose the senses and passions; it opposes a certain type of human reason that judges events by the light of prudence alone. Grounded in the folly of the cross, the Christian faith evaluates events in a manner opposed to the world's reason. This theological logic permits the believer to grasp the reasons behind such apparently irrational irruptions of violence as persecution.

> There is still one thing necessary to make our suffering perfect: to arm ourselves against the reasoning of the human mind opposed to the principles of faith, which teaches us to find glory in disdain, riches in poverty, life in death. It makes us judge things according to the truth and discover how according to the Prophets it must put an end to our evils, so that we will not let ourselves be beaten by what seems to be harshest to our senses and capable of making us afraid and horrified. Nothing seemed as odious as the death of Jesus Christ. Still, we have been redeemed by it. It will be by the same means, that is, by crosses, persecutions, and afflictions that our salvation will be achieved.[83]

In this perspective faith provides a global vision that interprets personal and social events in the light of the cross. The world's calculus of gain and loss is overturned by a vision of history that perceives salvation as the supreme good and which recognizes persecution for the truth as one of the prominent signs and means of this salvation. Just as it contradicts the evidence of the senses, the light of faith inaugurates a science of the cross that contradicts the most self-evident tenets of worldly creeds that conceive history in terms of personal success and social esteem.

Like faith the virtue of hope is reconfigured in the context of persecution. Still oriented toward the future, hope is no longer limited to its technical theological object, the enjoyment of the beatific vision of God in eternity; it is the confidence that God will protect and console the believer in the midst of oppression.

> Faith inspires a hope so firm in God's goodness that it not only leads us to believe that we will be happy in the future, if we remain faithful to its demands; it even convinces us that we are happy right at the present moment, when we feel that we lack everything and that there no longer remains any support and consolation from

human beings. It is then that we find everything in God, if we are not lacking faith. Hope then supports our soul like an unshakable anchor through all the tempests that temptation or persecution can arouse against us.[84]

If hope remains the believer's confidence in a future beatitude prepared by God, it acquires a new urgency and terrestrial application in the maelstrom of persecution.

Similarly charity is recast in the rhetoric of persecution and resistance. The virtue of charity is defined as the capacity to undergo martyrdom for the sake of the truth. "It is not excessive to ask Christians to say that if they do not have the occasion to suffer death for the sake of Jesus Christ, they should at least be disposed to do so. Charity must be strong enough in their hearts to maintain them in this disposition. It is necessary that in rest and peace, as well as in persecution, God sees that they seek only his glory, that they only work for his service, and that they are always ready to sacrifice everything out of love for him."[85] Like faith and hope, charity is reconstructed as a martial virtue, apt to arm the nun in enduring a persecution that has become the daily order of her convent. The supernatural love of God and neighbor emerges as a militant attachment to the truth of Christ's Gospel. This steely fidelity is inscribed within a broader ethics of martyrdom.

Like the virtues, the vices are refashioned in the framework of continual persecution. Although Mère Angélique de Saint-Jean occasionally condemns pride as the major vice,[86] it is fear that is named most frequently as the principal vice in the Christian life. While a certain fear of the Lord is salutary, the fear of possible future harm can easily paralyze the moral agent. "There are people who fear evils so strongly that just their fear of them knocks them down before the evils arrive. This fear greatly increases these evils, while we could say that the present evils are minor when considered in and of themselves. . . . Fear is the greatest of all evils because it has no limits. Present evils, on the other hand, are always limited and cannot harm us as much as can our apprehension about those that perhaps will never occur."[87] In a Christian life dominated by combat against omnipresent enemies devoted to one's destruction, fear can destroy the entire ensemble of virtues necessary to resist oppression. Rather than the natural virtue of courage, however, the antidote to fear is hope, the theological virtue planted by Christ's grace to strengthen the believer.

Several passages explicitly assimilate the vice of fear to cowardice. From the perspective of faith, persecution should occasion militant fidelity rather than flight. "When God permits us to be threatened with suffering, just as we are at present, we should not consider these types of burdens in a low and cowardly manner that would cause us fright and anxiety. On the contrary, we must gaze with admiration at the conduct of God toward us, waiting for everything that it pleases him to permit to occur to us."[88] Just as hope properly positions us before a future clouded by persecution, the fear of the coward creates a false future based on collapse in the face of opposition. In an ethics of spiritual combat, the preeminent vice is a fear that places material survival and popular approval before witness to the truth. In the presence of such a corrosive vice, the very possibility of martyrdom has disappeared.

The environment of persecution also shapes the philosophy of action advanced by the *Reflections*. Although the conferences cite the earlier cautious counsels of Mère Agnès, it proposes an ethics of militant resistance to all compromise with the opponents of Port-Royal. The morally astute nun is to refuse cooperation with civil and ecclesiastical authorities whose ultimate goal is the nun's submission to the iniquitous condemnation of Jansen. To pursue this conscientious objection against the unjust demands of a determined throne and episcopate, natural courage is of no avail. This posture of resistance must draw its moral resources from a spirituality of abandonment that can find union with God outside the usual ecclesiastical channels of sacramental mediation.

The uncompromising nature of the ethics of resistance proposed by the *Reflections* appears in numerous passages where Mère Angélique de Saint-Jean alters the directives of Mère Agnès she has just read to the assembled nuns. Repeatedly, the abbess removes the nuances of her aunt's counsels in favor of a simple, unreserved strategy of refusal. When Mère Agnès advises the nuns to refrain from all complaints, Mère Angélique de Saint-Jean admits that "I am very surprised by this opinion."[89] She explains that this counsel against complaining makes sense in a situation where one is surrounded by people who are sympathetic with one's plight. But since "we rarely have the occasion to make complaints in such a situation," complaints against injustice are more than understandable.[90]

On the neuralgic question of obedience to foreign superiors, Mère Agnès had advised a certain suppleness; the nuns should especially try to obey a superior who is governing her own convent in the manner proper to the rule of her order. No such accommodation survives in Mère Angélique de Saint-Jean's gloss. The abbess insists that the nuns should obey only when the superiors "only ask what conforms to what God obliges us to do."[91] Any command deviating from the rule the Port-Royal nuns have promised to follow must be stoutly resisted. The conscientious nun must decide "whether we are going to obey God or a creature."[92]

Where Mère Agnès had permitted a limited relationship with external priests for the purpose of sacramental confession, Mère Angélique de Saint-Jean condemns any conversation with foreign clerics. For an ostracized person in search of consolation, even the most anodyne conversation can lead to a manipulation of conscience. "It is a grave mistake to desire to seek some consolation in foreign spiritual directors on the pretext of only taking from their conversations what would be helpful for our support. That would be a way to lose ourselves to those who seek perhaps only one such occasion to insinuate themselves into our minds and spread their poison, disguised by an appearance of good will for our service."[93] The prudential code of material cooperation devised by Mère Agnès is transformed into a code of militant resistance by her niece.

The code of conscientious objection defended by the abbess reflects her intransigent position on collaboration with anti-Jansenist authorities since the first crisis of the signature in 1661. But it also reflects her personal experience of vacillation during her exile in the Annonciade convent in 1664–65. In an autobiographical passage she explains the skill of the psychological warfare waged by Port-Royal's persecutors. The willingness to engage in dialogue with others, accompanied by the inability to rely on God alone for guidance, easily leads to surrender motivated by fear.

> We are speaking by experience. . . . People who find themselves removed from all occupations can become too preoccupied by

considering only the faults and imperfections of their past life,
without addressing themselves to Jesus Christ, who can through
his grace provide them with a remedy for their affliction. They permit themselves to be overwhelmed by this view of things, which
beats them down into mistrust and convinces them that they do
not have enough proof that God was in them to persevere in the
state to which he himself had called them. So they wanted to seek
counsel and light elsewhere and consulted other persons instead of
those whom God had removed in order to be replaced by God himself in all things. This dangerous temptation can break down some
souls, when they let themselves go this way.[94]

This astute study of the psychological means by which the victim
can turn herself into the transgressor indicates how easily spiritual
practices can become tools to erode conscientious convictions. Virtues such as humility, patience, charity, and compunction for sin
can easily serve manipulation and mask a carefully cultivated cowardice. In Port-Royal's context of persecution, steadfast resistance
must govern the soul. Silence and speech become decisive arms in
the drama of submission and refusal.

To sustain the posture of uncompromising resistance, the nun
must draw on certain spiritual resources. The phenomenon of persecution should be interpreted as a call to martyrdom. The steadfast
virtues of the martyrs will unveil to the besieged nun the reasons for
the world's hatred of religious truth, the strategies for proper endurance, and the award awaiting the persecuted. "When we celebrate
the feasts of the Martyrs, we must let their example stir us up to
make a new effort to witness our loyalty to Jesus Christ, because we
are not less accountable than they were. Saint Paul desires that if we
have already suffered something, we should forget the past and endure courageously everything we have to suffer again, remembering
the palm and the victory that are promised."[95] While the world dismisses the persecuted as failures, the church's narrative of martyrdom discloses both the theological purpose of persecution and graced
emblems of resistance to oppression by the enemies of truth.

Allied to the theology of martyrdom is a spirituality of solitary
communion with God. The most obvious effects of interdict and excommunication, the deprivation of the Eucharist and sacramental

confession, would appear to destroy the spiritual life in as deeply sacramental a religion as Catholicism. The devastation wrought in a Counter-Reformation convent whose central devotion is perpetual adoration of the Blessed Sacrament is even more palpable. A major part of Mère Angélique de Saint-Jean's directives on strategies of resistance to persecution is to guide the nuns in accepting sacramental deprivation and in developing a more solitary, interior piety that will actually draw them closer to the God no longer communicated to them under sacramental signs.

Rather than constituting a cause for panic, the deprivation of the sacraments should serve as an opportunity for the oppressed nuns to discover more deeply the immediate presence of God to the soul. Since the nuns have been barred from the sacraments through no fault of their own, they should interpret this ban as an evil tolerated by God out of love for his faithful witnesses. Rather than distancing them from God, the censure should initiate them into a deeper, more immediate union with God through suffering and abandonment.

> We must not consider as losses what God has removed by his order.
> If we submit to this, we will find in the obedience we offer his will
> as much assistance as we appear to lose. Similarly we can say that
> God in his goodness has put us in a place where we must serve him
> and that he has given us numerous means to do so which we would
> not have encountered otherwise. . . . We must believe that the
> heavenly fire that descended apparently to steal certain goods will
> only change this assistance into something more spiritual. This
> will teach us to belong to God in a more perfect manner through
> suffering and privation rather than through peace and abundance.[96]

Instead of placing a further screen between the believer and God, the legal sanctions used by the opponents of Port-Royal have introduced the nuns to a more intimate union with Christ crucified in suffering and opprobrium.

In this new asacramental experience of God, the mediating role of the priest is fulfilled by Christ himself. Rather than provoking discouragement, the deprivation of sacramental confession and spiritual direction should intensify the nun's spiritual relationship with

Christ the high priest. "Instead of addressing ourselves to an earthly doctor who will only empoison our sores, let us go to the omnipotent doctor, revealing our wounds to him, exposing our soul to his grace. We know that he is the sovereign priest. Let us be satisfied with the advice he will give us."[97] Similarly, the deprivation of the Eucharist frees the nuns to discover God present in the interior tabernacle of her soul. The sacramental presence of Christ under the appearances of bread and wine now yields to a more internal presence of Christ that has dispensed with external mediation. "He [Christ] makes a tent in which he hides the presence of his grace, not in order to take it away from us entirely, but to humble us. Let us adore him under this tent, as we did under the species of the Blessed Sacrament."[98] Instead of declining, the prayer of adoration, which is the highest form of communion with God, is intensified by the capacity to discern and reverence Christ's presence in a purely spiritual, internal tabernacle that no external decree can abolish.

Despite her pleas to discover God more intimately through the new spiritual isolation caused by persecution, Mère Angélique de Saint-Jean recognizes that the prolonged oppression endured by the convent has made the hidden God seem even more distant. In the *Reflections* the incomprehensible nature of God is no longer a simple theological tenet or an insight acquired through contemplation; the experience of persecution has further obscured the essence of an already inscrutable deity. "Let us remember that he is a hidden God and that he is only hiding to give greater merit to our faith, which must seek and find him under the shadows of the imperfection of our neighbor."[99] As persecution turns the theological virtues into a set of martial postures, it transforms the perpetual alterity of God into the painful silence of a benevolent deity before the suffering of his innocent witnesses. Port-Royal's apophatic portrait of God is now embedded within the anguish of Job.

Epistemology of Doubt

Among the opuscules devoted to an ethics of resistance, *On the Danger of Hesitation and Doubt Once We Know Our Duty* possesses unusual philosophical interest. As in similar works Mère Angélique de Saint-Jean exhorts the nuns to remain firm in persecution and to refuse all compromise. But *On the Danger* explores the epistemology of resistance. The essay examines how the exercise of doubt can in certain situations pose a moral danger to the one engaged in it, because the exercise can destroy the resolve to resist oppression, which is clearly one's moral duty. Rather than being a disinterested exercise, doubt always arises in a relationship of power where oppressive majorities encourage an atmosphere of skepticism to corrode and eventually destroy the convictions of ostracized minorities. The oppressor often forces the persecuted minority to conduct its self-doubt in an uneven debate whose terms are determined by the more powerful party. In the context of the Port-Royal crisis, the conjugated powers of church and state insist on conducting the controversy on the grounds of loyalty and obedience, while the nuns' case for resistance makes sense only in the context of truth and faith. The exercise of doubt also opens the besieged minority to manipulation by an appeal to personal interests that are irrelevant to the truth-claims under discussion; the human desire for survival, esteem, and freedom is easily used by the oppressor to pressure the recalcitrant to retract their judgments at the conclusion of a period of doubt and hesitation.

At the center of *On the Danger*'s argument lies the thesis that persecution for the sake of truth is the normal, indeed graced, situation of the authentic disciple of Christ. Rather than being considered a cause for flight, the oppression of Port-Royal should be embraced as a mission given by God. "The servants of God know that they could never be in a greater state of assurance than when they have to suffer. When their enemies hold them in captivity, they find themselves in a greater liberty, being less in danger when they are in the greatest of dangers."[100] Since persecution for the sake of the Gospel, in this case for the sake of the truth concerning Christ's grace, represents the highest type of sanctity, it is a state that should be embraced with fervor rather than shunned.

This state of persecution is accompanied by an epistemological note of certitude. Citing Saint Bernard of Clairvaux, cofounder of the Cistercians, Mère Angélique de Saint-Jean insists that it is wrong to engage in any hesitation once a Christian knows her moral duty to resist evil. Furthermore, the decades-long theological dispute over the signature, the actual experience of persecution, and the personal spiritual experience of the nuns under interdict indicate that God's will in this matter is known with a high degree of certitude. "We should not hesitate when we are certain about what we should do, because we expose ourselves to lose more than we assuredly have through hesitation. . . . We ardently and confidently approve what we know with certitude that God approves."[101] To maintain the proper posture of resistance, the nun must conserve the certitude that her position on the quarrel of grace is correct and the certitude that God has called her to witness this truth by firm opposition to those who would deny or dilute the grace of Christ.

To destroy the certitude at the mental core of resistance, the enemies of Port-Royal attempt to provoke an attitude of doubt on the part of the recalcitrant nuns. One method used to arouse skepticism is to appeal to the value of compromise in resolving conflicts. Although emotionally attractive, such a plea for compromise already weakens the determination of the resister, since it suggests that something in the resister's position can be bargained away. "Perhaps it is a fault to want to leave this blessed state [of persecution] in order to enter into new deliberations over possible accommodations, which are always very dangerous to those who have right on their side. We can even endorse the proposition . . . that doing so would indicate that we have something to concede to our enemies."[102] The very willingness to engage in negotiations and to entertain the possibility of concessions is to treat one's previous position of refusal with an obvious skepticism. To conserve the certitude of one's God-given duty to refuse illegitimate commands to assent to a falsehood, the nun must dismiss any appeal to negotiation and compromise.

On the Danger analyzes at length the moral dangers posed by an invitation to dialogue that by its nature would tend to destroy the certitude of the resistant Augustinian and insinuate a corrosive doubt through the use of clever rhetoric. One of the essay's most telling arguments is that the proffered dialogue will never occur in terms of equality. Dominated by worldly ecclesiastics and politicians, the dialogue will inevitably force the recalcitrant nuns to reason according to the world's logic of prudence rather than according to the convent's logic of faith.

This [consultations] opens the door to completely human types of reasoning and to thoughts of flesh and blood. Since in these meetings they make a profession to examine everything, it seems that we would be disarming faith itself, which represses all considerations of nature in order to make us ponder only eternal objects. . . . We often speak without thinking through our greatest enemies, the senses, which borrow from reason what they need to plead their cause and which sometimes cover themselves with the most beautiful verbal appearances. They can fool us if we are not careful.[103]

This analysis points out that the moral danger of negotiation lies not only in the power imbalance between the majority and a minority; it also lies in the ability of the majority to frame the debate in terms of its own categories and interests. The language of nature, which privileges such prudential categories as survival, simply eliminates the faith-based categories of the minority, with their appeal to the truths of revelation. When negotiations are conducted in such a fashion, the minority will begin to doubt the veracity of its position; its surrender will inevitably follow.

Not only does the invitation to negotiation mask an unevenly matched conflict between the logic of the world and the logic of faith; it veils an appeal to the material desire for self-preservation. The insinuation of doubt on the propriety of the nuns' refusal to sign the formulary can easily place the desire to maintain the convent's survival over the duty to conserve the convent's devotion to the truth. "Our visible enemies want to ruin our monastery and our invisible enemies only use them and the fear we may have of losing it to ruin our faith. But our faith is worth more than a monastery and our conscience should be preferred to a building that in God's sight would only be our tomb if we ever entered it by wounding our conscience."[104] The doubt nurtured by the offer or actual exercise of negotiation is not morally neutral. It manipulates the basic emotion and vice of fear. Reversing the authentic hierarchy of goods, it privileges material security over spiritual fidelity. Distinctively modern, the passage also underscores that it is the conscience of the nuns, and not only the doctrinal truth concerning Christ's grace, that is being defended by the refusal to compromise.

Despite her critique of prudential arguments for a willingness to reconsider one's theological positions, Mère Angélique de Saint-Jean offers her own prudential arguments on the danger of engaging in a doubt generated by dialogue with the opponents of Port-Royal. In this realistic counsel the abbess warns that the nuns' enemies seek total capitulation to the condemnation of Jansenism; any concession will be only a first step toward final and complete surrender. "Whatever we might concede to them, we should not believe that impassioned enemies, such as the Jesuits, will be satisfied with it. They will only seem to be content at first with the smallest wounds we can inflict on ourselves in order to put us at ease to do greater damage to ourselves."[105] Every persecuted nun must recognize the true stakes involved in this campaign against the convent. Concessions granted by opponents through dialogue, amended phrases, and legal euphemisms are only pragmatic gestures patiently employed to erode the certitude of the resisters. The abbess dryly notes how irenic compromises by the nuns in the past were easily annulled by their persecutors. "Either the king does not find it right or the pope cannot consent to it."[106] The debates devised by the enemies of the convent are not a disinterested search for the truth regarding grace; they are carefully designed to plant a doubt within the nuns that will lead first to concessions and ultimately to the renunciation of their theological convictions.

As an antidote to the danger of doubt provoked by efforts at compromise, Mère Angélique de Saint-Jean counsels an intensified recourse to prayer. Instead of seeking illusory concessions, the persecuted minority should implore God for the grace to stiffen their resistance. "We know very well what God asks of us. Consequently we should have no other thought than to ask him for the grace to be able to do what he asks. Let us use the time we would have used for deliberation in order to pray. We will find a more solid joy in suffering than we would have found in efforts to discover means that would have spared us suffering."[107] The proper response to the ingenious efforts to insinuate doubt into the mind of the resister is a recommitment to the certitude of the duty of refusal, deepened by petitionary prayer to the God who originally commissioned the resister to a painful witness to the truth.

Complementing its philosophical argument on the moral perils posed by the exercise of doubt, *On the Danger* develops a theological argument citing various biblical narratives. The prophet Jeremiah refused to consult with others when he received the dangerous divine commission to condemn the sins of the nation.[108] Jesus Christ himself refused to enter into legalistic debate when he faced accusations on the eve of his death.[109] When the evangelist Saint John was imprisoned, he awaited God's intervention rather than engage others in human deliberation over possible strategies for escape.[110] In a vibrant Old Testament example, the divine anger struck Balaam for his repeated hesitations and efforts at reassurance once his mission clearly had been received from God.[111] Biblical narrative reinforces the duty to resist doubt concerning one's sacred obligations and in fact brands such skeptical hesitation as sinful.

A model of Jansenist rigorism, *On the Danger* insists that the moral duty to defend the truth regarding Christ's grace admits of no compromises. Even the willingness to engage in dialogue that might lead the nun to reconsider her refusal to sign the controversial formulary is condemned as sinful. As critics have long argued, the intransigence of Mère Angélique de Saint-Jean turned persecution into a self-fulfilling prophecy.[112] Many of the most acerbic passages in her essay and similar writings target Jansenist moderates who attempted to craft compromise formulas, established through negotiations with the opponents of Port-Royal, in order to resolve the convent's crisis. Rather than constituting a burden to be overcome through bilateral diplomacy, persecution is conceived by the abbess as a sacred gift to be avidly embraced and even sought after as a sign of divine election. In such an apotheosis of resistance, doubt and hesitation become vices to be suppressed. Dialogue itself acquires a whiff of the diabolic.

Even with its defensive closure of dialogue, *On the Danger* offers an original theory of doubt that transcends its immediate confines in the crisis of the signature. Germaine Grébil has classified the philosophy of the treatise as "Cartesian,"[113] but Mère Angélique de Saint-Jean's philosophy of doubt differs from Descartes's methodic doubt on several grounds. The doubt analyzed in *On the Danger* is not a speculative one, designed to generate metaphysical certitude; it is a practical doubt opposed to moral certitude in a religious matter. This doubt threatens to erode the moral certitude the resister has acquired through her faith (correctly ascribed to God's grace rather than to her own works), her vocation to suffer for truth, and her experience of persecution for that truth as a grace comparable to martyrdom. Rather than being a disinterested exercise to discover unshakable truth, doubt in these circumstances is a prelude to the destruction of the theological convictions that are central to one's faith and vocation. Furthermore, unlike Descartes, Mère Angélique de Saint-Jean carefully attends to the dynamics of power that control any exercise of doubt. To engage in doubt on the sovereign grace of Christ in terms set by the enemies of Port-Royal is not to pursue an open-ended theological debate on a point of doctrine; it is to surrender to a process of dialogue that will manipulate the minority's desire for survival and its inclination to obey religious and political authorities. The issue of doubt can be accurately perceived only when it is analyzed within the framework of the campaign of coercion in which it is embedded. In her analysis of doubt as a reflection of a conflict of powers and a conflict of opposed rationalities, Mère Angélique de Saint-Jean develops a theory of the mechanics of skepticism that differs from the rationalist paradigm of methodic doubt.

Anthropology of Victimhood

Written during Mère Angélique de Saint-Jean's exile in the Annonciade convent, *Reflections on the Conformity of the State of the Nuns of Port-Royal with That of Jesus Christ in the Eucharist* is one of Port-Royal's numerous spiritual treatises focused on the convent's central devotion: eucharistic adoration. Like Mère Agnès's earlier *Private Chaplet of the Blessed Sacrament*, the work analyzes the attributes of Christ present under the sacramental appearances of bread and wine. But the emphasis of *On the Conformity* differs from the contemplative perspective of Mère Agnès's treatise. *On the Conformity* establishes a detailed parallel between the sacrificial mode of existence exhibited by Christ in the immolation of the Eucharist and the sacrificial mode of existence occasioned by the state of persecution into which the Port-Royal nuns have been plunged. By elaborating on the similarity between divine and human natures in the annihilation that both undergo in their respective experiences of sacrifice, the nun shows the mutual identity of the divine and human natures in their status as victim. Rather than underscoring the radical opposition between the divine and the human, as do many other Port-Royal devotional treatises, *On the Conformity* evokes the commonality of their natures in such dark states as abandonment, annihilation, and destruction.

To develop its analogy between the eucharistic Christ and the persecuted nuns, *On the Conformity* adduces twenty-one attributes shared by both divine and human natures in the context of sacrifice. Strikingly, the first two attributes possess an anticlerical tinge. Both Christ and the dissenting nuns undergo sacrificial immolation through the agency of priests: "Jesus Christ in the Eucharist is immolated by priests and pastors; thus, we must accept the fact that it is our own pastors and ministers who sacrifice us."[114] The parallel suggests that the ecclesiastical hierarchy, which ritually sacrifices Christ in the Mass's representation of the drama of Calvary, is now actually sacrificing the recalcitrant nuns through the violence of exile and imprisonment. "Jesus Christ is distributed by their hands where they went and to whom they went; thus, we should not complain that he [Christ] gives them the authority over us to deliver us into the hands of unknown persons as they like and for as long as they like."[115] The victimization here involves the abolition of personal independence on the part of Christ and the persecuted nuns. A passivity imposed by violence becomes a common trait of their sacrificial mode of existence.

Many of the attributes catalogued in the parallels between the eucharistic Christ and the resistant nuns stress the extremity of the alteration of the divine and human natures effected by the cross and persecution. The Oratorian language of annihilation is employed to describe the violent death to self that unites the crucified Christ in the Eucharist with the besieged nun in persecution. "Jesus Christ in this sacrament only gives his life to souls by a species of annihilation of his proper will and the destruction of himself; thus, we should be consoled if we are no longer able to serve the souls he has entrusted to us by external assistance, since by dying to ourselves and suffering from it we can be more helpful to them than we have ever been."[116] One of the arguments raised by the nuns who were *signeuses* during the crisis of the signature and by many moderates who sought a compromise solution was that continuing the apos-

tolic works of Port-Royal (notably the school, publications, lay retreats, and sermons open to the public) trumped any concern for
doctrinal purity in a technical dispute over grace few Catholics
could fathom. As a rejoinder Mère Angélique de Saint-Jean insists
that uncompromising fidelity to the truth of the Gospel remains the
sole and urgent task of the morally upright nun. Only the rhetoric
of annihilation (anéantissement) can describe the total holocaust of
self that is the normal state of the disciple given to the sacrifice of
the cross.

Communal as well as individual, the sacrifice demanded of the
nuns entails the final destruction of the convent. Already in the
early conflicts of the 1660s Mère Angélique de Saint-Jean recognizes
that the conflict between the Port-Royal nuns and their opponents
over the nature of grace will lead to the destruction of the convent.
"The sacrifice [of the Eucharist] must cease before the last day. It is
proper that a convent that is completely consecrated to honoring
the Eucharist will be destroyed when he [Christ] desires it, because
it honors the Eucharist more worthily by destruction than it would
have done by survival. Sacrifice is worth more than simple adoration."[117] Instead of honoring the Blessed Sacrament by contemplative adoration, Port-Royal has now been called to participate viscer-
ally in the sacrifice at the heart of the Eucharist. Rather than to be
shunned, the destruction of the entire community of Port-Royal
under the blows of persecution is, like the death of Christ on the
cross, the logical consummation of a religious commitment that
prizes fidelity to the truth over self-preservation.

Another favored category of the spirituality of the école française, abandonment also characterizes the experience of sacrifice
undergone by Christ and the persecuted nuns. The apparent victory
of evil over good, accompanied by the ominous silence of God as the
innocent are destroyed, causes a sentiment of abandonment marked
by consternation as well as by a deeper confidence in God's hidden
providence. "Jesus Christ appears abandoned by his Father who does
not avenge the injuries he suffers. It should be our consolation that
we are treated like his Son and that by withdrawing the visible pro-
tection he had us feel in other circumstances, he gives us reason to
hope that we will receive much greater favors, which are the price of
sufferings we endure for his love."[118] What is most lacerating in the
experiences of the cross and of persecution is the palpable absence

of a God who is both omnipotent and just. Although the steely silence of God can lead the suffering innocent to a more spiritual hope, this silence during the annihilation of the just remains the darkest wound of the victimhood endured by Christ and the persecuted nuns.

Complementing the sentiment of abandonment is the experience of exile or dispossession undergone by both the Christ and the ostracized nuns. Christ is the warrior-king who advances in combat under the shelter of mobile tents; the persecuted Christian moves from one temporary shelter to another under the blows of incessant spiritual warfare.[119] As the eucharistic Christ is suspended above the altar in a dangling tabernacle, the censured nuns are exposed to the mockery of a society that contemns their intransigence.[120] The eucharistic Christ appears only in the sheltered confines of the sanctuary; the persecuted nuns must learn to draw support only from the invisible assistance of God.[121] The destruction of self caused by the violence of the cross and persecution necessitates an exile from one's previous history and social bonds. As the eucharistic Christ remains the lonely prisoner of the tabernacle in the isolated church sanctuary, the imprisoned nun finds herself alienated from the social sources of support and esteem that had once sustained her.

Several parallels between Christ and the Port-Royal nuns underscore the invisibility of those who undergo this violent consummation out of fidelity to God. It is only faith, not the senses, that can perceive the salvific nature of the sacrifice endured by persecuted innocents. "Jesus Christ is invisible and without any action of the senses; similarly we have become invisible to those who know us and have practically disappeared from human eyes. We are like the dead whom no one can approach."[122] The annihilation endured by Christ and his saints not only removes them from society; it renders them symbolically dead to those who once praised and embraced them. With its Neoplatonic echo this passage insists that the victimhood endured by Christ and his persecuted disciples is inaccessible to the external senses and the passions. It is a spiritual reality; only faith, centered on the mystery of the cross, can discern the nature and the grace of the suffering undergone by the innocent for the sake of truth.

On the Conformity also specifies the cause of the persecution unleashed against Port-Royal. It is their fidelity to Saint Augustine's doctrine of grace that has provoked the violent opposition of their tormentors in church and state. "Jesus Christ is offered [in the Eucharist] for everyone and in place of everyone. We are similar to him on this point, because in these circumstances we are victims who have been chosen to be immolated in the Passion by those who want to destroy all the disciples of Saint Augustine, over whom God has still not given them power."[123] The victimhood that envelops the persecuted nuns flows from an abuse of power by political and religious figures who have exceeded their authority in an attempt to destroy a religious movement falsely tarred with charges of heresy. The irony of this particular persecution is that the doctrine defended by the victimized group, namely the doctrine of Christ's grace as definitively interpreted by Saint Augustine, represents the soul of the Gospel that Catholic bishops and France's Most Christian King have sworn to uphold. As the Eucharist manifests the sacrifice of Christ on the cross to save sinful humanity, the persecuted nuns reveal in their trials the truth concerning the grace of the cross.

In its litany of correspondences between the crucified Christ and the persecuted convent, *On the Conformity* develops a philosophy of divine attributes and a philosophy of human nature based on the common category of victimhood. In his paschal mystery, made present through the celebration of the Eucharist, the divine person of Christ provides a portrait of God different from that proposed by traditional philosophical theology with its concept of an impassive, purely active God characterized by infinity, omnipotence, and satiety. Mère Angélique de Saint-Jean details a different set of attributes. Instead of omnipotence, Christ subjects himself to the ministrations of the priesthood. Instead of infinity, Christ is localized, even broken and imprisoned, in very specific places in the sanctuary. Instead of serene exemption from suffering, Christ experiences abandonment at the hands of God the Father as well as of humanity. The obedience, limitation, and abandonment manifest by Christ in the Passion not only indicate certain traits of his human nature; they evoke the suffering love at the center of the divine nature itself. Rather than celebrating divine impassivity, *On the Conformity* evokes more conflictual attributes of God gleaned from a focus on the atonement of Christ crucified. It is the sacrificial vic-timhood of Christ rather than the creation of the world that be-comes the privileged locus to explore the identity of God in terms of salient attributes.

Similarly, *On the Conformity* sketches a philosophical anthro-pology based on the fundamental datum of the sacrifice present in the persecution of Port-Royal. The basic identity of the Christian, indeed of the human person, is not to be found in the exercise of speculative intellect or in the cultivation of natural moral virtues such as prudence. It is martyrdom that reveals the sanctified human person to herself. It is in the experience of persecution that the human person begins to awaken to the cost of truth, the need of repentance, the logic of atonement, and the sacrificial price of au-thentic charity. Only victimhood can introduce the believer into the sacrificial heart of the Gospel, which is too often glimpsed from the exterior. Like the divine nature, human nature reveals its su-preme attributes, such as the capacity for self-donatory love, only from the interior of sacrificial victimhood. It is costly witness to the truth under violent duress, and not the serene capacity to think and choose, which reveals the highest attributes of humanity. It is mar-tyrdom alone that permits redeemed human nature to declare its noblest identity.

Despite the vividness of its presentation of divine and human attributes, *On the Conformity* never abandons the apophatic theol-ogy and anthropology that characterize Port-Royal. The divine es-sence revealed by the suffering of Christ on the cross can be known only by an intuition that eludes the senses and the passions. Al-though certain, the knowledge of God through faith transcends the limits of natural reason and of syllogistic demonstration. The di-vine nature disclosed by the cross is a nature on the verge of anni-hilation. Paradoxically, the divine essence shown forth in Christ's Passion appears antidivine: confined in space and time, oppressed, anguished. Only negative theology can evoke a divine essence so different from the standard metaphysical portrait of God. Similarly, the human essence revealed under the weight of persecution is a nature that flees and dissolves as it approaches its consummation in martyrdom. The categories of faculties and moral virtues can no longer describe it. Only the rhetoric of annihilation, abandonment, and destruction can evoke a human self destined to complete and violent dissolution. If the category of victimhood permits Mère Angélique de Saint-Jean to evoke common divine and human attributes, these remain the traits of a divine and a human essence that remain irreducibly opaque.

CONCLUSION

In the writings of Mère Angélique de Saint-Jean, the Augustinian philosophy of Port-Royal has become the doctrine of a party. The teaching of Jansen on concupiscence and the counsels of Saint-Cyran on access to the sacraments have acquired a clipped, rule-like quality. As the abbess guides a doomed convent into its obscure future, no ambiguity can be conceded to the actors in the convent's drama. The slightest compromise is promptly tagged as treason to the cause of truth.

In this sectarian environment, the philosophical resources of Port-Royal's complex Augustinian tradition have become pieces of intellectual armament. Augustine's dualistic metaphysics of the two opposed cities decodes the conflict between the convent's allies and critics as a stark struggle between God's servants and their enemies. Apparently apolitical virtues, such as monastic silence, are recast as weapons of resistance to the oppressor. In this framework of an apocalyptic battle between light and darkness, nuance disappears. One searches in vain for an echo of Mère Angélique Arnauld warning fellow members of the Jansenist circle that their vitriolic rhetoric is contradicting the very defense of charity they are trying to make. In the hands of her niece, Mère Agnès's moral casuistry, with its careful line-drawing between tolerable and intolerable material cooperation, is transmuted into a warning on collaboration with opponents who are literally agents of the devil. Even the simple act of doubt bears the mark of possible betrayal. Despite its originality, Mère Angélique de Saint-Jean's philosophical argument remains subordinated to the defense of a narrow set of doctrinal theses that have become routine at Port-Royal.

Another weakness tied to the sectarian cast of Mère Angélique de Saint-Jean's philosophy is the ethics of resistance it stoutly defends. Not only does the abbess explore the rules of action and the moral attitudes that should characterize the nun under duress; she repeatedly glorifies the state of the persecuted as an end in itself. When she sketches her anthropology of victimhood, the status of being persecuted unto death becomes a moral ideal. If in theory martyrdom is a grace granted by God in his obscure providence, in practice it is also a badge of honor to be relished by the faithful as a sign of divine favor and of moral superiority. Even apparently placid virtues, such as humility, are redefined to become dispositions of militant contestation. In this Corneillian ethics of combat, moral greatness can be founded only in the uncompromising refusal of a persecuted minority to grant the least concession to its opponents. Although the abbess often develops a plausible indictment of the abuses of power exercised by the convent's opponents, her ethics of resistance serves as a moral glorification of her community and its controversial theories. Self-exaltation is never far from the dualistic narrative of persecution and vicitimhood which frames her moral analysis.

Despite their polemical narrowness, the works of Mère Angélique de Saint-Jean provide a major contribution to the philosophical canon of Port-Royal. The scholarly quality of the abbess's argumentation merits consideration. Whereas other nuns at Port-Royal insisted on their adherence to an Augustinian philosophical tradition, their knowledge of the major works in this tradition is often spotty. Mère Angélique de Saint-Jean's knowledge, on the other hand, is impressively detailed. Her discussion of Augustine's theories shows firsthand knowledge of specific passages in *The City of God* and other works. Her grasp of the Augustinian monastic theology of Saint Bernard of Clairvaux is even more extensive. Her arguments on Jansen's theory of predestination or Arnauld's distinction between *droit* and *fait* invariably bear a precision that distinguishes them from the vaguer theological discussions of other prominent nuns.

The philosophical acumen of the abbess is not limited to her patristic erudition. She carefully demonstrates her positions by a logical presentation of justificatory reasons. The necessity of cultivating the monastic virtues in the Rule of Saint Benedict is justified by specific traits of the contemplative nun's vocation. The stiff counsels against collaboration with the opponents of Port-Royal are grounded on a thorough consideration of the probable consequences of such collaboration. Not without reason did contemporary critics dismiss her as too *raisonneuse,* too apt to justify every controversial position with a lawyerly armory of ecclesiastical precedents and logical arguments. But this tendency to provide detailed proof for her positions, especially her efforts to reduce contingent questions of moral action to matters of logical necessity, is precisely one of the traits that indicates the philosophical and not only the literary merit of her extensive corpus.

The philosophical pertinence of Mère Angélique de Saint-Jean's work also appears in her efforts to ground the moral concerns of the convent in broader categories of speculative philosophy. Her treatment of monastic virtues, for example, ties such virtues as silence and obedience to the anthropological issue of the contradictions of the human will. Her analysis of the asceticism proper to Port-Royal roots the moral struggles of the nuns in the larger metaphysical conflict of two kinds of love. Her strictures on cooperation with the enemy rest on an anthropology where the human person undergoes a victimhood analogous to that borne by the crucified Christ. While hundreds of Port-Royal tracts exhort to virtue, few make such an extensive effort to explain how particular moral actions or habits necessarily flow from specific facts of human nature.

Mère Angélique de Saint-Jean also makes a signal contribution to epistemology, especially in her treatise *On the Danger of Hesitation and Doubt.* In a period when Descartes's methodic doubt had acquired general philosophical prestige, even among certain partisans of Port-Royal, the abbess develops a different approach. Rather than being a neutral instrument for the acquisition of certain knowledge, doubt emerges as an intellectual exercise embedded in a network of power. It is not necessarily evidence that persuades the doubting agent to alter her opinions; force, threats, insinuation, promises, rhetorical skill, and emotional appeals can prove far more persuasive. The abbess's admonition to her subjects on the danger of doubt is obviously occasioned by the perceived danger of abandoning the convent's principles through an insidious campaign of persuasion by imposed preachers and confessors. But in its broader argument on the role of power and passions in the inauguration and conduct of doubt, the abbess's epistemology of doubt anticipates contemporary explorations on the often occult relationship between power and knowledge.

The same modernity marks another contribution of Mère Angélique de Saint-Jean's philosophy: her ethics of resistance to abuses of power by civil and ecclesiastical authorities. The problem of the proper ethical response to tyranny is an ancient one, but the abbess gives it a distinctively modern turn by insisting that there are matters so personal and interior that external authorities have no right to invade the privacy of subjects who are not otherwise engaged in the public disruption of order. Although the abbess's intransigent position through the various crises of the signature should not be too quickly assimilated to the classical liberal defense of the rights of conscience, since it is the erroneous judgment of throne and altar that justifies the resistance, her philosophy of resistance clearly limits the authority of the state to interfere with the private religious judgments of individuals.

Not only does the abbess provide a justification for the long resistance of the nuns to persecutory authorities; she develops a code of civil and ecclesiastical disobedience to express and discipline this resistance. Especially striking is the varied use of the contemplative arm of silence to avoid an erosion of conviction caused by correspondence with families, entreaties by friends in the convent parlor, or hostile spiritual advice offered by priests in the pulpit or confessional. A spirituality of asacramental communion with God provides the spiritual resources necessary for such a solitary civil disobedience to endure.

Possibly the greatest philosophical contribution made by Mère Angélique de Saint-Jean is the most elusive. It is the diffuse nihilism that marks her ethical and metaphysical reflection. Like her aunts, she defends an apophatic account of God's attributes clearly indebted to the tutelage of Bérulle and Saint-Cyran. But the use of negation and the argument that rational reflection must ultimately yield to the recognition of opaque mystery is not limited to philosophical theology. A proper understanding of human nature, illuminated by the mystery of the cross, leads to the annihilation of the human essence; the faculties, concepts, and passions of the human person fade before the impenetrability of his or her own nature in the act of self-immolation. Political philosophy no longer consists in the analysis of the quantifiable institutions of the state; it resides in the lacerating question of why the state and its allies in the church engage in such inexplicable acts of persecution. History is no longer the serene unfolding of the economy of salvation or of secular progress; it has become an enigma, a jagged drama of omens and crises that bear the obscure mark of the demonic.

This nihilistic theology, anthropology, and history reflect both the psychology of the abbess, who during her exile at the Annonciade convent underwent a crisis of faith where she understood empathetically the denial of human immortality by the materialists, and the sociology of the later Port-Royal, where abandonment by erstwhile allies in the renewed persecution plunged the convent into anomie. But the nihilism flavoring the abbess's philosophical perspective is more than a reflection of her dour personality or the bitter fortunes of an isolated convent. It represents yet another recasting of the humility the abbess, following Saint Bernard, makes so central in her ethics. Now noetic, this humility denies unaided human reason the capacity to construct a convincing portrait of God, the human soul, or terrestrial history. The inscrutable mystery of God, the violent contradictions of the soul, and the irrational vagaries of history remain a cipher to the reason unredeemed by faith. Even with the light of faith, redeemed reason can only glimpse God and humanity darkly through the annihilation of the cross. In anthropology as in theology, the greater truth lies in what cannot be justified and what cannot even be conceptualized by a human reason shattered by the Fall.

CHAPTER 5

CONCLUSION

A Nocturnal Philosophy

The philosophy developed by the Arnauld abbesses possesses more than a historical significance. It illuminates several concerns in contemporary philosophy. The writings of
the Port-Royal nuns indicate several directions for the contemporary effort to retrieve the heretofore neglected works
of women philosophers and to present them in an expanded
canon of philosophy. In their apophatic theory of divine attributes and their sectarian account of virtue, the nuns manifest
an affinity with certain Christian philosophers who attempt
to import explicitly theological categories into philosophical
reflection. The nuns' efforts to conceive personal freedom in
terms of the right to dissent is part of a distinctively modern project to limit the scope of political and ecclesiastical
power in the name of conscience.

The immense corpus of neo-Augustinian thought written by the Arnauld abbesses highlights certain issues in current efforts to present the work of early modern women
authors in an expanded canon of philosophy. First, it challenges too strict a division between philosophical and theological reflection. Mères Angélique, Agnès, and Angélique
de Saint-Jean are primarily religious writers who as abbesses

of a prominent convent under siege devote much of their writings to practical counsel for their subjects, other nuns, and laity under their spiritual direction. Their primary concerns are theological issues of grace, concupiscence, right doctrine, and ecclesiastical governance; their rhetoric is a theological one, bathed in scriptural and patristic references. But at the interior of theological reflection proper to a cloistered convent, the nuns develop arguments on perennial philosophical issues: the attributes of God, the nature of authentic virtue, the limits of authority, and the nature of personal freedom. As they exhort their listeners to cultivate the ascetical virtues and to negotiate the persecution occasioned by the quarrel over grace, the nuns defend a dualistic anthropology, sharply opposing the soul to the flesh, and an Augustinian philosophy of virtue, contesting the legitimacy of purely natural virtues in the name of an ethic based on the supernatural virtues infused by grace.

Like that of Augustine, Pascal, and Kierkegaard, the philosophy developed by the Port-Royal nuns disconcerts because it is an antiphilosophy. Its doctrine of the radical darkening of the human intellect by the Fall discounts the very effort of unaided human reason to grasp basic truths concerning God and the moral life. Engaging in philosophical debate, it undercuts the very legitimacy of the philosophical project in its ambition to provide a purely rational sketch of the real. Respecting such a fideist philosophy is central to understanding not only the Augustinian tradition, which from its inception has challenged the legitimacy of a humanistic philosophy in the name of the necessity of grace, but also the contribution of women to the philosophical tradition, since in the early modern period many women authors addressed philosophical questions at the interior of a theological or devotional inquiry. As Jacqueline Broad argues in her study of seventeenth-century British women philosophers, issues of Christian theology were the dominant concerns of the women engaged in philosophical speculation in this era.[1] The Arnauld abbesses were not the only women authors to bring a stern fideist edge to their scrutiny of a rationalist philosophy they considered the adversary of the Gospel.

The philosophy crafted by the Port-Royal nuns also highlights the issue of the site of philosophical reflection. Women philosophers of the early modern period have long been invisible to the canon because they were absent from the principal sites of the period's philosophical debates. Their exclusion from the university and the scientific academy ensured their invisibility to the chroniclers of academic philosophy. The convent represents one of the major sites in which women underwent an apprenticeship in theological and philosophical argument. During the seventeenth century many European women acquired the rudiments of neo-Scholastic philosophy through the catechetical instruction provided by convent schools. Both in its school and in the formation of its own nuns, Port-Royal promoted a complex Augustinian philosophy that was also a distinctively conventual philosophy. The virtues celebrated by the Port-Royal abbesses pivot around the monastic vows of poverty, chastity, and obedience. The cloistered virtues of silence and mortification acquire a new primacy. The critical treatment of the virtue of humility by the abbesses reflects their determination to safeguard the spiritual authority of the nun and to prevent the virtue of obedience from deteriorating into cowardice. The gendered philosophy developed by the Port-Royal nuns is contextual, rooted in the experience of women religious committed to a contemplative life. It is also rooted in the experience of a specific convent, determined to sustain the virtues of resistance in the midst of a persecution that had engulfed it.

In their apophatic account of divine attributes, the Arnauld abbesses exhibit an affinity with the "religious turn" that has characterized recent Continental phenomenology.[2] For both groups of writers, it is the negative theology of Christian mysticism that shapes their evocations of God. When Mère Agnès addresses God, she privileges what God is not: the incommunicable, the unlimited, and the ineffable. The contemplative experience of God points to what cannot be described or defined. The traces of divine immanence have been abolished in a theology that stresses almost exclusively the transcendence of God. Designated as wholly other, God can no longer be serenely recognized as the cause of the world and of the human person, since such affirmation runs the inevitable risk of projection of finite human qualities into the portrait of the being who is essentially other than human. The Augustinian anthropology of the Port-Royal nuns, with its emphasis on the corruption of the postlapsarian world and the concupiscence of the fallen human person, only deepens the chasm between a perfect Creator and a finite world long since fallen under the reign of sin.

The apophatic approach to the divine attributes also has clear implications for gender. The traditional Christian gendered portrait of God as Father finds itself relativized. Although God as Father and Son are clearly affirmed by the Port-Royal nuns, their references to God often emphasize the purely spiritual God who transcends, even on the level of metaphor, corporeal difference. In her letters Mère Angélique often invokes the mystery of God's essence and criticizes correspondents who too quickly detect divine causation behind a natural event or an internal inspiration. In her conferences Mère Angélique de Saint-Jean Arnauld d'Andilly emphasizes a humility that recognizes the incapacity of the human mind to grasp the essence of the divinity and the necessity for the mind to recognize the inscrutability of divine providence. The entire canon of Mère Agnès is suffused with an apophatic Oratorian spirituality that undercuts its metaphorical portraits of God's attributes by its recurrent appeals to God's absolute mystery. The gendered image of God as father and the political image of God as king are countered by a philosophy of God as that which eludes depiction and definition. The apophatic appeal to divine alterity unmasks the projection and idolatry that too easily taint sentimental or dogmatic evocations of God.

Especially significant is the philosophy of virtue proposed by the Port-Royal nuns. Faithful to a long ascetical tradition, the Arnauld abbesses exhort their subjects to perfect their moral character through the cultivation of specific virtues. It is a truism to note that the retrieval of virtue theory constitutes a major trait of contemporary moral philosophy during the past four decades.[3] In their own treatment of the virtues, however, the Port-Royal nuns differ sensibly from contemporary efforts to revive an ethics focused on virtue and character.

First, the Arnauld abbesses ally their treatment of virtue to their steely Augustinian anthropology of sin and grace. Along with other Christian and skeptical *moralistes* of the period, they reject the neoclassical account of virtue as false. The alleged fortitude, temperance, justice, and prudence of the good pagan are only masks of the vice of pride. Outward martial valor or abstemiousness cannot alter the destructive self-love that animates an unredeemed soul governed by sin rather than grace. The attempt of Christian neo-Stoics to baptize the alleged virtues of the naturally dutiful man is an illusion; the attempted self-salvation of the pagan Stoics through an act of self-will only closes them to the truth of their own grave sinfulness and the necessity of receiving salvation through Christ. The Jesuit effort to graft the theological virtues upon the natural goodness of the cardinal virtues is based on a false anthropology, since the radical concupiscence caused by the Fall and the vanity fueling the claim of possession of the cardinal virtues are ignored by the Jesuits in their overly optimistic account of human freedom and self-determination.

Each of the abbesses insists that the issue of virtue must be explored within the framework of the unmerited grace granted by God to the elect. It is the divine infusion of the theological virtues of faith, hope, and above all charity which permits the ensemble of moral virtues to flourish; rather than constituting the perfection of the natural moral virtues, the theological virtues constitute their ground and condition for existence. The moral virtues necessary for individual and social happiness can be grasped only within the theological framework of Fall, concupiscence, grace, election, and predestination. This theocentric account of the genesis and nature of the moral as well as theological virtues constitutes one of the most Augustinian traits of the philosophy developed at the convent of Port-Royal. The entire moral life, not only the more religious dimensions of this life, must be situated within the fundamental drama of Fall and redemption, a drama shrouded in the inscrutable decrees of an absolutely sovereign Godhead.

This Augustinian account of grace also highlights one of the fundamental weaknesses of the philosophy developed by the Arnauld abbesses: the inability to defend a plausible theory of freedom of the will. When challenged by a listener during her abbatial conferences, Mère Angélique stoutly rejects the argument that the sinful conduct of a nun might be due to predestination or to a lack of grace in which the nun has no fault. But in an anthropology that so emphasizes the determination of human moral action by divine causation, it is difficult to see how the moral freedom of the human agent remains more than nominal. In this area the abbesses progress little beyond the problems created by Jansen and Antoine Arnauld in their more erudite quarrels with fellow academic theologians. In the *Augustinus* and associated controversial opuscules, Jansen himself insisted that human beings remain free, but this freedom appears little more than a simple type of voluntariness. Unlike other animals, human beings possess the power to choose one course of action rather than another. Unlike nonrational beings, humans routinely engage in deliberation and election as they ponder their actions. But since their fundamental delectation (to love God or to love themselves) has been determined by another (God or Adam), their intellectual and volitional processes appear to fall short of authentic moral responsibility. The repeated insistence by Mère Angélique de Saint-Jean that the public virtues of the righteous are only expressions of God's sovereign grace at work within them easily dovetails with a theory of liberty that sees freedom as a grace-inspired liberation from damning vice rather than an internal exercise of self-determination or a morally imputable response to a divine initiative. The theocentrism of this account of virtue and freedom tends to crush the properly human and libertarian dimensions of the moral act as well as the act of salvation itself.

Second, the philosophy of virtue developed by the Port-Royal nuns is a contextual one. Rather than treating the desirable intellectual and moral habits for a universal human nature, the abbesses' discussion of virtues focuses on those habits of soul central for the specific vocation of a cloistered nun and of a cloistered nun called to endure the particular persecution shaking Port-Royal. In their writings the nuns provide scant analysis of the more universal virtues of justice or fortitude. The siege mentality of the convent rendered temperance and prudence suspect; these virtues could too easily be manipulated by the convent's adversaries into spiritual weapons to compel submission. The nuns argue at length how the monastic vows of poverty, chastity, and obedience foster their own distinctive set of virtues. Port-Royalist poverty entails the strict renunciation of private property, generosity toward the refugee, and abstemiousness in the use of food, drink, clothing, and housing. In the hands of Mères Angélique and Agnès, poverty emerges as an aesthetic virtue: a refined taste for sober architecture and furnishings. Port-Royalist obedience magnifies the reverence due the superior of the community in her role of spiritual director but qualifies the submission due the monarch and the episcopate in contested disciplinary judgments. Mère Angélique de Saint-Jean in particular stresses how obedience to the grace of Christ, as defended by the Augustinian party, trumps the deference due civil and ecclesiastical authorities. Silence is no longer a virtue of politeness and good social order; it becomes the condition for the flourishing of the adoration that constitutes the soul of the Port-Royal vocation and the experiential matrix of the nun's apophatic recognition of God. In this evocation of a virtue that is related to the context of a particular vocation and a particular community, the virtue theory of the Arnauld abbesses parallels the efforts of certain contemporary virtue ethicists to replace the unitary model of virtue proposed by certain classical authors with a more variable set of virtues reflecting the specific work, gender, or social milieu of the concrete human agent.[4]

In both its Augustinian orientation and its attention to religious-communitarian context, the virtue theory of the Port-Royal nuns bears certain resemblances to the sectarian moral philosophy proposed by Stanley Hauerwas and his associates.[5] Battling what they claim to be the illusions of natural law theory and the false universalism of much philosophical virtue theory, ethicians like Hauerwas argue that the particular set of virtues promoted by a given community reflects that community's distinctive vision of God and narrative of God's dealings with the members of the community. The community's rituals, sacred texts, and moral heroes shape the habits of mind considered virtuous and vicious by the community. For Christian churches the life, passion, and resurrection of Christ constitute the ultimate criterion and context for the determination of right action and virtuous habits for the members of the Christian community. In their perspective, the effort to find a universal ethic and ensemble of virtues for a humanity abstracted from its religious communities is illusory, since ethical principles emerge only within specific communities of memory and hope. The Arnauld abbesses' philosophy of virtue follows a similar logic. Moral virtue cannot be grasped independently of the biblical narrative of Fall and redemption, since the vice of pride animating alleged pagan virtue is disclosed only within an acknowledgment of concupiscence and the authenticity of the theological virtues is unveiled only within the acknowledgment of grace. Similarly the conventual virtues of poverty and humility cannot be properly interpreted apart from the evangelical counsels of Christ in the New Testament which inspired such virtues as part of the *imitatio Christi*. For the Port-Royal nuns as for the circle of Hauerwas, the virtues to be pursued within a given Christian community can neither be named nor comprehended apart from a broader communitarian account of discipleship, vocation, and the Kingdom of God.

Indisputably one of the most modern contributions of the Port-Royal nuns to philosophy is their defense of the right and duty of the conscientious moral agent to refuse to adhere to judgments he or she believes to be false. In his survey of Port-Royal philosophy, Antony McKenna underscores the contribution of the Arnauld abbesses to a modern theory of conscience: "For the first time in Catholic theology, the resistance of the nuns to the demand for condemnation of Jansenism in 1656 was founded on the definition of the rights of the individual conscience, a major step towards the formulation, in the following century (and following the writing of Pierre Bayle), of a doctrine of religious toleration."[6] Their defense of the freedom of the individual to dissent from political and ecclesiastical judgments must be carefully understood in terms of the theological context in which the nuns have framed it. For the Arnauld abbesses, the obligation to refuse to offer an unqualified signature to the throne's *formulaire* and its attendant papal censures flows from the duty of the Christian to defend religious truth, especially the truth at the heart of salvation: the grace of Christ. It is devotion to truth, not a libertarian defense of personal autonomy, which justifies the critique of civil and ecclesiastical power present in the nuns' defense of their resistance during the long crisis of the signature. The freedom to assent to or dissent from political and ecclesiastical judgments is subordinate to the duty to adhere to the truth concerning salvation, a truth central to one's eternal beatitude or damnation.

In their writings the Arnauld abbesses elaborate at length on the proper exercise of this freedom to dissent in the context of resistance to persecution by the throne and altar. Mère Angélique's letters to her brother Antoine Arnauld evoke the virtue of suffering for truth which must guide the embattled Christian attempting to defend the sovereignty of grace and the purity of Christian ethics against a lax court and religious establishment. They also argue that the manner of protesting injustice is just as central in the virtuous exercise of freedom as is the courage to refuse to subscribe to falsehoods. Forbearance rather than sarcasm must characterize the Christian's treatment of his or her enemies. Mère Agnès's spiritual writings place the virtue of suffering for the truth in a more mystical framework. Drawing on the Oratorian spirituality of *anéantissement,* she presents the mortal conflict with the world over the question of grace in terms of the annihilation of self into God which must characterize the will of the perfect nun. She balances this mystical account of the resistant soul with a pragmatic set of casuistic rules to guide the righteous nun through the trials of imprisonment, exile, and interdict. Her *Counsels on the Conduct Nuns Should Maintain* establishes boundaries between acceptable and unacceptable actions in cooperating with Port-Royal's tormentors as well as limning the necessary spiritual dispositions to endure the persecution occasioned by the crisis of the signature. More inclined to metaphysical speculation than her aunts, Mère Angélique de Saint-Jean incorporates the right and duty to dissent in the face of false judgment into a broader dualistic theory of human nature and history. The virtue of suffering for the truth reflects the more general duty for the soul to refuse all that comforts the body or flatters self-love. Persecution is the normal state of serious Christians, always a small minority even in the church, given the inevitable compromises made by the church and state to please a mediocre majority. Rather than being feared or weakened through compromise, persecution should be welcomed as the fate of the elect in the apocalyptic battle between light and darkness that will mark human history until the Parousia. Doubt, Cartesian or otherwise, must be firmly resisted as one adheres to one's religious convictions against the enticements of a persecutory world. A heroic ethics of resistance replaces the more prudent casuistry of her aunts in their common defense of the rights of conscience to oppose religious error and to resist the encroachments of civil and ecclesiastical powers into areas beyond their competence.

This richly textured defense of personal freedom in religious controversy is also a gendered one. The Arnauld abbesses' philosophy of resistance is tied to their defense of the broader right of women to participate in theological controversies; this participation in turn is embedded in the right of women to a theological culture. Unsurprisingly, critics condemned the Port-Royal nuns as *théologiennes*, women who engaged in theological questions beyond the ken of their sex. The arguments of the Port-Royal nuns against unqualified assent to the church's condemnation of Jansen reflect the sophisticated biblical and patristic culture the convent provided its nuns and lay pupils. The citations of de Sales, Avila, Antoine Arnauld, and Jansen himself (as author of *The Reform of the Interior Man*) are not ornamental; they reflect the controversial Augustinian culture nurtured by the nuns and their spiritual directors. The defense of the right of the nuns to dissent from the condemnation of Jansen also reflects the convent's defense of the right of women to exercise religious authority; it is the abbess, elected by her sisters rather than appointed by the throne, who serves as the convent's most authoritative spiritual guide. Assisted by confessors and chaplains of her own choice, she has the principal role in determining the proper lines of cooperation and resistance with external authorities who have erroneously judged the theories of Jansen and his disciples.

The abbesses's treatment of the virtues reflects this concern to safeguard the religious authority of women. Praising humility as a central Christian virtue, the abbesses insist that humility cannot be reduced to blind submission to political or ecclesiastical authorities. Authentic humility resides in the admission of one's utter dependence on God's action for one's creation, redemption, and sanctification; agreement with the condemnation of those who defend such humility's dependence on grace represents a violation rather than an expression of the virtue. Similarly, obedience is celebrated as a central virtue as well as a constitutive vow in religious life; accepting an order to engage in practices that violate the spirit and rule of the religious order one vowed to enter, however, represents a grave disobedience to God, whom one has promised to honor in a particular vocational path. Rather than opposing humility and obedience, resistance to oppressive authorities constitutes an exemplary exercise of humility and obedience by nuns trained by Port-Royal's theological culture to measure their beliefs and their actions by a doctrine of complete dependence on God's grace.

Perhaps the most striking trait of the Arnauld abbesses' philosophy is its nocturnal quality. The abbesses repeatedly allude to the unknowability of God, the obscurity of human history, and the illusions of human freedom and virtue. Critics have long dismissed this nocturnal note in the nuns' writings as a simple expression of Jansenist gloom or pessimism, but this nocturnal perspective reflects a thoroughgoing anthropology and epistemology of limit. Wounded by concupiscence, the human mind's efforts to prove the existence and attributes of God independently of divine revelation can lead only to assertions marked by their fragility and tentativeness. Even human nature is marked by obscurity. In their unredeemed state, the human faculties of intellect and will are so distorted by the darkness of sin, passion, and ignorance that they appear to be ruins of their original. In their redeemed state, those faculties are so united to God that the differentiated human self appears to disappear and only the language of negation can point to the *imago Dei*. A critical study of the alleged virtues of the good pagan of classical antiquity unmasks the omnipresence of the vice of pride, a vice itself hidden in the shadows of the demonic. As they contemplate the current state of Christendom, the Arnauld abbesses can perceive only the absence of God in a morally lax society governed by political expediency.

One can easily detect the intellectual sources of this nocturnal vision of God, the soul, and the world. Like other Jansenists, Saint-Cyran allied a philosophical Pyrrhonism, denying certitude to the claims of reason alone concerning God, with a fideism defending the certitude of propositions concerning God rooted in supernatural revelation. The Oratorian influence is also palpable. Through Bérulle, the old Pseudo-Dionysian apophatic theology finds a voice in the Port-Royal nuns, especially in the more contemplative writings of Mère Agnès. Through Condren, the spirituality of annihilation of the self transfers the categories of negative theology to descriptions of the human soul. The nuns' emphasis on the limitations of human knowledge and volition draws heavily upon the Augustinian doctrine of concupiscence. This nocturnal perspective, however, cannot be adquately explained by intellectual influences or by the nuns' membership in the embattled social class of the *noblesse de robe*.

Mère Angélique's insistence on the indecipherability of God's actions, Mère Agnès's evocation of God's negative names, and Mère Angélique de Saint-Jean's summons to resist a demonic contemporary world reflect an experience of persecution where both God and the soul are glimpsed through the prism of victimhood. It is Port-Royal's experience of exile, imprisonment, and excommunication which shapes the nocturnal images of God, the soul, and the virtues which haunt the Arnauld abbesses' philosophical inquiries.

APPENDICES

APPENDIX A

Lettres de la Mère Angélique Arnauld à Antoine Arnauld

In the following letters Mère Angélique Arnauld counsels her brother Antoine on the dispositions to adopt during periods of persecution. The letters were written during two crises in his life: the campaign against his book *On Frequent Communion* in 1644 and the revocation of his doctorate of theology by the Sorbonne faculty in 1655. In these letters Mère Angélique analyzes the virtue of suffering for the truth. She also admonishes her brother to adopt a more charitable tone in his philosophical and theological polemics.

The text of the letters is based on the print edition of Mère Angélique's correspondence: Mère Angélique Arnauld, *Lettres*, 3 vols. (Utrecht: Aux dépens de la Compagnie, 1742–44). The numbering of the letters follows the Utrecht edition. Punctuation and spelling have been modernized.

NO. 144

March 1644

Si vous pouviez voir, mon très cher Père, ce qui se passe dans mon coeur et dans mon esprit, vous connaîtriez que nuit et jour je me suis occupée de vous; et quoique ce ne soit pas sans de grands sentiments de tendresse et de douleur de notre séparation, néanmoins la vue que j'ai de la grande et singulière grâce que Dieu nous fait de souffrir pour la vérité essayant de servir les âmes qu'il a rachetées de son sang, surmonte tous mes sentiments; de sorte que je ne pense volontairement qu'au désir extrême et ardent que j'ai que vous souteniez cette tentation chrétiennement et saintement, afin que vous appreniez aux fidèles par votre persécution soutenue de la sorte, la pratique de la pénitence plus dignement que vous ne leur avez enseignée la théorie par votre Livre. Je sais, mon très cher frère, que vous avez ce dessein, mais dans de si tempestueuses rencontres notre esprit se distrait souvent; et l'esprit malin qui est plus au guet que jamais pour nous ravir les fruits que peuvent produire de si rares

et importantes occasions, essaie de nous diverter. Vous avez un bonheur que peu d'affligés ont, d'avoir des personnes qui veillent pour
vous, dans toute l'étendue de la vraie charité, de sorte que vous
n'avez qu'à prier Dieu, et à vous offrir sans cesse en sacrifice pour sa
gloire et le bien de son Église.

La divine providence a voulu que votre souffrance ait commencé
en ces jours que l'Église célèbre celle de notre Seigneur Jésus-Christ:
je dis commencé, parce que je ne vois pas quand elle finira. Mais
plus elle sera longue, et plus vous serez heureux. Je serais trop
contente si je pouvais vous accompagner et vous servir. Nous le serons toujours en esprit, avec plus d'affection que je ne vous puis exprimer. Toutes nos Soeurs vous en disent autant, non seulement les
cinq,[1] mais toutes les autres qui sont aussi touchées que nous et
prient pour vous de tout leur coeur. Je suis votre fille, votre soeur, et
votre mère. Que Notre Seigneur Jésus-Christ soit votre force, votre
espérance, votre repos, et votre unique amour, et qu'il occupe entiè-
rement votre esprit, le séparant de toutes les choses de la terre. Par-
donnez à mon extrême affection. La Mère Agnès vous envoie deux
petits Livres pour porter toujours sur vous, parce qu'elle craint que
vous n'ayez pas toujours commodément un bréviaire; au moins vous
en aurez la principale partie. Je vous conjure de prier le plus souvent
que vous pourrez, et de demander à Dieu ma conversion.

NO. 146

April 1644

Je n'ose vous écrire, mon très bon Père, de crainte de vous importu-
ner, encore que j'aie tous les jours le désir, pensant à vous incomparablement plus que je ne faisais lorsque j'avais le bien de vous voir
tous les jours, et avec une affection plus sensible. Quoiqu'elle me
tire souvent des larmes, je ne lasse pas d'avoir en même temps des
sentiments de joie mêlés dans celui de la douleur que j'ai, considé-
rant que vous êtes si heureux, non seulement de savoir, d'aimer et
d'enseigner, mais de souffrir pour la vérité. Je vous avoue que l'extrême affection que j'ai pour vous me fait craindre que vous ne lais-
siez échapper une occasion si précieuse, sans en tirer tous les avan-
tages que Dieu y présente. Vous avez vu de quelle sorte notre bon

1. The five sisters of Antoine Arnauld who were nuns at Port-Royal.

Père[2] s'est comporté. Je vous supplie, mon cher Père, d'y penser pour l'imiter; et surtout de beaucoup prier. Vous n'en travaillerez pas moins, quoique vous interrompiez souvent votre ouvrage pour prier. Au contraire vous acquérerez par une oraison courte, une nouvelle force et de nouvelles lumières pour faire bien et utilement.

Vous savez ce que l'on vous a tant dit, que si les Écrits n'étaient les fruits des prières et des larmes, ils étaient non seulement inutiles à ceux qui les lisaient, mais pernicieux à ceux qui les faisaient; et quand il arrive qu'on est obligé comme vous à des contestations, et à répondre à des personnes aussi déraisonables qu'injurieuses, on a besoin doublement de prier pour avoir la double grâce dont on a besoin, afin que l'on ne se laisse pas emporter aux sentiments de la nature. Je sais bien que par la grâce de Dieu vous n'êtes pas sensible à l'intérêt particulier; mais outré qu'il n'y a point de mal qui ne nous puisse arriver, si Dieu ne nous en préserve, il faut encore craindre de défendre l'intérêt de Dieu et de la vérité par la chaleur de la nature, plutôt que par celle du S. Esprit. J'ai une jalousie pour vous qui me rend importune. Ne me le pardonnez-vous pas? Je vous en supplie.

If faut que je vous dise encore ma peine de ce que vous ne vous rendez pas à sortir d'où vous êtcs. Car outre qu'il n'y a rien de pareil à obéir simplement, et que l'état où Dieu vous met, (que notre bon Père disait être pour lui celui de pénitent et ce que vous ne croyez pas moins pour vous) doit vous y obliger, il y a beaucoup de bonnes raisons pour le faire. Quoique j'admire et que je me tienne très obligée à la très grande charité de vos hôtes, néanmoins il ne faut pas qu'elle vous empêche de les quitter; puisqu'ils se doivent assurer qu'elle sera autant récompensée de Dieu, et reconnue de vous et de vos amis, que si elle avait duré jusqu'au bout, étant trop vrai qu'ils sont à lui dans la plénitude du coeur. Vous ferez mieux pour diverses raisons d'en sortir, et d'aller au lieu que vous savez. Vous y aurez aussi plus d'espace, ce qui vous sera nécessaire l'été; et vous serez assuré de n'apporter nulle incommodité, ce qui n'est pas où vous êtes, bien qu'elle soit reçue de très bon coeur. Enfin, mon très cher Père, je vous supplie très humblement de vous rendre à cela.

2. The letters' references to "our good Father" are to Jean Duvergier de Hauranne, abbé de Saint-Cyran (1581–1643), the spiritual director of Port-Royal and confidant of Mère Angélique.

Je vous envoie une croix; vous verrez bien qui vous l'a faite. Elle est pleine de reliques, et le dessus de paroles du S. Esprit, que N. a jugé qui vous seraient propres. Tout le monde prie Dieu pour vous, et vous salue. Nous avons fait un voeu de prier un an durant tous les jours S. Joseph, et dire les litanies de la Sainte Vierge. Je vous supplie de vous en souvenir et de prier avec nous: c'est à sept heures et demie du soir. Votre collègue nous a écrit deux Lettres admirables. Je prie Notre Seigneur qu'il vous fasse deux olives et deux chandeliers ardents dans sa maison.

NO. 147

April 1644

Nous avions, mon très cher Père, déjà résolu M. Singlin[3] et nous ce que vous désirez aussi bien que lui, et nous désirons autant qu'il nous sera possible reconnaître la très grande charité que ces bonnes personnes ont pour vous. Je prie Dieu de tout mon coeur, qu'il en soit lui-même la récompense. Ne craignez pas que je ne le témoigne comme je le ressens à la personne, lorsque je la verrai. À ce que nous voyons, si Dieu ne fait de grands changements, votre exil sera bien long. On voit clairement que le radoucissment qui avait paru n'a été que pour assoupir les bruits et faire croire à tout le monde qu'on était satisfait: mais dans la vérité on a autant de dessein de vous ruiner que jamais. Et de fait la Reine[4] a dit que le dernier Livre était pire que le premier et qu'elle ferait ce qu'elle pourrait pour les faire censurer à Rome. En quoi je vous estime heureux voyant clairement que Dieu vous prépare une longue souffrance par l'horrible opposition que l'on a à la vérité et qui a fait donner aux puissances de si mauvaises impressions.

3. Antoine Singlin (1607–64), a disciple of Saint-Cyran, was the chaplain of Port-Royal.
4. Queen Anne of Austria (1601–66), widow of Louis XIII and mother of Louis XIV, was the regent of France during the minority of Louis XIV. Mère Angélique had petitioned the queen to defend Antoine Arnauld and the Jansenists as the quarrel over the *Augustinus* (1640) intensified. The queen, however, turned against the movement and supported the campaign of her prime minister, Jules Cardinal Mazarin, against the Jansenists.

Tout mon désir est qu'il plaise à Dieu de vous remplir de plus en plus, non seulement de la connaissance de la vérité, mais d'un parfait amour qui vous la fasse pratiquer fidèlement, et de vous donner surtout une humble patience. Ce grand applaudissement de beaucoup de gens me déplaît; car bien que je sache que, grâce à Dieu, vous ne vous y arrêtez pas, et que vous connaissez aussi bien cette vérité que les autres, qu'il n'y a rien de nous en nous, et en toutes nos actions que le péché et la faiblesse, néanmoins j'éprouve tous les jours que notre nature corrompue ne laisse pas de prendre quelque secrète complaisance, dérobant ce que nous savons bien ne nous pas appartenir. Enfin, mon très cher, nous devons toujours trembler. Vous le savez incomparablement mieux que moi par la lumière de l'esprit, mais je le sais mieux que vous par l'expérience de ma grande corruption. Je voudrais bien que vous eussiez toutes vos Lettres, et que vous les lussiez souvent; vous y trouveriez toutes choses.

Je vous supplie de vous souvenir de toutes les pratiques de dévotion que notre bon Père avait dans sa prison. Car encore que je sois très aise que vous travailliez beaucoup, je crains toujours que vous ne priiez pas assez. Pardonnez-le moi, mon très cher, c'est que je suis si peu soigneuse de le faire quoique je sente palpablement que c'est la source de tout notre bien, qui est dans la grâce que Dieu veut que nous lui demandions sans cesse, que je crains toujours que les autres fassent comme moi, et qu'ils en reçoivent les dommages que j'expérimente tous les jours. Je vous regarde comme un homme qui est dans une affaire la plus importante qu'il puisse jamais avoir, où il y va de toute sa fortune, non seulement temporelle mais éternelle. Que s'il y a des actions uniques pour ménager notre éternité, celle où vous êtes est des plus singulières. Enfin, mon cher Père, vous êtes dans la possession du trésor qui a enrichi tous les Saints. Je prie Dieu de tout mon coeur qu'il vous fasse la grâce d'en faire un aussi saint usage dans la vraie humilité, sans laquelle les plus grand biens nous causent les plus grands maux.

NO. 149

May 1644

Encore que je ne dusse point, mon très cher Père, faire de réponse à votre dernière, néanmoins je ne puis m'empêcher de vous témoigner l'extrême consolation qu'elle me donne. Car bien que je ne vous flatte pas, ni moi-même, de croire que vos sentiments ne naissent que d'humilité, néanmoins je sais qu'ils sont humbles et produits de la grâce et miséricorde de Dieu, sans laquelle nous ne pouvons connaître nos défauts, principalement quand ils ne sont pas grossiers ni visibles aux yeux des hommes. J'ai une joie sensible, mon très cher frère, (je me puis m'empêcher de vous le dire encore une fois) des sentiments que Dieu vous donne, et qui procèdent de la vraie lumière de sa grâce qui vous fait connaître ce que lui doit un chrétien, un Prêtre, un Docteur; et un homme qu'il a daigné choisir pour défendre ses vérités, surtout celle de la nécessité de la pénitence et de la charité. Il vous fallait cette dernière grâce pour soutenir les premières, et surtout celle de souffrir persécution pour la justice.

Je vous confesse que j'ai toujours été inquiète depuis que je vous ai vu dans cette persécution, craignant qu'elle ne vous ennuyât, ou que vous ne la soutinssiez pas aussi humblement qu'a fait notre bon Père, qui l'a toujours prise comme vous savez pour un Purgatoire et qui désirait y mourir. Je crois que cela serait arrivé, mais Dieu ne l'a pas voulu pour l'honneur de la vérité et pour notre consolation, et vous voyez qu'il n'a guère tardé à le mettre dans le ciel. Encore que vous ne souffriez pas sensiblement, toutefois votre état est souffrant et ennuyant, et peut avec le temps devenir, si Dieu l'ordonne aussi, plus pénible. Mais tandis que Dieu vous tiendra dans l'état où il lui plaît de vous mettre, il sera toujours très bon pour votre âme; et je m'estime trop heureuse de souffrir avec vous, car j'ai une si grande tendresse pour vous que tout ce qui vous touche m'est extrêmement sensible.

Notre bonne mère qui vous a commandé en mourant de souffrir et de mourir pour la vérité, et à moi d'être votre mère, m'a comme laissé ce tendre amour qu'elle avait pour son Benjamin; et j'espère qu'elle m'obtiendra aussi de Dieu sa force, vous voyant souffrir d'aussi bon coeur et mourir si Dieu vous en rend digne, pour la vérité, comme elle l'a désiré. Je ne lasserai pas de prier Dieu qu'il fortifie de plus en plus sa grâce en vous, et je vous supplie, mon très cher Père, de le prier qu'il me convertisse et nous toutes. Nous ne correspondons point à la grande miséricorde que nous avons reçue de Dieu, de connaître la vérité et la pureté du Christianisme. J'ai bien envie, si Dieu le veut, que vous écriviez un Traité qui porte ce titre.

NO. 152

May 1644

Je vous envoie, mon très cher Père, votre Saint du mois, qui est le grand S. Athanase.[5] J'ai été fâchée que vous ne l'ayez pas eu pour son jour, mais en votre place ma Soeur Anne de l'Incarnation l'a honoré pour vous et a communié pour mieux prier pour vous, afin que Dieu vous rende imitateur de ce grand Saint. Il ne tiendra pas à vos adversaires qu'ils ne vous fassent autant souffrir, pourvu qu'il plaise à Dieu, comme je l'espère de son infinie miséricorde, de vous donner autant de grâces pour soutenir toutes les persécutions. Vous serez trop heureux, et vous aurez grande obligation de prier pour vos ennemis.

Je vous confesse ma faiblesse qui m'attendrit souvent jusqu'aux larmes, quand je pense qu'ils ne vous laisseront jamais en repos, et que sans miracle toute votre vie se passera dans de continuelles peines. Je ne lasse pas de bénir Dieu de tout mon coeur, sachant bien que c'est la meilleure fortune qui vous pouvait arriver; et je me souviens toujours de la bénédiction que notre bonne mère vous a donnée, en souhaitant à sa mort que vous mouriez pour la vérité. J'espère que vos souffrances donneront bénédiction à ce que vous avez déjà écrit, et à ce que Dieu vous fera la grâce d'écrire. Vous faites une promesse d'un Traité dont je souhaite beaucoup l'accomplissement, si Dieu le veut. Je vous supplie de le prier qu'il me convertisse: je vois tous les jours combien je suis loin de ce que je dois être pour porter dignement le nom de chrétienne. J'ai lu de la *Tradition*, tout du long, la Préface.[6] Elle m'a extrêmement consolée, me faisant voir plus que je n'avais jamais fait la grandeur et la sainteté du Christianisme.

Je vous envoie une Lettre qu'on vous a écrite d'Avignon. Nous devons beaucoup nous garder des louanges. Il faut louer Dieu de ses

5. Saint Athanasius (296–373), bishop of Alexandria, used Platonic categories to defend the divinity of Christ in his campaign against Arianism. Port-Royal paid particular honor to Saint Athanasius as the model of a Christian persecuted by bishops and emperor for his tenacious defense of doctrinal orthodoxy.

6. Antoine Arnauld, *La tradition de l'Église sur le sujet de la pénitence et de la communion.*

grâces et espérer en lui; mais il faut toujours bien craindre notre corruption, ce qui nous doit tenir dans une sainte crainte et défiance de nous-mêmes, surtout dans les choses extraordinaires, et ne témoigner nulle estime de ces choses, ni aussi trop de crainte, mais qu'on n'en tient compte, et les remettre toujours dans la voie de l'humilité et de la simplicité.

NO. 157

29 June 1644

Je vous remercie très humblement de votre dernière. Je vous supplie de croire, mon très cher, que ce m'est une dure mortification, lorsque je vous dis des choses que je me doute bien qui vous feront de la peine. L'état où vous êtes m'est déjà si pénible que je n'y pense point sans douleur. Toutefois Dieu me fait la grâce de le louer de vous voir dans la voie assurée du ciel, puisque vous portez la croix. L'extrême désir que j'ai que vous deveniez aussi saint que Dieu témoigne vous vouloir faire par sa miséricorde (comme il a paru par la conduite qu'il a tenue sur vous dès votre naissance) fait que je surmonte mon inclination de tendresse pour vous, en vous disant tout ce que je crains qui vous pourrait nuire. Il est vrai que tout le monde du dehors de céans savait où vous étiez. Je ne suis pas assurée de N. mais assurément il était à propos que vous changeassiez de logis. Je loue Dieu de ce que cela s'est fait, encore que j'appréhende qu'il vous ennuie dans une plus grande solitude.

Je prie Dieu qu'il vous augmente ses saintes grâces dont la moindre parcelle vaut mieux que toutes les consolations des créatures. Je ne saurais assez bénir Dieu de sa bonté et de la douceur dont il lui plaît d'user envers nous, en l'état où sont les choses, de n'avoir point voulu que nous eussions les cuisants soucis que nous aurions eus s'il avait autrement disposé des choses qu'il n'a fait. Car je vous confesse ma faiblesse: souvent il me vient de grandes appréhensions que l'état des choses ne change et que ne se rende plus pénible pour vous. Néanmoins j'espère en Dieu que s'il envoie des croix, (car jusqu'à cette heure nous n'en avons pas eu de véritables), sa bonté nous fera la grâce de les porter. Je vous envoie une lettre de M. Thomas que j'ai trouvée si chrétienne que j'ai cru que vous seriez bien aise de la voir. Pour moi je ne crains point la longueur des conten-tions, voyant bien qu'elle est inévitable; et je m'attends que vous y passerez votre vie: en quoi vous aurez le bonheur de ressembler à plusieurs Saints Pères. Je prie la bonté de Dieu que ce soit avec leur modestie, humilité et charité, afin qu'il vous sanctifie comme eux dans le combats.

Je vous ose supplier, mon très cher, de ne prendre jamais la plume ni la quitter sans prier Dieu. Je crois bien que vous le faites; mais comme je m'aperçois que ma promptitude me le fait souvent omettre dans mes actions mêmes les plus importantes, j'appréhende qu'il ne vous en arrive autant. J'ai encore à vous prier que vous lisiez tous les jours du vieux et du nouveau Testament; car je crains tou-jours que vous ne sachiez pas assez l'Écriture sainte, et que vos gran-des occupations ne vous fassent oublier de la lire. Or il me semble que vous ne devez non plus omettre de donner cette sainte nourri-ture à votre âme que le pain à votre corps, dont aucun travail, quel-que pressé qu'il soit, ne dispense. Je crois, mon très cher, que vous n'oubliez pas à prier pour moi. J'en ai un très grand besoin en mon particulier, reconnaissant tous les jours que je n'aime point Dieu, et que le peu que je fais est plus par une crainte intérieure que par une vraie charité. J'ai toujours cette crainte de la mort, et de la mort éternelle, sans que cela produise aucun effet, ne me séparant point des imperfections et attaches que j'ai à mes inclinations que je fuis sans cesse. Je vous le dis sincèrement et par la vraie connaissance que j'en ai, vous suppliant de prier Dieu qu'il daigne me regarder en sa miséricorde.

NO. 779

28 November 1655

Je loue Dieu, mon cher Père, de ce que vous n'êtes point abattu; et en vérité j'ose dire qu'il n'y a pas de quoi, puisque pour ce qui nous regarde il y a plus de bonheur que de malheur à souffrir l'injustice des hommes, car c'est un grand sujet d'espérer en la miséricorde de Dieu. Je vous supplie de ne vous point laisser emporter aux mouve-ments des hommes quoique touchés de zèle, parce que la patience et l'humilité chrétienne sont toujours les plus puissants moyens de glorifier Dieu et de défendre la vérité. Vous l'avez annoncée par sa seule grâce, et certes personne ne la peut ignorer, non plus que l'injustice qu'on lui fait aussi bien qu'à vous, qui serez trop heureux de lui sacrifier votre honneur et votre vie. Vous êtes proche de celui que Dieu vous a donné: n'écoutez que sa voix; et laissez celle des étrangers, quoique bons.

NO. 789

15 December 1655

L'insolente opiniâtreté avec laquelle on persécute la vérité et votre personne, mon très cher frère, m'afflige fort. J'ai eu peur, quoique je ne doive pas mesurer ma faiblesse avec votre force, que vous ne le soyez aussi un peu, et que le grand travail qui vous empêche souvent de dormir, affaiblissant votre corps, ne contribue aussi à la peine de l'esprit. D'ailleurs Dieu veut bien souvent que ceux à qui il donne plus de lumières, éprouvent qu'elles ne leur peuvent pas procurer les biens qu'elles leur font connaître. Il voudra peut-être que vous appreniez par experience ce que vous avez appris par les Lettres saintes, de la vérité que vous soutenez et pour laquelle vous souffrez.

Si cette science porte les hommes à s'humilier, l'expérience le fait encore mieux. Pourvu que nous soyons humbles, nous serons trop heureux: tous les maux nous seront utiles, puisqu'ils nous humilieront toujours davantage; et plus nous serons humbles, plus nous serons heureux, la sainteté étant aussi grande dans l'âme que l'humilité. J'avoue qu'il en faut beaucoup pour souffrir, comme if faut, la manière dont on traite la vérité et les personnes. La révolte que je sens dans mon esprit d'un procédé si injuste et si injurieux, me fait bien voir que je n'ai point d'humilité: ce qui me doit faire trembler, et vous supplier très humblement de la demander pour moi.

Je crois que la manière dont on agit ne fait point votre plus grande peine, mais ce sont plutôt les diverses propositions d'accommodement des amis qui embarrassent beaucoup, dans la crainte où vous êtes de trop déférer ou de trop résister en une chose aussi précieuse que la vérité, qui oblige à une grande fermeté et aussi à une grande humilité: mais cette dernière s'opposant à la cupidité nous préserve de ces agitations. Vous avez, par la grâce de Dieu, M. Singlin, que Dieu nous a donné et laissé afin de nous soutenir dans les mauvais jours. J'espère que Dieu vous déterminera et vous soutiendra par lui: c'est de quoi nous le supplierons sans cesse. Vos petites filles commencèrent hier une neuvaine pour vous. Enfin, mon cher Père, celui qui se confie en Dieu ne sera ni ébranlé ni confus. Tout le monde vous salue très humblement, et avec une affection que je ne puis exprimer.

NO. 792

22 *December 1655*

J'ai été en grande peine, mon très cher frère, que vous ne soyez arrivé trop tard; mais j'espère que, par la grâce de Dieu, il ne vous sera rien arrivé. Je vous renvoie la copie de la Lettre que vous avez écrite au sujet de l'épreuve où Dieu vous met. Elle est véritablement admirable; et j'ai une grande joie de savoir qu'elle est toute dans votre coeur. Avec ces dispositions que la grâce opère en vous, vous n'avez rien à craindre.

Je vous supplie très humblement que pour l'édification du prochain vous parliez toujours avec autant de modestie et d'humilité, et que votre promptitude naturelle ne vous fasse point trahir votre coeur, que je sais être constamment humble, doux et charitable, par la miséricorde de Dieu. Le démon en enrage, et c'est ce qui lui fait remuer quelquefois ce qui vous reste de naturel, pour couvrir en vous la grâce par ces défauts de nature, que j'ai bien plus grands que vous, n'étant pas si heureuse que d'avoir un si bon fonds. Cette vue me fait encore vous demander très humblement pardon de mon emportement, recommencé par trois fois, quoiqu'à chacune j'en ai eu des regrets. Bonjour, mon très cher Père. Je prie Dieu qu'il nous donne part à l'extrême douceur, retenue et sagesse du Bienheureux Évêque de Genève,[7] dont nous faisons aujoud'hui la mémoire.

---

7. François de Sales (1567–1622), bishop of Geneva, was the spiritual director and correspondent of Mère Angélique during the early phase of the reform of Port-Royal.

Appendix B

Mère Agnès Arnauld, *Pensées sur le chapelet secret du Saint-Sacrement*

Establishing the authentic text of the *Private Chaplet of the Blessed Sacrament* is problematic. Originally written in 1626 as a spontaneous autograph, the devotional treatise circulated in manuscript copies until 1633, when it became the object of ecclesiastical censure. In the ensuing pamphlet war, both critics and defenders of the *Chaplet* published divergent versions of the work. Its dense rhetoric further complicates the establishment and interpretation of the text. Clearly influenced by the Oratorian mysticism of Pierre de Bérulle and Charles de Condren, the *Chaplet* repeatedly uses periodic sentences, sentence fragments, parenthetical phrases, and the subjunctive mood to evoke a transcendent God who cannot be expressed in expository prose or in metaphors drawn from the world of creatures. Following the editorial judgment of Jean-Robert Armogathe in *"Le chapelet secret* de Mère Agnès Arnauld" (*XVIIe siècle* no. 170 [1991]: 77–86), we are using the version of the *Chaplet* published by François Pintherau in *Les reliques de Messire Jean Duvergier de Hauranne* ([Louvain, 1646], 432–38). Based on original manuscripts once owned by Jean Duvergier de Hauranne, abbé de Saint-Cyran, the preeminent defender of the *Chaplet*, the Pintherau version is as authoritative a copy of the treatise as we currently possess. In his *Discussion sommaire d'un livret intitulé "Le chapelet secret du très-saint Sacrement"; et de ce qui a esté escrit pour en défendre la doctrine* (Paris, 1635), Étienne Binet offers another early print version of the text. When Binet's version appears to offer a more accurate version of the text, I have placed his variant reading in brackets. Spelling and punctuation have been modernized.

Sur le premier attribut: Sainteté à Jésus-Christ!
Afin que Jésus-Christ soit au Très-Saint Sacrement en sorte qu'il ne sorte point de soi-même, c'est-à-dire que la société qu'il veut avoir

avec les hommes soit d'une manière séparée d'eux et résidente en lui-même, n'étant pas raisonnable qu'il approche [s'approche] de nous qui ne sommes que péché, et même en l'état de grâce, il n'y a rien en nous digne de la sainteté de Dieu, de façon que nous devrions dire au Très-Saint Sacrement ce que saint Pierre disait à Jésus-Christ: Retirez-vous de nous, Seigneur, car nous sommes pécheurs.

Sur le deuxième attribut: Vérité à Jésus-Christ!
Afin que Jésus-Christ se traite lui-même selon ses grandeurs, qu'il soit de tout ce qui lui appartient, que les âmes aillent à lui dans cette vérité, c'est-à-dire par lui-même, sans agir par leur être créé, parce que les bornes des âmes sont opposées à cette vérité, laquelle se doit regarder en Dieu, comme infinie de grandeur, sans limiter leurs usages envers lui, n'ayant que la conduite de l'esprit de Dieu, qui est cet esprit de vérité qui les puisse rendre dignes de l'adorer dans la même vérité qu'il demande d'elles.

Sur le troisième attribut: Liberté à Jésus-Christ!
Afin que Jésus-Christ ne dépende plus que de lui-même et [en] ce que sa miséricorde lui a donné des règles et des pensées d'accommodement aux hommes, vouloir que son être soit le principe de tous les mouvements, et que comme il est de soi-même, il soit aussi pour soi-même et dans cette pensée renoncer à toutes les promesses de Dieu, en tant que promesses qui semblent porter engagement et ne les vouloir recevoir, que comme partant du mouvement libre de Jésus-Christ.

Sur le quatrième attribut: Existence à Jésus-Christ!
Afin que Jésus-Christ s'établisse dans tout ce que les âmes sont, qu'il ne souffre point la subsistence de sa [la] créature, qu'il soit tout ce qu'il veut être et fasse disparaître tout autre être, comme le soleil efface toute autre lumière qu'il soit pour être et que la fin de son établissement soit pour lui, et non pour l'avantage de l'âme qui le porte.

Sur le cinquième attribut: Suffisance à Jésus-Christ!
Afin que Jésus-Christ prenne en soi-même tout ce qui est dû à une capacité, à une dignité et grandeur infinie, comme la science [la

sienne], qu'il ne soit point en indigence, au regard des hommes qui ne lui rendent pas ce qu'ils lui doivent, qu'il soit enrichi de ses propres trésors et que se reposant dans son tout, il paraisse glorieusement désintéressé des usages des hommes.

Sur le sixième attribut: Satiété à Jésus-Christ!
Afin que Jésus-Christ ne souffre point de délai dans l'accomplissement de ses desseins, qu'il donne lieu à l'instinct de son être, qui est de consumer tout en soi-même, comme le souverain être, qu'il demeure en lui-même qui est le pain de vie, et qu'il ne s'engage point dans la disette des hommes pour rien désirer d'eux, qu'il prenne rassasiement dans le contentement divin et dans la vue de sa propre gloire.

Sur le septième attribut: Plénitude à Jésus-Christ!
Afin que Jésus-Christ ait son compte en toutes choses, que l'effusion de ses grâces retourne à lui-même, que la réception des âmes soit un rejaillissement en lui par une entière référence, qu'il ne donne rien qu'à soi-même et pour soi-même et ne souffre plus de déchet dans la capacité de la créature qui ne peut porter qu'il ne soit pleinement en elle.

Sur le huitième attribut: Éminence à Jésus-Christ!
Afin que Jésus-Christ entre en tous ses droits, qu'il s'élève glorieusement dans toutes les prééminences, qu'il fasse une séparation de grandeur entre lui et la créature, que les âmes acceptent leurs bassesses en hommage de [à] cette grandeur, qu'il soit un Dieu Dieu, c'est-à-dire, se tenant dans ses grandeurs divines selon lesquelles il ne peut être tenu dans rien moindre que lui.

Sur le neuvième attribut: Possession à Jésus-Christ!
Afin que Jésus-Christ s'approprie les âmes, qu'il les réfère à soi, que les âmes relèvent de lui et prennent vie en lui, et que tous leurs usages soient les siens; en ce qu'elles doivent recevoir mouvement de lui, ainsi rien n'est digne de l'être, et il faut que les âmes adorent en Jésus-Christ la possession qu'il a de lui-même et qu'elles n'aient point de vue, qu'il [s'il] lui plaît, de le posséder ou non, étant assez qu'il se possède lui-même.

Sur le dixième attribut: Règne à Jésus-Christ!
Afin que Jésus-Christ prenne son royaume et qu'il demeure dans la condition de sa nature qui est de régner et de mettre toutes choses sous ses pieds, que les créatures demeurent dans l'incapacité qu'elles ont d'être comparées à Dieu, que sa magnificence soit élevée sur tous les cieux, qu'il soit dans le zèle [le ciel] de sa gloire, qu'il anéantisse toute puissance et qu'il fasse venir le sceptre de sa divinité, établissant son règne et faisant vivre son nom de la vie qu'il a de lui-même, sans qu'il ait besoin que les âmes consentent à son règne.

Onzième attribut: Inaccessibilité à Jésus-Christ!
Afin que Jésus-Christ demeure en lui-même laissant la créature dans l'incapacité [qu'elle a] de l'approcher, que tout ce qu'il est n'ait point de rapport à nous, que son inaccessibilité l'empêche de sortir de soi-même, que les âmes renoncent à la rencontre de Dieu et consentent qu'il demeure dans le lieu propre à la condition de son être qui est un lieu inaccessible à la créature dans lequel il reçoit la gloire de n'être accompagné que de son essence seule.

Douzième attribut: Incompréhensibilité à Jésus-Christ!
Afin que Jésus-Christ demeure dans ses voies, qu'il les connaisse lui seul et qu'il ne rend [rende] compte qu'à lui-même des desseins qu'il prend sur ses créatures, que les âmes se rendent à l'ignorance et qu'elles aiment le secret des conseils de Dieu, qu'elles renoncent à la manifestation des choses cachées de Dieu, en tant qu'elles doivent demeurer dans la seule science divine.

Treizième attribut: Indépendance à Jésus-Christ!
Afin que Jésus-Christ agisse comme première cause sans assujettissement aux fins qu'il s'est donné à lui-même, en sorte qu'encore que ce sacrement soit un signe d'amour, il en tire, s'il veut, un effet de justice, qu'il n'ait point d'égard à ce que les âmes méritent, mais qu'il fasse tout selon lui et que les âmes renoncent au pouvoir qu'elles ont d'assujettir Dieu, en ce qu'étant en grâce, il leur a promis de se donner à elles; qu'elles ne fondent point leurs espérances sur cela, mais demeurent dans une bienheureuse incertitude, qui honore l'indépendance de Dieu.

Quatorzième attribut: Incommunicabilité à Jésus-Christ!
Afin que Jésus-Christ ne se rebaisse point dans des communications disproportionnées à son infinie capacité, que les âmes demeurent dans l'indignité qu'elles portent d'une si divine communication, qu'elles laissent leur être à Dieu, non pas pour recevoir participation du sien, mais pour honorer l'excellence de son incommunicabilité, par la communication du peu que nous sommes, s'estimant heureusement assez partagées de n'avoir aucune part aux dons de Dieu, pour sa joie, qu'ils soient si grands, que nous n'en soyons pas capables.

Quinzième attribut: Illimitation à Jésus-Christ!
Afin que Jésus-Christ agisse dans l'étendue divine, qu'il ne lui importe ce qui arrive de tout ce qui est fini, qu'il ruine tout ce qui limite ses desseins, que les âmes pour l'honorer dans cette perfection rompent leurs liens, qu'elles ne se tiennent pas dans leurs pensées, ni dans leurs vues, qu'elles se précipitent dans la vastitude des desseins de Dieu, renonçant à toutes fins finies, que Jésus-Christ enferme tout en soi et qu'il ne soit enfermé en [de] rien, mais atteigne d'un bout à l'autre pour exécuter tout ce qu'il lui plaira.

Seizième attribut: Inapplication à Jésus-Christ!
Afin que Jésus-Christ s'occupe de lui-même et qu'il ne donne point dans lui d'être aux néants, qu'il n'ait égard à rien qui se passe hors de lui, que les âmes ne se présentent pas à lui pour l'objet de son application, mais plutôt pour être rebutées par la préférence qu'il doit à soi-même, qu'elles s'appliquent et se donnent à cette inapplication de Jésus-Christ, aimant mieux être exposées à son oubli, qu'étant en son souvenir lui donner sujet de sortir de l'application de soi-même pour s'appliquer aux créatures.

APPENDIX C

Mère Angélique de Saint Jean Arnauld d'Andilly, *Sur le danger qu'il y a d'hésiter et de douter, quand une fois l'on connaît son devoir*

Sur le danger is a treatise written to discourage the Port-Royal nuns against any compromise with the opponents of the convent during the successive crises of the signature. In this work Mère Angélique de Saint-Jean explains how the act of doubt is inscribed within a framework of power. The enemies of Port-Royal are encouraging the nuns to doubt their controversial beliefs in order to weaken and ultimately destroy the convent's adherence to the neo-Augustinian theories of the Jansenist circle. Never a neutral act, the willingness to doubt under persecution can lead only to moral surrender to the oppressor. Using the rhetoric of a legal brief, the treatise cites biblical and patristic precedents to justify the nun's admonition against doubt and compromise.

The French text is that of the first print edition: Mère Angélique de Saint-Jean, *Sur le danger qu'il y a d'hésiter et de douter, quand une fois l'on connaît son devoir,* in *Vies intéressantes et édifiantes des religieuses de Port-Royal et de plusieurs personnes qui leur étaient attachées* (Utrecht: Aux dépens de la Compagnie, 1750). The numbering follows the original 1750 edition; spelling has been modernized.

I.

Il n'y a rien de si périlleux dans les affaires de Dieu que de faire des avances. Car comme dans les moindres rencontres nous ne pouvons rien sans lui, et encore davantage dans celles qui le regardent, c'est assez pour tomber que de faire un pas contre son ordre, et sans qu'il nous le fasse faire lui-même. C'est ainsi que les affaires toutes de Dieu deviennent les nôtres, et que nous les rendons toutes humaines en y agissant par nous-mêmes: ce qui fait que Dieu cesse de nous secourir. Nous demeurerions invincibles si nous nous tenions toujours fermes dans le poste où il nous a mis. Car Dieu ne pouvant jamais être surmonté, nous ne pouvons l'être qu'en nous éloignant de lui. Et il faut qu'il y ait quelque chose de nous, quand nous sommes vaincus où que nous tombons, selon que dit le Prophète, *inpingentes in viis suis*,[1] par où il nous montre qu'on ne tombe jamais, tandis qu'on demeure dans la voie de Dieu, puisque chacun ne tombe que dans la sienne, *inpingentes in viis suis*.

II.

C'est ce qui fait que les serviteurs de Dieu ne se croient jamais en plus grande assurance, que lorsqu'ils n'ont qu'à souffrir, et que leurs ennemis les tenant en captivité ils se trouvent dans une plus grande liberté, étant moins en danger dans les plus grands dangers. Car comme ils ne craignent pas le mal que les hommes leur font, selon le précepte de l'Évangile, mais seulement celui qu'ils peuvent faire, en les mettant dans l'impuissance d'agir au dehors pas eux-mêmes, on les empêche de s'affaiblir, et en les faisant souffrir, on les fortifie. Si bien que nos propres ennemis, quand nous sommes à Dieu comme il faut, lors même qu'il leur laisse faire ce qu'ils veulent, nous rendent insurmontables et nous aident à les vaincre. Ils se ruinent en pensant nous ruiner, et ils nous élèvent au-dessus de leurs têtes en pensant nous abattre sous leurs pieds.

III.

C'est donc peut-être une faute que de vouloir sortir de cet heureux état, afin d'entrer dans de nouvelles délibérations d'accommodement, qui sont toujours très dangereuses à ceux qui ont l'avantage de leur côté. Et on ne peut même en agréer la proposition, tant s'en faut qu'on puisse la faire, qu'on ne témoigne en quelque manière qu'on a quelque chose à accorder à ses ennemis. Il n'y a point d'accommodement sans cela. C'est *pourquoi il n'y a plus lieu de consulter quand il n'y a plus lieu de relâcher: de même qu'il ne sert de rien de parler du prix d'une marchandise qu'on ne veut pas vendre.* Quand tout est fait, il n'y a donc plus rien à faire. Or c'est ce que nous avons témoigné en cent rencontres qu'on ne pouvait plus rien demander, parce que nous ne pouvions plus rien accorder: que nous

---

1. Jer. 18:15: "They have stumbled in their ways."

avons peut-être baissé au-delà de ce que nous pouvions, mais qu'as-surément nous ne pouvons baisser advantage.

IV.

Voilà donc la règle de Saint Bernard: *nemo super bis quae certae sunt haesitet:*[2] qu'on n'hésite point quand on est assuré de ce qu'il faut faire, parce qu'on s'expose à perdre l'avantage qu'on a d'être as-suré en hésitant. Quand on doute, il sert beaucoup de délibérer, afin de ne douter plus; mais quand on ne doute point, on apprend à dou-ter en délibérant. Si donc la délibération est nécessaire, elle ôte le doute: si elle est inutile, elle peut le faire venir. C'est pourquoi ap-prouvons hardiment et avec assurance ce que nous savons avec as-surance que Dieu approuve, comme dit le même père: *approbemus indubitanter que placere scimus Deo indubitanter.*[3] Or nous savons bien ce que Dieu demande de nous. N'ayons donc point d'autre pen-sée que de lui demander la grâce de pouvoir faire ce qu'il demande. Employons à prier le temps que nous employerions à délibérer, et nous trouverons une joie plus solide dans la souffrance, que nous n'en aurions à trouver des moyens de ne point souffrir.

V.

Ce n'est pas, comme nous avons dit, que ces sortes de consultations et de déliberations ne puissent être nécessaires, mais il est vrai qu'il n'y a rien qui nous mette plus en danger de nous affaiblir, et qui ouvre plus la porte à des raisonnements tout humains et aux pen-sées de la chair et du sang. Car comme dans ces rencontres on fait profession d'examiner tout, il semble que nous désarmions la foi, qui réprimerait tous les sentiments de la nature, pour ne nous faire regarder que des objects éternels, et qu'afin de négliger rien et de peser tout. Nous parlons souvent sans y penser avec nos plus grands ennemis, qui sont nos sens qui empruntent de la raison de quoi plai-der leur cause, et qui se couvrent quelquefois des plus belles appa-

2. Saint Bernard of Clairvaux: "No one hesitates about those things which are certain."
3. Saint Bernard of Clairvaux: "Let us approve without any doubt what it has pleased God to let us know undoubtedly."

rences du monde, et qui peuvent nous tromper, si nous ne nous tenons bien sur nos gardes.

VI.

Il ne faut pas s'étonner si de grands serviteurs de Dieu et les personnes les plus éclairées se trouvent quelquefois dans des difficultés insurmontables dans ces sortes de délibérations, dans lesquelles on est obligé de déférer beaucoup à la raison et aux apparences, qui sont le plus souvent opposées aux lumières de la foi, qu'il est impossible de perdre de vue sans qu'on s'égare. Que si cela arrive à ceux qui sont les plus savants dans la tradition de l'Église et dans la science des Pères, que fera-ce de ceux qui l'ignorent?

Quand vous ne pourrez plus parler aux personnes qui vous aideront à prendre un bon conseil, quand vous n'entendrez que des personnes suspectes, vous serez réduites à prendre conseil de vous-même ou de vos ennemis, et vous ne retirerez point peut-être d'autre avantage de vous être vues ensemble, et d'avoir conféré sur une matière qui ne demande point de nouveau conseil, que de vous affaiblir les unes les autres.

VII.

La charité qu'on porte aux autres fait qu'on est plus sensible à leurs maux, et s'il y en a une seule de faible, il peut y avoir danger que la compassion fasse entrer la faiblesse jusque dans le coeur. La prudence chrétienne demande que pour le moins nous ne recherchions point tout ce qui pourrait nous attendrir dans un temps où nous avons besoin, pour ainsi dire, d'une certaine dureté qui nous rende comme insensibles à toute sorte de maux, pour ne ressentir que ceux que souffre la vérité et l'Église.

Au reste comme nous sommes entre les mains de nos ennemis, et qu'il est périlleux de leur demander ces sortes de grâces, ils ne nous les accorderont qu'autant qu'ils croiront qu'elles pourront leur être avantageuses. Si nous demeurons aussi fermes qu'auparavant, ce leur fera un prétexte de nous persécuter encore advantage, comme ayant abusé de cette prétendue grâce qu'ils nous auront accordée, et ayant manqué à la parole que nous avons donnée de voir ensemble ce qui se pourrait faire, ce qui leur faisait espérer que nous avions eu pour le moins la pensée de pouvoir faire quelque chose de plus que nous avons fait.

VIII.

Mais quelque chose que nous puissions leur accorder, il ne faut pas croire que des ennemis passionnés comme sont les Jésuites s'en contentent. Ils ne se contenteraient d'abord des plus légères blessures, que nous pourrions nous faire, que pour nous porter ensuite avec plus de facilité à nous en faire de plus grandes. Nous savons bien qu'on n'aura pas de peine à se dédire de tout ce qu'on nous aura promis. Ou le Roi ne l'aura pas trouvé bon, ou le Pape n'aura pu y consenter. On nous obligera encore de faire un second pas, et nous le ferons peut-être, afin de n'avoir pas fait inutilement le premier.

Concevons donc une bonne fois que nos ennemis veulent nous perdre à quelque prix que ce soit, et qu'il n'y a que Dieu seul qui puisse les en empêcher, afin que nous n'ayons recours qu'à lui seul. Nos ennemis visibles veulent ruiner notre monastère, et nos ennemis invisibles ne se servent d'eux et de la crainte que nous pourrions avoir de le perdre, que pour ruiner notre foi. Mais, notre foi vaut mieux qu'un monastère, et notre conscience est à préférer à une maison qui ne serait devant Dieu que notre propre tombeau, si nous y rentrions jamais en blessant notre conscience.

IX.

Ne consultons donc point ce que nous pouvons faire pour sauver notre maison, puisque notre salut consiste à rien faire.

Jésus-Christ dans l'Évangile n'a point consulté jusqu'où il pouvait se relâcher pour éviter la fureur des Juifs. Et comment aurait-il consulté dans sa Passion où il n'a point parlé. Il n'a pas seulement ouvert la bouche pour se défendre, lors même qu'il en était pressé par les juges, et il n'a rompu son silence, quand il a commencé de souffrir, que pour rendre témoignage à la vérité de son père. C'est là où il a parlé: c'est là où il a répondu clairement à ce qu'on lui demandait s'il était le Christ; et il a ajouté qu'on le verrait venir un jour sur les nuées avec majesté pour juger le monde, ce qu'on ne me lui demandait pas, au lieu que nous faisons le contraire: car nous parlons peut-être plus qu'il ne faut pour nous défendre, et nous parlons peut-être moins qu'il ne faut pour rendre gloire à la vérité.

X.

Saint Jean n'a point consulté ce qu'il pourrait faire pour sortir de prison, et Jésus-Christ lui rend ce glorieux témoignage, que ses ennemis ont fait de lui ce qu'ils ont voulu: *fecerunt de illo quaecumque voluerunt.*[4] C'est qu'il savait bien qu'il n'avait rien à faire, et qu'il était plus entre les mains de Dieu qu'en celles de ses ennemis. C'est pourquoi il s'abandonnait en effet à la conduite de Dieu, en s'abandonnant à la puissance des hommes qui dépend toujours de celle de Dieu.

Jérémie, qui a été la figure de Jésus-Christ et de Saint-Jean, était si éloigné de consulter ce qu'il pouvait faire pour avoir la paix, qu'il n'avait perdue que parce qu'il était fidèle à Dieu, qu'il proteste ne s'être lui-même aperçu du dessein que ses ennemis avaient de le perdre: *non cognovi cum cogitaverunt super me consilia dicentes,* etc.[5] Ce n'est pas qu'il eût si peu d'esprit, qu'il ne remarquât ou qu'il ne pût remarquer ce que faisaient ses ennemis, mais il était si rempli de l'esprit de Dieu qu'il ne se mettait point en peine de tout ce qu'ils lui pouvaient faire, et que même il n'y pensait pas.

XI.

Lorsque Saint Pierre et Saint Jean, ayant été mal traités par les prêtres ensuite du miracle du boiteux, rapportèrent en pleine assemblée des fidèles ce qui s'était passé, il n'est pas dit qu'ils délibérèrent pour voir ce qu'il y avait à faire (car en effet il n'y avait rien à faire que de tout souffrir) mais qu'ils addressèrent tous à Dieu, et le prièrent de leur donner la force de parler avec toute liberté: *Et nunc Domine respice in minas eorum, et da servis tuis cum omni fiducia loqui verbum tuum.*[6] Voilà le fruit et l'utilité des saintes assemblées, non pas pour consulter dans de telles rencontres, mais pour prier avec plus d'ardeur et avec plus d'efficacité, qui est toujours plus grande quand l'union est plus grande. C'est comme cela qu'il est bon de s'assembler quand on le peut, afin de s'entr'enflammer à la prière et de faire une sainte violence à Dieu, à laquelle il ne peut résister, ainsi que remarque Tertullien parlant des assemblées des premiers chrétiens.[7] Mais quand c'est la cause de Dieu même qui nous empêche

---

4. Matt. 17:12: "They did to him whatever they pleased."

5. Jer. 11:19: "I did not know that it was against me they drew up their schemes, saying . . ."

6. Acts 4:29: "And now, Lord, look upon their threats and grant to your servants to speak your word with all fidelity."

7. See Tertullien, *Apologia,* chap. 39, no. 2.

de nous assembler, pour laquelle seule nous nous assemblerions, l'union des coeurs suffit. Et quoique les lieux soient différents, Jésus regarde ces prières comme une seule prière, parce que les coeurs ne sont pas différents, et qu'elle ne part que d'un même esprit.

XII.

La colombe de l'Évangile ne consulte point, parce qu'elle n'est que simple.[8] Je sais bien que la prudence du serpent y est aussi conseillée, mais elle n'est louable que quand on expose tout le corps pour sauver la tête qui est Jésus-Christ, et il ne faut point consulter pour cela.

Balaam se vit sur le point d'être tué par l'Ange, il ne s'exposa à ce danger que pour avoir consulté Dieu une seconde fois.[9] Car quand il nous a fait connaître sa volonté, c'est quelquefois le tenter que de lui demander encore ce qu'il veut.

Ce Prophète ayant été mandé par le Prince des Moabites de l'aller trouver pour maudire le people d'Israël, il recût l'ordre de Dieu de n'y point aller et de ne point maudire ce people, *noli ire cum eis*.[10] Cela devait suffire à Balaam. Mais, comme on lui envoya de nouveaux ambassadeurs, et que leurs présents et leurs promesses le tentèrent, il voulut consulter Dieu encore une fois: *manete hic*, leur dit-il, *hac nocte, et scire queam quid mibi rursum respondeat Dominus*.[11] Dieu lui permit d'y aller, mais il lui permit dans sa colère, parce qu'il méritait d'être aveuglé, ayant reçu déjà la lumière de Dieu de chercher encore une nouvelle lumière. Il pensa donc être tué de l'Ange dès la sortie, et ce voyage fut la cause de sa ruine. Que s'il est si périlleux de douter quand on ne doit plus douter, lors même qu'on ne consulte que Dieu, que ferait-ce de consulter les hommes de ce que nous ferons, quand Dieu a eu la bonté de nous assurer lui-même tant de fois de ce que nous avons à faire.

8. See Matt. 10:16.

9. See Num. 22:22–35.

10. Num. 22:12: "Do not go with him."

11. Num. 22:19: "Let us stay here this night so that I may know what else the Lord will tell me."

NOTES

1. Mary Warnock, *Women Philosophers* (London: J. M. Dent, 1996), xxxii. For a rebuttal of this rationalistic criterion of inclusion, see Eileen O'Neill, "Early Modern Philosophers and the History of Philosophy," *Hypatia*: 20:3 (2005): 185–97.

2. See Charles-Augustin Sainte-Beuve, *Port-Royal*, 3 vols., ed. Maxime Leroy (Paris: Gallimard, 1953–55), and Henry de Montherlant, *Port-Royal* (Paris: Gallimard, 1954).

3. The following works illustrate this retrieval of philosophical *salonnières*: Jacqueline Broad, *Women Philosophers of the Seventeenth Century* (Cambridge: Cambridge University Press, 2002); John J. Conley, *The Suspicion of Virtue: Women Philosophers in Neoclassical France* (Ithaca: Cornell University Press, 2002); Erica Harth, *Cartesian Women: Versions and Subversions of Rational Discourse in the Old Regime* (Ithaca: Cornell University Press, 1992).

4. Two organizations have rendered distinguished service in encouraging and diffusing scholarly research on the writings of the Port-Royal nuns. Founded in 1913, the Société des Amis de Port-Royal sponsors an annual colloquium and a scholarly journal, *Chroniques de Port-Royal*, which are indispensable sources of the latest developments in Port-Royal scholarship. Dating back to an early society founded in 1802, the Société de Port-Royal administers the Bibliothèque de Port-Royal, a Parisian research library housing the world's major collection of Port-Royal manuscripts and print material. Two recent initiatives have also encouraged access to and scholarly analysis of the works of the Port-Royal nuns. *Éditions Phénix* has published facsimile editions of rare out-of-print Port-Royal works. Its 2003 re-edition of the three volumes of Mère Angélique's *Lettres* (Utrecht, 1742–44), with a new preface by Jean Lesaulnier, is a major achievement. Directed by Jean Lesaulnier, *Collection univers de Port-Royal*, published by Éditions Nolin, is a series that has published contemporary monographs, collections, and reference works on Port-Royal.

5. This historical sketch of Port-Royal is indebted to the following sources: Jérôme Besoigne, *Histoire de l'abbaye de Port-Royal*, 6 vols. (Cologne: Aux dépens de la Compagnie, 1752); Charles Clémencet, *Histoire*

générale de Port-Royal, 10 vols. (Amsterdam: J. Vanduran, 1755–57); Louis Cognet, *La réforme de Port-Royal: 1591–1618* (Paris: Sulliver, 1950); William Doyle, *Jansenism: Catholic Resistance to Authority from the Reformation to the French Revolution* (New York: St. Martin's Press, 2000); Cécile Gazier, *Histoire du monastère de Port-Royal* (Paris: Perrin, 1929); Sainte-Beuve, *Port-Royal; Dictionnaire de Port-Royal,* ed. Jean Lesaulnier and Antony McKenna (Paris: Champion, 2004).

6. Apophatic theology, also called negative theology, attempts to describe God in terms of what God is not rather than positively in terms of what God is. It privileges such negative attributes of God as infinity and illimitability. Drawing on the apophatic tradition of Plotinus, Pierre de Bérulle (1575–1629) applied negative theology to the attributes of Christ. He stressed humiliation, abasement, and self-abandonment as key traits of the Incarnation. Accentuating the apophatic strain of Bérulle's theology, Charles de Condren (1588–1641) designated self-annihilation (*l'anéantissement du soi*) as the central trait of a perfected spiritual life.

7. In *De concordia libertii arbitrii cum divinae gratiae* (1588), Luis de Molina argued that through his *scientia media* God knows from all eternity the moral character, the actual free acts, and the possible free acts of each human agent. Although the human agent cannot save himself or herself due to the sinfulness and engrained concupiscence of postlapsarian humanity, God's grace of salvation is related to the moral character and history of each agent and can be made actual (efficacious) only by the free act of this agent.

8. The *querelle de la grâce* bitterly divided the Catholic Church at the end of the sixteenth century. One theological school championed the doctrine of efficacious grace, according to which God saves the elect by granting grace to those predestined for salvation. This grace unerringly achieves its end and depends on divine sovereignty rather than on human merit for its operation. Another school championed the doctrine of sufficient grace, according to which God provides the grace sufficient for salvation, but in order for this grace to become efficacious, it must be accepted by an act of free will by the individual human person. This school interpreted predestination as rooted in God's eternal knowledge of the merits of each creature. This quarrel between the two schools became a bitter struggle between the Dominican and Jesuit orders, since the Dominican Bañez and the Jesuit Molina became the leading spokesmen for the two opposed schools. With the Jesuits denouncing the Dominicans as Calvinists who denied free will and the Dominicans denouncing the Jesuits as Pelagians who denied the necessity of grace, the Vatican intervened. The *Congregation de auxiliis* (1598–1607) permitted representatives of the opposed schools to debate the question of

grace in the presence of successive popes and curial officials, but the Vatican concluded that the controversy had no clear resolution. Both schools could continue to maintain their positions on condition that they clearly affirm the necessity of both divine grace and human volition in the act of salvation and that they refrain from denouncing their opponents as heretics. Given the continuing violence of the *querelle*, the Holy Office in 1611 forbade public disputation on the issue of grace, but the ban was ineffective in preventing new outbreaks of the quarrel, such as the Jansenist-Jesuit dispute over the theology of the *Augustinus*.

9. Innocent X, *Cum occasione*, in *The Church Teaches: Documents of the Church in English*, ed. John F. Clarkson et al. (St. Louis: Herder, 1960), 249–50.

10. On December 3–4, 1563, the Council of Trent promulgated a decree mandating the reform of religious orders along the following lines: strict observance of cloister; abolition of personal possessions; minimum age limits for religious profession (sixteen) and for accession to abbatial office (forty). In 1570, Jérôme Souchier, abbot-general of the Cistercians, promulgated the *Ordinationes*, which specified how the Tridentine reforms were to be practiced in Cistercian communities.

11. See Catherine Villanueva Gardner, *Women Philosophers: Genre and the Boundaries of Philosophy* (Boulder, Colo.: Westview Press, 2004), 1–11.

12. See F. Ellen Weaver, *The Evolution of the Reform of Port-Royal: From the Rule of Cîteaux to Jansenism* (Paris: Beauchesne, 1978), and *La Contre-Réforme et les constitutions de Port-Royal* (Paris: Cerf, 2002).

13. This sketch of the Arnauld family history is indebted to the following sources: Alexander Sedgwick, *The Travails of Conscience: The Arnauld Family and the Ancien Régime* (Cambridge: Harvard University Press, 1998); *Dictionnaire de Port-Royal*, ed. Lesaulnier and McKenna; Jean Lesaulnier, ed., *Images de Port-Royal* (Paris: Nolin, 2002).

14. See Lucien Goldmann, *Le Dieu caché; Étude sur la vision tragique dans les "Pensées" de Pascal et dans le théâtre de Racine*, 3rd ed. (Paris: Gallimard, 1955).

15. See Victor Cousin, *Jacqueline Pascal: Premières études sur les femmes illustres et la société du XVIIe siècle*, 4th ed. (Paris: Didier, 1861); M. P. Faugère, *Lettres, opuscules et mémoires de Madame Périer et de Jacqueline, soeurs de Pascal, et de Marguerite Périer, sa nièce* (Paris: A. Vaton, 1845); Blaise Pascal et al., *Oeuvres complètes avec tous les documents biographiques et critiques; Les oeuvres d'Étienne, de Gilberte et de Jacqueline Pascal et celles de Marguerite Périer; La correspondance des Pascal et des Périer*, 4 vols., ed. Jean Mesnard (Paris: Desclée de Brouwer, 1964–92).

16. See Jacqueline Pascal, *A Rule for Children and Other Writings*, trans. and ed. John J. Conley (Chicago: University of Chicago Press, 2003); Frédéric Delforge, *Jacqueline Pascal, 1625–1661* (Paris: Nolin, 2002); Robert Leuenberger, *Jacqueline Pascal: Die Schwester des Philosophen* (Zurich: Theologischer Verlagen, 2002).

17. See Soeur Jacqueline de Sainte-Euphémie Pascal, *Écrit de Mademoiselle Jacqueline Pascal sur le mystère de la mort de Notre-Seigneur J.-C.* and *Relation de la Soeur Jacqueline de Sainte-Euphémie Pascal concernant la Mère Marie-Angélique*, in Faugère, *Lettres, opuscules*, 157–76, 223–27.

18. See Soeur Jacqueline de Sainte-Euphémie Pascal, letter to Gilberte Pascal Périer, 25 September 1647, in Faugère, *Lettres, opuscules*, 309–12.

19. See William Ritchey Newton, *Sociologie de la communauté de Port-Royal: Histoire, économie* (Paris: Klincksieck, 1999), 59–65.

20. See Dom Charles Clémencet, *Histoire littéraire des religieuses de Port-Royal des Champs*, Ms. Maz 4538.

21. See Thomas M. Carr, *Voix des abbesses du Grand Siècle: La prédication au féminin à Port-Royal* (Tübingen: Narr, 2006), 1–25.

22. Bernard Chédozeau, "Idéal intellectuel et vie monastique à Port-Royal," *Chroniques de Port-Royal* 37 (1997): 68–69.

23. See Philippe Sellier, *Le siècle de Saint-Augustin* (Paris: Champion, 2000).

24. See Madeleine de Souvré, marquise de Sablé, letter to Cardinal de Rispigliosi, BNF Ffr. 10583, f.6.

25. Gazier, *Histoire du monastère de Port-Royal*, 171.

26. Cornelius Jansenius, *De la réformation de l'homme intérieur*, trans. Robert Arnauld d'Andilly (Paris: Veuve J. Camusat, 1642).

27. See Saint-Cyran, *Lettres chrétiennes et spirituelles* (Paris: Veuve Martin Durand, 1645).

28. Saint-Cyran, *Théologie familière*, 5th ed. (Paris: Jean Le Mire, 1644), 76–77.

29. Soeur Jacqueline de Sainte-Euphémie Pascal, letter to Soeur Angélique de Saint-Jean, 23 June 1661, in Faugère, *Lettres, opuscules*, 402–14.

30. See Antoine Arnauld, *Phantôme du jansénisme ou justification des prétendus jansénistes* (Cologne: Chez Nicolas Schouten, 1686), and Pierre Nicole, *Les imaginaires ou lettres sur l'hérésie imaginaire* (Liège: Chez Adolphe Beyers, 1667).

31. See Leszeck Kolakowski, *God Owes Us Nothing: A Brief Remark on Pascal's Religion and the Spirit of Jansenism* (Chicago: University of Chicago Press, 1995).

32. See Isaac Habert, *La défense de la foi de l'Église et de l'ancienne doctrine de la Sorbonne, touchant les principaux points de la grâce, prêchée dans l'église de Paris* (Paris: T. Blaise, 1644).

33. The *Rule of Saint Augustine* refers to nine disparate texts written by Augustine during his episcopacy at Hippo (396–430) in order to provide guidance for male and female monastic communities under his supervision. Unlike the elaborate constitutions of later religious orders, Augustine's texts provide brief, hortatory advice on the virtues and dispositions to be cultivated in monastic communities.

34. See Saint John Climacus, *L'èchelle sainte, ou les degrés pour monter au ciel,* trans. Robert Arnauld d'Andilly (Paris: Pierre Le Petit, 1653).

35. The *solitaire* Antoine Le Maître played a central role in nurturing the convent's devotion to the person and works of Saint Bernard. See Antoine Le Maître, *La vie de S. Bernard, premier abbé de Clairvaux et père de l'église* (Paris: Antoine Vitré, 1648).

36. First published in 1609, *L'introduction à la vie devote* immediately established François de Sales as the preeminent spiritual writer in the French Counter-Reformation. His letters of spiritual direction to Mère Angélique Arnauld were treasured by the convent. The most philosophical of his works, *Traité de l'amour de Dieu* (1616), developed a neo-Augustinian philosophy of love rooted in the conflict between the delectation of earthly things and the delectation of celestial things.

37. A French translation of the works of Saint Teresa of Avila first appeared in 1601: Teresa of Avila, *Oeuvres de la Mère Thérèse de Jésus,* 3 vols., trans. Jean de Brétigny (Paris: G. de la Noüe, 1601). Robert d'Andilly later provided a new translation: Saint Teresa of Avila, *Oeuvres de Sainte Thérèse d'Avila,* trans. Robert d'Andilly (Paris: P. Le Petit, 1670). For a contemporary discussion of the status of Teresa of Avila as a philosopher, see Pierre-Jean Labarrière, "Thérèse d'Avila: Docteur de l'Église," *Études* 357 (1982): 391–402; and Mary Ellen Waithe, "Roswitha of Gondersheim, Christine of Pisan, Margaret More Roper, and Teresa of Avila," in *A History of Women Philosophers,* vol. 2, ed. Mary Ellen Waithe (Dordrecht: Kluwer, 1989), 309–17.

38. See Jean Orcibal, "Le Bérullisme," in *La spiritualité de Saint-Cyran avec ses écrits de piété inédits* (Paris: Librairie Philosophique J. Vrin, 1962), 9–12.

39. Jean du Vergier de Hauranne, abbé de Saint-Cyran, *Théologie familière,* cited in Orcibal, 1–2.

40. Antony McKenna, "Port-Royal," in *Routledge Encyclopedia of Philosophy* (London: Routledge). Retrieved June 14, 2005, from http://www.rep.routledge.com/article/DA063SECT2.

41. Jean du Vergier de Hauranne, abbé de Saint-Cyran, *De la grâce de Jésus-Christ, de la liberté chrétienne et de la justification,* in Orcibal, *La spiritualité de Saint-Cyran,* 233.

42. See Louis Cognet, *Le jansénisme,* 7th ed. (Paris: Presses universitaires de France, 1995), 7–18.

43. The author of numerous theological tracts, Antoine Arnauld coauthored two major philosophical treatises: *La logique ou l'art de penser* (1662), which attempted to substitute a Cartesian logic for the neo-Aristotelian logic of the French university; and *Grammaire générale et raisonnée* (1660), which explored the symmetry between the laws of language and the laws of thought. A major participant in the philosophical disputes of the period, he wrote the Fourth Objection to Descartes's *Meditations* (1641), a series of letters to Leibniz on metaphysics, and *Traité des vraies et fausses idées* (1683) against Malebranche's epistemology.

44. The genesis of Blaise Pascal's two prominent philosophical works, *Lettres provinciales* (1656–57) and *Pensées* (published posthumously in 1670), is closely tied to the Port-Royal convent. In composing *Lettres provinciales* he visited the *solitaires* Arnauld and Nicole at their Port-Royal residence to consult the documentation they had assembled on moral casuistry. In the spring of 1658 Pascal presented at Port-Royal a lecture that outlined the apology for the Christian faith on which he had begun to work. The unfinished notes and drafts for this monumental work of apologetics would be known posthumously as Pascal's *Pensées.*

45. A *solitaire* and schoolmaster at Port-Royal's *petite école* for boys, Pierre Nicole was the coauthor of *La logique, ou l'art de penser* (1662) and the leading moralist of the Port-Royal circle. His fourteen-volume *Essais de morale* (1671–1715) combated libertinism.

46. A *solitaire* and schoolmaster in the *petites écoles,* Claude Lancelot coauthored *Grammaire générale et raisonnée* (1660), which offered a quasi-Cartesian explanation of the relationship between language and thought. A distinguished pedagogue and grammarian, Lancelot wrote numerous works on methods for the teaching of Greek, Latin, Spanish, and Italian.

47. A *solitaire* and schoolmaster, Nicolas Fontaine translated numerous patristic writings into French. His translations of the early monastic theologian Cassian's *Conférences* (1663) and *Institutions* (1667) were especially influential. In addition he translated the works of Augustine, Gregory the Great, and Leo the Great. His translations of Eastern church fathers, notably Clement of Alexandria, Basil, and Gregory of Nazianzus, introduced the Port-Royal community to a Platonic philosophical tradition broader than the Augustinian tradition of the West.

48. The three texts are Mère Angélique Arnauld, *Lettres à Antoine Arnauld;* Mère Agnès Arnauld, *Le chapelet secret du Saint-Sacrement;* Mère Angélique de Saint-Jean Arnauld d'Andilly, *Sur le danger qu'il y a d'hésiter et de douter, quand une fois l'on connaît son devoir.*

49. For a more extensive discussion of the complexity and perils of characterizing Port-Royal's philosophy as Cartesian, see Tad M. Schmaltz, "What Has Cartesianism to Do with Jansenism?" *Journal of the History of Ideas* 60:1 (1999): 37–56.

50. Daniella J. Kostroun, "Undermining Obedience in Absolutist France: The Case of the Port-Royal Nuns, 1609–1709" (Ph.D. diss., Duke University, 2000), 12.

Chapter Two MÈRE ANGÉLIQUE ARNAULD

1. Sources for this biographical sketch include the following: Fabian Gastellier, *Angélique Arnauld* (Paris: Fayard, 1998); Jean Lesaulnier et al., "La Mère Angélique Arnauld (1591–1661)," *Chroniques de Port-Royal* no. 41 (1992); Perle Bugnion-Secrétan, *La Mère Angélique Arnauld 1591–1661 d'après ses écrits* (Paris: Cerf, 1991); Jean Lesaulnier, "Arnauld, Jacqueline, en religion Marie-Angélique de Sainte Madeleine, dite la Mère Angélique," in *Dictionnaire de Port-Royal*, ed. Jean Lesaulnier and Antony McKenna (Paris: Champion, 2004), 91–97.

2. The future Mère Angélique studied Plutarch in the celebrated Amyot French translation: *Les oeuvres morales et meslées de Plutarque translatées du grec en français*, trans. Jacques Amyot (Paris: M. de Vascosan, 1572).

3. Jean de Brisacier, S.J., *Le jansénisme confondu* (Paris: Florentin Lambert, 1651), 6.

4. See François Boulêtreau, "La charité de la Mère Angélique," *Chroniques de Port-Royal* no. 41 (1992): 171–94.

5. Mère Angélique Arnauld to Anne of Austria, queen-mother of France, 25 May 1661, *LMMA* 3: 539.

6. Ibid., 3: 541–42.

7. See Mère Angélique Arnauld, *Relation écrite par la Mère Marie-Angélique Arnauld de ce qui est arrivé de plus considérable dans Port-Royal*, ed. Jean Lesaulnier, *Chroniques de Port-Royal* no. 41 (1992): 7–93.

8. See Mère Angélique Arnauld, *Relation écrite par la Mère Angélique Arnauld*, ed. Louis Cognet (Paris: Grasset, 1949).

9. See Mère Angélique Arnauld, *Lettres de la Révérende Mère Marie-Angélique Arnauld, abbesse et réformatrice de Port-Royal*, 3 vols. (Utrecht: Aux dépens de la Compagnie, 1742–44). Elsewhere cited as *LMMA*. For a literary analysis of the correspondence, see Mary Rowan, "Angélique Arnauld's Web of Feminine Friendships: Letters to Jeanne de Chantal and the Queen of Poland," in *Les Femmes au grand siècle; Le Baroque; Musique et*

littérature; Musique et liturgie, ed. David Wetsel et al. (Tübingen: Narr, 2003), 53–59.

10. See Jean Mesnard, "Pour une édition critique des Lettres de la Mère Angélique," *Chroniques de Port-Royal* no. 41 (1992): 211–26.

11. Mère Angélique Arnauld to Marie-Louise de Gonzague, queen of Poland, 12 December 1652, *LMMA* 2: 232.

12. Mère Angélique Arnauld to Marie-Louise de Gonzague, queen of Poland, 28 March 1651, *LMMA* 1: 551.

13. See Mère Angélique Arnauld to François de Fleury, 24 July 1653, *LMMA* 2: 352–53.

14. See Mère Angélique Arnauld, *Entretiens ou conférences de la Révérende Mère Marie-Angélique Arnauld, abbesse et réformatrice de Port-Royal* (Bruxelles: A. Boudet, 1757). Hereafter cited as *EC.*

15. See Thomas M. Carr, "Avez-vous lu la Règle? Les instructions sur la Règle de la Mère Angélique," *Chroniques de Port-Royal* no. 52 (2003): 207–20.

16. Mère Angélique Arnauld, *Instructions de la Mère Angélique sur quelques chapitres de S. Bénôit,* BNF Ms. Ffr. 17794, vol. 5, 26.

17. Mère Angélique Arnauld to Soeur Anne de Sainte-Magdeleine Halley, 21 August 1636, *LMMA* 1: 85–86.

18. Mère Angélique Arnauld to Mère de Saint-Maur de Chiverney, prioress of Gif, 23 December 1651, *LMMA* 2: 18–19.

19. Mère Angélique Arnauld to Robert Arnauld d'Andilly, 13 November 1639, *LMMA* 1: 178–79.

20. See Blaise Pascal, letter no. 4 to Charlotte de Roannez, October 1656, *L'oeuvre de Pascal,* ed. Jacques Chevalier (Paris: Gallimard, 1950), 286–88.

21. Mère Angélique Arnauld to Madame de Bellisi, 23 April 1656, *LMMA* 3: 220.

22. Mère Angélique Arnauld to Marie-Louise de Gonzague, queen of Poland, 8 August 1653, *LMMA* 2: 358–59.

23. Mère Angélique Arnauld to Marie-Louise de Gonzague, queen of Poland, 21 May 1654, *LMMA* 2: 498.

24. Mère Angélique Arnauld to Marie-Louise de Gonzague, queen of Poland, 12 November 1655, *LMMA* 3: 98.

25. Mère Angélique Arnauld to Marie-Louise de Gonzague, queen of Poland, 27 November 1653, *LMMA* 2: 398.

26. Mère Angélique Arnauld to Madame de Sablé, 4 June 1660, *LMMA* 3: 490.

27. Mère Angélique Arnauld to Marie-Louise de Gonzague, queen of Poland, 18 August 1656, *LMMA* 3: 285.

28. Mère Angélique to Madame de Bellisi, 14 October 1655, *LMMA* 3: 79.

29. Mère Angélique Arnauld to a boarding pupil, 16 November 1650, *LMMA* 1: 517–18.

30. Mère Angélique Arnauld to Madame Allen, 12 May 1655, *LMMA* 2: 611.

31. Mère Angélique Arnauld to Marie-Louise de Gonzague, 31 December 1653, *LMMA* 2: 410.

32. Mère Angélique Arnauld to Anne de Rohan, princesse de Guéménée, 15 November 1629, *LMMA* 1: 179–80.

33. Mère Angélique Arnauld to Mère Agnès, March 1652, *LMMA* 2: 66–67.

34. See Mère Angélique Arnauld to Monsieur de Sévigné, 27 January 1661, *LMMA* 3: 511–12.

35. Mère Angélique Arnauld to a nun in Picardy, 11 October 1656, *LMMA* 3: 295.

36. Mère Angélique Arnauld to Soeur Suzanne de Sainte-Cécile Robert, 25 June 1648, *LMMA* 1: 376–77.

37. See Mère Angélique Arnauld to Marie-Louise de Gonzague, 12 December 1653, *LMMA* 2: 403–5.

38. See Mère Angélique to Monsieur de Sévigné, December 1660, *LMMA* 3: 498–500.

39. Mère Angélique Arnauld to Mademoiselle de Luzanci, 7 September 1650, *LMMA* 1: 494.

40. Mère Angélique Arnauld to Marie-Louise de Gonzague, queen of Poland, 11 August 1656, *LMMA* 3: 281–82.

41. The term *sectarian* is used here in the sense given to it by the sociologist of religion Ernst Troeltsch (1865–1923). According to Troeltsch, Christian communities organize themselves according to "church" or "sect" patterns. The churches try to incorporate the larger society and support an ethics of compromise with certain questionable moral practices, such as warfare or usury. The sects stand aloof from the larger society, focus on small groups, and develop an ethics that contests the sinful compromises of the larger world. With their theology of the small elect, their criticism of moral casuistry, and their disdain for the moral compromises of the episcopacy and the throne, Port-Royal clearly operated according to a sectarian ecclesiology.

42. Mère Angélique Arnauld to Soeur Angélique de Sainte-Thérèse, end of year 1656, *LMMA* 3: 325.

43. Mère Angélique Arnauld to Antoine Arnauld, early 1644, *LMMA* 1: 246.

44. Mère Angélique Arnauld to Antoine Arnauld, April 1644, *LMMA* 1: 251.

45. Mère Angélique Arnauld to Mère Marie de Sainte-Magdeleine du Fargis, prioress of Port-Royal des Champs, 25 April 1661, *LMMA* 3: 527.

46. Mère Angélique Arnauld to Anne of Austria, queen-mother of France, 25 May 1661, *LMMA* 3: 539–40.

47. Mère Angélique Arnauld to Monsieur Macquet, chaplain to Annonciades of Boulogne, 6 March 1643, *LMMA* 1: 233.

48. Mère Angélique Arnauld to Monsieur Macquet, chaplain to Annonciades of Boulogne, 27 February 1643, *LMMA* 1: 231.

49. See Mère Angélique Arnauld to Monsieur Macquet, chaplain to Annonciades of Boulogne, May 1646, *LMMA* 1: 291–93.

50. See Mère Angélique Arnauld to Marie-Louise de Gonzague, queen of Poland, 24 March 1656, *LMMA* 3: 198–200.

51. Mère Angélique Arnauld to Antoine Arnauld, November 1651, *LMMA* 1: 603–4.

52. Mère Angélique Arnauld to Jean-François de Gondi, archbishop of Paris, 17 December 1651 and January 1652, *LMMA* 2: 10–12 and 34–35.

53. See Mère Angélique Arnauld to Catherine de Morant, abbess of Gif, 8 July 1653, *LMMA* 2: 341–43.

54. See Mère Angélique Arnauld to Marie-Louise de Gonzague, queen of Poland, 10 July 1653, *LMMA* 2: 343–45.

55. Mère Angélique Arnauld to François de Fleury, 10 July 1653, *LMMA* 2: 346.

56. Mère Angélique Arnauld to Monsieur Macquet, chaplain to Annonciades of Boulogne, 7 June 1650, *LMMA* 1: 478–79.

57. Mère Angélique Arnauld to Soeur Angélique de Sainte-Agnès de Marle de la Falaise, end of year 1655, *LMMA* 3: 141–42.

58. See Mère Angélique Arnauld to Antoine Arnauld, December 1652, *LMMA* 2: 235–36.

59. Mère Angélique Arnauld to the Ursulines of Rouen, 15 June 1655, *LMMA* 3: 12.

60. Mère Angélique Arnauld to Madame de Bellisi, 7 October 1657, *LMMA* 3: 431.

61. Mère Angélique Arnauld to the superior of the Annonciades of Boulogne, 14 May 1640, *LMMA* 1: 188–89.

62. Mère Angélique Arnauld to Monsieur Macquet, chaplain to Annonciades of Boulogne, 4 January 1635, *LMMA* 1: 51.

63. See ibid., 48–50.

64. Mère Angélique Arnauld to Madame de Mornay de Villarceaux, abbess of Gif, 16 September 1650, *LMMA* 1: 503.

65. See Mère Angélique Arnauld to Marie-Louise de Gonzague, queen of Poland, 12 November 1655, *LMMA* 3: 97–99.

66. See Mère Angélique Arnauld to Marie-Louise de Gonzague, queen of Poland, 23 June 1656, *LMMA* 3: 264–66.

67. See Mère Angélique Arnauld to Marie-Louise de Gonzague, queen of Poland, 11 August 1656, *LMMA* 3: 280–83.

68. Mère Angélique Arnauld to Marie-Louise de Gonzague, queen of Poland, 20 January 1655, *LMMA* 2: 560.

69. Mère Angélique Arnauld to Marie-Louise de Gonzague, queen of Poland, 16 December 1655, *LMMA* 3: 121.

70. Ibid., 121–22.

71. See Mère Angélique Arnauld to Marie-Louise de Gonzague, queen of Poland, 1 April 1655, *LMMA* 2: 586–92.

72. Mère Angélique Arnauld to Marie-Louise de Gonzague, queen of Poland, 5 November 1655, *LMMA* 3: 88–89.

73. Mère Angélique Arnauld, *EC*, 254.

74. Mère Angélique Arnauld, *EC*, 2.

75. Mère Angélique Arnauld, *EC*, 30.

76. Mère Angélique Arnauld, *EC*, 71.

77. Mère Angélique Arnauld, *EC*, 33.

78. Mère Angélique Arnauld, *EC*, 34.

79. Mère Angélique Arnauld, *EC*, 344.

80. Mère Angélique Arnauld, *EC*, 77.

81. Mère Angélique Arnauld, *EC*, 417.

82. Mère Angélique Arnauld, *EC*, 408.

83. Mère Angélique Arnauld, *EC*, 232.

84. Mère Angélique Arnauld, *EC*, 27.

85. Mère Angélique Arnauld, *EC*, 17.

86. See Mère Angélique Arnauld, *EC*, 292–93.

87. Mère Angélique Arnauld, *EC*, 68.

88. Mère Angélique Arnauld, *EC*, 68–69.

89. Mère Angélique Arnauld, *EC*, 365.

90. Mère Angélique Arnauld, *EC*, 108.

91. Mère Angélique Arnauld, *EC*, 33.

92. Mère Angélique Arnauld, *EC*, 141.

Chapter Three   MÈRE AGNÈS ARNAULD

1. Sources for this biographical sketch include the following: Perle Bugnion-Secrétan, *Mère Agnès Arnauld, 1593–1672: Abbesse de Port-Royal*

(Paris: Cerf, 1996); Philippe Sellier et al., "La Mère Agnès Arnauld (1593–1672)," *Chroniques de Port-Royal* no. 43 (1994); Jean Lesaulnier, "Arnauld, Jeanne, en religion Jeanne-Catherine de Sainte-Agnès de Saint-Paul, dite la Mère Agnès," in *Dictionnaire de Port-Royal,* ed. Jean Lesaulnier and Antony McKenna (Paris: Champion, 2004), 98–101.

2. See Mère Angélique Arnauld, *Relation écrite par la Mère Angélique Arnauld de ce qui est arrivé de plus considérable dans Port-Royal,* ed. Jean Lesaulnier, *Chroniques de Port-Royal* no. 41 (1992): 24.

3. Two early accounts of the *Private Chaplet* recount the history of its composition: Catherine Le Maître, "Relation de ce qui est arrivé depuis jusqu'en 1636," and Mère Angélique de Saint-Jean Arnauld d'Andilly, "Relation de l'origine et de la querelle du *Chapelet secret* du très Saint-Sacrement," ·*Mémoires pour servir à l'histoire de Port-Royal et à la vie de la Révérende Mère Marie-Angélique de Sainte-Magdeleine Arnauld réformatrice de ce monastère,* 3 vols. (Utrecht: Aux dépens de la Compagnie, 1742), 1: 419–55, 456–75.

4. "La censure des docteurs de la Sorbonne (8 juin 1633)," cited by Jean Orcibal in *Les origines du jansénisme,* 5 vols. (Paris: J. Vrin, 1947–62), 2: 311.

5. See Mère Angélique Arnauld, *Relation,* 58.

6. This viewpoint is clearly represented in Cécile Gazier, *Histoire du monastère de Port-Royal* (Paris: Perrin, 1929), 58–69.

7. See Jean du Vergier de Hauranne, abbé de Saint-Cyran, *Examen d'une apologie qui a été faite pour servir de défense à un petit livre intitulé Le chapelet secret du Très-Saint Sacrement* (Paris, 1634).

8. See Claude Séguenot, *Élévation d'esprit à Jésus-Christ Notre Seigneur au Très-Saint Sacrement, contentant divers usages de grâces sur ses perfections divines* (n.p., 1633).

9. See Mère Angélique Arnauld, *Relation,* 71–72.

10. See F. Ellen Weaver, *La Contre-Réforme et les constitutions de Port-Royal* (Paris: Cerf, 2002), 92–113.

11. Mère Agnès Arnauld to Jacqueline Pascal, 25 February 1650, *LMAA* 1: 167.

12. Mère Agnès Arnauld to Jacqueline Pascal, 5 August 1650, *LMAA* 1: 173.

13. Mère Agnès Arnauld to Jacqueline Pascal, 4 November 1650, *LMAA* 1: 177–78.

14. Mère Agnès Arnauld to Antoine Arnauld, 6 December 1644, *LMAA* 1: 116.

15. Mère Agnès Arnauld, "Déclaration de la Mère Agnès au subject des calumnies du Père Brisacier," 30 January 1652, *LMAA* 1: 227.

16. Mère Agnès Arnauld to Antoine Arnauld, 6 September 1644, *LMAA* 1: 115–17.

17. Mère Agnès Arnauld to Monsieur de Sévigné, 20 February 1668, *LMAA* 2: 253–55.

18. Mère Agnès Arnauld to Antoine Arnauld, May 1666, *LMAA* 2: 230–34.

19. Linda Timmermans, "La 'Religieuse Parfaite' et la théologie: L'attitude de la Mère Agnès à l'égard de la participation aux controverses," *Chroniques de Port-Royal* no. 43 (1994): 108.

20. Mère Agnès Arnauld to Madame de Foix, coadjutor abbess of abbey of Saintes, 10 December 1662, *LMAA* 2: 76.

21. Mère Agnès Arnauld to Louis XIV, 6 May 1661, *LMAA* 1: 494–95.

22. See Jean Mesnard, "Mère Agnès femme d'action," *Chroniques de Port-Royal* no. 43 (1994): 66–67.

23. See Mère Agnès Arnauld, *Le chapelet secret du Saint-Sacrement*, P.R. Ms. 8. Cited afterwards as *CS*. The text is reprinted by Jean-Robert Armogathe in "*Le chapelet secret* de Mère Agnès Arnauld," *XVIIe siècle* no. 170 (1991): 83–86. An extensive secondary literature has been devoted to the analysis of the *Chaplet*. See Jean Orcibal, *Les origins du jansénisme*, 5 vols. (Paris: Vrin, 1947–48), 1: 305–34; Louis Cognet, "*Le chapelet secret du Saint-Sacrement*," *Bulletin de la Société des Amis de Port-Royal* no. 2 (1951): 3–14; K. Kawamata, "Deux chapelets de Port-Royal," *Bulletin d'études françaises* (Dokkyo University) no. 16 (1985): 1–18; no. 17 (1986): 1–35; no. 18 (1987): 1–26; Armogathe, "*Le chapelet secret*," 77–86; Jean Lesaulnier, "*Le chapelet secret* de la Mère Angès Arnauld," *Chroniques de Port-Royal* no. 43 (1994): 9–23.

24. See Mère Agnès Arnauld, *L'image d'une religieuse parfaite et d'une imparfaite, avec les occupations intérieures pour toute la journée* (Paris: Charles Savreux, 1665). Cited afterwards as *IRP*.

25. See Bernard Chédozeau, "Aux sources du *Traité de l'oraison* de Pierre Nicole: Martin de Barcos et Jean Desmarets de Saint-Sorlin lecteurs des *Occupations intérieures* de la Mère Agnès Arnauld," *Chroniques de Port-Royal* no. 43 (1994): 123–34.

26. See Martin de Barcos, abbé de Saint-Cyran, *Les sentiments de l'abbé Philérème sur l'oraison mentale* (Cologne: P. Du Marteau, 1696), and Jean Desmarets de Saint-Sorlin, *Le chemin de la paix et celui de l'inquiétude*, vol. 1 (Paris: C. Audinet, 1665).

27. See Pierre Nicole, *Traité de l'oraison divisé en sept livres* (Paris: Josset, 1679).

28. See Mère Agnès Arnauld, *Les constitutions du monastère de Port-Royal du Saint-Sacrement* (Mons: Gaspard Migeot, 1665). Cited afterwards

as *CPR*. Although the first edition of the Constitutions carries the imprint of the Belgian Catholic publishing firm Gaspard Migeot and the stamped approval of Spain's King Philip (then ruling Belgium as part of the Spanish Lowlands), the book was actually published by the Protestant firm of Daniel Ezevier in Amsterdam. Jansenist authorities probably used this subterfuge to deflect the charges of Calvinism already launched against the convent.

29. See Mère Agnès Arnauld, *L'esprit du monastère de Port-Royal*, in *Constitutions du monastère de Port-Royal du Saint-Sacrement* (Mons: Gaspard Migeot, 1665), 397–422. Cited afterwards as *EPR*.

30. See Mère Agnès Arnauld, *Avis donnés par la Mère Catherine Agnès de Saint-Paul Arnauld, Sur la conduite que les religieuses devoient garder, au cas qu'il arrivât du changement dans le gouvernement de sa maison* (n.p., 1718), 81–108. Cited afterwards as *ACR*.

31. Mère Agnès Arnauld, *Lettres de la Mère Agnès Arnauld, abbesse de Port-Royal*, 2 vols., ed. Prosper Faugère (Paris: Benjamin Duprat, 1858). Cited elsewhere as *LMAA*.

32. See Mère Agnès Arnauld, *De l'amour qu'on doit avoir pour la croix de Jésus-Christ*, in *Recueil de divers traits de piété*, 2nd ed., ed. Jean Hamon (Paris: Desprez, 1675), 1: 397–423.

33. See Mère Agnès Arnauld, *Explication de la Règle par la Mère Agnès*, BNF Ms. Ffr. 19714.

34. *CS* no. 11.

35. *CS* no. 12.

36. *CS* no. 13.

37. *CS* no. 14.

38. *CS* no. 15.

39. *CS* no. 16.

40. *CS* no. 11.

41. *CS* no. 12.

42. *CS* no. 13.

43. *CS* no. 14.

44. *CS* no. 15.

45. *CS* no. 16.

46. *CS* no. 1.

47. *CS* no. 4.

48. *CS* no. 8.

49. *CS* no. 3.

50. *CS* no. 9.

51. See Étienne Binet, *Discussion sommaire d'un livret intitulé "Le chapelet secret du très-saint Sacrement"* (Paris, 1635).

52. See Louis Cognet, *"Le chapelet secret du Saint-Sacrement,"* 10–14.

53. See Armogathe, *"Le chaplet secret de Mère Agnès Arnauld,"* 80–82.

54. *IRP*, 7.
55. *IRP*, 10.
56. *IRP*, 17.
57. *IRP*, 21.
58. *IRP*, 24–25.
59. *IRP*, 30–31.
60. *IRP*, 31.
61. *IRP*, 35.
62. *IRP*, 43.
63. *IRP*, 44.
64. *IRP*, 48.
65. *IRP*, 49.
66. *IRP*, 53.
67. *IRP*, 55.
68. *IRP*, 55.
69. *IRP*, 61.
70. *IRP*, 78.
71. *IRP*, 88.
72. *IRP*, 94.
73. *IRP*, 100.
74. *IRP*, 126.
75. *IRP*, 127.
76. *IRP*, 101.
77. *IRP*, 148.
78. *IRP*, 155.
79. *IRP*, 160–61.
80. *IRP*, 165.
81. See Bernard Chédozeau, "Idéal intellectuel et vie monastique à Port-Royal," *Chroniques de Port-Royal* no. 37 (1988): 71–73. Chédozeau argues that Mère Agnès abandons her earlier mystical emphasis in favor of an intellectualist, moralist spirituality in her later works.
82. *EPR*, 398.
83. *EPR*, 398.
84. *EPR*, 398.
85. *EPR*, 399.
86. *EPR*, 398–99.
87. *EPR*, 414.
88. *EPR*, 399.
89. *EPR*, 399.
90. *EPR*, 408.
91. *EPR*, 413.
92. *EPR*, 400–401.

93. *EPR*, 404.

94. *EPR*, 411.

95. *EPR*, 411.

96. Mère Angélique Arnauld modified the original 1646 architectural plans of Antoine le Pautre for the Port-Royal de Paris convent church by insisting on the simplification of the columns, statuary, niches, glass, and arches. As a result, a baroque church in the "Jesuit" style was transformed into an austere neo-Cistercian temple for plain and transparent worship. For a discussion of this transformation, see Weaver, *La Contre-Réforme*, 82–87.

97. *EPR*, 411.

98. *EPR*, 411.

99. *CPR*, 59.

100. See *CPR*, 60–62.

101. *CPR*, 74.

102. *CPR*, 99.

103. *CPR*, 101.

104. *CPR*, 105.

105. *CPR*, 43.

106. *CPR*, 45.

107. *CPR*, 46.

108. For a discussion on the legal restrictions placed on nuns' access to the Bible during this period, see Chédozeau, "Idéal intellectual," 58–71.

109. See *CPR*, 159–60.

110. *CPR*, 54.

111. *CPR*, 56.

112. See *CPR*, 169–79.

113. See *CPR*, 172.

114. *CPR*, 170.

115. *CPR*, 179.

116. *CPR*, 38.

117. *CPR*, 2.

118. *CPR*, 9.

119. *CPR*, 12–13.

120. *CPR*, 273.

121. *ACR*, 82–83.

122. *ACR*, 83.

123. See *ACR*, 84–86.

124. The religious vow of poverty traditionally meant that while individual members of the religious order had renounced their right to personal property, the order itself could own collective property in its own name. The women belonging to the second order of the Franciscans, popularly

known as Poor Clares (after their foundress, Saint Clare), however, renounced communal as well as personal property in order to practice complete dependence on divine providence.

125. *ACR*, 89.

126. *ACR*, 91.

127. See *ACR*, 93–96.

128. See *ACR*, 86–88.

129. See *ACR*, 98–102.

130. *ACR*, 97.

131. *ACR*, 104.

132. *ACR*, 104.

133. *ACR*, 82.

134. *ACR*, 88.

135. *ACR*, 108.

136. *ACR*, 94.

137. *ACR*, 95–96.

138. *ACR*, 91.

139. *ACR*, 83.

140. *ACR*, 94–95.

141. *ACR*, 107.

142. *ACR*, 104.

Chapter Four MÈRE ANGÉLIQUE DE SAINT-JEAN ARNAULD
D'ANDILLY

1. Sources for this biography include Jean Orcibal, *Port-Royal
entre le miracle et l'obéissance: Flavie Passart et Angélique de St.-Jean
Arnauld d'Andilly* (Paris: Desclée de Brouwer, 1957); Brigitte Sibertin-Blanc,
"Angélique de Saint-Jean Arnauld d'Andilly d'après sa correspondance de
1624–1669" (thesis, École des Chartres, 1962); François Gazier et al., "Mère
Angélique de Saint-Jean Arnauld d'Andilly," *Chroniques de Port-Royal*
no. 35 (1985); F. Ellen Weaver-Laporte, "Arnauld d'Andilly, Angélique de
Saint-Jean," in *Dictionnaire de Port-Royal,* ed. Jean Lesaulnier and Antony
McKenna (Paris: Champion, 2004), 103–6.

2. René Rapin, *Mémoires du P. René Rapin de la Compagnie de Jésus
sur l'église et la société, la cour, la ville, et le jansénisme,* 3 vols. (Paris:
Gaume et Duprey, 1865), 1: 443.

3. Thomas du Fossé, *Mémoires pour servir à l'histoire de Port-Royal*
(Cologne: Aux dépens de la Compagnie, 1739), 378.

4. Madame de Sévigné to Madame de Grignan, 29 November 1679, in Marie de Rabutin-Chantal, marquise de Sévigné, *Lettres*, 3 vols., ed. Émile Gérard-Gailly (Paris: Gallimard, 1953–63), 2: 517.

5. See Mère Angélique Arnauld, *Relation écrite par la Mère Marie-Angélique Arnauld de ce qui est arrivé de plus considérable dans Port-Royal*, ed. Jean Lesaulnier, *Chroniques de Port-Royal* no. 41 (1992): 11–93.

6. See Mère Angélique de Saint-Jean Arnauld d'Andilly, *Relation ou histoire suivie de la Mère Marie-Angélique Arnauld*, in *Mémoires pour servir à l'histoire de Port-Royal et à la vie de la Révérende Mère Marie-Angélique de Sainte-Magdeleine Arnauld, réformatrice de ce monastère* (Utrecht: Aux dépens de la Compagnie, 1742), 1: 7–261.

7. See F. Ellen Weaver, "Angélique de Saint-Jean: Abbesse et 'mythographe' de Port-Royal," *Chroniques de Port-Royal* no. 35 (1985): 93–108, and Jean Lesaulnier, "Deux siècles d'historiographie port-royaliste," in *Images de Port-Royal*, ed. Jean Lesaulnier (Paris: Nolin, 2002), 225–45.

8. Du Fossé, *Mémoires pour servir*, 380.

9. For a catalogue of the criticisms of her personality offered by members of the Port-Royal circle, see Brigitte Sibertin-Blanc, "Biographie et personnalité de la séconde Angélique," *Chroniques de Port-Royal* no. 35 (1985): 74–82.

10. Cited by Sibertin-Blanc, ibid., 84.

11. See Mère Angélique de Saint-Jean Arnauld d'Andilly, *Relation de captivité*, ed. Louis Cognet (Paris: Gallimard, 1954).

12. Ibid., 66–68.

13. Soeur Angélique de Saint-Jean Arnauld d'Andilly to Mademoiselle de Bagnols, 14 May 1661, *LMASJ*, P.R. Let 358, 28.

14. See Soeur Angélique de Saint-Jean Arnauld d'Andilly to Antoine Arnauld, 5 November 1661, *LMASJ*, P.R. Let 358, 42.

15. Soeur Angélique de Saint-Jean Arnauld d'Andilly to Antoine Arnauld, 28 December 1668, *LMASJ*, P.R. Let 358, 176.

16. Soeur Angélique de Saint-Jean Arnauld d'Andilly to Madame la marquise de Sablé, 2 September 1669, *LMASJ*, P.R. Let 358, 180.

17. Soeur Angélique de Saint-Jean Arnauld d'Andilly to Antoine Arnauld, July 1666, *LMASJ*, P.R. Let 358, 121.

18. See Soeur Angélique de Saint-Jean Arnauld d'Andilly to unspecified addressee, 28 November 1661, *LMASJ*, P.R. Let 358, 47.

19. Soeur Angélique de Saint-Jean Arnauld d'Andilly to unspecified addressee, 28 November 1661, *LMASJ*, P.R. Let 358, 47.

20. Sibertin-Blanc, "Biographie et Personnalité," 83.

21. See Soeur Angélique de Saint-Jean Arnauld d'Andilly to Mère de Maurisse, 10 November 1670, *LMASJ*, P.R. Let 359, 192.

22. See Soeur Angélique de Saint-Jean Arnauld d'Andilly to Mademoiselle de Bagnols, 11 July 1674, *LMASJ*, P.R. Let 359, 265, and to Madame de Fonspertuis, 8 July 1675, *LMASJ*, P.R. Let 359, 304.

23. Soeur Angélique de Saint-Jean Arnauld d'Andilly to Gilberte Pascal Périer, 18 October 1671, *LMASJ*, P.R. Let 359, 210.

24. Soeur Angélique de Saint-Jean Arnauld d'Andilly to Mademoiselle de Bagnols, 11 July 1674, *LMASJ*, P.R. Let 359, 265.

25. Soeur Angélique de Saint-Jean Arnauld d'Andilly to Mademoiselle de Courcelles, 14 August 1676, *LMASJ*, P.R. Let 359, 366.

26. Soeur Angélique de Saint-Jean Arnauld d'Andilly to Mademoiselle de Bagnols, 4 September 1675, *LMASJ*, P.R. Let 359, 314.

27. Mère Angélique de Saint-Jean Arnauld d'Andilly to Henry Arnauld, bishop of Angers, 20 May 1679, *LMASJ*, P.R. Let 359, 473.

28. Mère Angélique de Saint-Jean Arnauld d'Andilly to Pope Innocent XI, 29 May 1679, *LMASJ*, P.R. Let 359, 474.

29. Mère Angélique de Saint-Jean Arnauld d'Andilly to Louis XIV, king of France, 5 February 1680, *LMASJ*, P.R. Let 360, 551.

30. Mère Angélique de Saint-Jean Arnauld d'Andilly to Monsieur Grenet, curé of Saint-Benoît and ecclesiastical overseer of Port-Royal, 19 April 1680, *LMASJ*, P.R. Let 360, 524.

31. Mère Angélique de Saint-Jean Arnauld d'Andilly to Madame de Fonspertuis, February 1680, *LMASJ*, P.R. Let 360, 514.

32. See Mère Angélique de Saint-Jean Arnauld d'Andilly to François de Harlay de Champvallon, archbishop of Paris, 1 September 1681, *LMASJ*, P.R. Let 360, 586.

33. Mère Angélique de Saint-Jean Arnauld d'Andilly to Madame de Fonspertuis, 18 January 1684, *LMASJ*, P.R. Let 360, 894.

34. Mère Angélique de Saint-Jean Arnauld d'Andilly to Mademoiselle de Bagnols, 29 May 1683, *LMASJ*, P.R. Let 369, 814.

35. The *régale* was an ancient privilege of the French king which permitted him to enjoy the revenues of certain dioceses in the Paris area during the interim period between the death of one bishop and the installation of his successor. In 1673 Louis XIV attempted to exercise the *régale* in all dioceses under French control upon the death of their bishops. Condemned by Pope Innocent XI as a violation of earlier treaties and declarations of ecumenical councils, the king's expansion of the *régale* provoked the pope's refusal to consecrate the king's nominees for dioceses. Louis XIV in turn took measures against papal authority, culminating in the passage of the "Gallican articles" by the French Assembly of Clergy in 1682. The articles limited papal rights in the affairs of the French church and exalted the rights of the king in both spiritual and temporal matters. The Jansenists and their allies

in the episcopate generally sided with the Vatican in this controversy, further increasing the French throne's hostility.

36. Mère Angélique de Saint-Jean Arnauld d'Andilly to Madame de Fonspertuis, 17 November 1681, *LMASJ*, P.R. Let 360, 614. See 1 John 2:17–19.

37. Cited by Germaine Grébil, "L'image de Mère Angélique de Saint-Jean au XVIIIe siècle," *Chroniques de Port-Royal* no. 35 (1985): 113.

38. See Mère Angélique de Saint-Jean Arnauld d'Andilly, *Discours de la Révérende Mère Marie Angélique de S. Jean, Abbesse de P.R. des Champs, sur la Règle de S. Benoît* (Paris: Osmont et Delespine, 1736). Hereafter cited as *DRSB*. This edition of Mère Angélique de Saint-Jean's commentary on the Rule of Saint Benedict, the only extant edition, must be read with caution, since the editors interpolated several passages from Mère Angélique Arnauld's early commentary on the Rule of Saint Benedict into the text.

39. See Mère Angélique de Saint-Jean Arnauld d'Andilly, *Conférences de la Mère Angélique de Saint-Jean sur les Constitutions du monastère de Port-Royal du Saint-Sacrement*, 3 vols., ed. Dom Charles Clémencet (Utrecht: Aux dépens de la Compagnie, 1760). Hereafter cited as *CCPR*.

40. See Mère Angélique de Saint-Jean Arnauld d'Andilly, *Réflexions de la R. Mère Angélique de S. Jean Arnauld, Abbesse de P.R. des Champs, Pour préparer ses soeurs à la persecution, conformément aux Avis que la R. Mère Agnès avait laissés sur cette matière aux religieuses de ce monastère* (n.p., 1737). Hereafter cited as *RPR*.

41. See Mère Angélique de Saint-Jean Arnauld d'Andilly, *Relation de captivité*.

42. See Mère Angélique de Saint-Jean Arnauld d'Andilly, *Discours de la R. M. Angélique de S. Jean, appellés Miséricordes, ou Recommendations, faites en chapitre, de plusieurs personnes unies à la Maison de Port-Royal des Champs* (Utrecht: C. Le Fevre, 1735). For a study of the social genesis of the genre of "miséricordes," see Thomas M. Carr, "Grieving Family and Community Ties at Port-Royal: Les Miséricordes of Angélique de Saint-Jean," in *La Rochefoucauld; Mithridate; Frères et soeurs; Les Muses soeurs*, ed. Claire Carlin (Tübingen: Narr, 1998), 171–79.

43. See Mère Angélique de Saint-Jean Arnauld d'Andilly, *Petit écrit de la Mère Angélique de Saint Jean, Sur la conformité de l'état où est réduit P.R. à l'état de Jésus-Christ dans l'Eucharistie*, in *Vies intéressantes et édifiantes des religieuses de Port-Royal et de plusieurs personnes qui leur étaient attachées* (Utrecht: Aux dépens de la Compagnie, 1750), 1: 250–56. Hereafter cited as *SC*.

44. See Mère Angélique de Saint-Jean Arnauld d'Andilly, *De la nécessité de défendre l'Église chacun en sa manière*, in *Vies intéressantes et édifiantes*, 1: 256–88.

45. See Mère Angélique de Saint-Jean Arnauld d'Andilly, *Réflexions de la Mère Angélique de Saint-Jean Arnauld d'Andilly, Sur le danger qu'il y a d'hésiter et de douter, quand une fois l'on connaît son devoir,* in *Vies intéressantes et édifiantes,* 1: 289–97. Hereafter cited as *DHD.*

46. See Mère Angélique de Saint-Jean Arnauld d'Andilly, *Relation ou histoire suivie de la Mère Marie-Angélique Arnauld,* in *Mémoires pour servir à l'histoire de la vie de la Mère Marie-Angélique de Sainte-Magdeleine Arnauld réformatrice de ce monastère* (Utrecht: Aux dépens de la Compagnie, 1742), 1: 7–261.

47. See Mère Angélique de Saint-Jean Arnauld d'Andilly et al., *Mémoires pour servir à l'histoire de la vie de la Mère Marie-Angélique de Sainte-Magdeleine Arnauld réformatrice de ce monastère,* 3 vols. (Utrecht: Aux dépens de la Compagnie, 1742).

48. See Mère Angélique de Saint-Jean Arnauld d'Andilly et al., *Nécrologie de l'abbaye de Notre-Dame de Port-Royal-des-Champs, ordre de Cîteaux, Institut du Saint-Sacrement, qui contient les éloges historiques avec les épitaphes des fondateurs et bienfaiteurs de ce monastère,* ed. Dom Antoine Rivet de La Grange (Amsterdam: N. Potgieter, 1733).

49. Cited by Grébil, "L'images," 116.

50. Religieuses de Port-Royal, *Exercises de piété à l'usage des religieuses de Port-Royal du Saint-Sacrement* (Paris: Au Désert, 1787).

51. See Mère Angélique de Saint-Jean Arnauld d'Andilly, *Lettres de la Mère Angélique de Saint-Jean,* P.R. Let 358–361. Elsewhere cited as *LMASJ.*

52. See Mère Angélique de Saint-Jean Arnauld d'Andilly, *De la direction,* P.R. Ms. 175, 4.

53. Ibid., 97.

54. See Mère Angélique de Saint-Jean Arnauld d'Andilly, *Pensées sur divers sujets,* P.R. Ms. 130.

55. See Mère Angélique de Saint-Jean Arnauld d'Andilly, *Récit fidèle des miracles et visions de la Soeur Flavie écrit par la Mère Angélique de S. Jean,* P.R. Let 361, appendix.

56. For an analysis of the historical genesis of the Rule of Saint Benedict, see Adalbert de Vogüé, *The Rule of Saint Benedict: A Doctrinal and Spiritual Commentary* (Kalamazoo, Mich.: Cistercian Publications, 1983).

57. See Hildegarde of Bingen, *Explanation of the Rule of Saint Benedict,* trans. Hugh Feiss (Toronto: Peregrina, 1990).

58. *DRSB,* 4. See Matt. 20:16.

59. *DRSB,* 53–54.

60. *DRSB,* 243.

61. *DRSB,* 248–49.

62. *DRSB,* 267–68.

63. *DRSB,* 407. See Phil. 2:6–8.

64. *DRSB*, 311–12.
65. *DRSB*, 326–27.
66. *DRSB*, 358.
67. *DRSB*, 381.
68. *DRSB*, 473.
69. Although she had read the *City of God* in the Latin original, Mère Angélique de Saint-Jean often cites the standard modern French translation of the work by François de Belleforest, with annotations by Gentian Hervet and a commentary on Augustine by Juan Luis Vives. First published in 1570 in Paris, this version of the *Cité de Dieu* underwent numerous re-editions throughout the seventeenth century.
70. *CCPR*, 1: 33.
71. *CCPR*, 1: 321–22.
72. *CCPR*, 1: 384. See Heb. 9:14.
73. *CCPR*, 1: 386. See Isa. 55:11.
74. *CCPR*, 1: 52.
75. *CCPR*, 1: 775–76.
76. *RPR*, 57.
77. *RPR*, 16–17.
78. *RPR*, 205–6.
79. *RPR*, 20–21.
80. *RPR*, 20.
81. *RPR*, 288–89.
82. *RPR*, 168.
83. *RPR*, 160.
84. *RPR*, 161.
85. *RPR*, 31.
86. See *RPR*, 242.
87. *RPR*, 25–26.
88. *RPR*, 71.
89. *RPR*, 82–83.
90. *RPR*, 83–84.
91. *RPR*, 105.
92. *RPR*, 105.
93. *RPR*, 112–13.
94. *RPR*, 116–17.
95. *RPR*, 319. See 1 Thess. 1:4.
96. *RPR*, 222–23.
97. *RPR*, 113.
98. *RPR*, 292.
99. *RPR*, 286.
100. *DHD*, 290.

101. *DHD*, 291.

102. *DHD*, 290.

103. *DHD*, 291–92.

104. *DHD*, 294.

105. *DHD*, 293.

106. *DHD*, 293. See Jer. 16:1–13.

107. *DHD*, 291.

108. See *DHD*, 295.

109. See *DHD*, 294. This refers to the silence of Christ during the interrogations by Caiaphas and Pilate shortly before his execution.

110. See *DHD*, 295. See Matt. 11:2–6.

111. See *DHD*, 296–97. See Num. 22:9–12.

112. One of the most influential is Sainte-Beuve, who in his monumental *Port-Royal* depicts Mère Angélique de Saint-Jean Arnauld d'Andilly as a stubborn ideologue who systematically seeks confrontation "due to a certain demon of contestation." See this portrait of the nun in Charles-Augustin Sainte-Beuve, *Port-Royal*, 3 vols., ed. Maxime Leroy (Paris: Gallimard, 1953–55), 2: 703–37.

113. See Grébil, "L'image," 30.

114. *SC*, 251.

115. *SC*, 251.

116. *SC*, 252.

117. *SC*, 253.

118. *SC*, 252.

119. See *SC*, 255.

120. See *SC*, 254–55.

121. See *SC*, 255.

122. *SC*, 251.

123. *SC*, 252–53.

Chapter Five   CONCLUSION

1. See Jacqueline Broad, *Women Philosophers of the Seventeenth Century* (Cambridge: Cambridge University Press, 2002).

2. For a critical study of this theological turn in recent Continental philosophy, see Dominique Janicaud, ed., *Phenomenology and the Theological Turn: The French Debate* (New York: Fordham University Press, 2001). Discussed in this volume, the recent work of Jean-Luc Marion, Jean-Louis Chrétien, and Jean-François Courtine illustrates the renewed interest in negative theology, which Marion would prefer to recast in Pseudo-Dionysius's category of "mystical theology."

3. Representative works in the recent retrieval of virtue ethics are Julia Driver, *Uneasy Virtue* (Cambridge: Cambridge University Press, 2001); Philippa Foot, *Natural Goodness* (Oxford: Clarendon Press, 2001); Peter Geach, *The Virtues* (Cambridge: Cambridge University Press, 1977).

4. Among recent efforts to develop a more contextualist and pluralist account of virtue, see Christine Swanton, *Virtue Ethics: A Pluralistic View* (Oxford: Oxford University Press, 2003).

5. Major works in which Hauerwas defends a theological-contextual theory of virtue are *A Community of Character* (Notre Dame, Ind.: University of Notre Dame Press, 1981) and *The Peaceable Kingdom: A Primer in Christian Ethics* (Notre Dame, Ind.: University of Notre Dame Press, 1986).

6. Antony McKenna, "Port-Royal," in *Routledge Encyclopedia of Philosophy* (London: Routledge). Retrieved 14 June 2005 from http://www.rep.routledge.com/article/DA063SECT2.

WORKS CITED

Armogathe, Jean-Robert. "*Le chapelet secret* de Mère Agnès Arnauld." *XVIIe siècle* no. 170 (1991): 77–86.

Arnauld, Mère Agnès. *Avis donnés par la Mère Catherine Agnès de Saint-Paul, Sur la conduite que les religieuses doivent garder, au cas qu'il arrivât du changement dans le gouvernement de sa maison.* N.p., 1718.

———. *Les constitutions du monastère de Port-Royal du Saint-Sacrement.* Mons: Gaspard Migeot, 1665.

———. *De l'amour qu'on doit avoir pour la croix de Jésus-Christ.* In *Recueil de divers traités de piété.* 2nd ed. Edited by Jean Hamon, 1: 397–423. Paris: Desprez, 1675.

———. *Explication de la Règle par la Mère Agnès.* BNF Ms. Ffr. 19714.

———. *Lettres de la Mère Agnès Arnauld, abbesse de Port-Royal.* Edited by Prosper Faugère. 2 vols. Paris: Benjamin Duprat, 1858.

———. *L'image d'une religieuse parfaite et d'une imparfaite, avec les occupations intérieures pour toute la journée.* Paris: Charles Savreux, 1665.

———. *Pensées sur le chapelet secret du Saint-Sacrement.* P.R. Ms. 8.

Arnauld, Mère Angélique. *Entretiens ou conférences de la Révérende Mère Marie-Angélique Arnauld, abbesse et réformatrice de Port-Royal.* Brussels: A. Boudet, 1757.

———. *Lettres de la Révérende Mère Marie-Angélique Arnauld, abbesse et réformatrice de Port-Royal.* 3 vols. Utrecht: Aux dépens de la Compagnie, 1742–44.

———. *Relation écrite par la Mère Angélique Arnauld.* Edited by Louis Cognet. Paris: Grasset, 1949.

———. *Relation écrite par la Mère Marie-Angélique Arnauld de ce qui est arrivé de plus considérable dans Port-Royal.* Edited by Jean Lesaulnier. *Chroniques de Port-Royal* 41 (1992): 7–93.

Arnauld, Antoine. *Phantôme du jansénisme ou justification des prétendus jansénistes.* Cologne: Chez Nicolas Schouten, 1686.

Arnauld, Antoine, and Claude Lancelot. *Grammaire générale et raisonnée.* Paris: P. Le Petit, 1660.

Arnauld, Antoine, and Pierre Nicole. *La logique, ou l'art de penser.* Paris: C. Savreux, 1662.

Arnauld d'Andilly, Mère Angélique de Saint-Jean. *Conférences de la Mère Angélique de Saint Jean sur les Constitutions du monastère de Port-Royal du Saint Sacrement.* Edited by Dom Charles Clémencet. 3 vols. Utrecht: Aux dépens de la Compagnie, 1760.

———. *De la direction.* P.R. Ms. 175, 4.

———. *De la nécessité de défendre l'Église chacun en sa manière.* In *Vies intéressantes et édifiantes des religieuses de Port-Royal et de plusieurs personnes qui leur étaient attachées.* 1: 256–88. Utrecht: Aux dépens de la Compagnie, 1750.

———. *Discours de la Révérende Mère Marie Angélique de S. Jean, Abbesse de P.R. des Champs, sur la Règle de S. Benoît.* Paris: Osmont et Delespine, 1736.

———. *Discours de la R. M. Angélique de S. Jean, appellés Miséricordes, ou Recommandations, faites en chapitre, de plusieurs personnes unies à la Maison de Port-Royal des Champs.* Utrecht: C. Le Fevre, 1735.

———. *Lettres de la Mère Angélique de Saint-Jean.* Edited by Rachel Gillet. P.R. Let 358–61.

———. *Mémoires pour servir à l'histoire de Port-Royal et à la vie de la Révérende Mère Marie Angélique de Sainte Magdeleine Arnauld, réformatrice de ce monastère.* 3 vols. Utrecht: Aux dépens de la Compagnie, 1742.

———. *Nécrologie de l'abbaye de Notre-Dame de Port-Royal-des-Champs, ordre de Cîteaux, Institut du Saint-Sacrement, qui contient les éloges historiques avec les épitaphes des fondateurs et bienfaiteurs de ce monastère.* Edited by Dom Antoine Rivet de La Grange. Amsterdam: N. Potgieter, 1733.

———. *Pensées sur divers sujets.* P.R. Ms. 130.

———. *Petit écrit de la Mère Angélique de Saint Jean, Sur la conformité de l'état où est réduit P.R. à l'état de Jésus-Christ dans l'Eucharistie.* In *Vies intéressantes et édifiantes des religieuses de Port-Royal et de plusieurs personnes qui leur étaient attachées.* 1: 250–55. Utrecht: Aux dépens de la Compagnie, 1750.

———. *Récit fidèle des miracles et visions de la Soeur Flavie écrit par la Mère Angélique de S. Jean.* P.R. Let 361, appendix.

———. *Réflexions de la Mère Angélique de Saint-Jean Arnauld d'Andilly, Sur le danger qu'il y a d'hésiter et de douter, quand une fois l'on connaît son devoir.* In *Vies intéressantes et édifiantes des religieuses de Port-Royal et de plusieurs personnes qui leur étaient attachées.* 1: 289–97. Utrecht: Aux dépens de la Compagnie, 1750.

———. *Réflexions de la R. Mère Angélique de S. Jean Arnauld, Abbesse de P.R. des Champs, Pour préparer ses soeurs à la persecution, conformé-*

ment aux Avis que la R. Mère Agnès avait laissés sur cette matière aux religieuses de ce monastère. N.p., 1737.

———. *Relation de captivité.* Edited by Louis Cognet. Paris: Gallimard, 1954.

———. *Relation ou histoire suivie de la Mère Marie-Angélique de Sainte-Magdeleine Arnauld réformatrice de ce monastère.* 1: 7–261. Utrecht: Aux dépens de la Compagnie, 1742.

Augustine, Saint. *De la cité de Dieu.* Translated by François de Belleforest. Paris: Nicolas Chesneau, 1570.

Besoigne, Jérôme. *Histoire de l'abbaye de Port-Royal.* 6 vols. Cologne: Aux dépens de la Compagnie, 1752.

Binet, Étienne. *Discussion sommaire d'un livret intitulé "Le chapelet secret du très-saint Sacrement."* Paris, 1635.

Boulêtreau, François. "La charité de la Mère Angélique." *Chroniques de Port-Royal* 41 (1992): 171–94.

Broad, Jacqueline. *Women Philosophers of the Seventeenth Century.* Cambridge: Cambridge University Press, 2002.

Bugnion-Secrétan, Perle. *Mère Agnès Arnauld, 1593–1672; Abbesse de Port-Royal.* Paris: Cerf, 1996.

———. *La Mère Angélique Arnauld, 1591–1661, après ses écrits.* Paris: Cerf, 1991.

Carr, Thomas M. "Grieving Family and Community Ties at Port-Royal: Les Miséricordes of Angélique de Saint-Jean." In *La Rochefoucauld; Mithridate; Frères et soeurs; les Muses soeurs,* edited by Claire Carlin, 171–79. Tübingen: Narr, 1988.

———. *Voix des abbesses du Grand Siècle: La prédication au féminin à Port-Royal.* Tübingen: Narr, 2006.

Chédozeau, Bernard. "Aux sources du *Traité de l'oraison* de Pierre Nicole: Martin de Barcos et Jean Desmarets de Saint-Sorlin lecteurs des *Occupations intérieures* de la Mère Agnès Arnauld." *Chroniques de Port-Royal* 43 (1994): 123–34.

———. "Idéal intellectual et vie monastique à Port-Royal." *Chroniques de Port-Royal* 37 (1997): 57–74.

The Church Teaches: Documents of the Church in English. Edited by John F. Clarkson et al. St. Louis: Herder, 1960.

Clémencet, Charles. *Histoire générale de Port-Royal.* 10 vols. Amsterdam: J. Vanduran, 1755–57.

———. *Histoire littéraire des religieuses de Port-Royal des Champs.* Ms. Maz 4538.

Cognet, Louis. "*Le chapelet secret* du Saint-Sacrement." *Bulletin de la Société des amis de Port-Royal* no. 2 (1951): 3–14.

———. *Le jansénisme.* 7th ed. Paris: Presses Universitaires de France, 1995.

———. *La réforme de Port-Royal: 1591–1618.* Paris: Sulliver, 1950.

Conley, John J. *The Suspicion of Virtue: Women Philosophers in Neoclassical France.* Ithaca: Cornell University Press, 2002.

Cousin, Victor. *Jacqueline Pascal: Premières études sur les femmes illustres et la société du XVIIe siècle.* 4th ed. Paris: Didier, 1861.

Delforge, Frédéric. *Jacqueline Pascal, 1625–1661.* Paris: Nolin, 2002.

Desmarets de Saint-Sorlin, Jean. *Le chemin de la paix et celui de l'inquiétude.* Vol. 1. Paris: C. Audinet, 1665.

Dictionnaire de Port-Royal. Edited by Jean Lesaulnier and Antony McKenna. Paris: Champion, 2004.

Doyle, William. *Jansenism: Catholic Resistance to Authority from the Reformation to the French Revolution.* New York: St. Martin's Press, 2000.

Driver, Julia. *Uneasy Virtue.* Cambridge: Cambridge University Press, 2001.

Du Fossé, Thomas. *Mémoires pour servir à l'histoire de Port-Royal.* Utrecht: Aux dépens de la Compagnie, 1739.

Foot, Philippa. *Natural Goodness.* Oxford: Clarendon Press, 2001.

François de Sales. *Oeuvres.* Edited by André Ravier. Paris: Gallimard, 1992.

Gastellier, Fabian. *Angélique Arnauld.* Paris: Fayard, 1998.

Gazier, Cécile. *Histoire du monastère de Port-Royal.* Paris: Perrin, 1929.

Geach, Peter. *The Virtues.* Cambridge: Cambridge University Press, 1977.

Goldmann, Lucien. *Le Dieu caché: Étude sur la vision tragique dans les "Pensées" de Pascal et dans le théâtre de Racine.* 3rd ed. Paris: Gallimard, 1955.

Grébil, Germaine. "L'image de Mère Angélique de Saint-Jean au XVIIIe siècle." *Chroniques de Port-Royal* 35 (1985): 110–25.

Habert, Isaac. *La défense de la foi de l'Église et de l'ancienne doctrine de la Sorbonne, touchant les principaux points de la grâce, prêchée dans l'église de Paris.* Paris: T. Blaise, 1644.

Harth, Erica. *Cartesian Women: Versions and Subversions of Rational Discourse in the Old Regime.* Ithaca: Cornell University Press, 1992.

Hauerwas, Stanley. *A Community of Character.* Notre Dame, Ind.: University of Notre Dame Press, 1981.

———. *The Peaceable Kingdom: A Primer in Christian Ethics.* Notre Dame, Ind.: University of Notre Dame Press, 1986.

Hildegarde of Bingen. *Explanation of the Rule of Saint Benedict.* Translated by Hugh Feiss. Toronto: Pergrina, 1990.

Janicaud, Dominique, ed. *Phenomenology and the Theological Turn: The French Debate.* New York: Fordham University Press, 2001.

Jansenius, Cornelius. *De la réformation de l'homme intérieur.* Translated by Robert Arnauld d'Andilly. Paris: Veuve J. Camusat, 1642.

John Climacus, Saint. *L'échelle sainte, ou les degrés pour monter au ciel.* Translated by Robert Arnauld d'Andilly. Paris: Pierre Le Petit, 1653.

Kawamata, K. "Deux chapelets de Port-Royal." *Bulletin d'études françaises* (Dokkyo University) 16 (1985): 1–18; 17 (1986): 1–35; 18 (1987): 1–26.

Kolakowski, Leszeck. *God Owes Us Nothing: A Brief Remark on Pascal's Religion and the Spirit of Jansenism.* Chicago: University of Chicago Press, 1995.

Kostroun, Daniella J. "Undermining Obedience in Absolutist France: The Case of the Port-Royal Nuns." Ph.D. diss., Duke University, 2000.

Labarrière, Pierre-Jean. "Thérèse d'Avila: Docteur de l'Église." *Études* 357 (1982): 391–402.

Le Mâitre, Antoine. *La vie de S. Bernard, premier abbé de Clairvaux et père de l'église.* Paris: Antoine Vitré, 1648.

Lesaulnier, Jean. "Arnauld, Jeanne, en religion Jeanne-Catherine de Sainte-Agnès de Saint-Paul, dite la Mère Agnès." In *Dictionnaire de Port-Royal,* edited by Jean Lesaulnier and Antony McKenna, 98–101. Paris: Champion, 2004.

———. "*Le chapelet secret* de la Mère Agnès Arnauld." *Chroniques de Port-Royal* 43 (1994): 9–23.

———. "Deux siècles d'historiographie port-royaliste." In *Images de Port-Royal,* edited by Jean Lesaulnier, 225–45. Paris: Nolin, 2002.

Leuenberger, Robert. *Jacqueline Pascal: Die Schwester des Philosophen.* Zurich: Theologischer Verlagen, 2002.

McKenna, Antony. "Port-Royal." In *Routledge Encyclopedia of Philosophy.* London: Routledge. Retrieved 14 June 2005 from http://www.rep. routledge.com/article/DA063SECT2.

Mesnard, Jean. "Mère Agnès femme d'action." *Chroniques de Port-Royal* 43 (1994): 66–67.

———. "Pour une édition critique des lettres de la Mère Angélique." *Chroniques de Port-Royal* 41 (1992): 211–26.

Montherlant, Henry de. *Port-Royal.* Paris: Gallimard, 1954.

Newton, William Ritchey. *Sociologie de la communauté de Port-Royal: Histoire, économie.* Paris: Klincksieck, 1999.

Nicole, Pierre. *Les imaginaires ou lettres sur l'hérésie imaginaire.* Liège: Chez Adolphe Beyers, 1667.

O'Neill, Eileen. "Early Modern Philosophers and the History of Philosophy." *Hypatia* 20:3 (2005): 185–97.

Orcibal, Jean. *Les origines du jansénisme.* 5 vols. Paris: J. Vrin, 1947–62.

———. *Port-Royal entre le miracle et l'obéissance: Flavie Passart et Angé-lique de St.-Jean Arnauld d'Andilly.* Paris: Desclée de Brouwer, 1957.

———. *La spiritualité de Saint-Cyran avec ses écrits de piété inédits.* Paris: Librairie Philosophique J. Vrin, 1962.

Pascal, Blaise. *L'Oeuvre de Pascal.* Edited by Jacques Chevalier. Paris: Galli-mard, 1950.

———, et al. *Oeuvres complètes avec tous les documents biographiques et critiques; Les oeuvres d'Étienne, de Gilberte et de Jacqueline Pascal et celles de Marguerite Périer; la correspondence des Pascal et des Périer.* 4 vols. Edited by Jean Mesnard. Paris: Desclée de Brouwer, 1964–92.

Pascal, Jacqueline. *Lettres, opuscules et mémoires de Madame Périer et de Jacqueline, soeurs de Pascal, et de Marguerite Périer, sa nièce.* Edited by M. P. Faugère. Paris: A. Vaton, 1845.

———. *A Rule for Children and Other Writings.* Translated and edited by John J. Conley. Chicago: University of Chicago Press, 2003.

Plutarch. *Les oeuvres morales et meslées de Plutarque translatées du grec en français.* Translated by Jacques Amyot. Paris: M. de Vascosan, 1572.

Rapin, René. *Mémoires du P. René Rapin de la Compagnie de Jésus sur l'église et la société, la cour, la ville, et le jansénisme.* 3 vols. Paris: Gaume et Duprey, 1865.

Rowan, Mary. "Angélique Arnauld's Web of Feminine Friendships: Letters to Jeanne de Chantal and the Queen of Poland." In *Les femmes au grand siècle; Le Baroque; Musique et literature; Musique et liturgie,* edited by David Wetsel et al., 53–59. Tübingen: Narr, 2003.

Saint-Cyran, Jean du Vergier de Hauranne, abbé de. *Examen d'une apologie qui a été faite pour servir de défense à un petit livre intitulé Le chape-let secret du Très-Saint Sacrement.* Paris, 1633.

———. *Lettres chrétiennes et spirituelles.* Paris: Veuve Martin Durand, 1645.

———. *Théologie familière.* 5th ed. Paris: Jean Le Mire, 1644.

Saint-Cyran, Martin de Barcos, abbé de. *Les sentiments de l'abbé Philérème sur l'oraison mentale.* Cologne: P. Du Marteau, 1696.

Sainte-Beuve, Charles-Augustin. *Port-Royal.* 3 vols. Edited by Maxime Leroy. Paris: Gallimard, 1953–55.

Schmaltz, Tad M. "What Has Cartesianism to Do with Jansenism?" *Journal of the History of Ideas* 60:1 (1999): 37–56.

Sedgwick, Alexander. *The Travails of Conscience: The Arnauld Family and the Ancien Régime.* Cambridge: Harvard University Press, 1998.

Séguenot, Claude. *Élévation d'esprit à Jésus-Christ Notre Seigneur au très-saint Sacrement, contenant divers usages de grâces sur ses perfections divines.* N.p., 1633.

Sellier, Phillipe. *Le siècle de Saint-Augustin*. Paris: Champion, 2000.

Sévigné, Marie de Rabutin-Chantal, marquise de. *Lettres*. 3 vols. Edited by Émile Gérard-Gailly. Paris: Gallimard, 1953–63.

Sibertin-Blanc, Brigitte. "Angélique de Saint-Jean Arnauld d'Andilly d'après sa correspondence de 1624–1669." Thesis, École des Chartres, 1962.

———. "Biographie et personnalité de la séconde Angélique." *Chroniques de Port-Royal* 35 (1985): 74–82.

Swanton, Christine. *Virtue Ethics: A Pluralistic View*. Oxford: Oxford University Press, 2003.

Teresa of Avila. *Oeuvres de la Mère Thérèse de Jésus*. 3 vols. Translated by Jean de Brétigny. Paris: G. de la Noüe, 1601.

———. *Oeuvres de Sainte Thérèse d'Avila*. Translated by Robert Arnauld d'Andilly. Paris: P. Le Petit, 1670.

Timmermans, Linda. "La 'Religieuse Parfaite' et la théologie: L'attitude de la Mère Agnès à l'égard de la participation aux controverses." *Chroniques de Port Royal* 43 (1994): 108.

Villanueva Gardner, Catherine. *Women Philosophers: Genre and the Boundaries of Philosophy*. Boulder, Colo.: Westview Press, 2004.

Vogüé, Adalbert de. *The Rule of Saint Benedict: A Doctrinal and Spiritual Commentary*. Kalamazoo, Mich.: Cistercian Publications, 1983.

Waithe, Mary Ellen. "Roswitha of Gondersheim, Christine of Pisan, Margaret More Roper, and Teresa of Avila." In *A History of Women Philosophers*, vol. 2, edited by Mary Ellen Waithe. Dordrecht: Kluwer, 1989.

Warnock, Mary. *Women Philosophers*. London: J.M. Dent, 1996.

Weaver, F. Ellen. "Angélique de Saint-Jean: Abbesse et 'mythographe' de Port-Royal." *Chroniques de Port-Royal* 35 (1985): 93–108.

———. *La Contre-Réforme et les constitutions de Port-Royal*. Paris: Cerf, 2002.

———. *The Evolution of the Reform of Port-Royal: From the Rule of Cîteaux to Jansenism*. Paris: Beauchesne, 1978.

Weaver-Laporte, F. Ellen. "Arnauld d'Andilly, Angélique de Saint-Jean." In *Dictionnaire de Port-Royal*, edited by Jean Lesaulnier and Antony McKenna, 103–6. Paris: Champion, 2004.

INDEX

abandonment, spiritual, 6, 34, 47–48; Mère Agnès on, 128, 131, 173; Mère Angélique on, 56, 75; Mère Angélique de Saint-Jean on, 183, 216, 219, 227–30

abbess, 2, 4, 193, 197

absolutism, 12, 22, 24

adoration, 7, 37; Mère Agnès on, 115–16, 119, 129, 132–35, 142–45, 161, 168, 173–74; Mère Angélique on, 49, 66, 95–96, 107; Mère Angélique de Saint-Jean on, 205, 220, 226–32, 243

Ad sacram (Alexander VII), 11

aesthetics, 47, 73, 74, 87, 150, 166, 243

Against Spain (Arnauld the Elder), 21

Alexander VII, pope, 11, 13, 124

Allen, Madame, 70

alterity, divine, 130–35, 188, 220, 240

analogy, 132

Anne of Austria, queen and regent of France, 10, 54, 57, 80–81

annihilation, spiritual, 6, 245; Mère Agnès on, 115–17, 128, 129, 133–34, 137, 141, 143–44, 170, 174; Mère Angélique on, 60, 76–77, 92, 99; Mère Angélique de Saint-Jean on, 202, 226–32, 236

Annonciades, 89–91, 182–83, 195, 226, 235

anthropocentrism, 135–45

anthropology, 95, 239, 247; Arnauld abbesses on, 122, 132, 138, 139, 145, 151–52, 226–31, 233

Apologies for Jansenius (Antoine Arnauld), 9, 59, 79, 81

Apology Made to Defend a Small Book Entitled "Private Chaplet of the Blessed Sacrament" (Saint-Cyran), 119

apophaticism, 24–25, 27, 35–36, 37, 40, 237, 239–40, 243, 274n6; and Mère Agnès, 119, 128–35, 146–53, 171; and Mère Angélique, 107; and Mère Angélique de Saint-Jean, 188, 211, 220, 235

Aristotelianism, 85

Arnauld, Anne-Eugénie de l'Incarnation, 22, 177, 179

Arnauld, Antoine the Elder, 20–23, 24, 43–46

Arnauld, Antoine the Younger: and Mère Agnès, 121–24, 126, 129, 130; and Mère Angélique, 52–53, 59, 77–84, 86; and Mère Angélique de Saint-Jean, 177, 180, 182, 183, 185, 189, 233; and philosophy, 244, 246, 250; and Port-Royal, 2, 9, 11–12, 14–17, 19, 20, 23, 31, 36–37

Arnauld, Catherine de Sainte-
Félicité Marion, 22, 44–46, 114,
177
Arnauld, Henry, bishop of Angers,
19, 23–24, 127, 177, 188–89
Arnauld, Jacqueline-Marie (*known
in religion as* Mère Angélique).
See Arnauld, Mère Marie-
Angélique de Sainte-
Magdeleine
Arnauld, Jeanne (*known in religion
as* Mère Agnès). *See* Arnauld,
Mère Catherine-Agnès de
Saint-Paul
Arnauld, Madeleine de Sainte-
Christine, 22
Arnauld, Marie de Sainte-Claire, 22
Arnauld, Mère Catherine-Agnès de
Saint-Paul (*known as* Mère
Agnès): biography of, 114–27;
on character, 146–53; on divine
attributes, 130–35; critical
evaluation of, 171–74; and
Mère Angélique; 44, 48, 50, 51,
59, 73; and Mère Angélique de
Saint-Jean, 176, 180, 192, 194,
206, 208, 210, 216–17, 226; on
monastic constitutions,
153–63; and philosophy, 237,
240, 243, 245, 248; and Port-
Royal, 1, 3, 4, 6, 7, 9, 10, 15, 16,
19, 22, 27–38; on resistance,
163–70; on virtue, 135–45;
writings of, 128–30, 260–65
Arnauld, Mère Marie-Angélique de
Sainte-Magdeleine (*known as*
Mère Angélique): on authority,
88–93; biography of, 43–55;
conferences of, 60, 93–106;
correspondence of, 56–60,
61–93, 250–60; on divine

attributes, 61–65, 93–96; on
education, 86–88; critical
evaluation of, 106–12; on grace,
84–85, 103–6; and Mère Agnès,
113–22, 170; and Mère
Angélique de Saint-Jean, 180,
192; and philosophy, 237, 240,
243, 248, 250–60; and Port-
Royal 1, 3, 4, 5, 6, 9, 16, 19, 20,
22, 27–38; rationalism of,
101–3; on vice, 100–101; on
virtue, 65–84, 96–100; writings
of, 55–60
Arnauld d'Andilly, Mère Angélique
de Saint Jean: on anthropology,
226–32; biography of, 176–93;
critical evaluation of, 232–36;
on epistemology, 220–26; and
Mère Agnès, 124, 126; and
Mère Angélique, 55–56, 59–60,
61–93, 93–106, 106–12; and
philosophy, 237, 240, 242, 243,
245, 248; and Port-Royal, 1, 4,
14, 16, 17, 19, 22, 24, 27–38; on
resistance, 210–20; on virtue,
197–210; writings of, 193–97,
266–72
Arnauld d'Andilly, Anne-Marie, 176
Arnauld d'Andilly, Catherine de
Sainte-Agnès, 176
Arnauld d'Andilly, Catherine Le
Fèvre de la Broderie, 23, 176
Arnauld d'Andilly, Marie-Angélique
de Sainte-Thérèse, 126
Arnauld d'Andilly, Marie-Charlotte
de Sainte-Claire, 126
Arnauld d'Andilly, Robert, 23, 30,
52, 55, 62, 176
Arnauld family, 7, 19–27
asceticism, 86–88, 92, 99–100, 198,
234, 237

Asseline, Eustache de Saint-Paul, 115

Assembly of Bishops, 13

Assembly of Clergy, 53

attributes, divine, 27–28, 61–65, 93–96, 117, 130–35, 146, 171, 235, 237

Augustine of Hippo, Saint: disciples of, 27–38, 129; Mère Agnès on, 122–23, 130, 162; Mère Angélique on, 46, 51, 57, 77, 79, 104, 110; Mère Angélique de Saint-Jean on, 177, 186, 191, 205–10, 230, 233; and Port-Royal, 1, 9, 23; Rule of: 33, 198, 277n33

Augustinianism: and Arnauld abbesses: 27–38, 237–48; and Mère Agnès, 122–23, 129–30, 138, 144–45, 146–53, 172; and Mère Angélique, 51–52, 59, 82, 85, 96–100, 104, 106–12; and Mère Angélique de Saint-Jean, 187, 191, 194, 197, 198, 203, 205–10; 232–36; and Port-Royal, 1, 3, 4, 7, 8, 9, 23

Augustinus (Jansen): and Arnauld abbesses, 53, 81, 106, 119, 124, 180, 184; and Jansenism, 7–8, 9, 10, 11, 12, 14, 30, 32

authority, 41–42, 237, 246; Mère Agnès on, 125–26, 153–63, 163–70, 174; Mère Angélique on, 88–93, 109–10; Mère Angélique de Saint-Jean on, 197, 205, 235

Autobiography of Teresa of Avila, 115

Babylon, 204, 207

Bagnols, Gabrielle du Gué de, 184–85, 187–88, 191–92, 196

Bail, Louis, 187

Balaam, 225

Barcos, Martin de, abbé de Saint-Cyran, 128

Barrême, René, 118

Basil, Saint, 198

Basile, Father, 46

Bayle, Pierre, 244

Bellegarde, Olivier de, archbishop of Sens, 49–50, 118–19

Bellisi, Madame de, 87

Benedict of Nursia, Saint, Rule of, 6, 32–33; Mère Agnès on, 120, 130, 158, 167; Mère Angélique on, 46, 59, 60; Mère Angélique de Saint-Jean on, 191, 193, 197–205, 233

Benedictines, 4, 19, 114, 149, 155, 157, 170, 198

Bernard of Clairvaux, Saint, 33, 59, 123, 130, 221, 233, 236

Bérulle, Pierre de: 6, 7, 35, 37, 247; Arnauld abbesses and, 92, 115, 128, 131, 141, 168, 235

Bible: and Mère Agnès, 147–48, 157–58, 169–70; and Mère Angélique, 57, 88, 95, 104; and Mère Angélique de Saint-Jean, 210, 225; and Port-Royal, 16, 23

Bibliothèque de la Société de Port-Royal, 129, 193, 196, 197

Binet, Étienne, 59, 119, 134

Blessed Virgin Mary, 103

body, 138–39

Boileau-Despréaux, Nicolas, 37

Bologna, Concordat of, 5

Bossuet, Jacques-Bénigne, bishop of Meaux, 126, 127

Boucherat, Dom Nicolas II, abbot-general of Cistercians, 47

Boulart de Ninvilliers, Mère
    Élisabeth de Sainte-Anne, 17,
    18
Boulehart, Dame Jeanne, abbess of
    Port-Royal, 45, 114
Boulêtreau, François, 53
Briascier, Jean de, 59, 78, 82, 108,
    123
Broad, Jacqueline, 238
Brussells, 60

Calvin, Jean, 9, 81
Calvinism, 19, 20, 24
Canfield, Benoît de, 6
Carasse, Father, 35
Carmelites, 34, 100
Carr, Thomas M., 26, 60
Cartesianism, 40, 152, 225, 245
Cassian, John, 198
casuistry, 12, 24, 38, 245; and
    Arnauld abbesses, 53, 82, 108,
    129, 163, 173, 194, 210
Catherine de Medici, queen of
    France, 19–20
Catholicism, 3, 32, 36; and Mère
    Agnès, 115, 150, 153, 159; and
    Mère Angélique, 67, 78, 98, 103
causation, 24–41, 84–85, 111–12
certitude, 221–22, 224–26, 234, 247
character, moral, 146–53, 240
charity: Mère Agnès on, 130,
    141–42, 144, 147–48, 172; Mère
    Angélique on, 68–69, 79, 99,
    101; Mère Angélique de Saint-
    Jean on, 206, 212, 215
Charron, Pierre, 35
Chédozeau, Bernard, 28, 128, 157
Chevreuse, 4, 6, 48, 115, 123, 127,
    188, 192
Christian and Spiritual Letters
    (Saint-Cyran), 9, 30
Christology, 74, 91, 141–42

Cistercians, 4, 5, 7, 19; and Mère
    Agnès, 130, 141–42, 144,
    147–48, 172; and Mère
    Angélique, 44, 46, 48, 49, 51,
    100; and Mère Angélique de
    Saint-Jean, 198, 201, 221
Cîteaux, 4, 5, 48
City of God (Augustine), 32, 191,
    206–7, 233, 294n69
classicism, 96–97
Clémencet, Dom Charles, 26
Clement IX, pope, 15–16, 17, 127
Clement XI, pope, 17, 193
Climacus, Saint John, 33, 59
cloister, 4, 55, 98, 152, 238, 242–43
Cognet, Louis, 36, 55, 134
Colbert, Jean-Baptiste, 127
concupiscence: Augustinian
    doctrine of, 3, 70, 239, 247;
    Mère Agnès on, 122, 130, 144,
    146, 152, 172; Mère Angélique
    on, 94, 104, 106, 111; Mère
    Angélique de Saint-Jean on,
    187–88, 194, 198, 209–10
Condren, Charles de, 6, 35, 60,
    116–17, 131, 141, 247
*Conferences on the Constitutions
    of the Monastery of Port-Royal*
    (Mère Angélique de Saint-Jean
    Arnauld d'Andilly), 193, 196,
    205–10
conferences, abbatial, 1, 18, 26–27,
    158–59, 191, 193, 210
confession, 9, 51, 79, 120, 160,
    166–67, 206, 208–9, 217
Confessions (Augustine), 31, 57
conscience, 1, 11, 17, 22, 237, 244;
    Mère Agnès on, 126, 164, 167,
    169, 170; Mère Angélique on,
    38, 56; Mère Angélique de
    Saint-Jean on, 181, 195, 216–18,
    223, 235

Constitutions of the Monastery of Port-Royal of the Blessed Sacrament, The (Mère Agnès Arnauld), 15, 113, 120–21, 123, 126, 128, 191, 196, 201
contemplation, 86, 145, 154, 165
contempt of world, 75–76, 168
Contes, Jean-Baptiste de, grand vicar of archdiocese of Paris, 14, 187
contextualism, 145, 174, 242–43
contrition, 7, 51, 79, 120, 208–9
convent, 1, 3, 65, 174, 238–39; school: 8, 52–53, 121, 155–56, 177, 223–24; virtues of: 135–45, 233–34, 242–43
conversion, 72–73, 104–6, 173, 194
cooperation, moral, 163–70, 172–73, 216–17, 234, 245–46
Cornelius the centurion, 105–6
Cornet, Nicolas, 10
Counsels on the Conduct Which the Nuns Should Maintain in the Event of a Change in the Government of the Convent (Mère Agnès Arnauld), 114, 129, 163–70, 172, 176, 191, 193, 210, 245
Counter-Reformation, 21, 134, 148, 157
courage, 97
cowardice, 212, 216, 218, 239
Crisis of Signature: and Jansenism, 13–14, 17–18, 24, 28, 37–38, 245; and Mère Agnès, 125, 127; and Mère Angélique, 54; and Mère Angélique de Saint-Jean, 180–81, 186–87, 217, 221, 223, 225, 227, 235
Cum occasione (Innocent X), 10, 11, 12, 82

Daniel the prophet, 66
D'Aumont, Anne Herrault de Cheverny, marquise, 82
Defense of the Nuns of Port-Royal (Sainte-Marthe), 123
De Ligny, Mère Madeleine de Sainte-Agnès, 14
deontology, 142, 210–20
De Paul, Saint Vincent, 10
De Sales, Saint François, 6, 20, 33–34, 37, 47–48, 55, 59, 115, 130, 246
Descartes, René, 23, 25, 28, 36, 40, 225–26, 234
Desert Fathers, 23, 46
Des Esserts, Madame, 58
Desmarets de Saint-Sorlin, Jean, 128
D'Estrées, Angélique, abbess of Maubuission, 44–45, 47–48
detachment, spiritual, 57
determinism, 111–12, 162, 241–42
Deus absconditus, 4, 127, 220
direction, spiritual, 1, 122–23, 129–30, 184, 187, 191, 243
Discourses of Mère Angélique de Saint-Jean Called "Miséricordes." See *Miséricordes* (Mère Angélique de Saint-Jean Arnauld d'Andilly)
Discourses on the Rule of Saint Benedict (Mère Angélique de Saint-Jean Arnauld d'Andilly), 193, 196, 197–205
Dorotheus, Saint, 158
doubt, 220–26, 233–34, 245
dowry, 155
droit/fait distinction: and Jansenism 11–12, 14, 15, 17, 23, 36–38; and Arnauld abbesses, 54, 124, 180–82, 233

dualism, 32, 66, 76, 138, 205–10,
    232–33, 245
Du Fargis, Mère Marie de Sainte-
    Madeleine d'Angennes, 16, 17
Du Fossé. *See* Thomas du Fossé
Duval, André, 118

école française, 35, 115, 228
Edict of Nantes, 21
education, 52, 86–88, 121, 155–56
egalitarianism, 149–53, 156, 163
election, divine, 3, 8, 67–68, 108,
    153, 194, 197–204, 210, 225;
    of abbess, 48–49, 88–91, 121,
    159–60, 169
*Elevation of Spirit to Our Lord
    Jesus Christ* (Séguenot) 119
eminence, 132–33
epistemology, 40, 61, 110, 176,
    220–26, 247
essence, divine, 35, 107, 117, 130,
    133–34, 231–32, 240
Esther, Book of, 191, 193, 196
ethics, 2, 240; of Mère Agnès,
    135–45, 163–70, 170; of Mère
    Angélique, 73–77, 89; of Mère
    Angélique de Saint-Jean, 194,
    215–16, 232–36
Eucharist, 117–19, 130–35, 226–32
Eudes de Sully, bishop of Paris, 4
*Exercises of Piety for the Use of
    Port-Royal*, 196
existence, 132–33
*Explanation of the Rule of Saint
    Benedict* (Mère Agnès
    Arnauld), 130

faith, 97–98, 144, 147–48, 182,
    211–13, 222, 226, 229
*Faithful Narrative of the Miracles
    and Visions of Soeur Flavie*

    (Mère Angélique de Saint-Jean
    Arnauld d'Andilly), 197
fallibilism, 11
Faugère, Armand-Prosper, 129
fear, 86–87, 212, 215–26
fideism, 35–36, 110, 147, 238, 247
Five Propositions, 10–11, 15, 53–54,
    82, 83, 124–25, 180–81, 184,
    186–87
Fleury, François, 57, 83
Foix, Madame Françoise III de,
    abbess of Abbey aux Dames,
    127
Fonspertuis, Angélique Crespin de,
    187, 190, 191, 196
Fontaine, Nicolas, 37, 278n47
forgiveness, 93
formulary: crisis of, 12–13, 14,
    15–16, 31; and Arnauld
    abbesses 54, 124–27, 180–81,
    184, 223, 244–45
Francis I, king of France, 5
freedom: and Jansenism, 3, 7, 9, 10,
    31–32, 36, 40; Mère Agnès on,
    121, 148–49, 153–63, 172, 174;
    Mère Angélique on, 62, 84,
    96–97, 103–6, 111–12; Mère
    Angélique de Saint Jean on,
    191, 199–200, 205, 213;
    philosophy of, 237, 241–42,
    244–45
Froidmont, Liber, 119
Fronde, 13, 53, 123

Gallet, Rachel, 129
Gallicanism, 10, 12, 15
Garlande, Mathilde de, 4
Gazier, Cécile, 30
gender, 4, 41–42, 88–93, 109–10,
    153–63, 173–74, 240, 245–46
generosity, 97

genre, literary, 2, 18, 39, 194
Goldmann, Lucien, 24
Gondi, Jean-François de, archbishop
    of Paris, 48, 49, 82, 108
Gondi, Paul de, archbishop of, 57
Gonzague, Marie-Louise de, queen
    of Poland, 56, 57, 64, 66–68,
    70–71, 75, 89, 91–93, 127
grace: efficacious, 12, 30–31, 36,
    72–73, 77–79, 82–85, 103–6,
    110, 123; and Jansenism, 2, 3,
    7, 8, 10, 33, 38; Mère Agnès on,
    140, 152, 161–62, 164, 168,
    172; Mère Angélique on, 53,
    83, 97; Mère Angélique de
    Saint Jean on, 180–81, 197,
    198, 203, 207–10, 221, 230;
    philosophy and, 238, 240–41
Grandeurs of Jesus, The (Bérulle),
    115
gratitude, 148
Grenada, Venerable Luis, 84
Guéménée, Anne de Rohan,
    princesse de, 72
Guise, Charles, duc de, 20

Habert, Isaac, 10, 32
Halley, Soeur Anne de Sainte-
    Magdeleine, 61
Hallier, François, 9
Hamon, Jean, 57, 130
Harlay de Champvallon, François
    de, archbishop of Paris, 16, 188,
    189
Hauerwas, Stanley, 243–44
Henri IV, king of France, 5, 21, 24,
    44
hermeneutics, 38–42, 82, 170, 213
Hidden God, The (Goldmann),
    24–25
Hildegarde of Bingen, 198

Hodencq, Alexandre de, 14
holiness, 132–33
Holy Communion, 7, 51, 79, 120,
    136, 166, 206, 208–9
Homilies of Saint John Chrysostom,
    158
hope, 66–68, 97–98, 108, 211,
    214–15
Huguenots, 17, 20, 22
humanism, 212, 238
humility, 33, 239, 244, 246; Mère
    Agnès on, 117, 132, 140, 141,
    145, 172; Mère Angélique on,
    70, 95, 99; Mère Angélique de
    Saint Jean, 198–205, 236

illimitability, divine, 131–32
*Image of a Perfect and an Imperfect
    Nun, The* (Mère Agnès
    Arnauld), 15, 113, 126, 128,
    135–45, 171–72
inaccessibility, divine, 2, 131–32
Incarnation, 115, 144, 202
incommunicability, divine, 131–32
incomprehensibility, divine: Mère
    Agnès on, 131–32, 135, 146,
    151, 174; Mère Angélique on,
    61–65, 93–96, 107; and Port-
    Royal, 1, 2, 7, 35–36, 41, 247
independence, divine, 131–32
Index of Forbidden Books, 119
In eminenti (Urban VIII), 9
infallibilism, 11, 103
Innocent X, pope, 10, 14, 82, 83, 124
Innocent XI, pope, 17, 189, 192
Inquistion, Holy Office of, 9
Institut du Saint-Sacrement, 7,
    49–51, 116–17, 120
intention, 60
interdict, 129, 195, 204, 210, 218,
    222

Interesting and Edifying Lives of the Nuns of Port-Royal, 196
Interior Castle (Teresa of Avila), 115
Introduction to the Devout Life (François de Sales), 33–34, 59
Israel, 204

Jansen, Cornelius, bishop of Ypres: and Mère Agnès, 119, 124–25, 130, 163, 164; and Mère Angélique, 50, 51, 52–53, 54, 59, 77, 79, 81, 104; and Mère Angélique de Saint-Jean, 181, 182, 186–87, 232, 233; and Port-Royal, 7–9, 11, 14, 15–16, 17, 30, 246
Jansenism, 7, 11–15, 16–19, 22–25, 29, 31–32, 247; and Mère Agnès, 119, 123, 124, 147, 163; and Mère Angélique, 52, 57, 59, 77, 81–84, 103, 106–12; and Mère Angélique de Saint-Jean, 193, 195, 224
Jansenism Confounded (Brisacier), 59
Jeremiah the prophet, 225
Jesuits: and Jansenism, 3, 7–9, 12, 19–21, 24, 29, 35, 38, 241; and Mère Agnès, 118, 134; and Mère Angélique, 46, 51, 52–53, 54, 57, 73, 78, 82, 86, 87; and Mère Angélique de Saint-Jean, 185, 224
Jesus Christ: and resistance, 202, 207–8, 215, 220, 225, 226–32, 244; states of, 116–19, 125, 130–35, 141–42, 161, 167, 169–70; and virtue, 60, 74, 92–93, 102–6

John the Evangelist, Saint, 225
Josse, Marguerite, 58
journée du guichet, 46, 115

Kolakowski, Leszeck, 32
Kostroun, Daniella, 41

Ladder of Perfection (John Climacus), 33, 59
La Mothe-Arnauld, Antoine, 19–20
Lancelot, Claude, 37, 57, 278n46
language, 166, 201
Largentier, Dom Denis, abbot of Clairvaux, 46
La Rochefoucauld, François VI, duc, 37
La Trémoïlle, Marguerite-Marie de, abbess of Lys, 118
law, 25–27, 44, 90–91, 128–29, 153–63, 174, 243
laxism, 9, 12, 51, 194, 245, 247
Le Maître, Antoine, 23, 55–56, 59, 121, 122, 177
Le Maître, Catherine de Saint-Jean Arnauld, 22, 23, 58
Le Maître, Isaac, 23
Le Maître de Saci, Isaac, 16, 19, 23, 24, 123, 177, 184
Le Maître de Sérincourt, Simon, 23, 177
Leo X, pope, 5
Le Pautre, Antoine, 288n96
Lesaulnier, Jean, 55, 179
Les nouvelles ecclésiastiques, 196
Le Tardif, Mère Marie-Geneviève de Saint-Augustin, 6, 49, 116, 117
Le Tellier, Michel, chancellor of France, 127
Letters of Mère Agnès Arnauld, Abbess of Port-Royal, 129–30

Letters to a Duke and Peer (Antoine Arnauld), 59

libertinism, 87

Life of Saint Bernard, The (Antoine Le Maître), 59

Ligue, Catholic, 21

Lives of the Desert Fathers, The, 59, 158

Longueville, Anne-Geneviève de Bourbon, duchesse de, 13, 118, 127, 192

Louis of France, Saint, 92–93

Louis of Grenada, Venerable, 59, 158

Louis XIII, king of France, 6, 24, 48, 176

Louis XIV, king of France, 12, 15–18, 24, 125–26, 150, 184–85, 189–90, 192

Louvain, 50, 119

love, 101, 130, 137–38, 205–7, 215, 230

Luke, Saint, 105

Luaznci, Mademoiselle de, 75–76

Luzancy, Henri-Charles de, 23, 176–77

Malebranche, Nicolas, 23, 28, 112

Marion, Simon, 44, 114

Marle de la Falaise, Soeur Angélique de Sainte-Agnès, 85

Marly, Mathieu de, 4

Mars Gallicus (Jansen), 8

martyrdom, 204–5, 216, 218, 226, 231, 233

Mary Magdalene, Saint, 169–70

Maubuisson, abbey of, 44–45, 47–48, 115

Maurisse, Mère de, prioress of Saint-Martin, 187

maxime, 25

Mazarin, Jules, cardinal, 10, 12, 13

McKenna, Antony, 35–36

meditation, 64–65, 121, 134–35, 148–49, 156–57

Memoirs to Be Used for the History of Port-Royal, 196

Mesnard, Jean, 55, 126

metaphysics, 40, 109, 112, 205–10, 232

miracle of Holy Thorn, 12, 63, 182

Miséricordes (Mère Angélique de Saint-Jean Arnauld d'Andilly), 194–95, 196

Molina, Luis de, 7, 8, 274n7

monasticism, 175–76, 197–205, 239, 243–44

Montaigne, Michel de, 2, 35

Montherlant, Henry de, 2

Moral Theology of the Jesuits (Antoine Arnauld and Hallier), 9

Morant, Mère Catherine de, abbess of Gif, 56–57, 82, 91

mortification, 100

mysticism, 102–3, 116, 118, 134–35, 157, 170, 239

nature, 223, 227, 230, 231, 235, 247

Navarre, Collège de, 20

Necrology of Port-Royal, 196

Neoplatonism, 32, 34, 35, 135, 213, 229

New Testament, 23

Nicole, Pierre, 17, 31, 128, 278n45

nihilism, 235

Nijmegen, treaties of, 16–17, 188

Nivelle, Dom Pierre de, abbot of Cîteaux, 6, 48

noblesse de robe, 19, 24–27, 248

nonsigneuses, 14, 15, 126, 182, 183

obedience, 75, 172, 195, 199–201, 205, 230, 239, 242–43, 246

occasionalism, 112

Of Direction (Mère Angélique de Saint-Jean Arnauld d'Andilly), 197

Office of the Blessed Sacrament (Antoine Le Maître), 59

Of Frequent Communion (Antoine Arnauld), 9, 30, 31, 36, 52, 59, 81, 123

Of Grace and Free Will (Bernard of Clairvaux), 33

Of the Grace of Jesus Christ, Of Christian Liberty, and Of Justification (Saint-Cyran), 36

Of the Love of God (Bernard of Clairvaux), 33

Of the Love One Must Have for the Cross of Jesus Christ (Mère Agnès Arnauld), 130

omnipotence, divine, 72, 112, 141

On Free Will (Augustine), 32

On the Danger of Hesitation and Doubt Once One's Duty Is Known (Mère Angélique de Saint-Jean Arnauld d'Andilly), 41, 220–26; text of, 266–72

On the Mystery of the Passion of Our Lord Jesus Christ (Soeur Jacqueline de Sainte-Euphémie), 25

Oratorians: and Port-Royal 6, 7, 35, 240, 245, 247; spiritual influence of, 50, 60, 115–18, 128, 135, 141, 178, 202, 227

Orcibal, Jean, 35

Orléans, Gaston-Jean-Baptiste de France, duc d', 8, 176

Pachomius, Saint, 198

Paradise of Prayers, The (Grenada), 84

Parlement of Paris, 20

Pascal, Blaise: and Arnauld abbesses, 53, 59, 62, 77, 79, 82, 127, 129; and Jansenism, 2, 8, 12, 25, 28, 31, 278n44

Pascal, Soeur Jacqueline de Sainte-Euphémie, 8, 14, 16, 25–26, 31, 121–22, 180–81

Passart, Soeur Catherine de Sainte-Flavie, 182, 185

Passion of Christ, 144, 230

passions, 146–52, 201, 213, 235, 247

Path of Peace and the Path of Inquietude, The (Desmarets de Saint-Sorlin), 128

Path of Perfection, The (Teresa of Avila), 115

patience, 70–72, 109, 170

patristics, 8, 32, 35, 46, 51, 57, 77, 110, 158

Paul of Tarsus, Saint, 79, 97, 130, 207

Pavillon, Nicolas, bishop of Alet, 15, 127

Peace of Church, 15–16, 17, 20, 127, 187, 188, 197

Pelagianism, 8, 10–11, 32, 84

Pembroke, Archange de, 6, 46, 115

penance, 100

Perdeau, Mère Dorothée, 14

Péréfixe, Hardouin de Beaumont de, archbishop of Paris, 14, 127, 182, 184

perfection, moral, 135–45, 173

Périer, Gilberte Pascal, 127

Périer, Marguerite, 12

Perpetual Faith of the Church in the Eucharist (Antoine Arnauld), 20

persecution, 244–45; Mère Agnès and, 124, 126–27, 129, 163–70, 173; Mère Angélique and, 53, 56, 80, 108; Mère Angélique de Saint-Jean and, 175–76, 179, 189, 192, 195, 204, 210–20, 220–26, 236

Peter, Saint, 12

petites écoles, 7, 16, 23, 52, 53, 121, 178

Phillip II, king of Spain, 54

philosophy, 2, 3, 59, 110–12, 130, 147, 170–74, 211, 220–26; Augustinian, 27–38, 209–10, 232–36, 237–48

piety, 65–66, 92, 131, 147–48, 219

Plutarch, 44

Poligné, Father, 190

Pomponne, Henri-Charles Arnauld de, 24, 177

Poor Clares, 165

Port-Royal, 1, 2, 70, 228, 233; constitutions of, 153–63, 175–76; history of, 4–19, 43–55, 114–27, 176–92

Port-Royal (Sainte-Beuve), 2, 295n112

portrait moral, 25

poverty, 5, 33; Arnauld abbesses on, 73–74, 100, 108, 141, 150–51, 165, 172, 243–44

power, 89–93, 127, 139, 160, 226, 233–35

pragmatism, 207

predestination, 3, 8, 9, 233

pride, 79–80, 100–101, 139, 140, 144, 212, 215, 243, 247

primitivism, 87

Private Chaplet of the Blessed Sacrament (Mère Agnès Arnauld), 35, 41, 50, 55, 178, 226; Mère Agnès and, 113, 117–19, 123, 128, 130–35, 171, 178, 226; text of, 261–65

Protestantism, 20, 98, 103

providence, divine, 147, 228

Provincial Letters (Pascal), 12, 30, 31, 53, 59, 79

prudence: 1, 191–92, 214, 222, 224

Pseudo-Dionysius, 35, 247

Pyrrhonism, 36, 247

querelle de la grâce, 9, 83, 222, 274n8

Quesnel, Pasquier, 195

Racine, Jean, 37

Racine, Mère Agnès de Sainte-Thècle, 17

Rantzau, Mère Marguerite Elisabeth de, 183

Rapin, René, 177

rationalism, 101–3, 226, 238

reason, 200, 213–14, 247

Reflections on the Conformity of the State of the Nuns of Port-Royal with That of Jesus Christ in the Eucharist (Mère Angélique de Saint-Jean Arnauld d'Andilly), 195, 196, 226–32

Reflections to Prepare the Nuns for Persecution, in Conformity with the "Counsels" Mère Agnès Left on This Matter to the Nuns of This Monastery (Mère Angélique de Saint-Jean Arnauld d'Andilly), 194, 210–20

reform, monastic: Mère Agnès on, 114–17, 118, 120–21, 130; Mère Angélique on, 46–48, 49, 51–53, 57, 88; Mère Angélique de Saint-Jean on, 178–79, 187, 191; of Port-Royal, 4, 6, 26
Reform of the Interior Man, The (Jansen), 30, 52, 59, 246
régale, 192, 291n35
religion, virtue of, 140
Report of Captivity (Mère Angélique de Saint-Jean Arnauld d'Andilly), 183, 194, 196
Report or Documented History of Mère Marie-Angélique (Mère Angélique de Saint-Jean Arnauld d'Andilly), 178, 195
Report Written by Mère Angélique Arnauld Concerning the Major Occurrences at Port-Royal, 55–56, 118, 178
reputation, 139
resistance, 77–84, 106–12; to persecution, 125, 163–70, 173, 176, 181, 210–20, 220–26, 232–33, 239
reverence, 136, 139–40, 145
Revocation of the Edict of Nantes, 20
Richelieu, Armand du Plessis, duc de, cardinal, 8, 13, 51, 120
rights, 88–91, 128–29, 153–63, 164, 170, 174, 191, 193
rigorism, 10; of Mère Angélique, 51, 57, 66, 68, 74; of Mère Angélique de Saint-Jean, 191, 194, 205, 208, 209
Ritchey Newton, William, 26
Rivet de la Grange, Dom Antoine, 196

Rule for Children (Soeur Jacqueline de Sainte-Euphémie Pascal), 16, 25, 121
Rule of Saint Benedict. See Benedict of Nursia, Saint, Rule of
Rule of the Master, 198

Sablé, Madeleine de Souvré, marquise de, 30, 37, 67–68, 122, 185–86
sacraments, 7, 9, 10; Mère Agnès on, 120, 128, 169, 170; Mère Angélique on, 51; Mère Angélique de Saint-Jean on, 176, 195, 206, 208–9, 219–20
sacrifice, 226–32
Saint-Antoine-des-Champs, Abbey of, 44
Saint Bartholomew's Day Massacre, 20
Sainte-Beuve, Charles Augustin, 2, 16, 18
Sainte-Beuve, Jacques de, 57
Saint-Cyr, Abbey of, 44, 48, 114–15
Saint-Cyran, Jean du Vergier de Hauranne, abbé de: and Mère Agnès, 119, 120, 121, 123, 130, 136, 160; and Mère Angélique, 50, 51–52, 55, 73, 77, 81, 87, 104, 108; and Mère Angélique de Saint-Jean, 189, 195, 206, 208, 232, 235; and philosophy, 247; and Port-Royal, 7, 8, 9, 18, 34–36
Sainte-Marthe, Claude de, 123
salon, 2–3
salvation, 104–6, 199, 213, 244
sectarianism, 232, 237, 243, 281n41
Séguenot, Claude, 118, 119
self-knowledge, 72–73
Sellier, Philippe, 29

senses, 213–14, 229
Sentiments of Abbé Philérème on Mental Prayer (Barcos), 128
Sévigné, Marie de Rabutin, marquise de, 37, 177
Sévigné, René Renaud de, 74, 75
Sibertin-Blanc, Brigitte, 187
signeuses, 14, 15, 126, 182, 197, 227
silence, virtue of, 6, 86, 165, 201, 205, 232
Simple Theology (Saint-Cyran), 9–10, 30–31, 35
sin, 8, 240–41
Singlin, Antoine, 7, 52, 55, 59, 121–23, 180
skepticism, 98, 103, 226
Socrates, 72
solitaires: and Arnauld abbesses, 52–53, 122, 127, 177, 178, 192; and Port-Royal, 7–9, 16–17, 23, 30, 37
solitude, 142–43
Sorbonne: and Arnauld abbesses 48, 50, 118–19, 123, 128, 196; and Jansenism 6, 10, 11–12, 17, 21
soul, 138, 247
sovereignty, divine, 7, 61–65, 71, 95, 241
Spinoza, Baruch, 112
Spirit of the Monastery of Port-Royal, The (Mère Agnès Arnauld), 113, 129, 146–53
Spiritual Doctrine of Saint Dorotheus, The, 158
spirituality, 115, 120, 128, 202, 228
Steps of Humility (Bernard of Clairvaux), 33, 59
Stoicism, 44, 85, 241
submission, religious, 136
suffering for truth, 77–84, 108, 219, 226, 229, 244

Suffren, Jean, 115
Summary Discussion of a Booklet Entitled "Private Chaplet of the Blessed Sacrament" (Binet), 59, 119
Suireau, Mère Marie des Anges, 10, 53
superstition, 102, 103

Tard, monastery of, 116, 120
Teresa of Avila, Saint, 23, 33–34, 54, 59, 91, 115, 130, 158, 246
Théméricourt, Marie-Scolastique Le Sesne de, 129
theocentrism, 64, 65–69, 99, 107, 108–9, 128, 135–45, 171–74, 241–42
theology: 39, 237–38, 245–46; and Mère Agnès, 124, 129, 159, 170, 174; and Mère Angélique, 69–73; and Mère Angélique de Saint-Jean, 209, 236
Thomas du Fossé, Pierre, 177, 179–80
Thoughts on Various Subjects (Mère Angélique de Saint-Jean Arnauld d'Andilly), 197
Three Conferences on the Necessity to Defend the Church (Mère Angélique de Saint-Jean Arnauld d'Andilly), 195
Timmermans, Linda, 124
toleration, 21
transcendence, 119, 239
translation, 4, 39
Treatise on Prayer (Nicole), 128
Treatise on Virginity (Augustine), 31
Trent, Council of, 6, 15, 89, 103, 121, 143, 159, 208–9

truth: Mère Agnès on, 132, 158, 164; Mère Angélique on, 80, 83, 111; Mère Angélique de Saint Jean on, 215, 218, 221–24, 228

ultramontanism, 21
Unigenitus (Clement XI), 193
Urban VIII, pope, 9, 48
Ursulines, 86–87
Utrecht, 56, 59, 129, 196

Vatican, 5, 14, 15, 17, 44, 46, 49, 119
via negativa, 25, 35, 239; Mère Agnès on, 131–32, 135, 148, 171; Mère Angélique on, 61–65, 107, 110–11
vices, 57, 100–101, 140, 167, 202, 212, 215–16, 225
victimhood, 226–32, 233
Villanueva Gardner, Catherine, 18
Vineam Domini Sabaoth (Clement XI), 17
virtues: Mère Agnès on, 126, 135–53, 167–68, 171–72; Mère Angélique on, 57, 65–88,

96–100, 108–9; Mère Angélique de Saint-Jean on, 191–94, 197–205, 211–15, 240–43, 247; Port-Royal and, 1, 27–28, 31–34, 240–43, 247
Visitation order, 14, 126
vocation, 88, 154–55, 174
voluntarism, 57, 60, 62–63, 207, 242, 247
vows, monastic, 73–77, 174

Warnock, Mary, 2
Weaver, F. Ellen, 18–19, 121, 179
will: divine: 61–65, 88, 132, 136, 147; human, 57, 69, 132, 147–48, 199–203, 212, 234, 241–42, 247
wisdom, 131
women, 2–3, 41–42, 88–93, 109–10, 128–29, 153–63, 173–74, 205, 237–48

Zamet, Sébastien, bishop of Langres, 6, 49–51, 55, 116–20, 178, 194
zeal, religious, 137, 172

JOHN J. CONLEY, S.J.,

is Bernard P. Knott Chair of Philosophy

and Theology at Loyola College in Maryland.